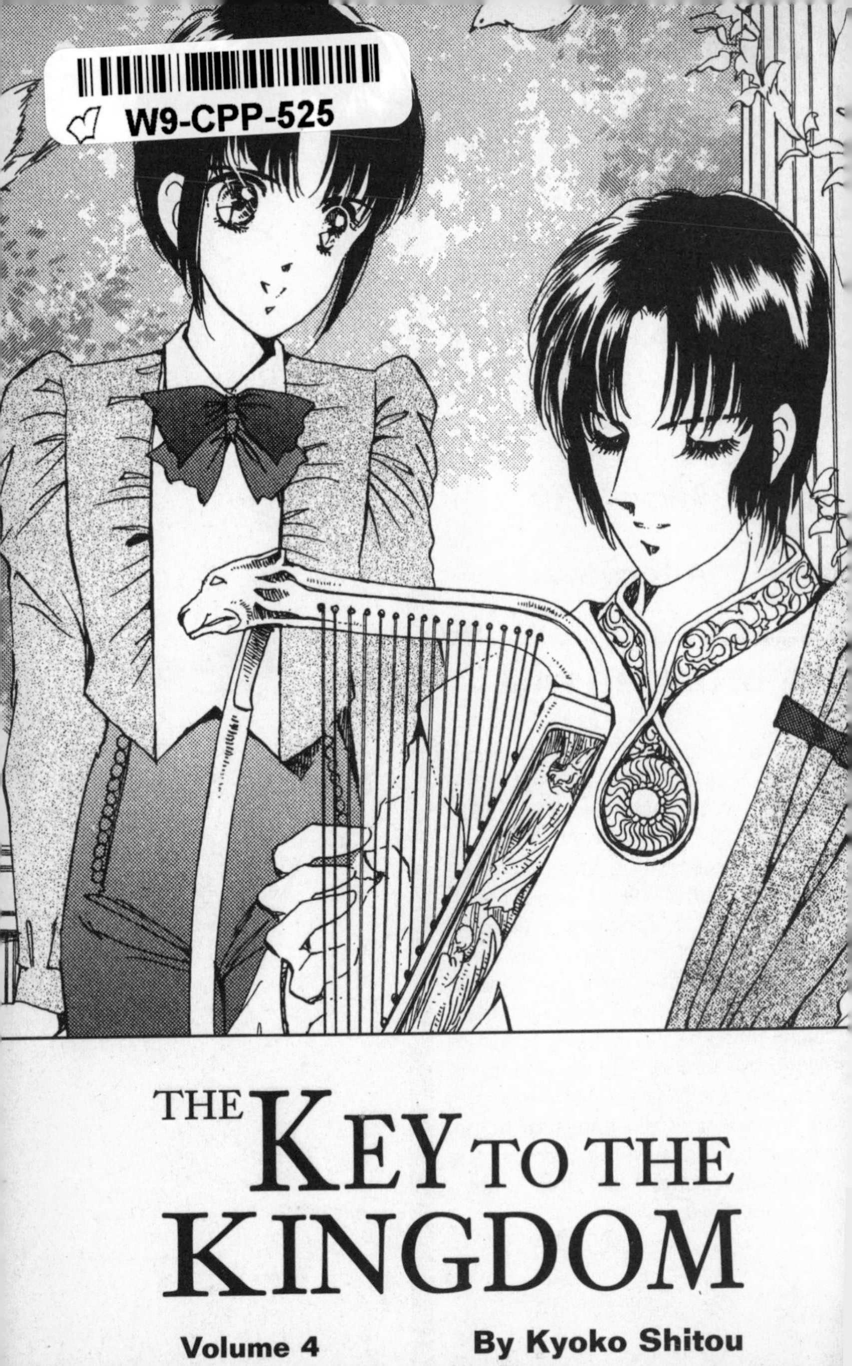

THE KEY TO THE KINGDOM

Volume 4

By Kyoko Shitou

CONTENTS

THE STORY SO FAR:

The five candidates for the throne continue their quest for the Key to the Kingdom. While Asta and Badd head for Beltos to the north, Leticia and Asloane search for the "Invisible Tower" to the west and east, respectively. Meanwhile, General Bardus goes south and Duke Alan chooses to remain near the Imperial City. Leticia is told by the Dragon Man, Gaius, that she is to be the one to ascend the throne. As for Asloane, he discovers a 300-year-old painting in the basement of his ancestral home, one that sends a warning across the centuries to beware the Dragon Men, Gaius and Ceianus!

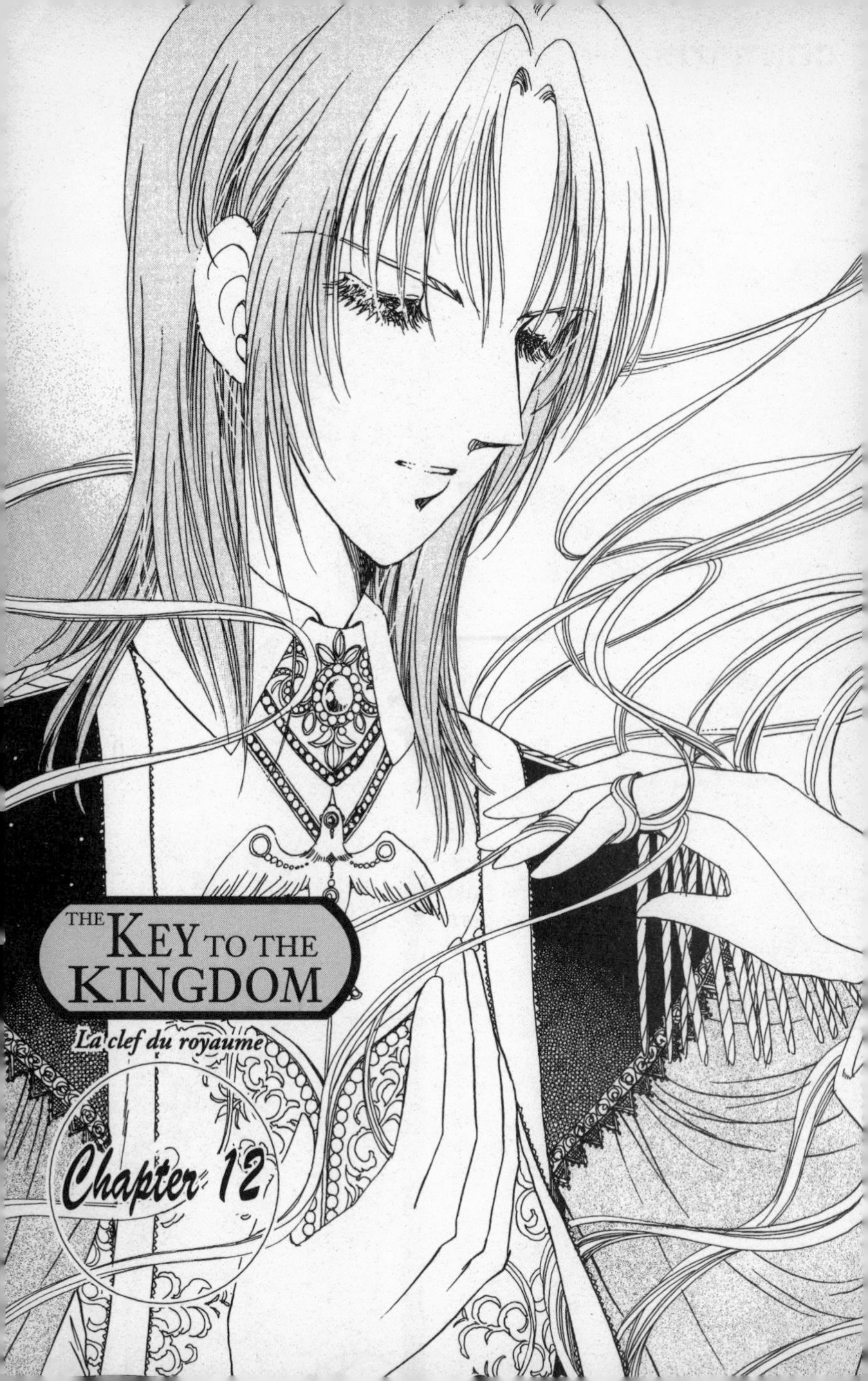
THE KEY TO THE KINGDOM
La clef du royaume
Chapter 12

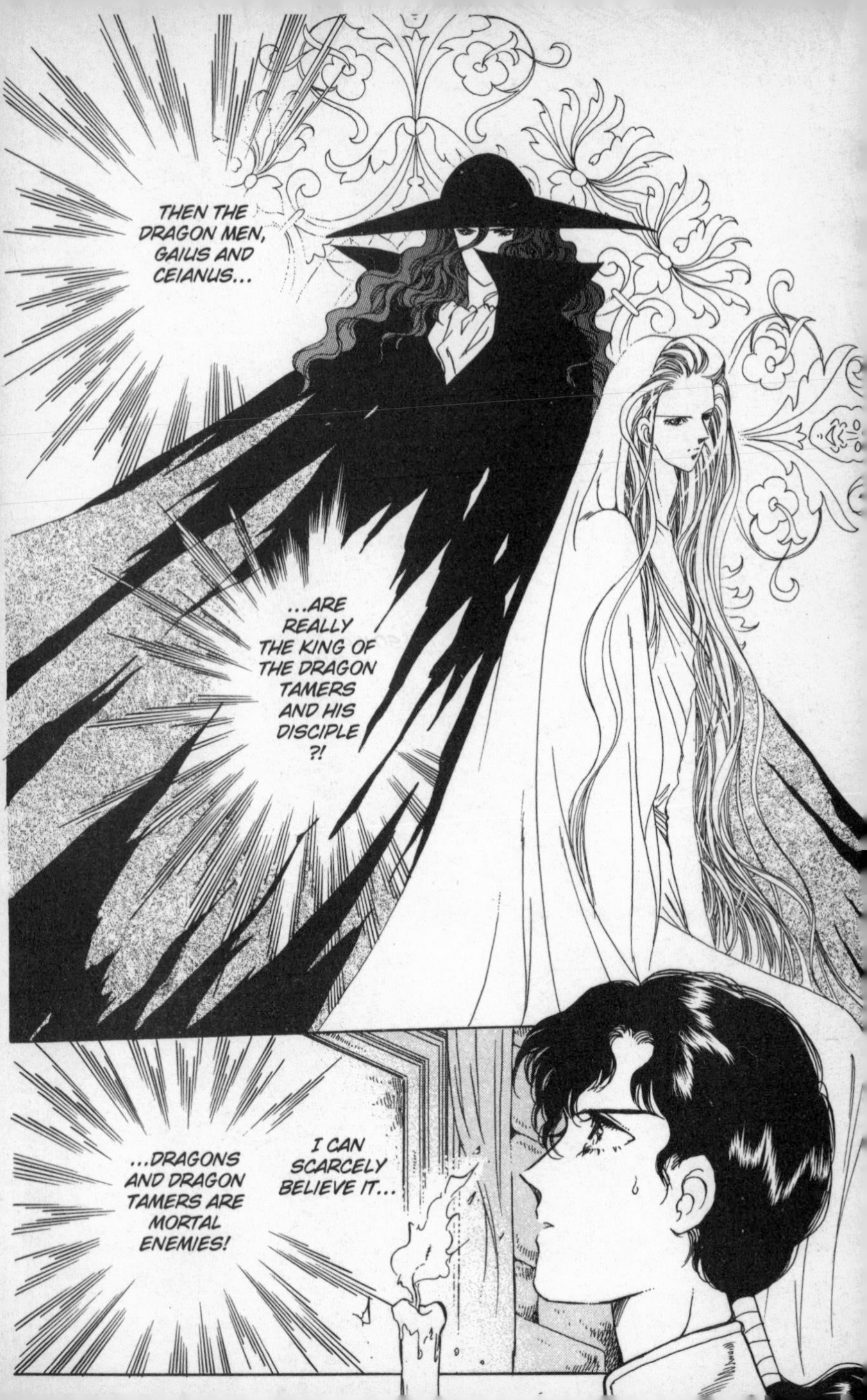
THEN THE DRAGON MEN, GAIUS AND CEIANUS...
...ARE REALLY THE KING OF THE DRAGON TAMERS AND HIS DISCIPLE ?!
I CAN SCARCELY BELIEVE IT...
...DRAGONS AND DRAGON TAMERS ARE MORTAL ENEMIES!

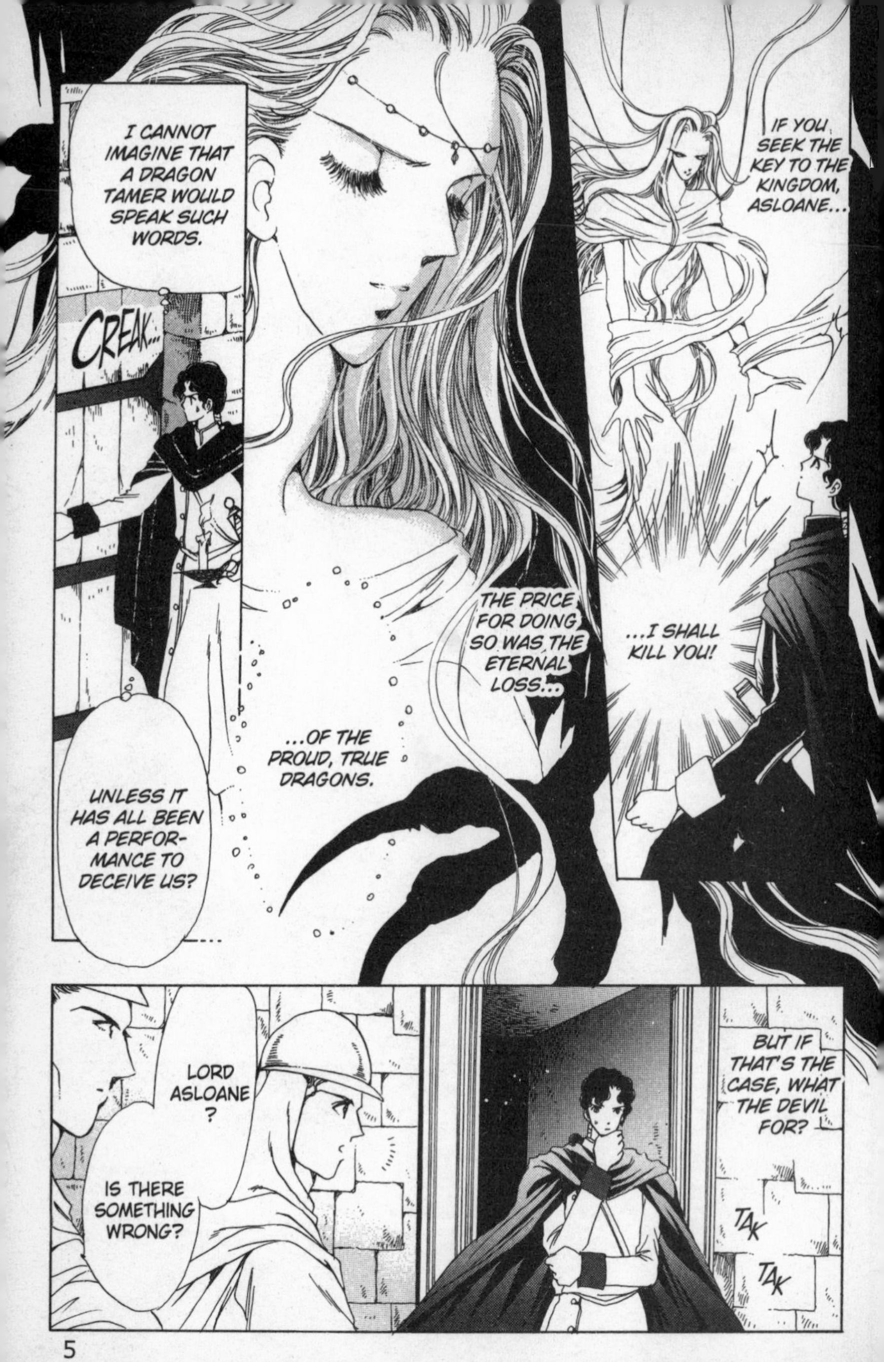
IF YOU SEEK THE KEY TO THE KINGDOM, ASLOANE...
...I SHALL KILL YOU!
THE PRICE FOR DOING SO WAS THE ETERNAL LOSS...
...OF THE PROUD, TRUE DRAGONS.
I CANNOT IMAGINE THAT A DRAGON TAMER WOULD SPEAK SUCH WORDS.
CREAK...
UNLESS IT HAS ALL BEEN A PERFORMANCE TO DECEIVE US?
BUT IF THAT'S THE CASE, WHAT THE DEVIL FOR?
TAK
TAK
LORD ASLOANE?
IS THERE SOMETHING WRONG?

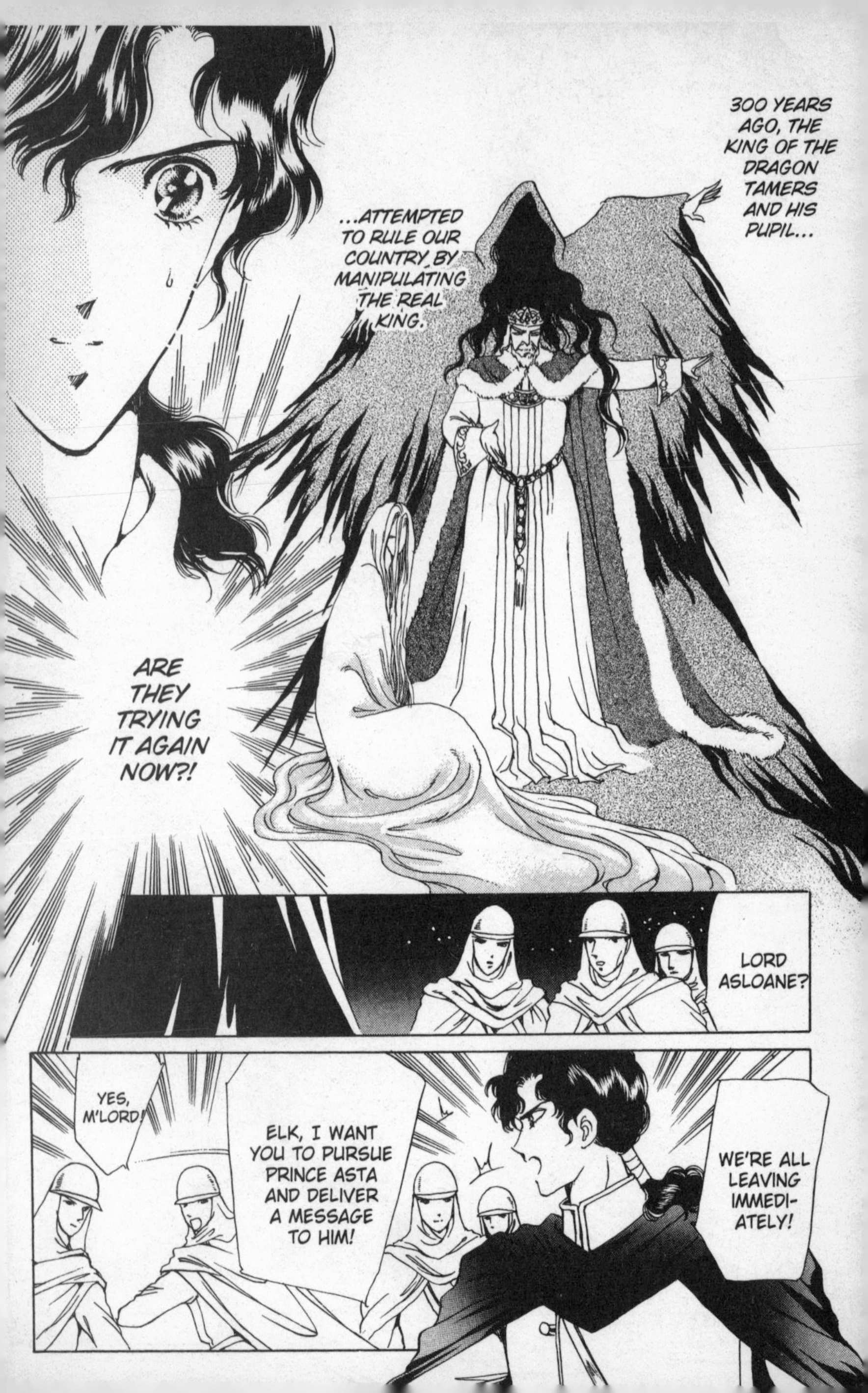
300 YEARS AGO, THE KING OF THE DRAGON TAMERS AND HIS PUPIL...
...ATTEMPTED TO RULE OUR COUNTRY BY MANIPULATING THE REAL KING.
ARE THEY TRYING IT AGAIN NOW?!
LORD ASLOANE?
WE'RE ALL LEAVING IMMEDI-ATELY!
ELK, I WANT YOU TO PURSUE PRINCE ASTA AND DELIVER A MESSAGE TO HIM!
YES, M'LORD!

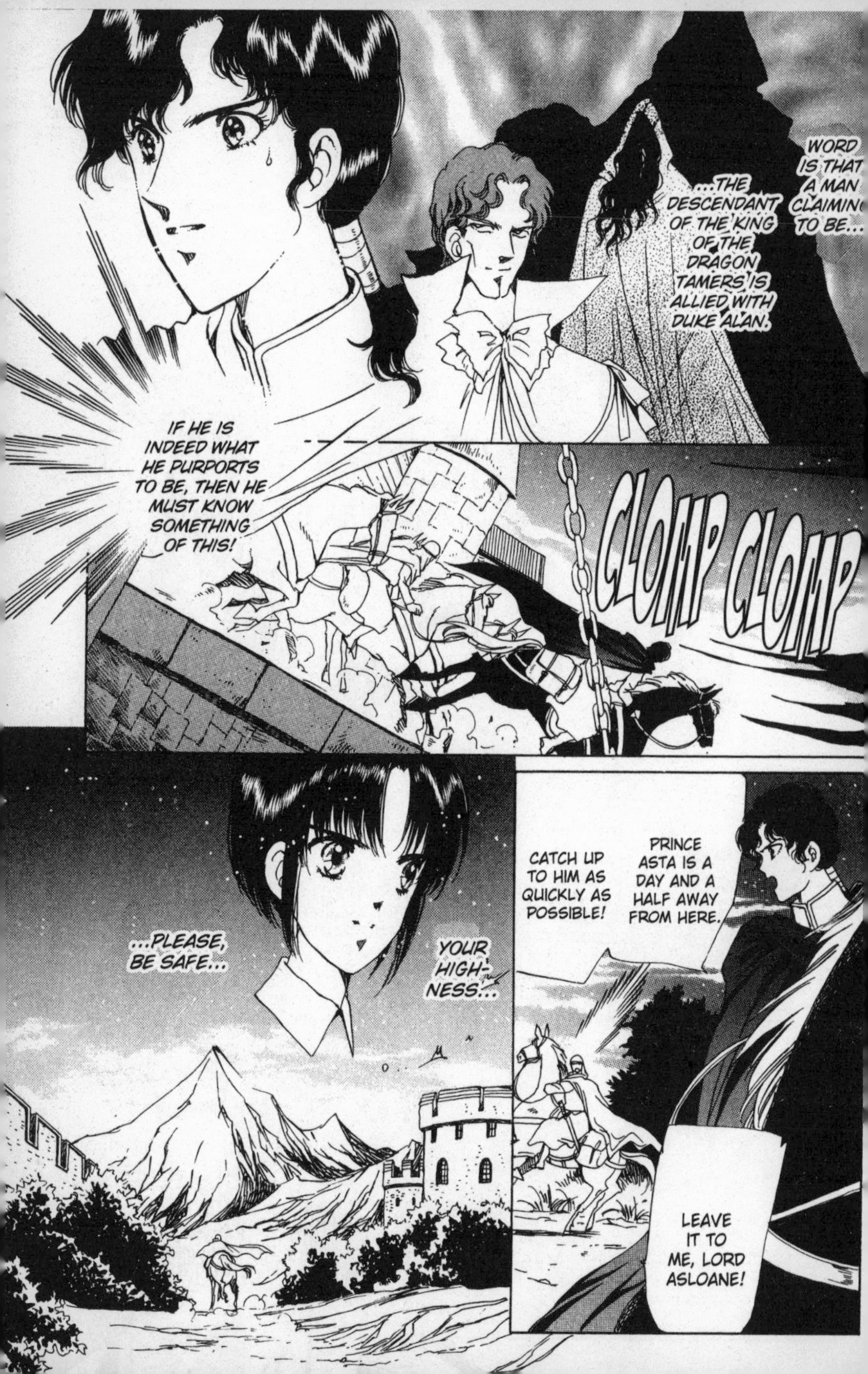
WORD IS THAT A MAN CLAIMING TO BE...
...THE DESCENDANT OF THE KING OF THE DRAGON TAMERS IS ALLIED WITH DUKE ALAN.
IF HE IS INDEED WHAT HE PURPORTS TO BE, THEN HE MUST KNOW SOMETHING OF THIS!
CLOMP CLOMP
PRINCE ASTA IS A DAY AND A HALF AWAY FROM HERE.
CATCH UP TO HIM AS QUICKLY AS POSSIBLE!
LEAVE IT TO ME, LORD ASLOANE!
YOUR HIGH-NESS...
...PLEASE, BE SAFE...

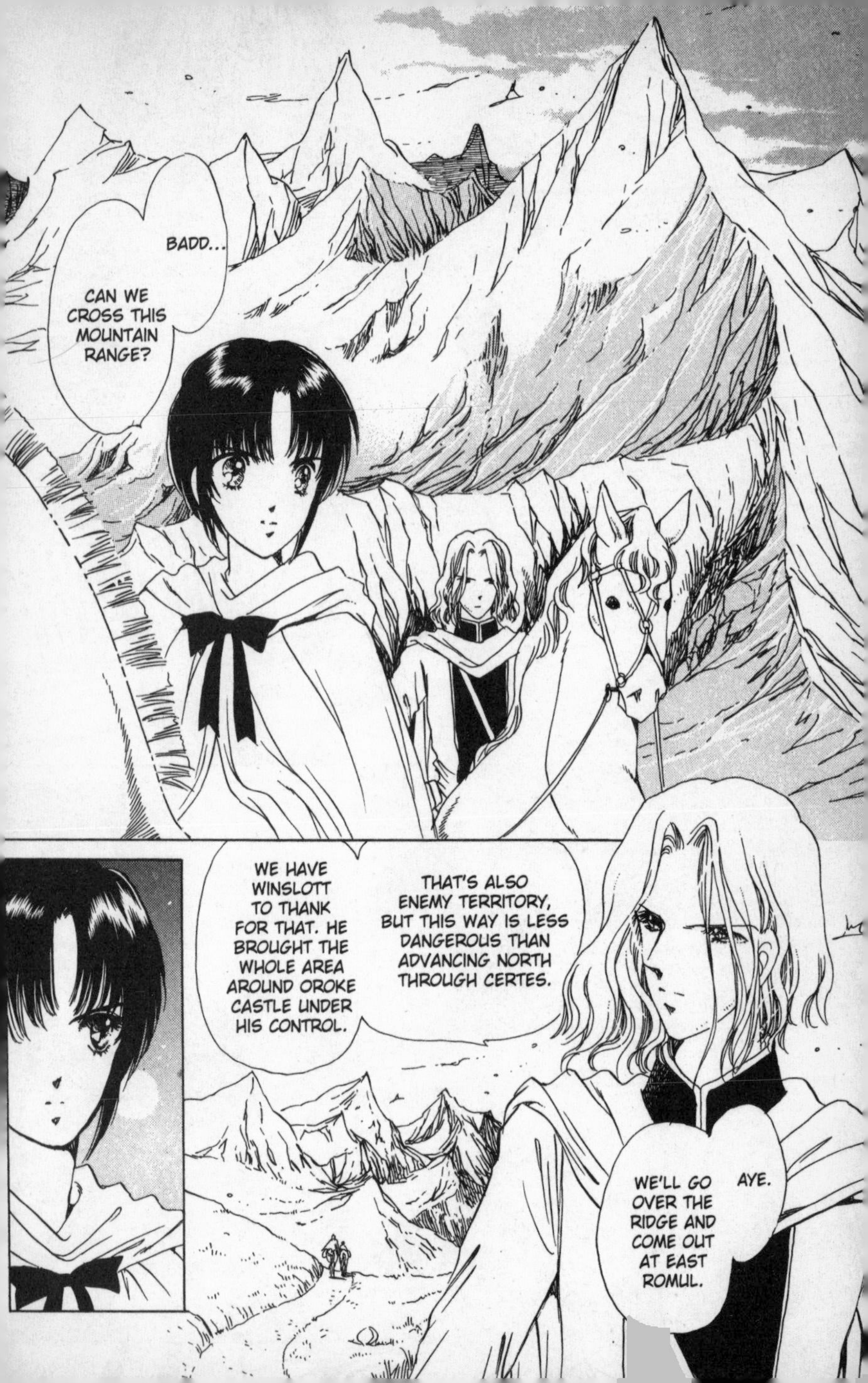
BADD...
CAN WE CROSS THIS MOUNTAIN RANGE?
AYE.
WE'LL GO OVER THE RIDGE AND COME OUT AT EAST ROMUL.
THAT'S ALSO ENEMY TERRITORY, BUT THIS WAY IS LESS DANGEROUS THAN ADVANCING NORTH THROUGH CERTES.
WE HAVE WINSLOTT TO THANK FOR THAT. HE BROUGHT THE WHOLE AREA AROUND OROKE CASTLE UNDER HIS CONTROL.

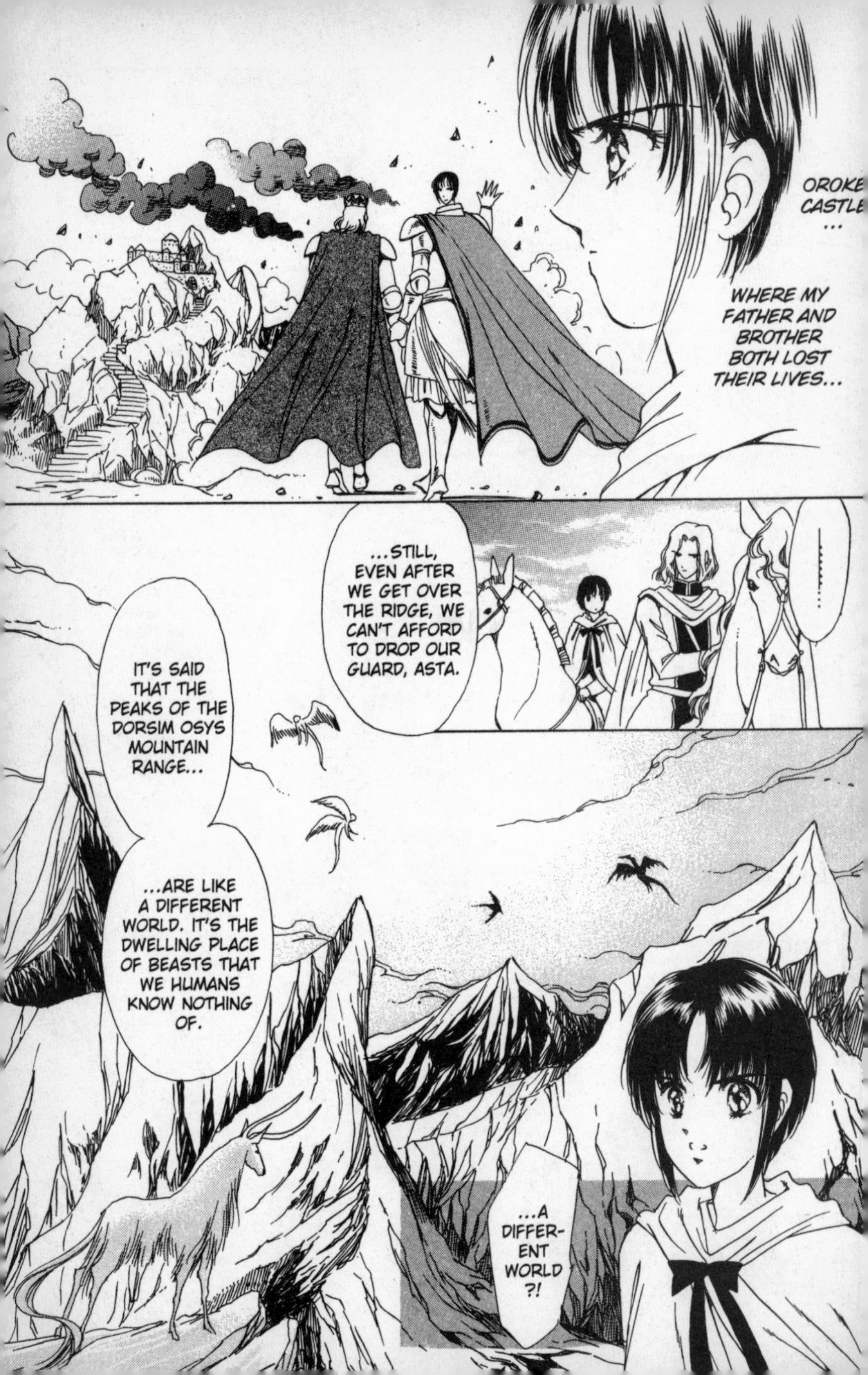
OROKE CASTLE ...
WHERE MY FATHER AND BROTHER BOTH LOST THEIR LIVES...
......
...STILL, EVEN AFTER WE GET OVER THE RIDGE, WE CAN'T AFFORD TO DROP OUR GUARD, ASTA.
IT'S SAID THAT THE PEAKS OF THE DORSIM OSYS MOUNTAIN RANGE...
...ARE LIKE A DIFFERENT WORLD. IT'S THE DWELLING PLACE OF BEASTS THAT WE HUMANS KNOW NOTHING OF.
...A DIFFER-ENT WORLD ?!

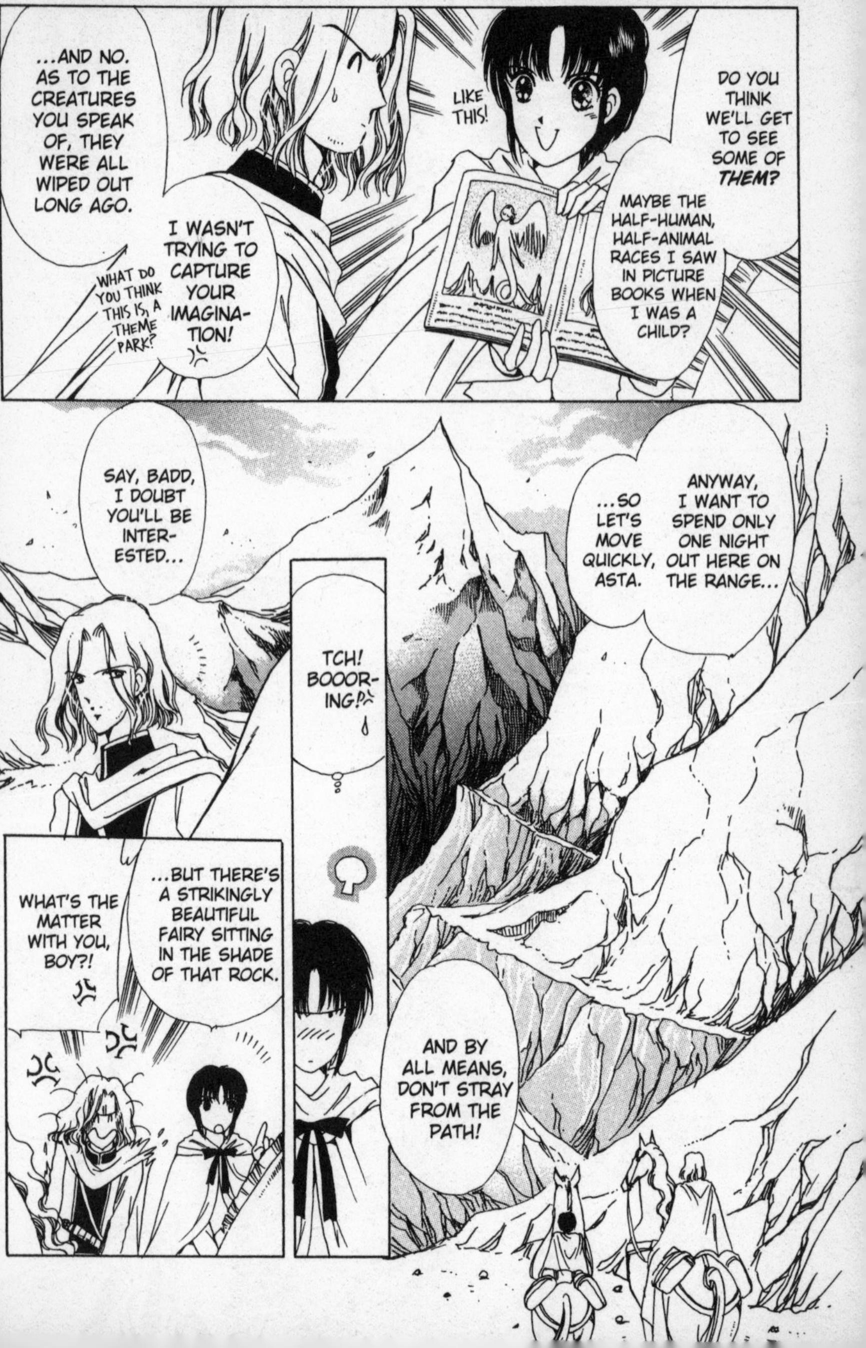
DO YOU THINK WE'LL GET TO SEE SOME OF *THEM?*
LIKE THIS!
MAYBE THE HALF-HUMAN, HALF-ANIMAL RACES I SAW IN PICTURE BOOKS WHEN I WAS A CHILD?
...AND NO. AS TO THE CREATURES YOU SPEAK OF, THEY WERE ALL WIPED OUT LONG AGO.
I WASN'T TRYING TO CAPTURE YOUR IMAGINATION!
WHAT DO YOU THINK THIS IS, A THEME PARK?
ANYWAY, I WANT TO SPEND ONLY ONE NIGHT OUT HERE ON THE RANGE...
...SO LET'S MOVE QUICKLY, ASTA.
AND BY ALL MEANS, DON'T STRAY FROM THE PATH!
TCH! BOOORING!
SAY, BADD, I DOUBT YOU'LL BE INTERESTED...
...BUT THERE'S A STRIKINGLY BEAUTIFUL FAIRY SITTING IN THE SHADE OF THAT ROCK.
WHAT'S THE MATTER WITH YOU, BOY?!

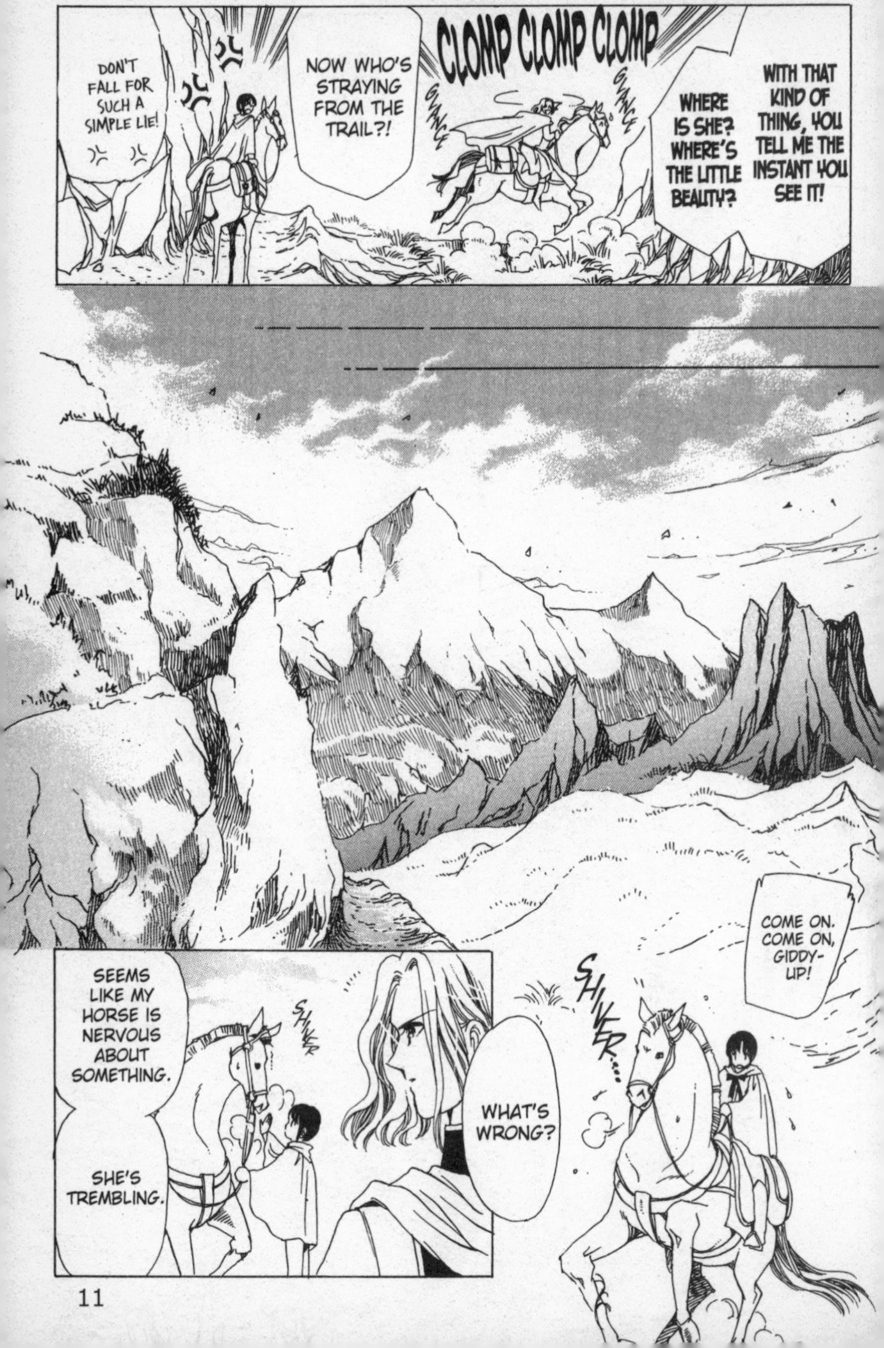
WITH THAT KIND OF THING, YOU TELL ME THE INSTANT YOU SEE IT!
WHERE IS SHE? WHERE'S THE LITTLE BEAUTY?
CLOMP CLOMP CLOMP
GLANCE
GLANCE
NOW WHO'S STRAYING FROM THE TRAIL?!
DON'T FALL FOR SUCH A SIMPLE LIE!
COME ON. COME ON, GIDDY-UP!
SHIVER....
WHAT'S WRONG?
SEEMS LIKE MY HORSE IS NERVOUS ABOUT SOMETHING.
SHIVER
SHE'S TREMBLING.

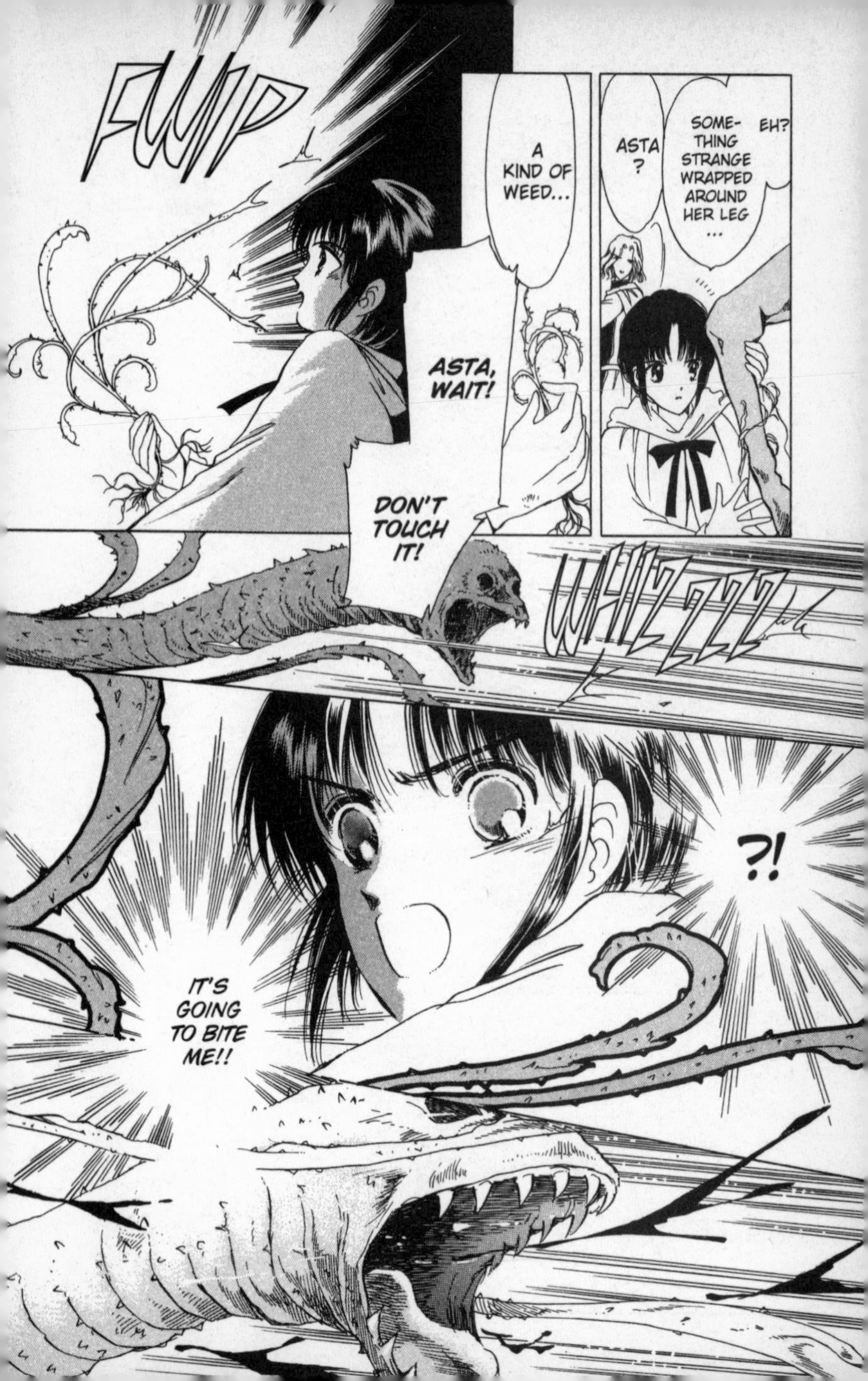
EH?
SOME-THING STRANGE WRAPPED AROUND HER LEG ...
ASTA ?
A KIND OF WEED...
ASTA, WAIT!
DON'T TOUCH IT!
FWIP
WHIZZZZ
?!
IT'S GOING TO BITE ME!!

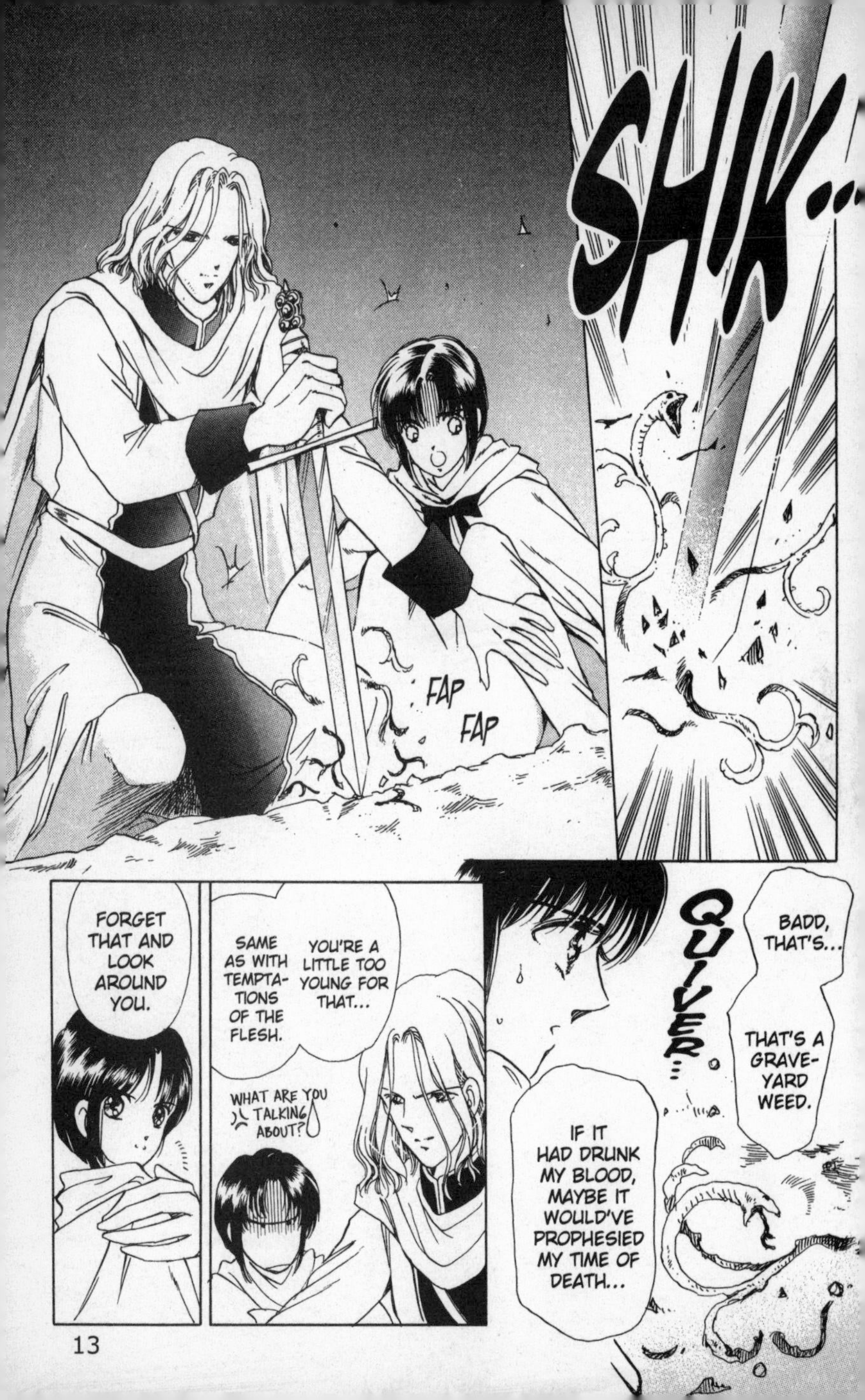
SHIK...
FAP
FAP
QUIVER...
BADD, THAT'S...
THAT'S A GRAVE-YARD WEED.
IF IT HAD DRUNK MY BLOOD, MAYBE IT WOULD'VE PROPHESIED MY TIME OF DEATH...
YOU'RE A LITTLE TOO YOUNG FOR THAT...
SAME AS WITH TEMPTA-TIONS OF THE FLESH.
WHAT ARE YOU TALKING ABOUT?
FORGET THAT AND LOOK AROUND YOU.

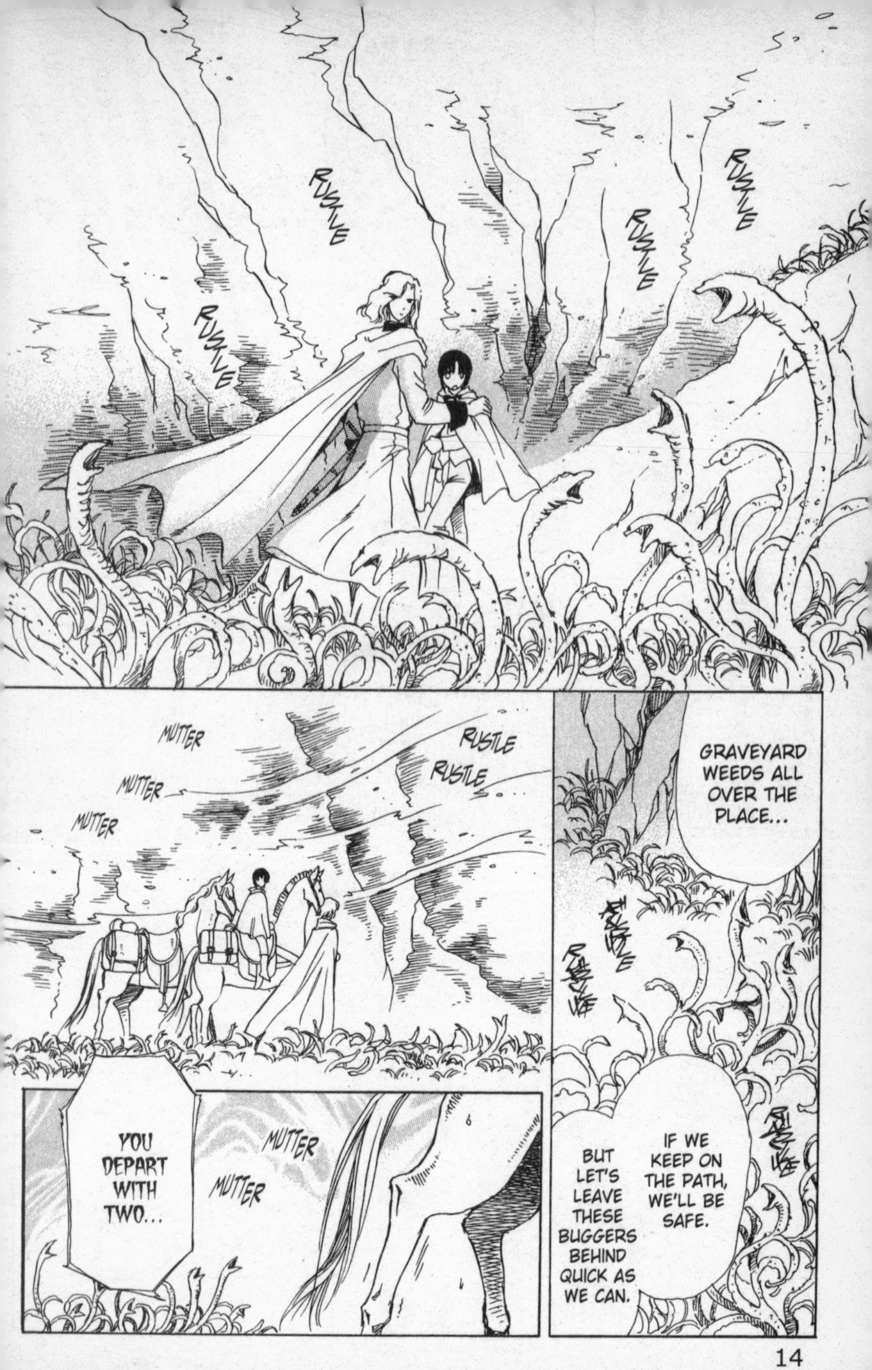
RUSTLE
RUSTLE
RUSTLE
RUSTLE
GRAVEYARD WEEDS ALL OVER THE PLACE...
IF WE KEEP ON THE PATH, WE'LL BE SAFE.
BUT LET'S LEAVE THESE BUGGERS BEHIND QUICK AS WE CAN.
RUSTLE
RUSTLE
MUTTER
MUTTER
MUTTER
YOU DEPART WITH TWO...
MUTTER
MUTTER

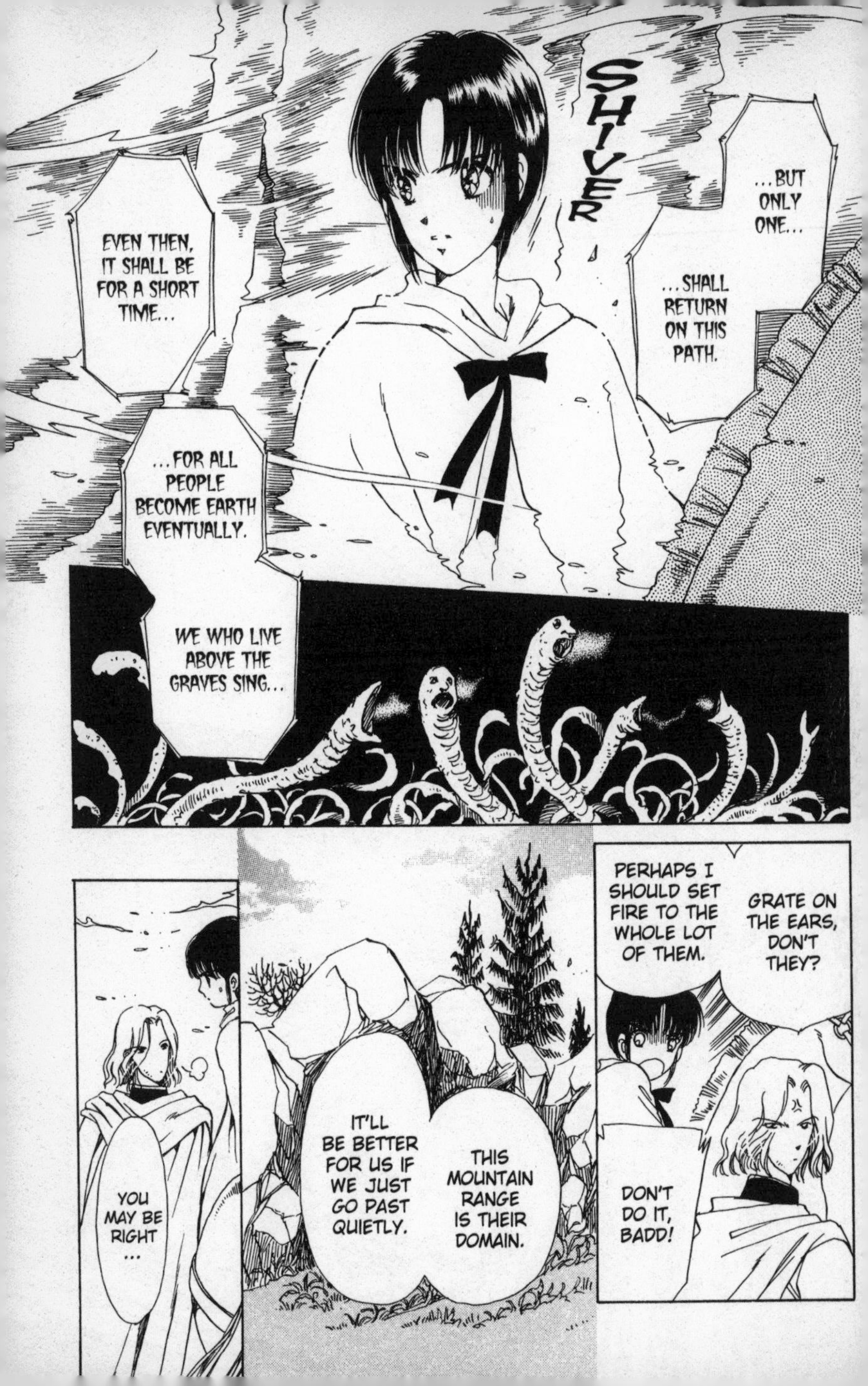
SHIVER
...BUT ONLY ONE...
...SHALL RETURN ON THIS PATH.
EVEN THEN, IT SHALL BE FOR A SHORT TIME...
...FOR ALL PEOPLE BECOME EARTH EVENTUALLY.
WE WHO LIVE ABOVE THE GRAVES SING...
GRATE ON THE EARS, DON'T THEY?
PERHAPS I SHOULD SET FIRE TO THE WHOLE LOT OF THEM.
DON'T DO IT, BADD!
THIS MOUNTAIN RANGE IS THEIR DOMAIN.
IT'LL BE BETTER FOR US IF WE JUST GO PAST QUIETLY.
YOU MAY BE RIGHT...

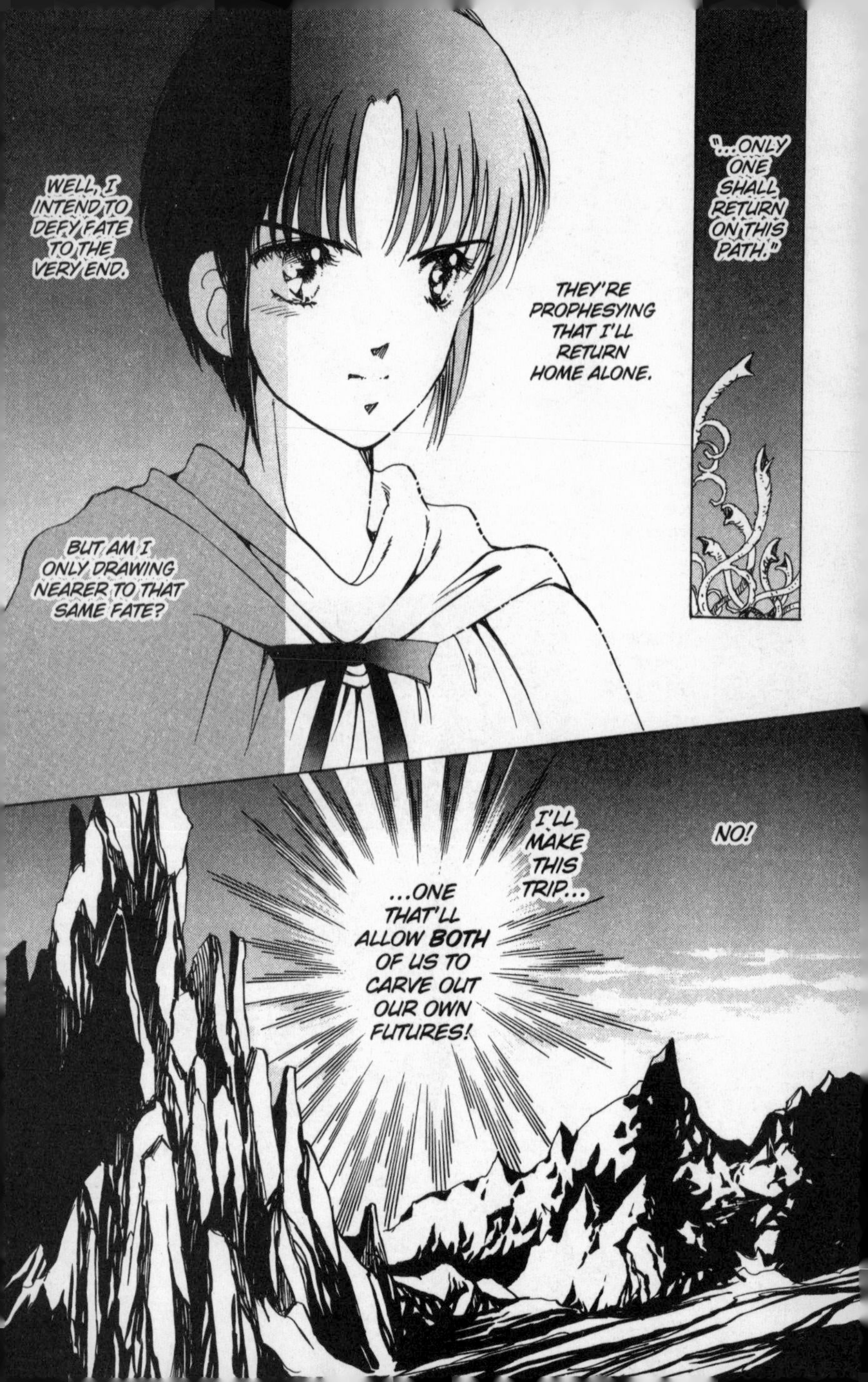
"...ONLY ONE SHALL RETURN ON THIS PATH."
THEY'RE PROPHESYING THAT I'LL RETURN HOME ALONE.
WELL, I INTEND TO DEFY FATE TO THE VERY END.
BUT AM I ONLY DRAWING NEARER TO THAT SAME FATE?
NO!
I'LL MAKE THIS TRIP...
...ONE THAT'LL ALLOW **BOTH** OF US TO CARVE OUT OUR OWN FUTURES!

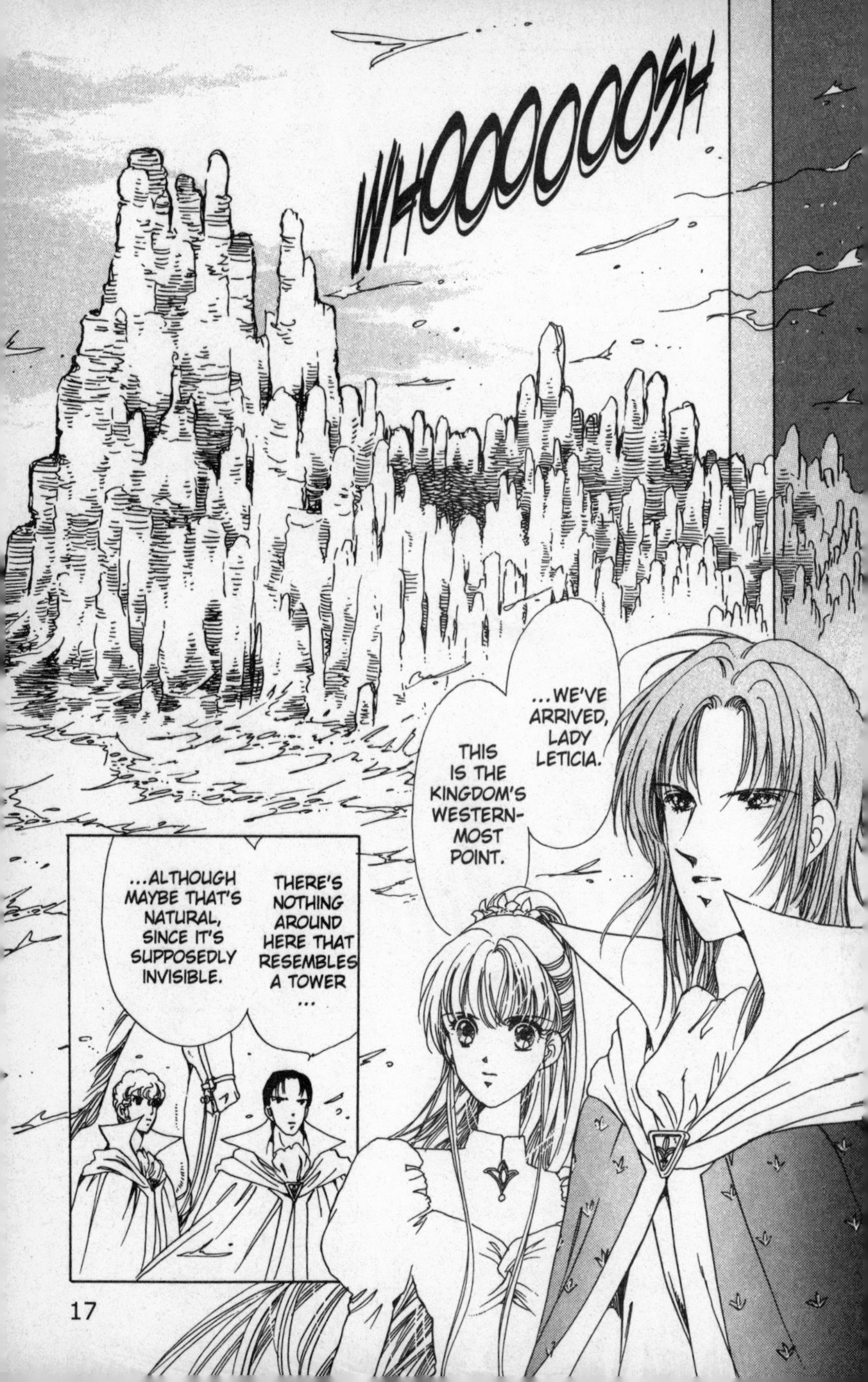
WHOOOOOOOSH
...WE'VE ARRIVED, LADY LETICIA.
THIS IS THE KINGDOM'S WESTERN-MOST POINT.
THERE'S NOTHING AROUND HERE THAT RESEMBLES A TOWER ...
...ALTHOUGH MAYBE THAT'S NATURAL, SINCE IT'S SUPPOSEDLY INVISIBLE.

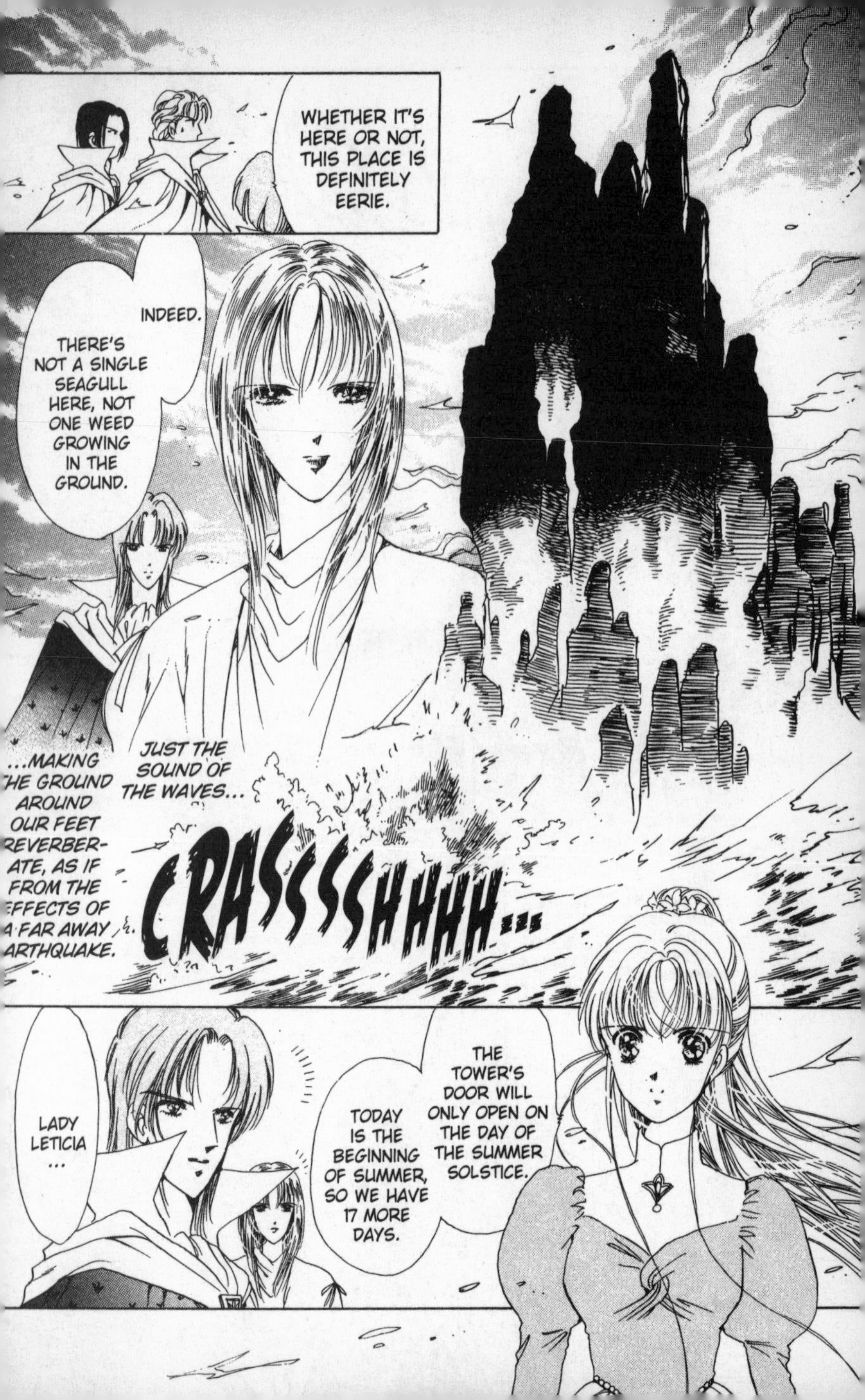
WHETHER IT'S HERE OR NOT, THIS PLACE IS DEFINITELY EERIE.
INDEED.
THERE'S NOT A SINGLE SEAGULL HERE, NOT ONE WEED GROWING IN THE GROUND.
JUST THE SOUND OF THE WAVES...
...MAKING HE GROUND AROUND OUR FEET REVERBER-ATE, AS IF FROM THE FFECTS OF A FAR AWAY ARTHQUAKE.
CRASSSSHHHH...
THE TOWER'S DOOR WILL ONLY OPEN ON THE DAY OF THE SUMMER SOLSTICE.
TODAY IS THE BEGINNING OF SUMMER, SO WE HAVE 17 MORE DAYS.
LADY LETICIA ...

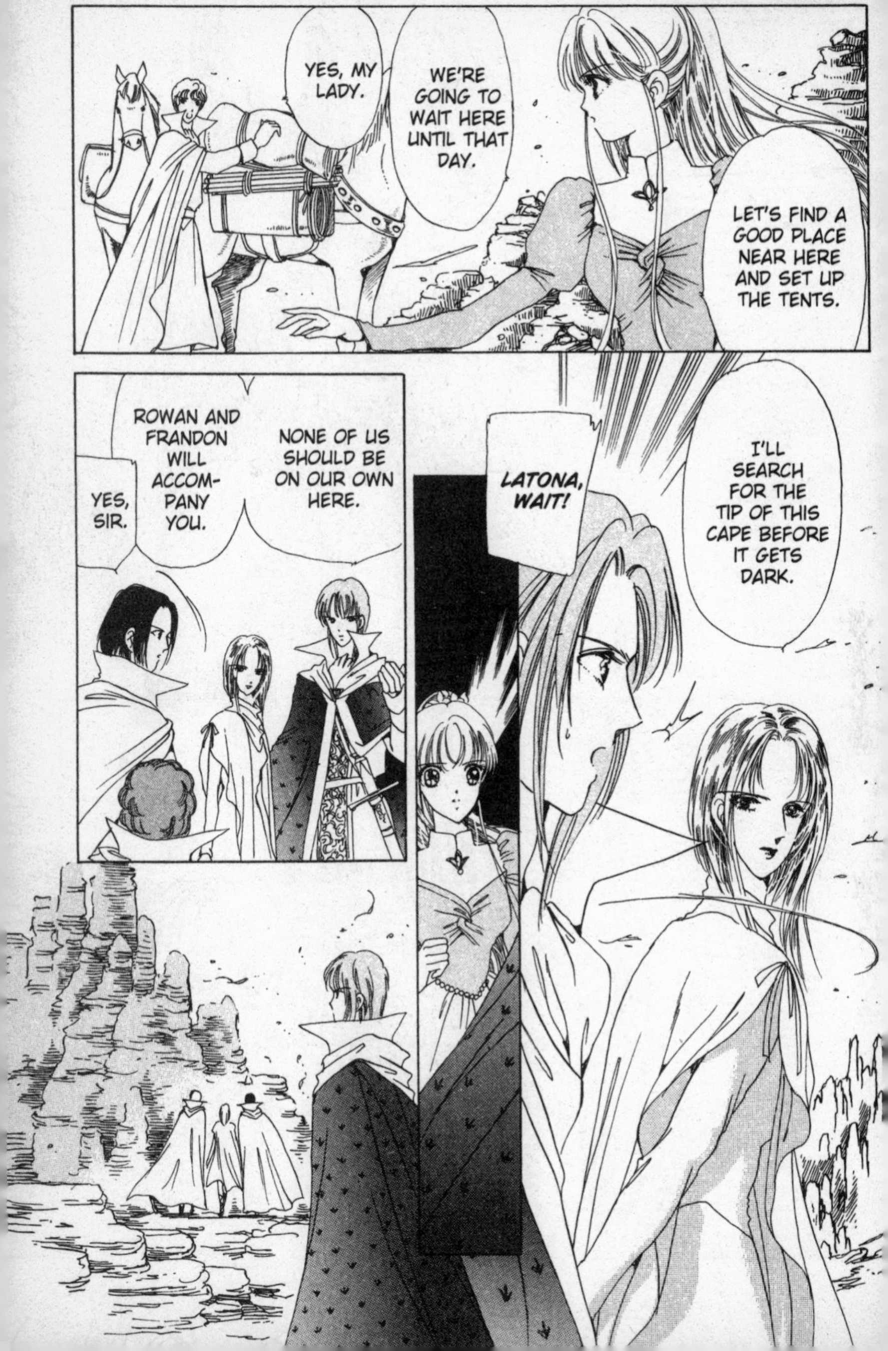
LET'S FIND A GOOD PLACE NEAR HERE AND SET UP THE TENTS.
WE'RE GOING TO WAIT HERE UNTIL THAT DAY.
YES, MY LADY.
I'LL SEARCH FOR THE TIP OF THIS CAPE BEFORE IT GETS DARK.
LATONA, WAIT!
NONE OF US SHOULD BE ON OUR OWN HERE.
ROWAN AND FRANDON WILL ACCOMPANY YOU.
YES, SIR.

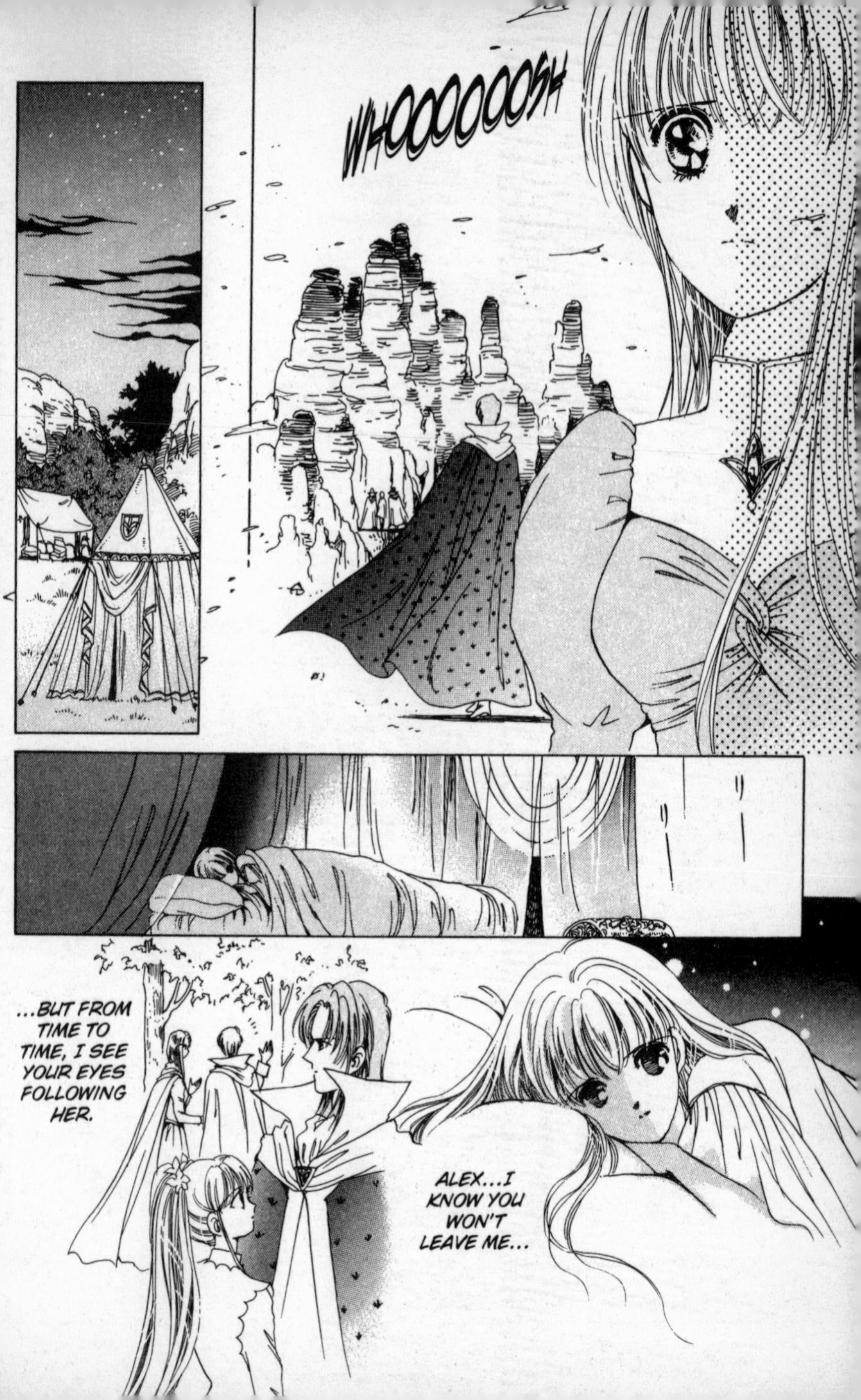
WHOOOOOOSH
ALEX...I KNOW YOU WON'T LEAVE ME...
...BUT FROM TIME TO TIME, I SEE YOUR EYES FOLLOWING HER.

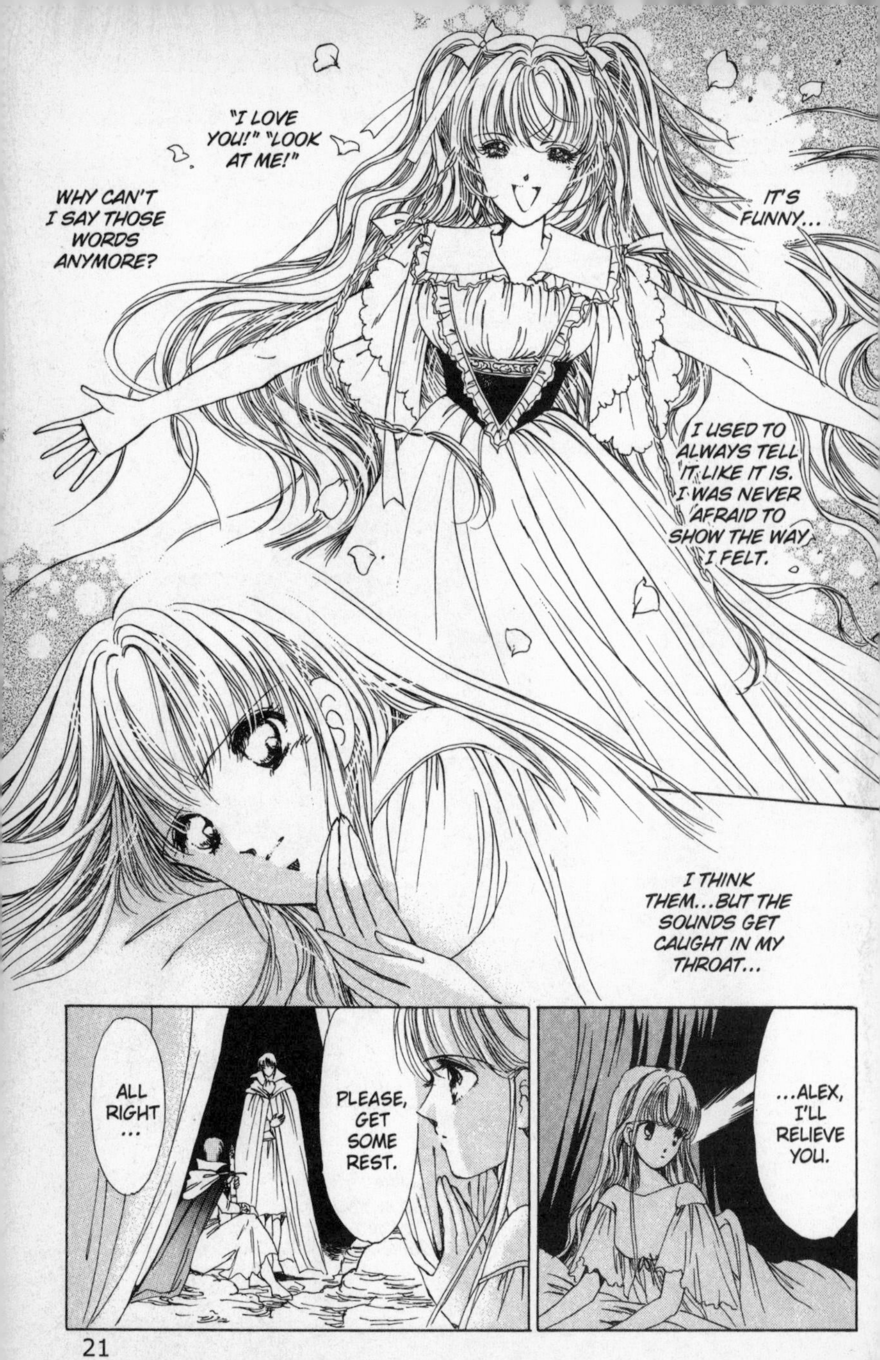
IT'S FUNNY...
I USED TO ALWAYS TELL IT LIKE IT IS. I WAS NEVER AFRAID TO SHOW THE WAY I FELT.
"I LOVE YOU!" "LOOK AT ME!"
WHY CAN'T I SAY THOSE WORDS ANYMORE?
I THINK THEM...BUT THE SOUNDS GET CAUGHT IN MY THROAT...
...ALEX, I'LL RELIEVE YOU.
PLEASE, GET SOME REST.
ALL RIGHT...

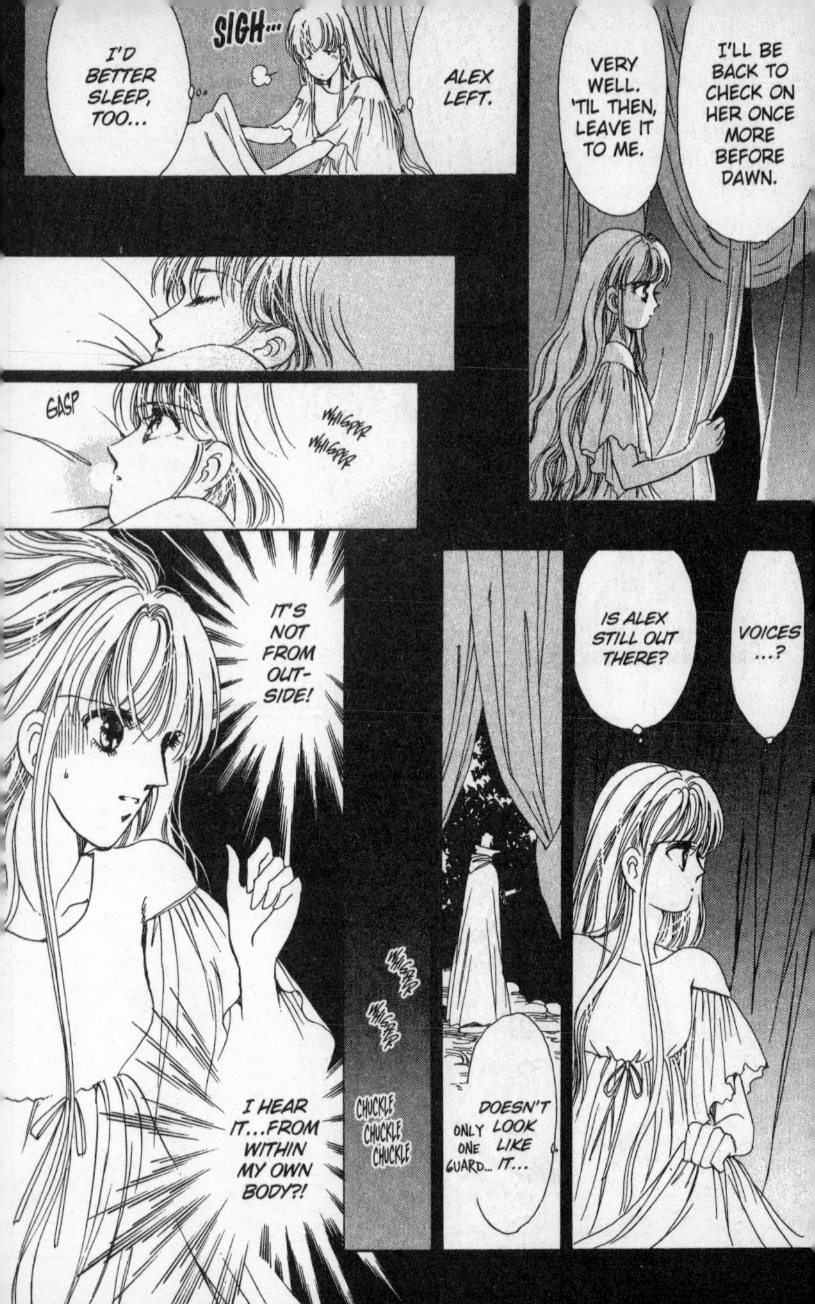
I'LL BE BACK TO CHECK ON HER ONCE MORE BEFORE DAWN.
VERY WELL. 'TIL THEN, LEAVE IT TO ME.
ALEX LEFT.
SIGH...
I'D BETTER SLEEP, TOO...
WHISPER
WHISPER
GASP
VOICES ...?
IS ALEX STILL OUT THERE?
DOESN'T LOOK LIKE IT...
ONLY ONE GUARD...
WHISPER
WHISPER
CHUCKLE CHUCKLE CHUCKLE
IT'S NOT FROM OUT-SIDE!
I HEAR IT...FROM WITHIN MY OWN BODY?!

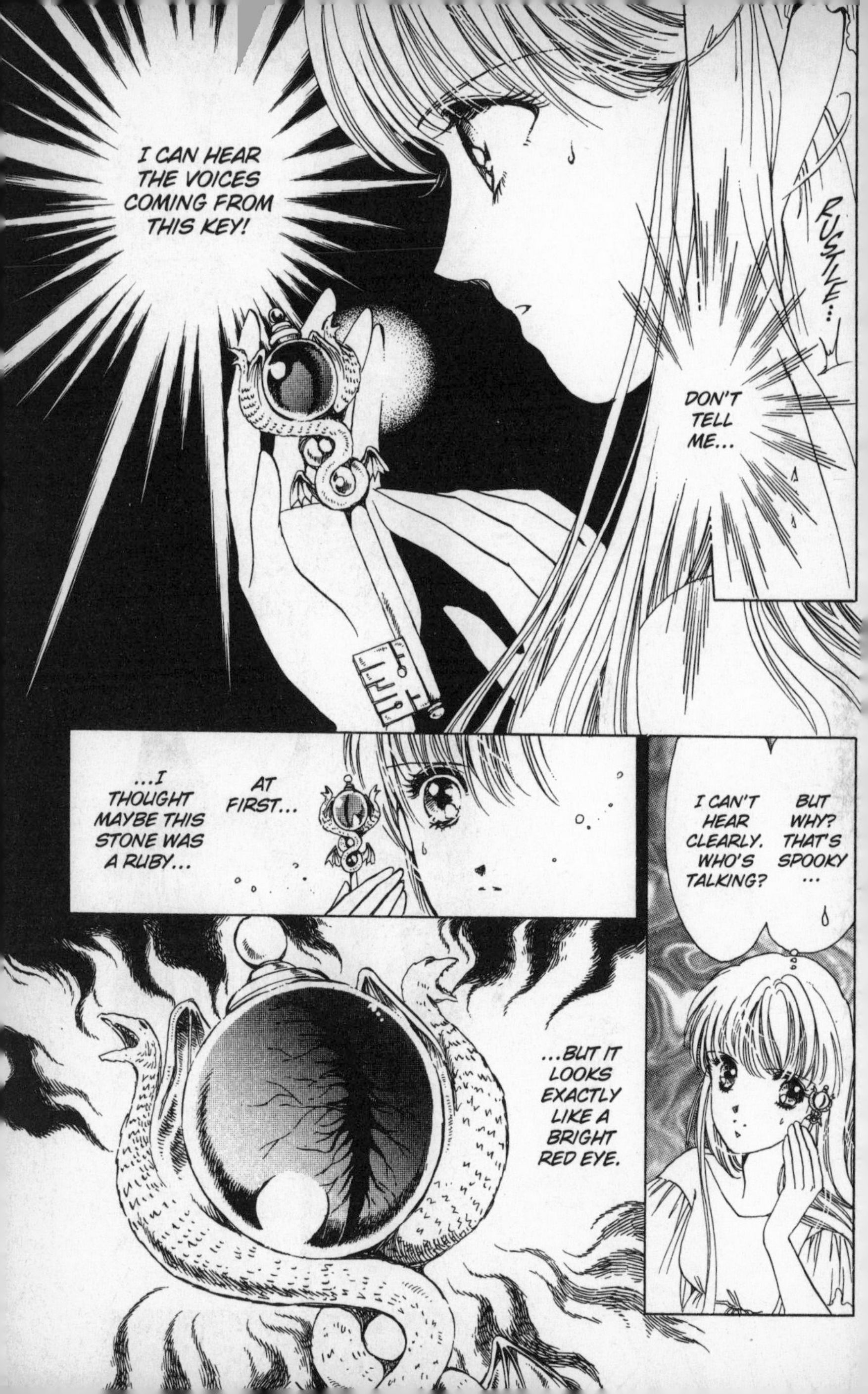

RUSTLE...
DON'T TELL ME...
I CAN HEAR THE VOICES COMING FROM THIS KEY!
BUT WHY? THAT'S SPOOKY...
I CAN'T HEAR CLEARLY. WHO'S TALKING?
AT FIRST...
...I THOUGHT MAYBE THIS STONE WAS A RUBY...
...BUT IT LOOKS EXACTLY LIKE A BRIGHT RED EYE.

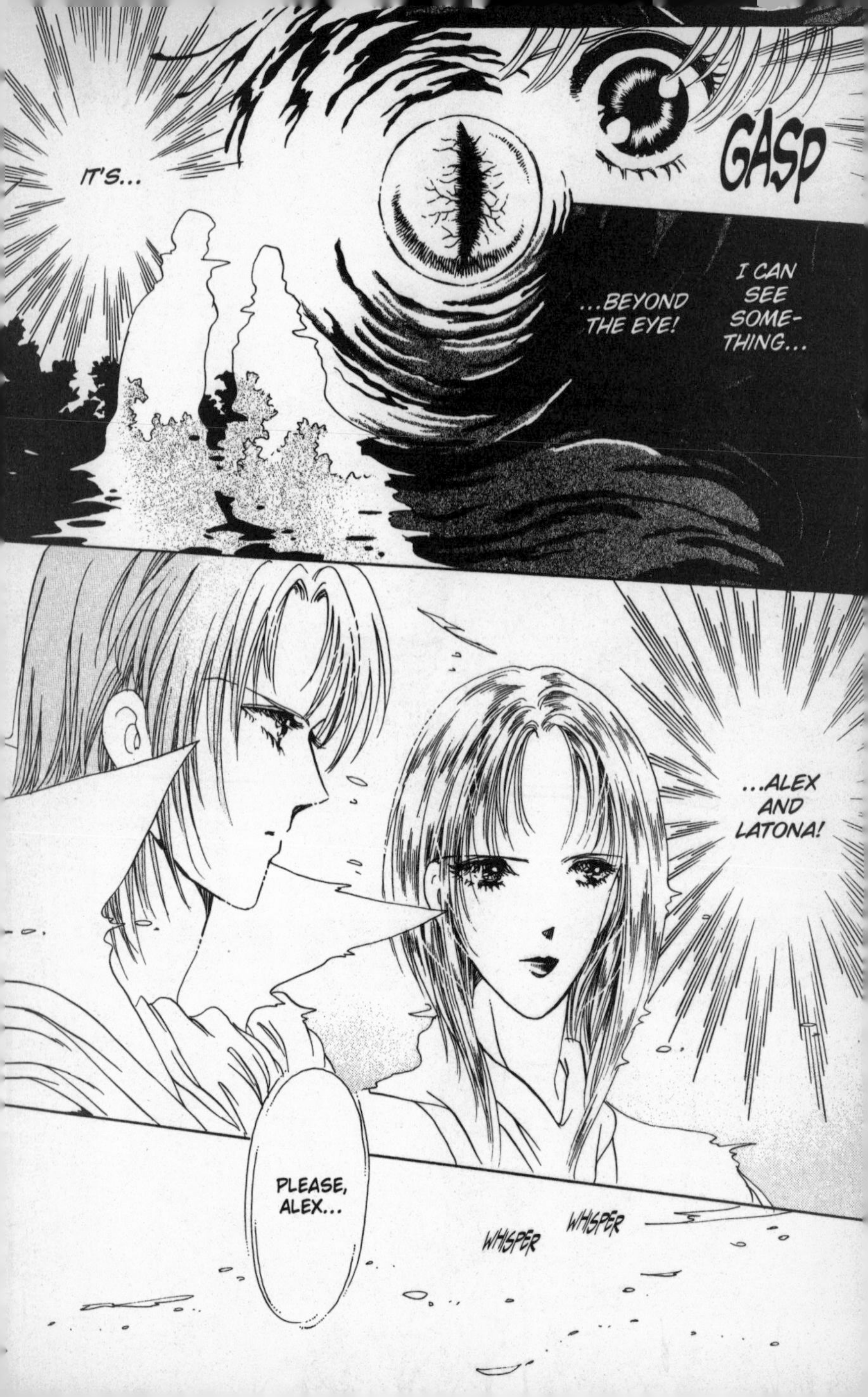
GASP
I CAN SEE SOME-THING...
...BEYOND THE EYE!
IT'S...
...ALEX AND LATONA!
WHISPER
WHISPER
PLEASE, ALEX...

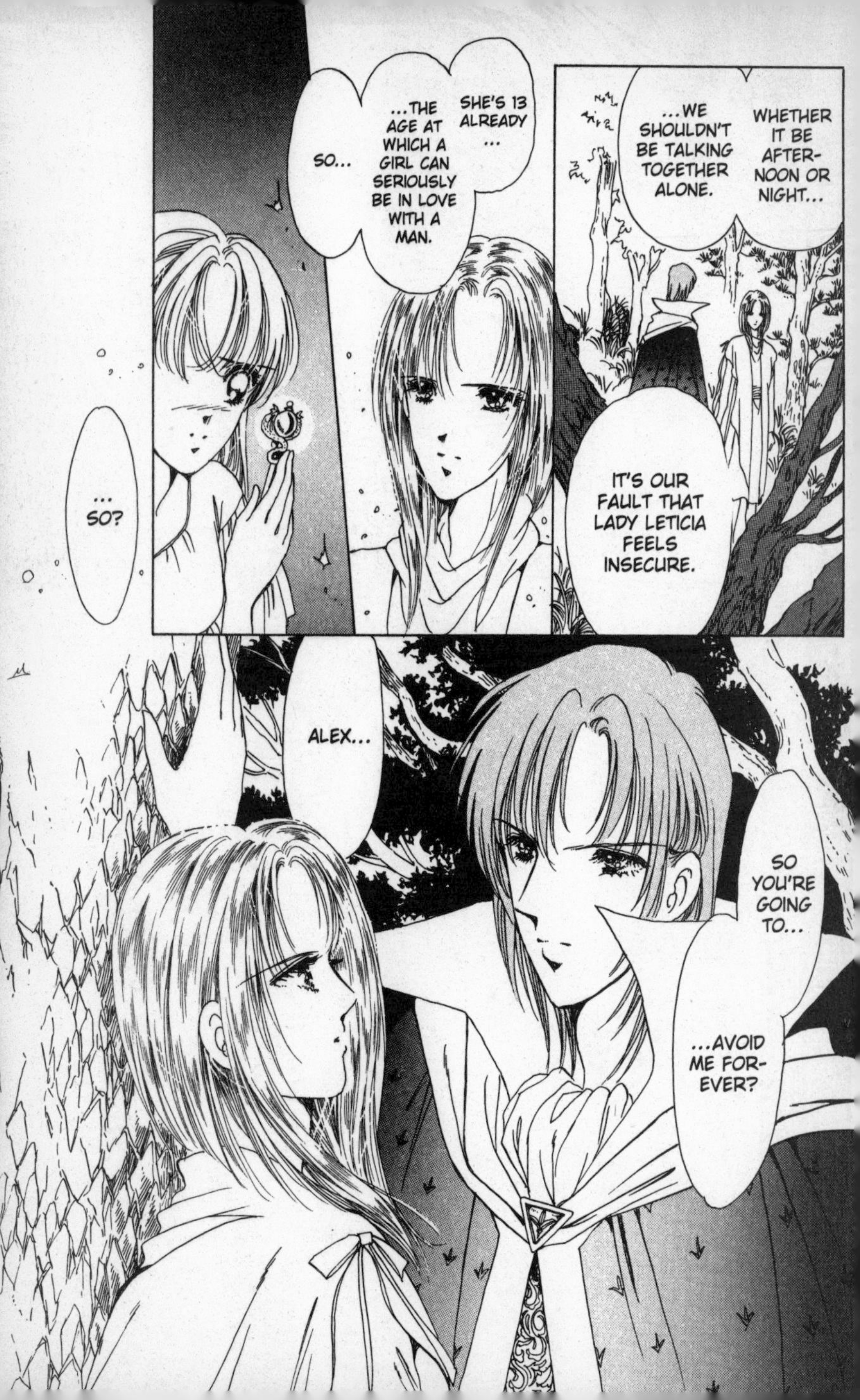

WHETHER IT BE AFTER-NOON OR NIGHT...
...WE SHOULDN'T BE TALKING TOGETHER ALONE.
IT'S OUR FAULT THAT LADY LETICIA FEELS INSECURE.
SHE'S 13 ALREADY...
...THE AGE AT WHICH A GIRL CAN SERIOUSLY BE IN LOVE WITH A MAN.
SO...
...SO?
ALEX...
SO YOU'RE GOING TO...
...AVOID ME FOR-EVER?

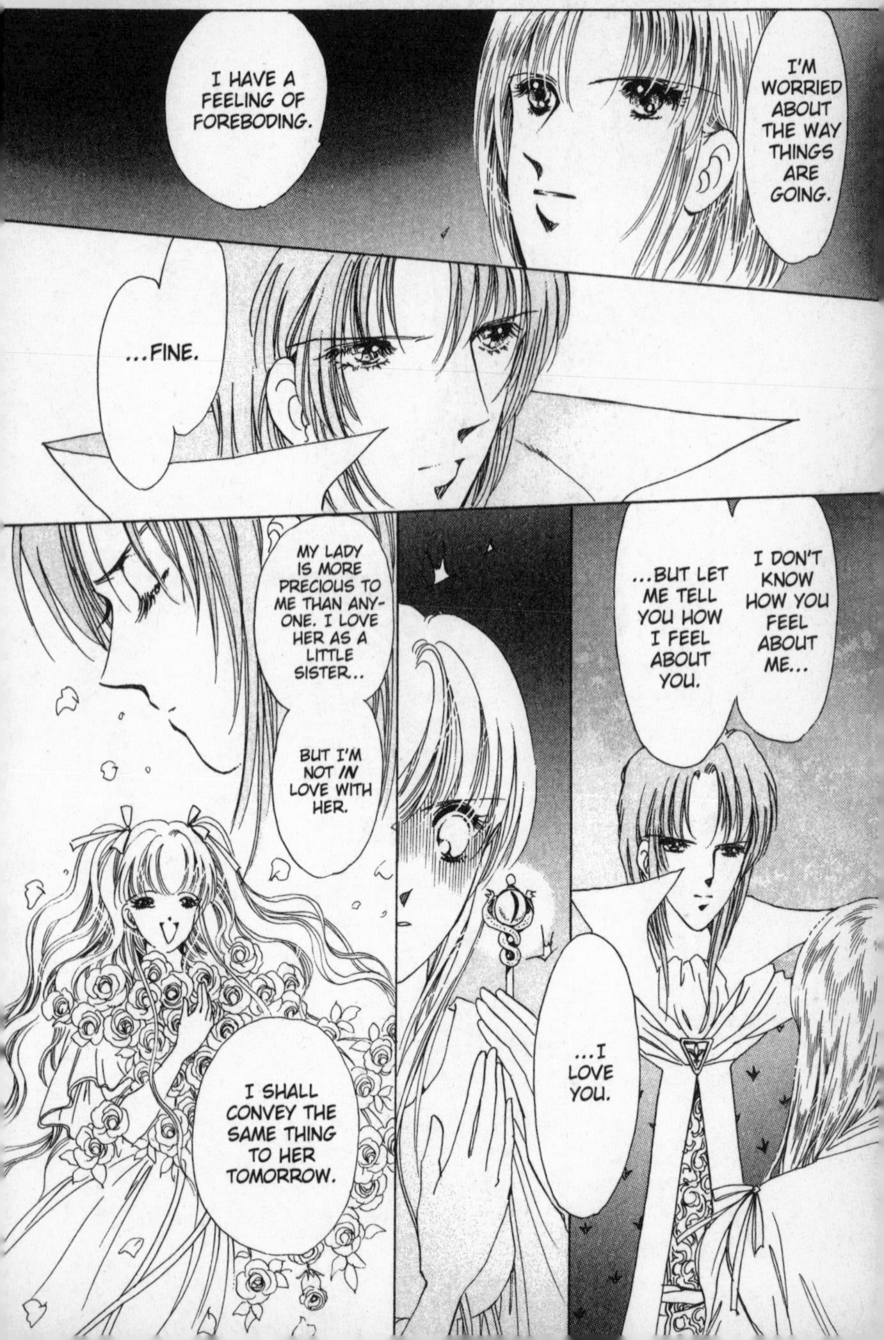
I'M WORRIED ABOUT THE WAY THINGS ARE GOING.
I HAVE A FEELING OF FOREBODING.
...FINE.
I DON'T KNOW HOW YOU FEEL ABOUT ME...
...BUT LET ME TELL YOU HOW I FEEL ABOUT YOU.
...I LOVE YOU.
MY LADY IS MORE PRECIOUS TO ME THAN ANY-ONE. I LOVE HER AS A LITTLE SISTER...
BUT I'M NOT *IN* LOVE WITH HER.
I SHALL CONVEY THE SAME THING TO HER TOMORROW.

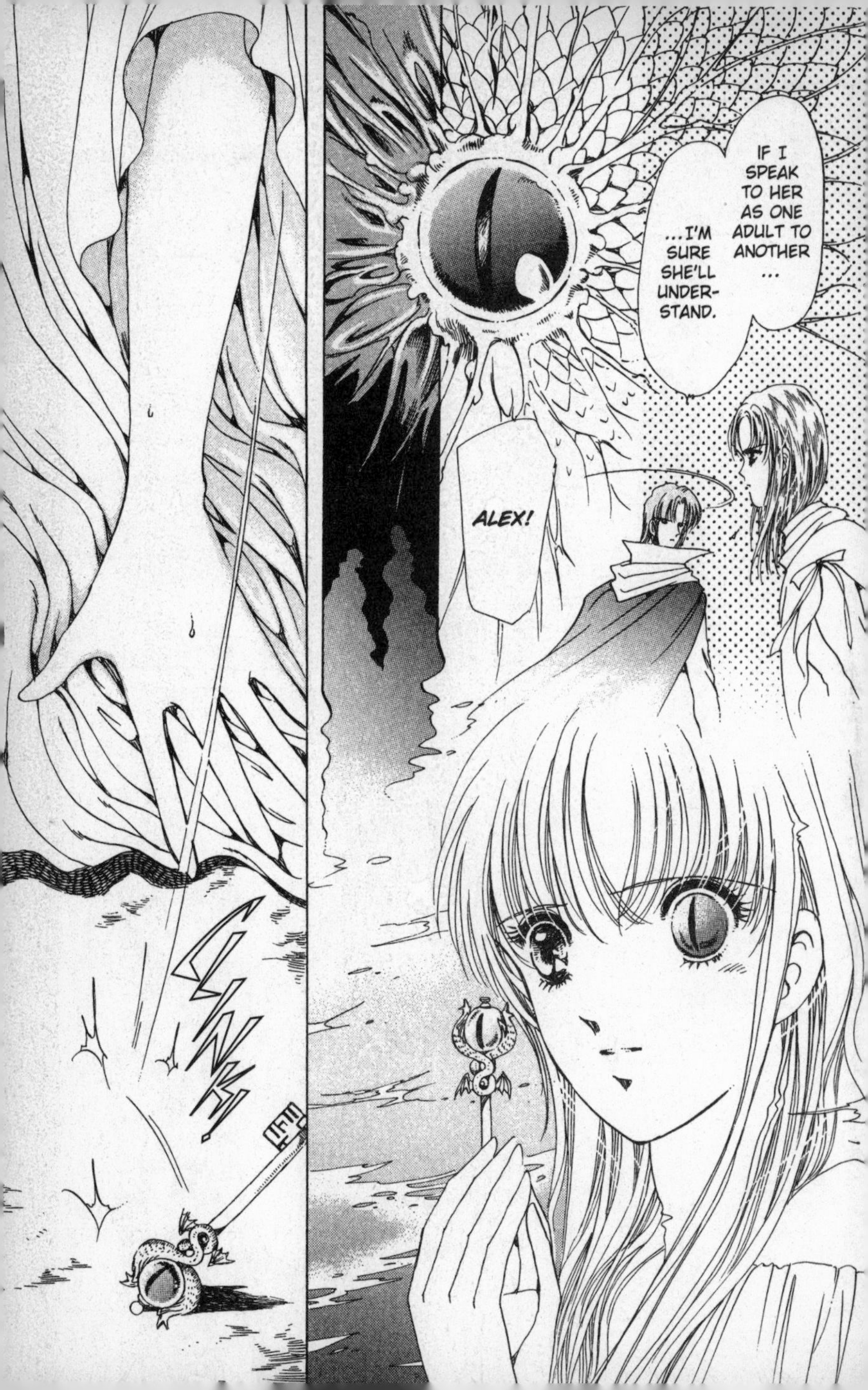
IF I SPEAK TO HER AS ONE ADULT TO ANOTHER ...
...I'M SURE SHE'LL UNDER-STAND.
ALEX!
CLINK!

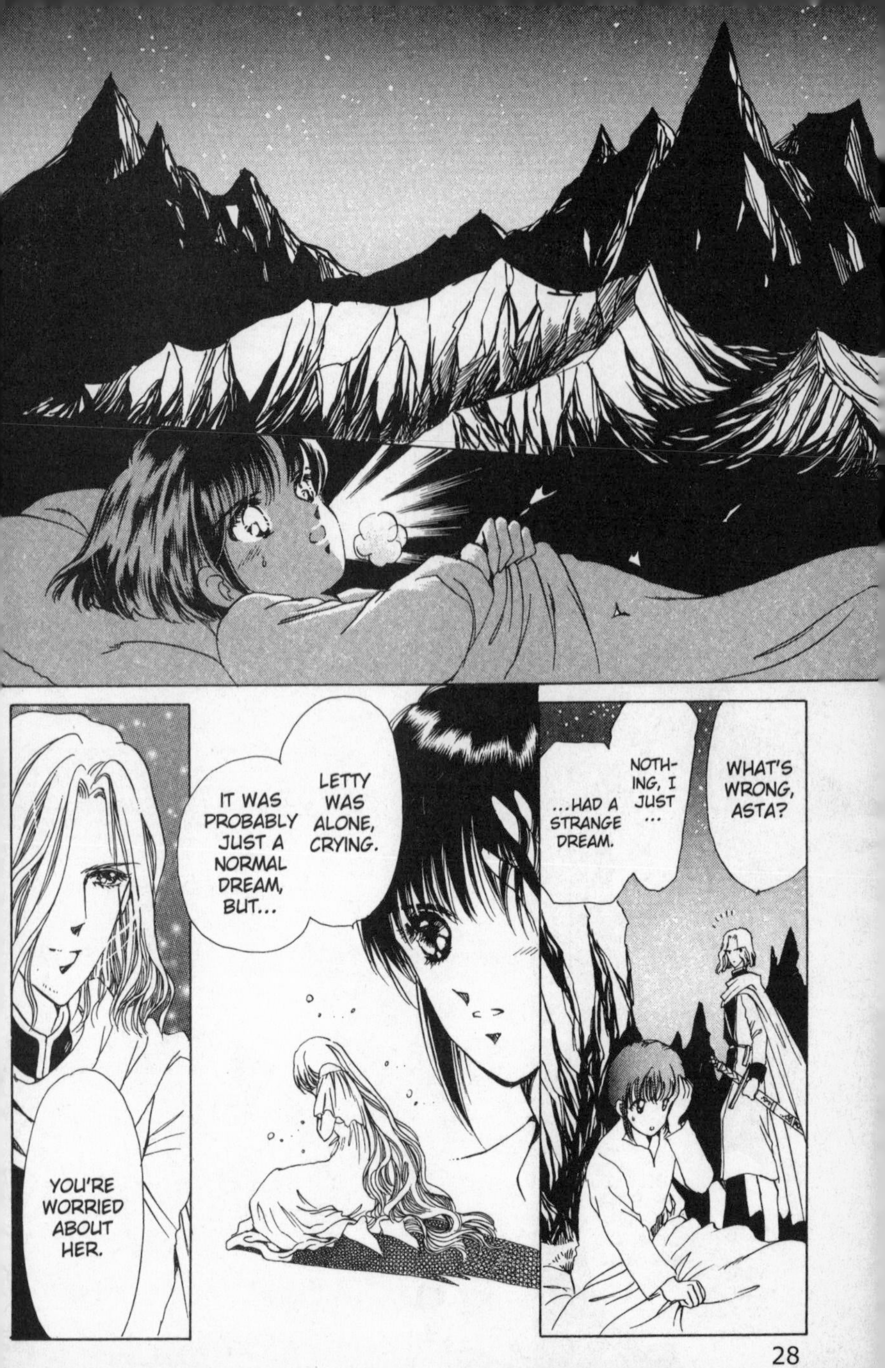
WHAT'S WRONG, ASTA?
NOTH-ING, I JUST ...
...HAD A STRANGE DREAM.
LETTY WAS ALONE, CRYING.
IT WAS PROBABLY JUST A NORMAL DREAM, BUT...
YOU'RE WORRIED ABOUT HER.

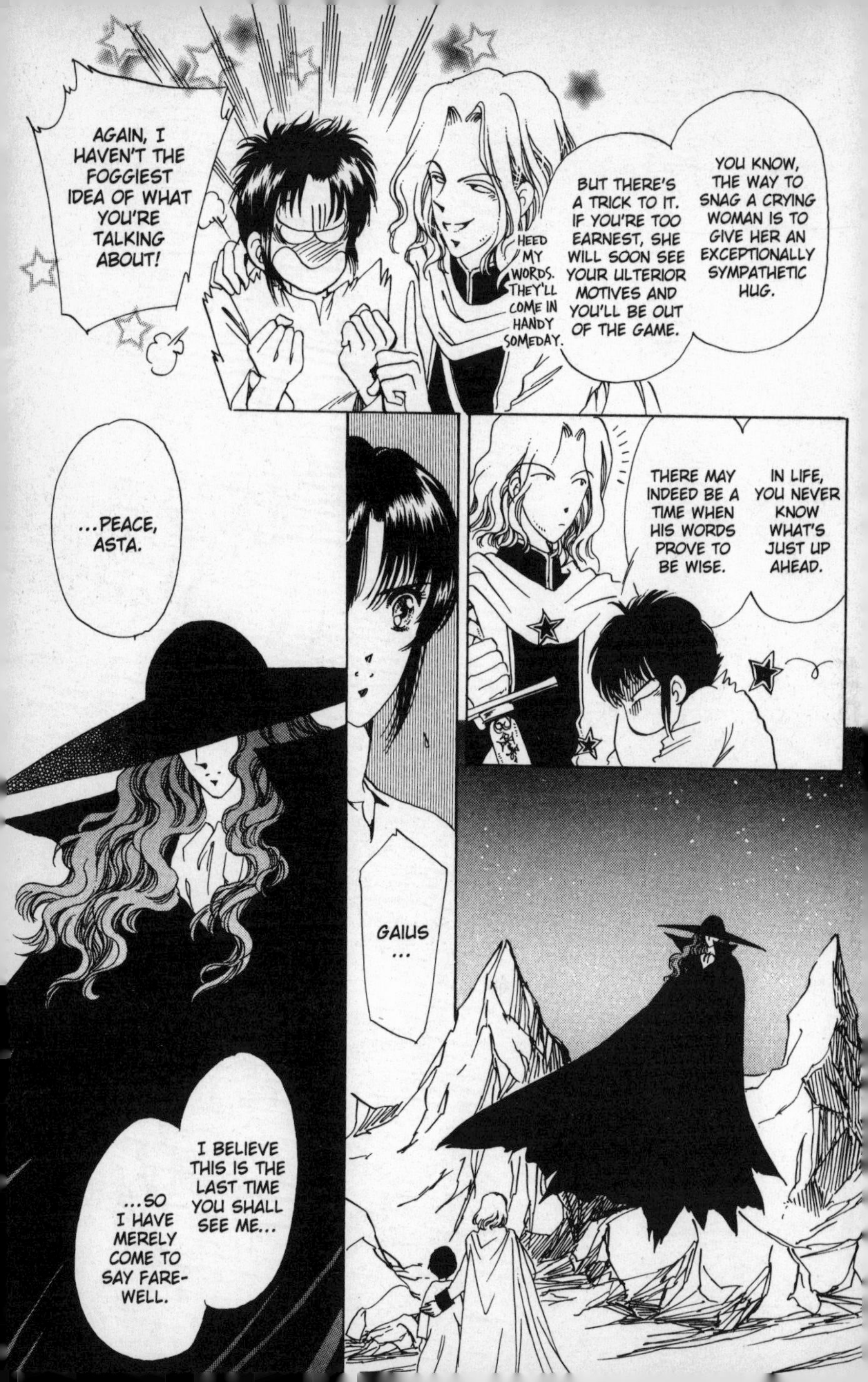
YOU KNOW, THE WAY TO SNAG A CRYING WOMAN IS TO GIVE HER AN EXCEPTIONALLY SYMPATHETIC HUG.
BUT THERE'S A TRICK TO IT. IF YOU'RE TOO EARNEST, SHE WILL SOON SEE YOUR ULTERIOR MOTIVES AND YOU'LL BE OUT OF THE GAME.
HEED MY WORDS. THEY'LL COME IN HANDY SOMEDAY.
AGAIN, I HAVEN'T THE FOGGIEST IDEA OF WHAT YOU'RE TALKING ABOUT!
IN LIFE, YOU NEVER KNOW WHAT'S JUST UP AHEAD.
THERE MAY INDEED BE A TIME WHEN HIS WORDS PROVE TO BE WISE.
GAIUS ...
...PEACE, ASTA.
I BELIEVE THIS IS THE LAST TIME YOU SHALL SEE ME...
...SO I HAVE MERELY COME TO SAY FARE-WELL.

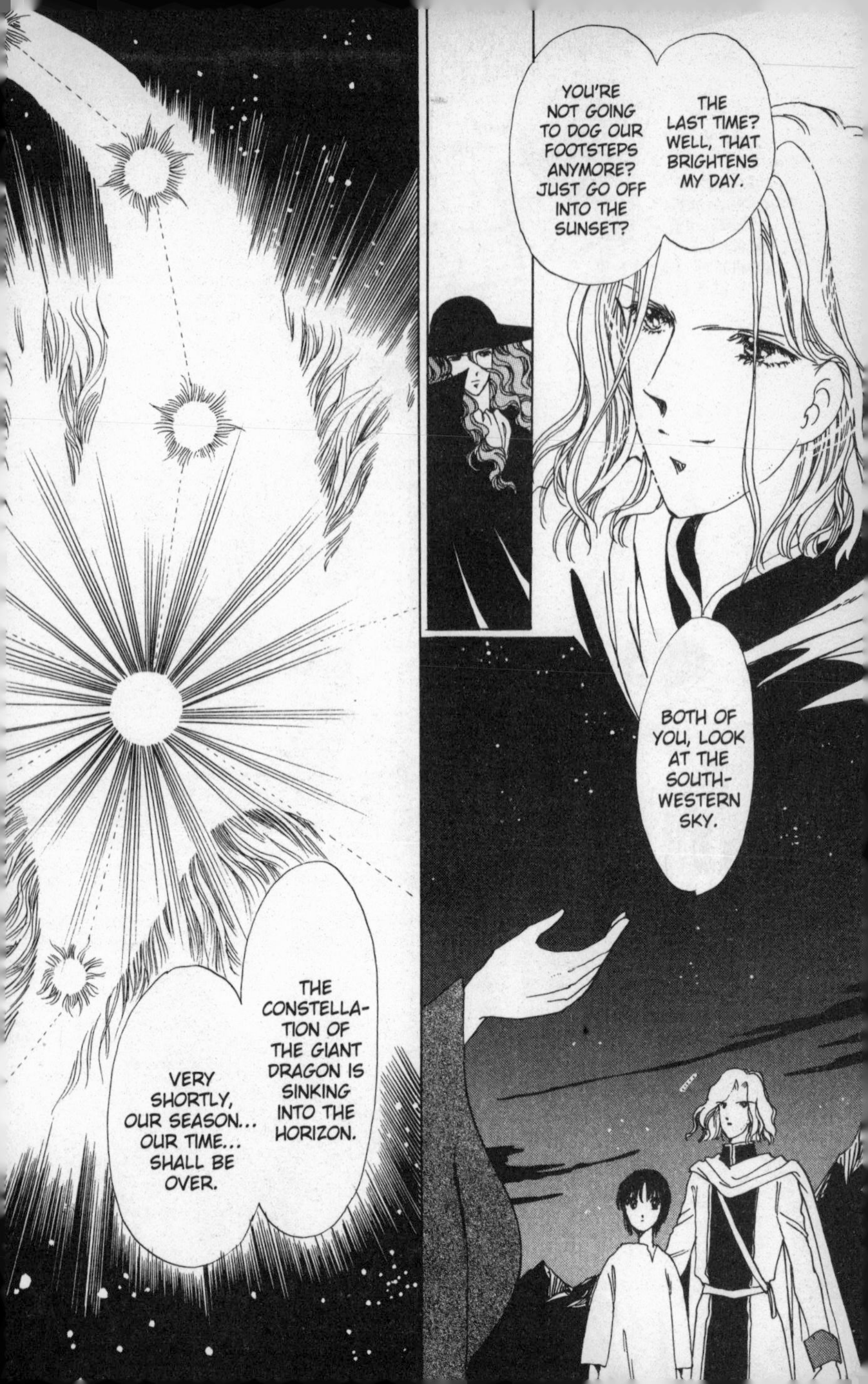
THE LAST TIME? WELL, THAT BRIGHTENS MY DAY.
YOU'RE NOT GOING TO DOG OUR FOOTSTEPS ANYMORE? JUST GO OFF INTO THE SUNSET?
BOTH OF YOU, LOOK AT THE SOUTH-WESTERN SKY.
THE CONSTELLATION OF THE GIANT DRAGON IS SINKING INTO THE HORIZON.
VERY SHORTLY, OUR SEASON... OUR TIME... SHALL BE OVER.

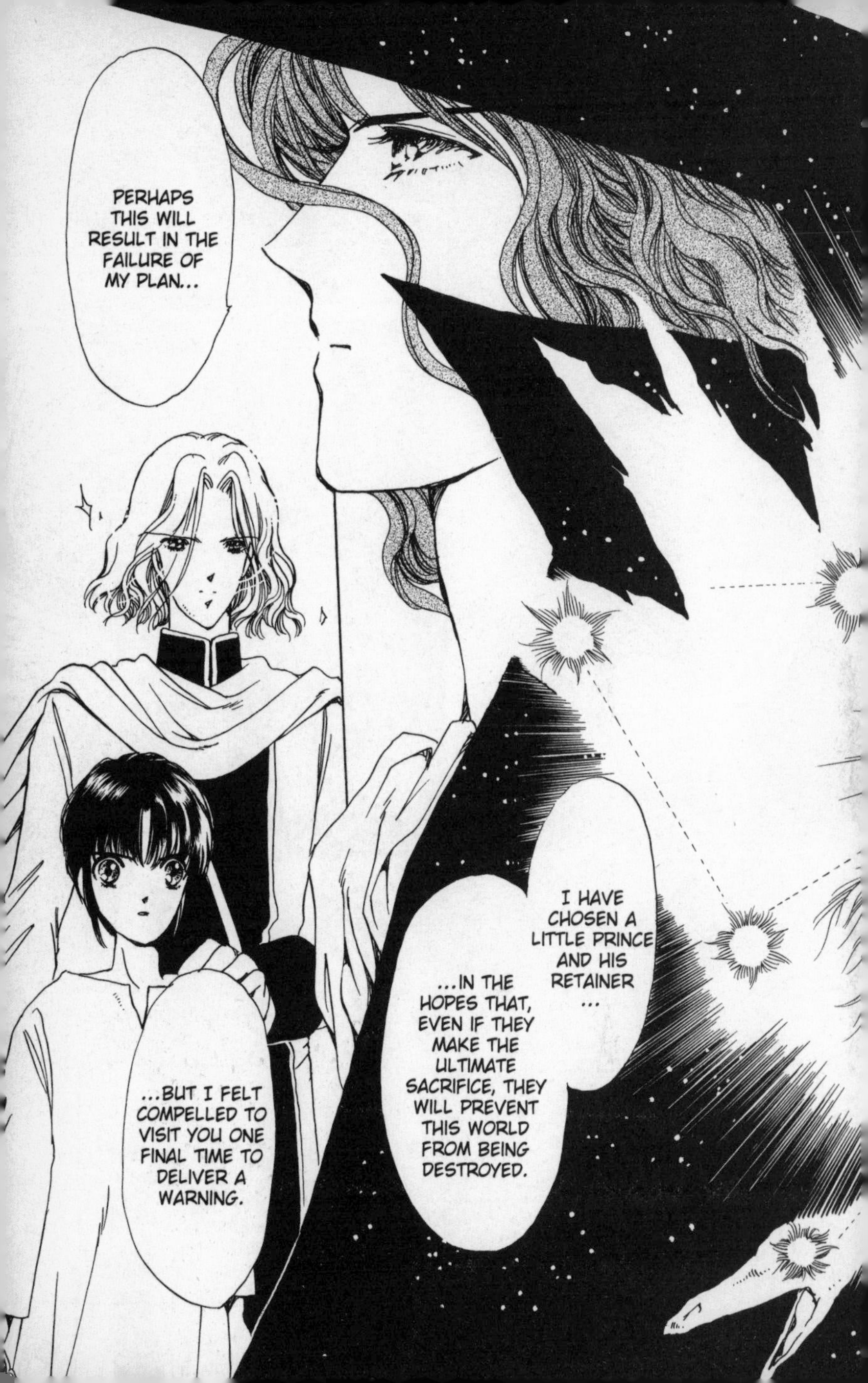
PERHAPS THIS WILL RESULT IN THE FAILURE OF MY PLAN...
...BUT I FELT COMPELLED TO VISIT YOU ONE FINAL TIME TO DELIVER A WARNING.
I HAVE CHOSEN A LITTLE PRINCE AND HIS RETAINER ...
...IN THE HOPES THAT, EVEN IF THEY MAKE THE ULTIMATE SACRIFICE, THEY WILL PREVENT THIS WORLD FROM BEING DESTROYED.

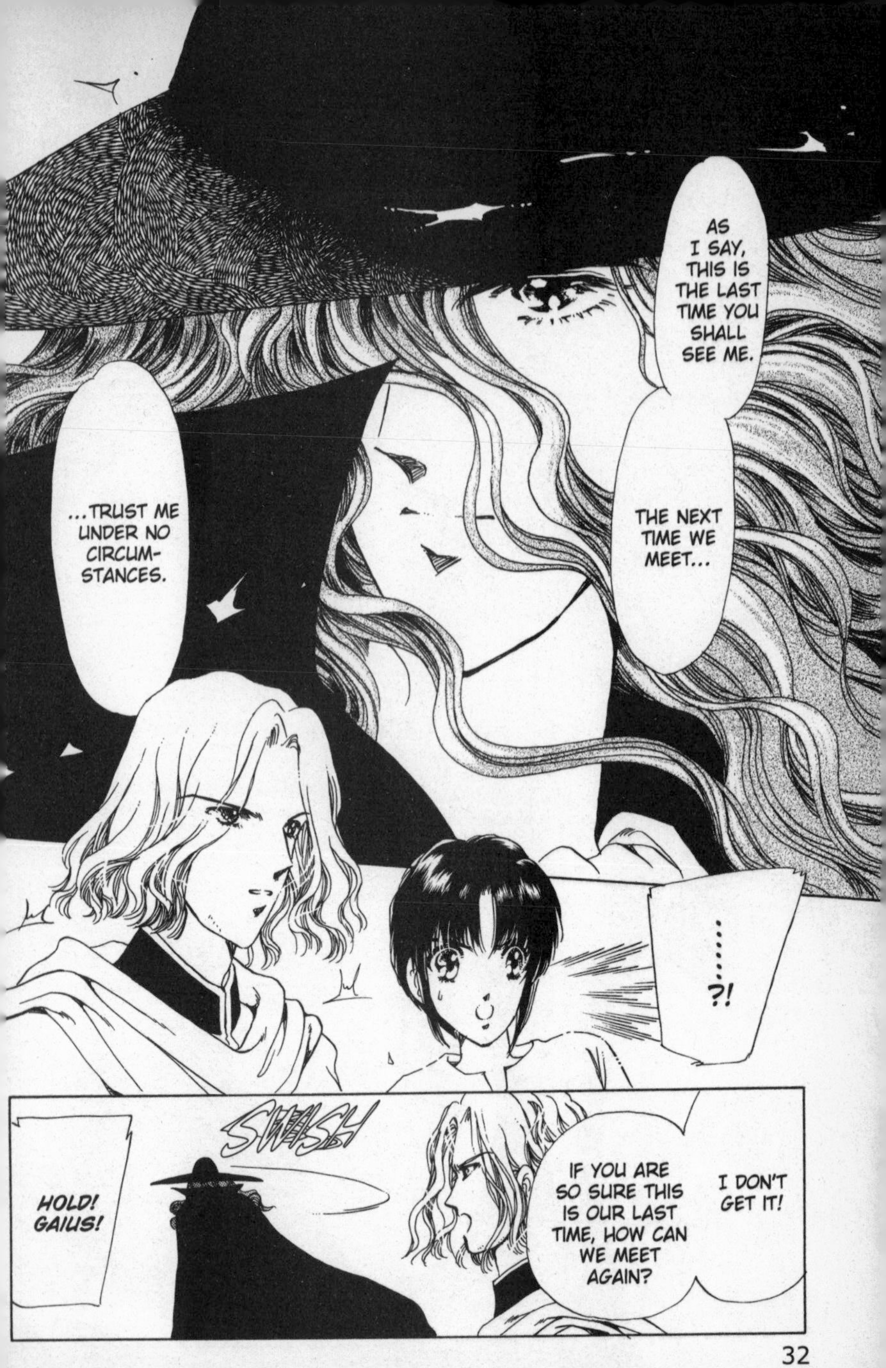
AS I SAY, THIS IS THE LAST TIME YOU SHALL SEE ME.
THE NEXT TIME WE MEET...
...TRUST ME UNDER NO CIRCUM-STANCES.
......?!
I DON'T GET IT!
IF YOU ARE SO SURE THIS IS OUR LAST TIME, HOW CAN WE MEET AGAIN?
SWISH
HOLD! GAIUS!

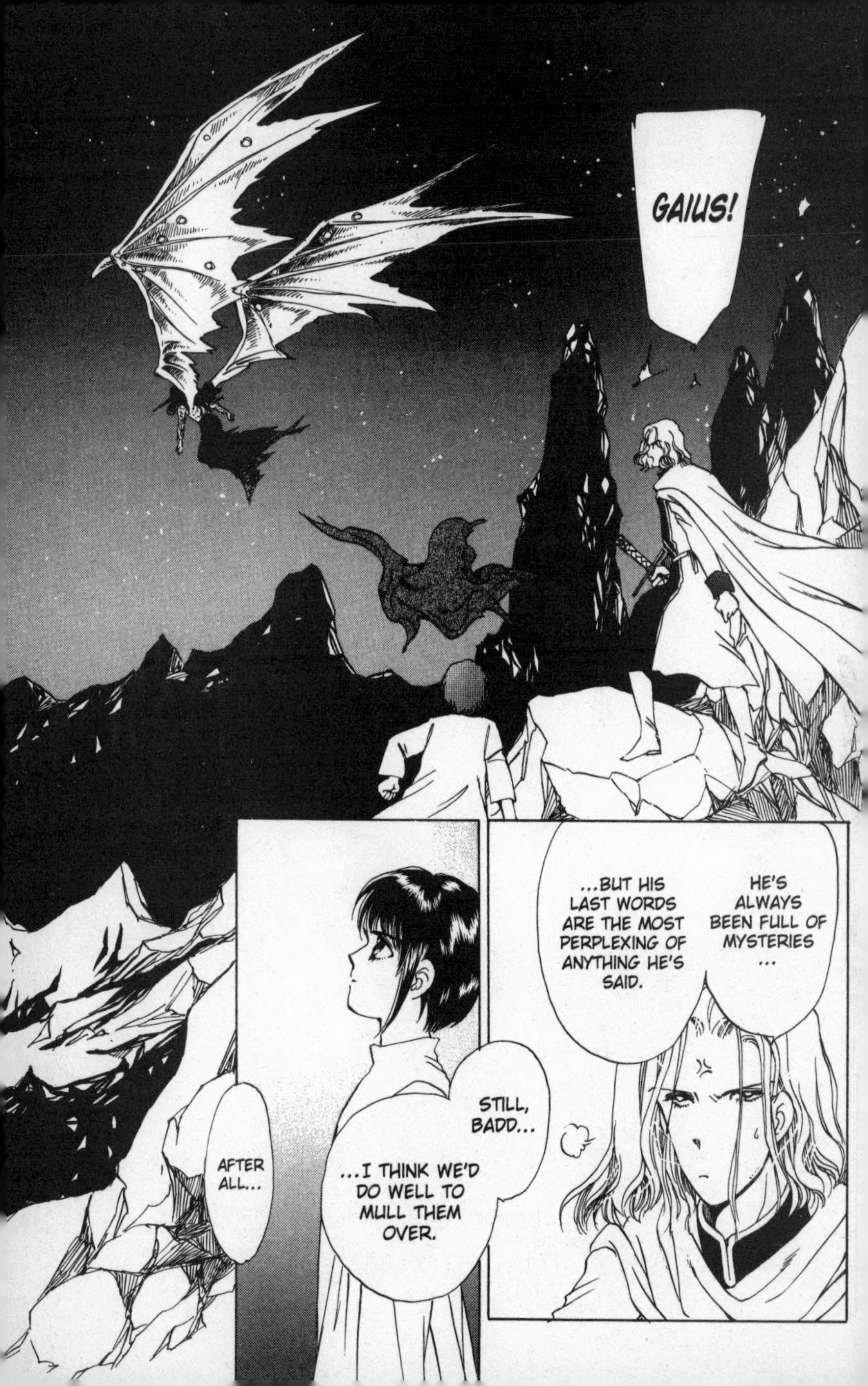
GAIUS!
HE'S ALWAYS BEEN FULL OF MYSTERIES...
...BUT HIS LAST WORDS ARE THE MOST PERPLEXING OF ANYTHING HE'S SAID.
STILL, BADD...
...I THINK WE'D DO WELL TO MULL THEM OVER.
AFTER ALL...

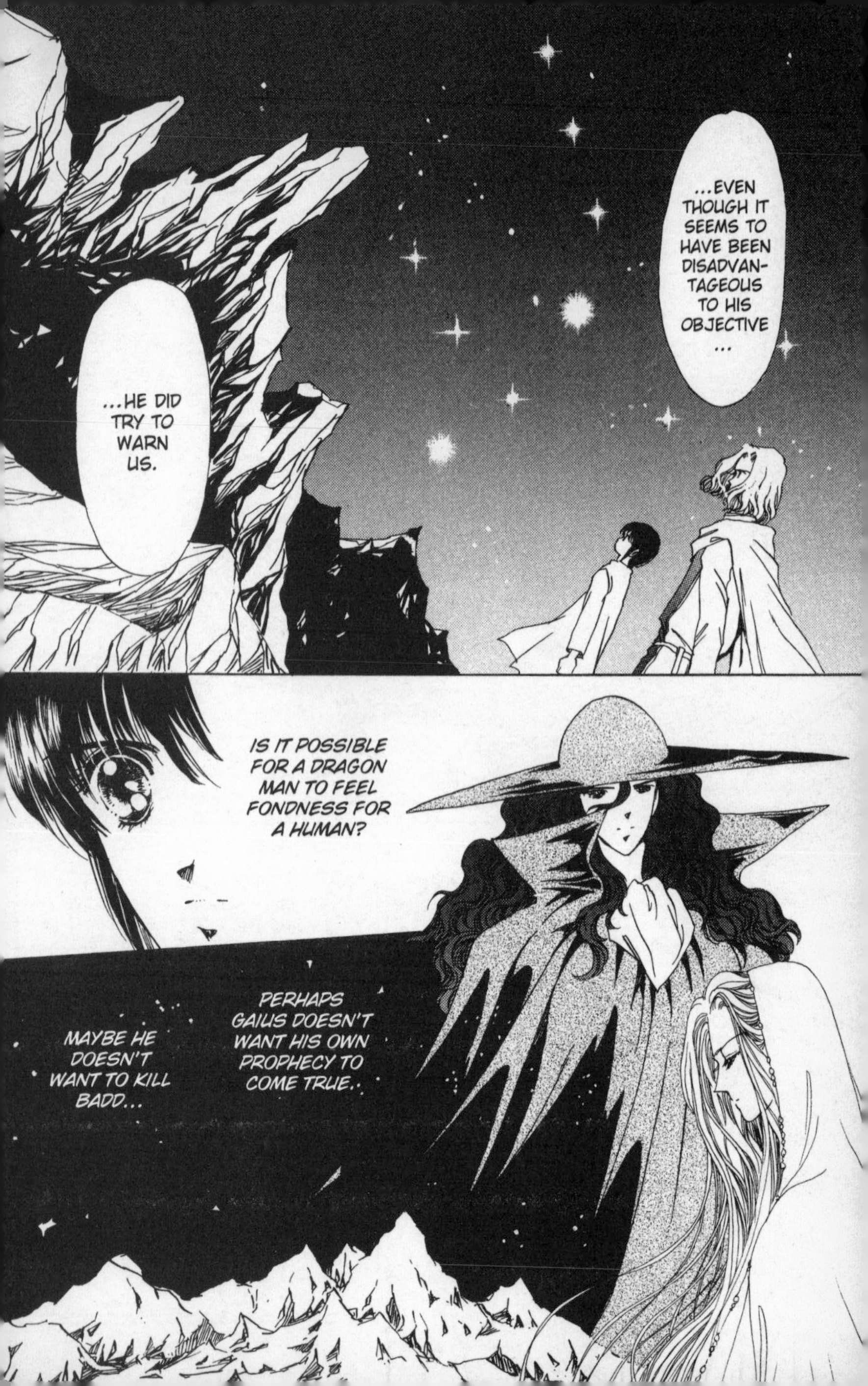
...EVEN THOUGH IT SEEMS TO HAVE BEEN DISADVANTAGEOUS TO HIS OBJECTIVE...
...HE DID TRY TO WARN US.
IS IT POSSIBLE FOR A DRAGON MAN TO FEEL FONDNESS FOR A HUMAN?
PERHAPS GAIUS DOESN'T WANT HIS OWN PROPHECY TO COME TRUE..
MAYBE HE DOESN'T WANT TO KILL BADD...

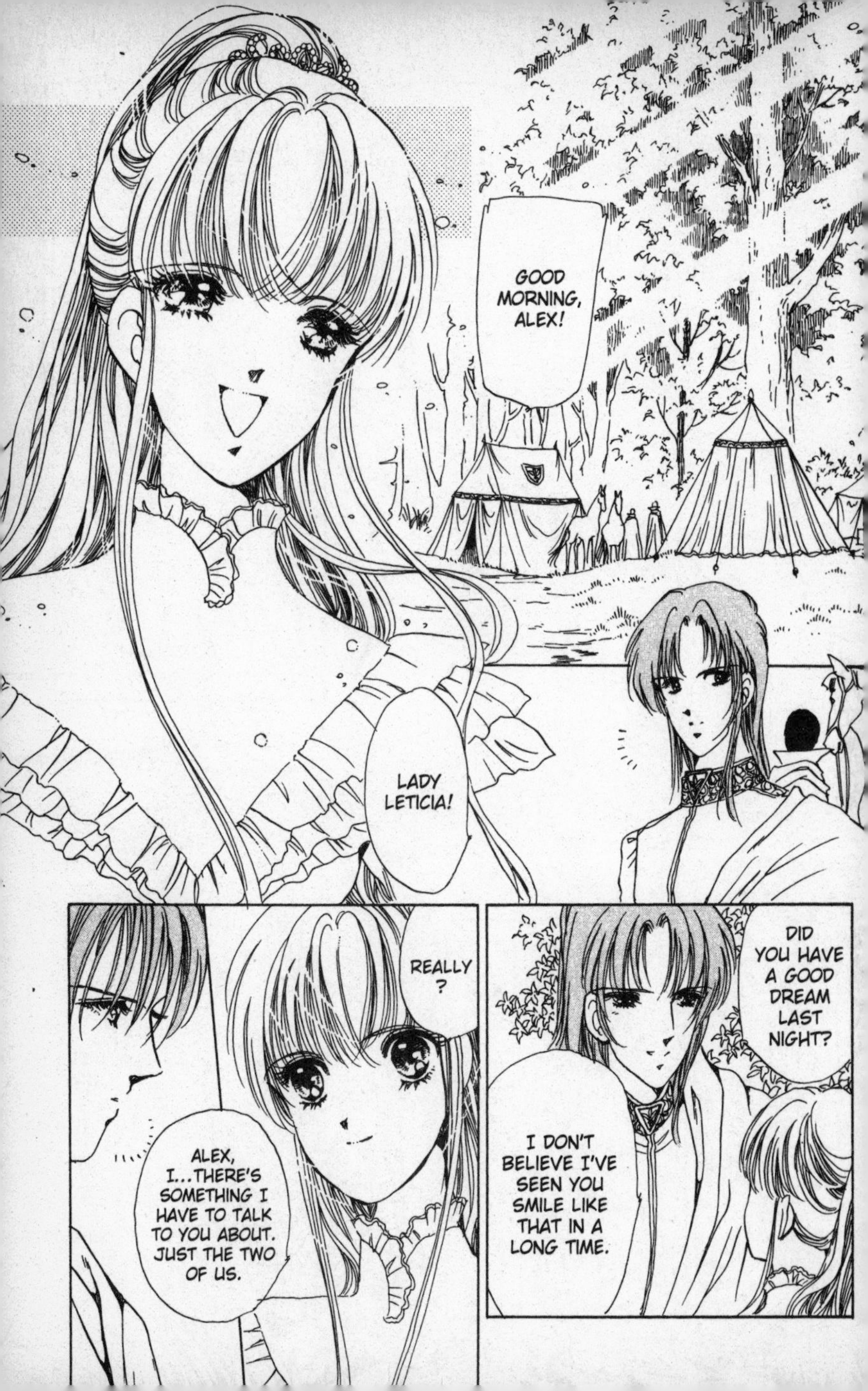
GOOD MORNING, ALEX!
LADY LETICIA!
DID YOU HAVE A GOOD DREAM LAST NIGHT?
I DON'T BELIEVE I'VE SEEN YOU SMILE LIKE THAT IN A LONG TIME.
REALLY?
ALEX, I...THERE'S SOMETHING I HAVE TO TALK TO YOU ABOUT. JUST THE TWO OF US.

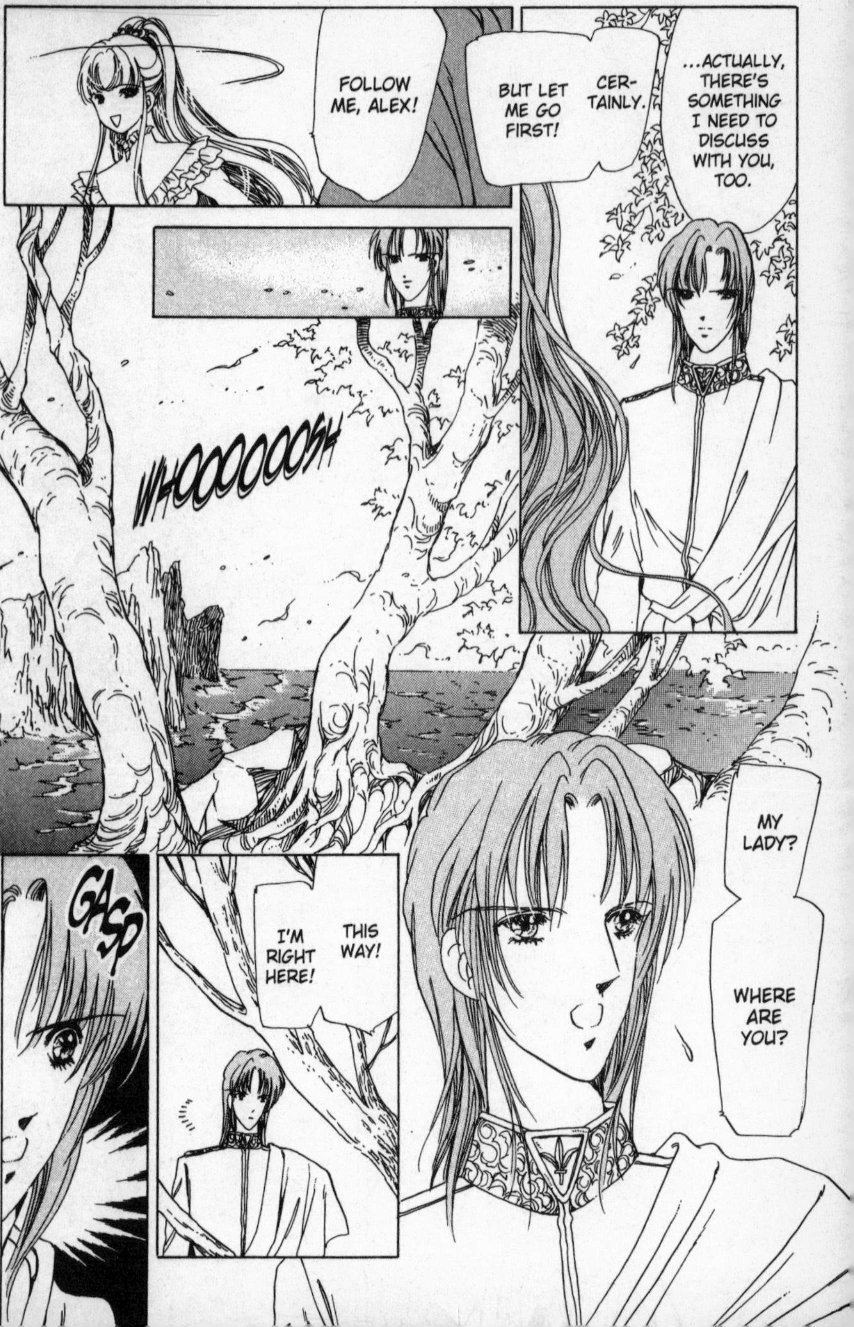

...ACTUALLY, THERE'S SOMETHING I NEED TO DISCUSS WITH YOU, TOO.
CER-TAINLY.
BUT LET ME GO FIRST!
FOLLOW ME, ALEX!
WHOOOOOOSH
MY LADY?
WHERE ARE YOU?
THIS WAY!
I'M RIGHT HERE!
GASP

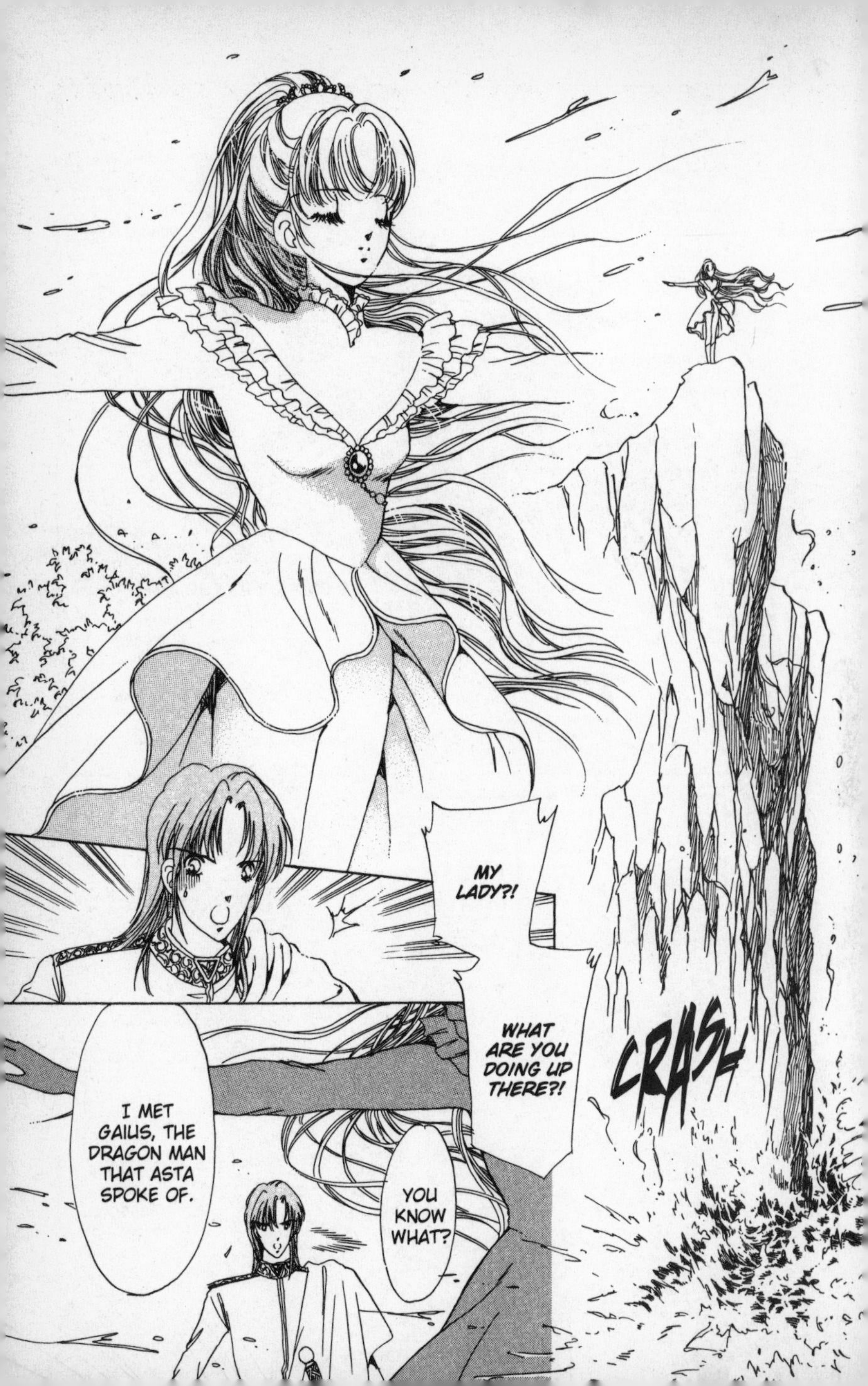
MY LADY?!
WHAT ARE YOU DOING UP THERE?!
CRASH
YOU KNOW WHAT?
I MET GAIUS, THE DRAGON MAN THAT ASTA SPOKE OF.

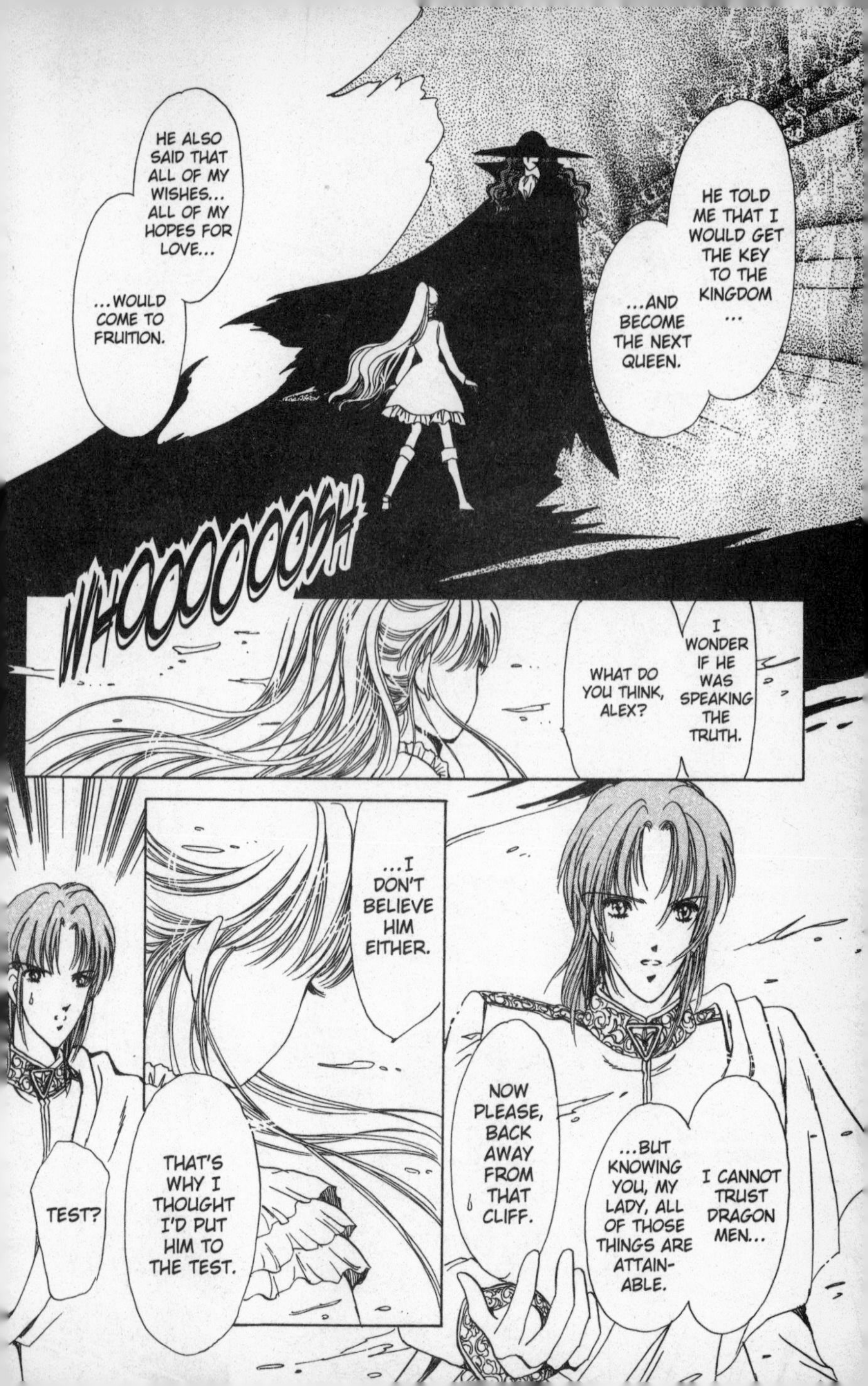
HE TOLD ME THAT I WOULD GET THE KEY TO THE KINGDOM ...
...AND BECOME THE NEXT QUEEN.
HE ALSO SAID THAT ALL OF MY WISHES... ALL OF MY HOPES FOR LOVE...
...WOULD COME TO FRUITION.
WHOOOOOOSH
I WONDER IF HE WAS SPEAKING THE TRUTH.
WHAT DO YOU THINK, ALEX?
I CANNOT TRUST DRAGON MEN...
...BUT KNOWING YOU, MY LADY, ALL OF THOSE THINGS ARE ATTAIN-ABLE.
NOW PLEASE, BACK AWAY FROM THAT CLIFF.
...I DON'T BELIEVE HIM EITHER.
THAT'S WHY I THOUGHT I'D PUT HIM TO THE TEST.
TEST?

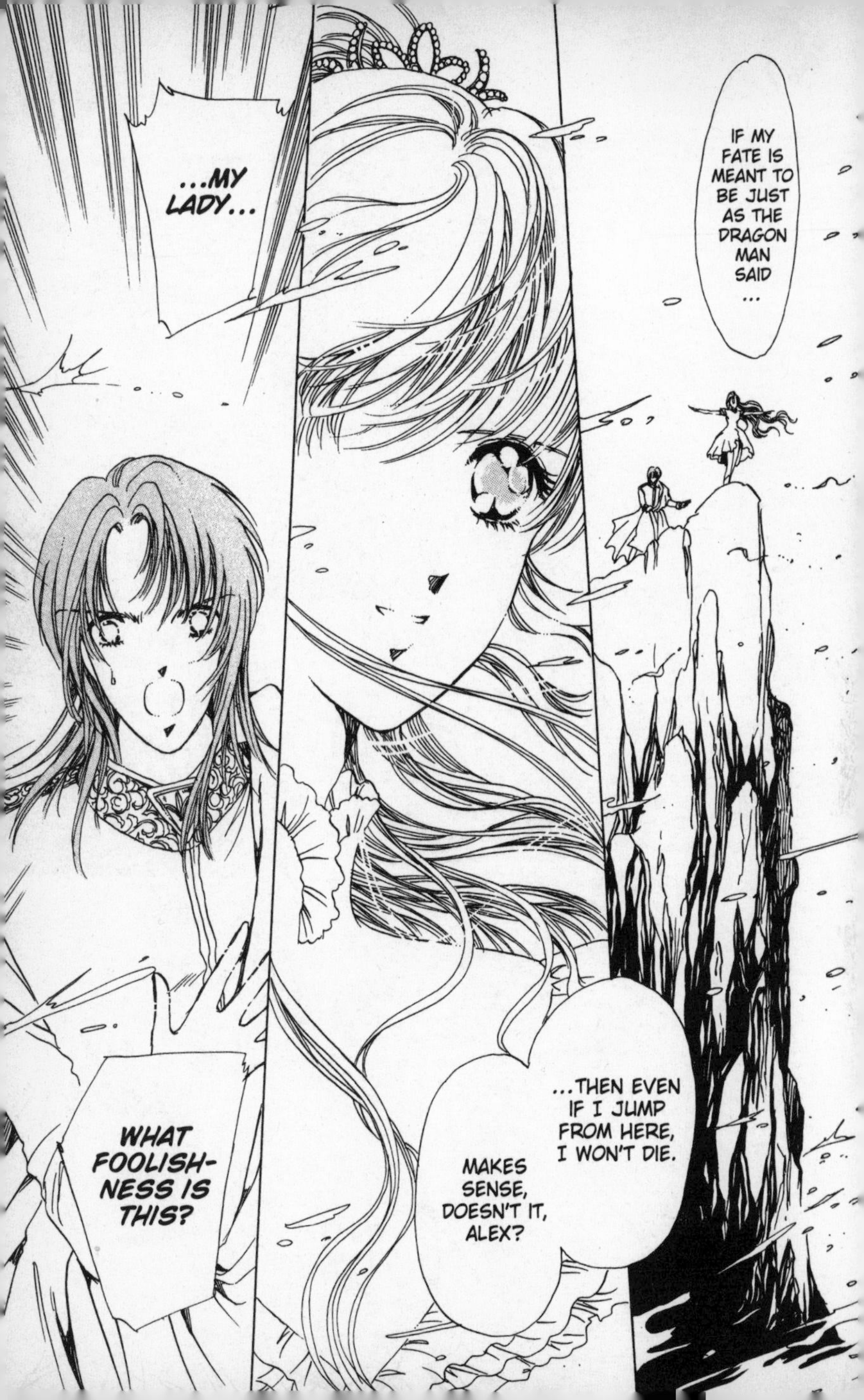
IF MY FATE IS MEANT TO BE JUST AS THE DRAGON MAN SAID ...
...THEN EVEN IF I JUMP FROM HERE, I WON'T DIE.
MAKES SENSE, DOESN'T IT, ALEX?
...MY LADY...
WHAT FOOLISH-NESS IS THIS?

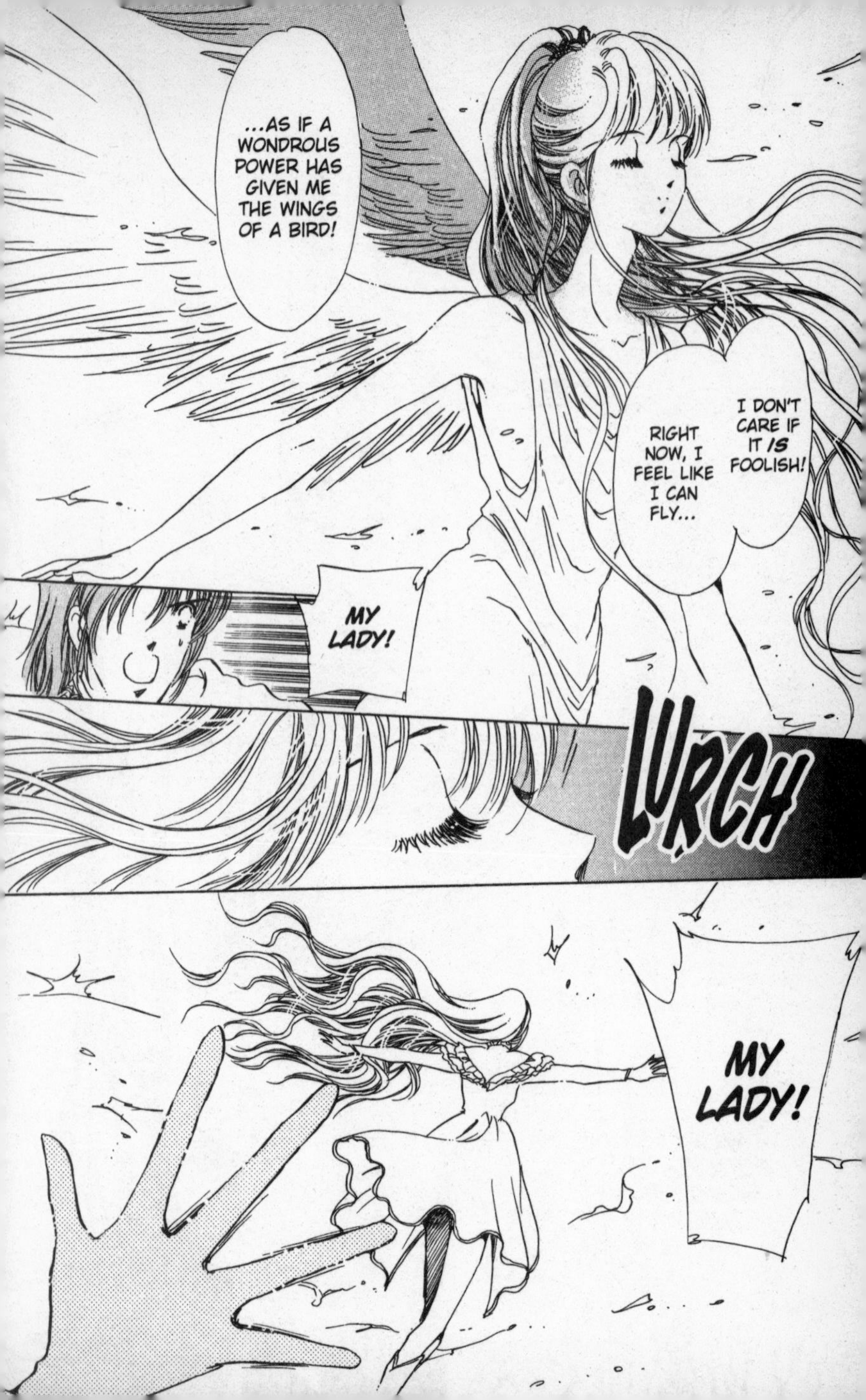
I DON'T CARE IF IT IS FOOLISH!
RIGHT NOW, I FEEL LIKE I CAN FLY...
...AS IF A WONDROUS POWER HAS GIVEN ME THE WINGS OF A BIRD!
MY LADY!
LURCH
MY LADY!

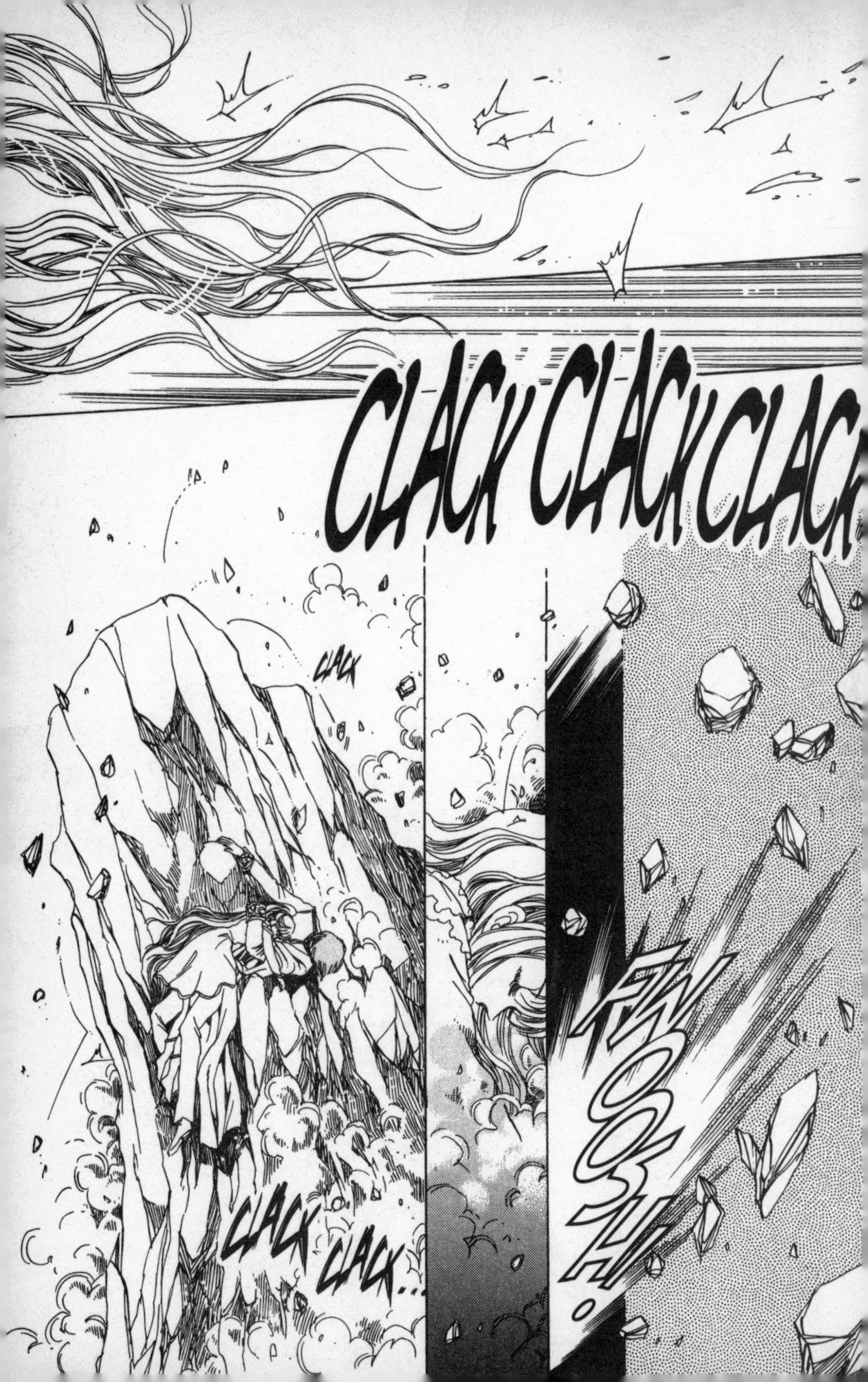
CLACK CLACK CLACK
FWOOSH!
CLACK
CLACK
CLACK...

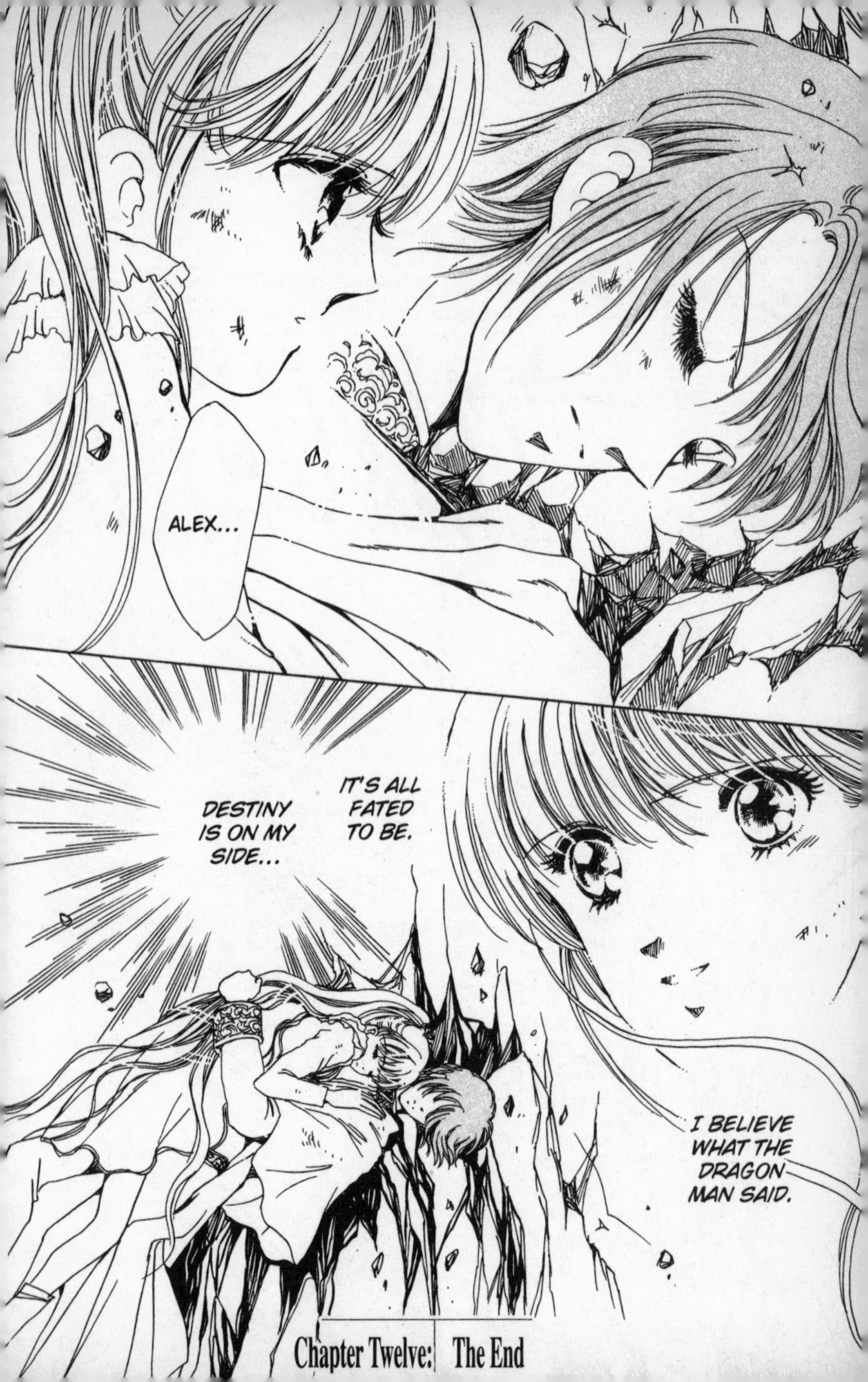
ALEX...
IT'S ALL FATED TO BE.
DESTINY IS ON MY SIDE...
I BELIEVE WHAT THE DRAGON MAN SAID.

Chapter Twelve: The End

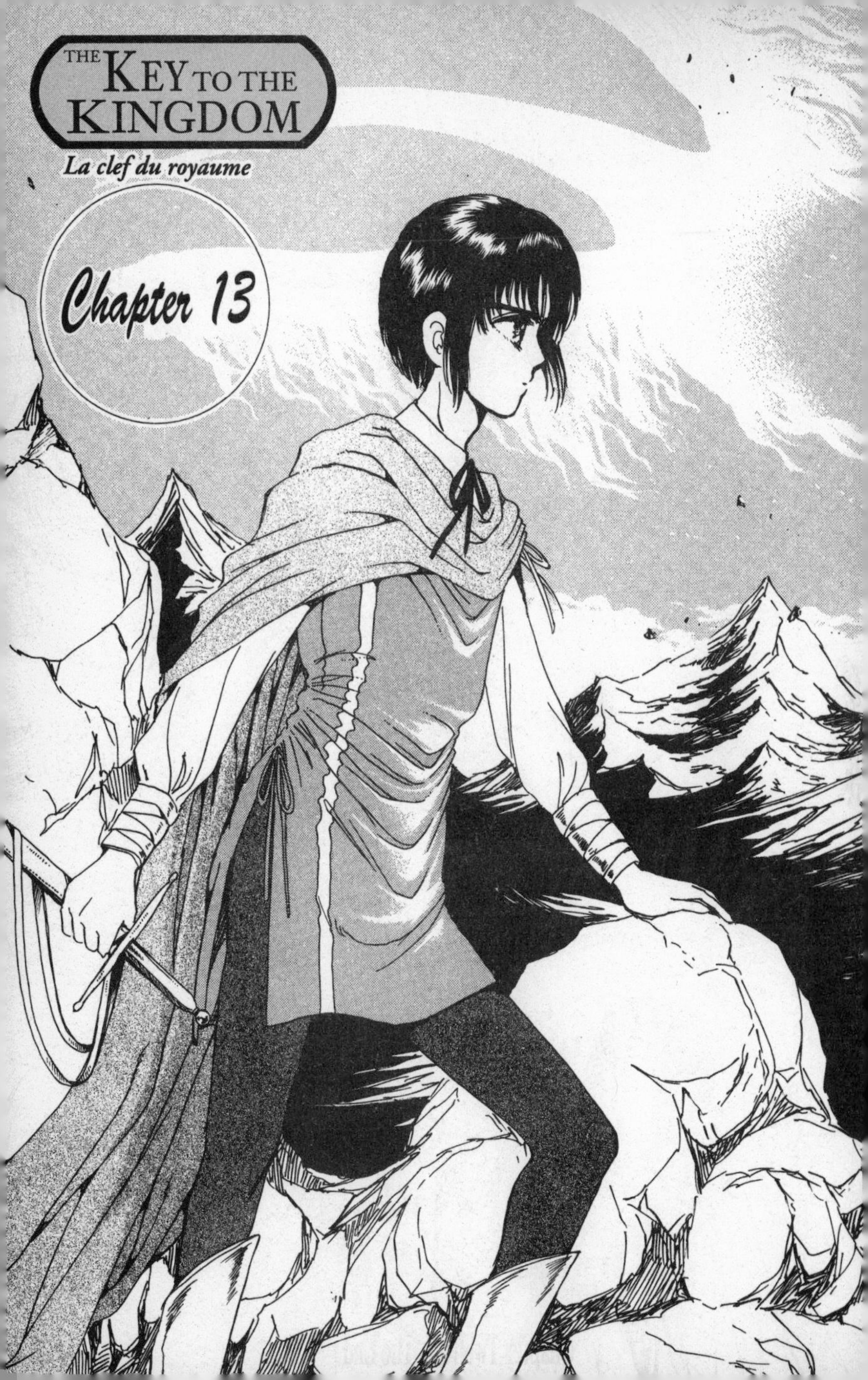
THE KEY TO THE KINGDOM
La clef du royaume
Chapter 13

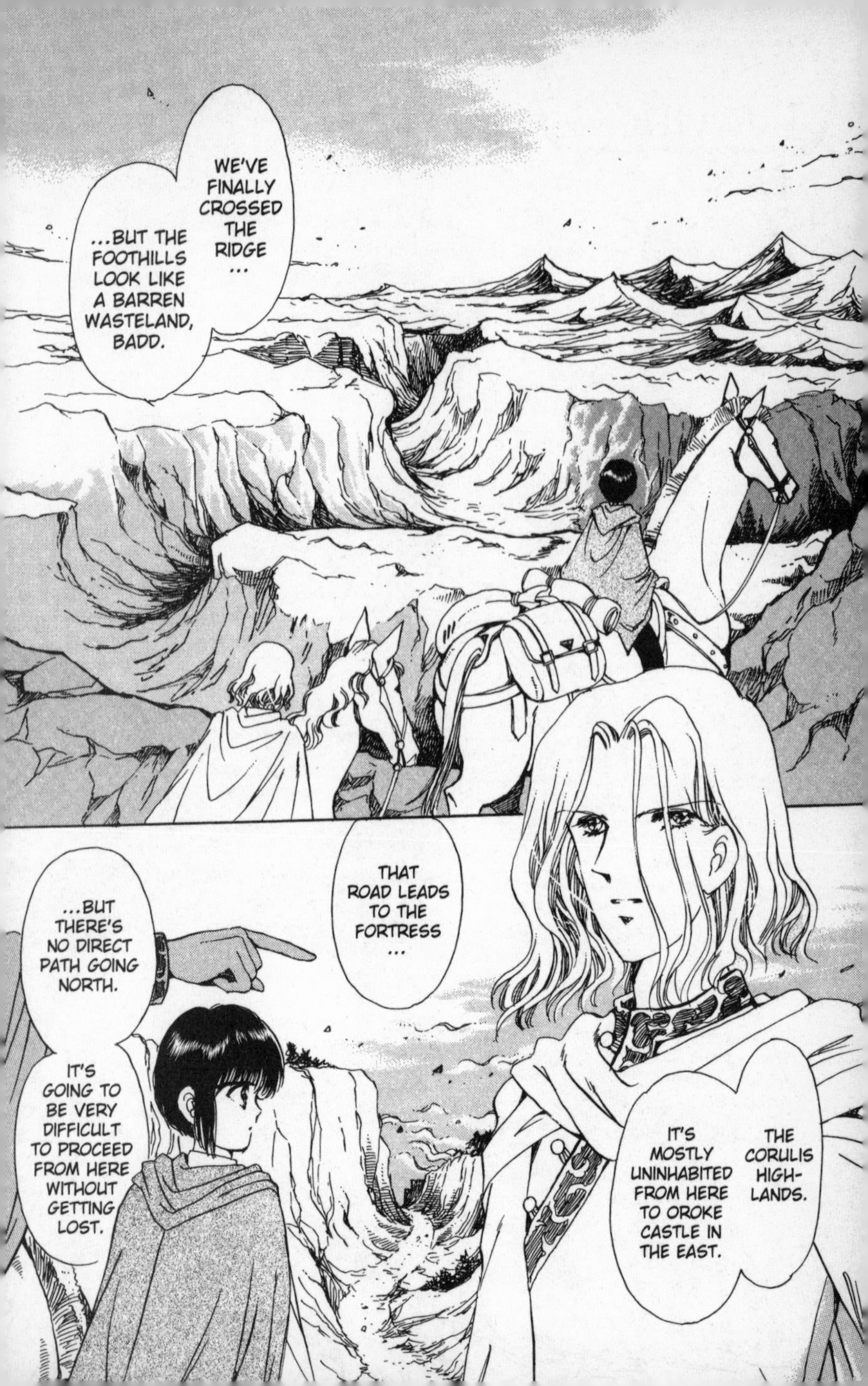
WE'VE FINALLY CROSSED THE RIDGE ...
...BUT THE FOOTHILLS LOOK LIKE A BARREN WASTELAND, BADD.
THAT ROAD LEADS TO THE FORTRESS ...
...BUT THERE'S NO DIRECT PATH GOING NORTH.
THE CORULIS HIGH-LANDS.
IT'S MOSTLY UNINHABITED FROM HERE TO OROKE CASTLE IN THE EAST.
IT'S GOING TO BE VERY DIFFICULT TO PROCEED FROM HERE WITHOUT GETTING LOST.

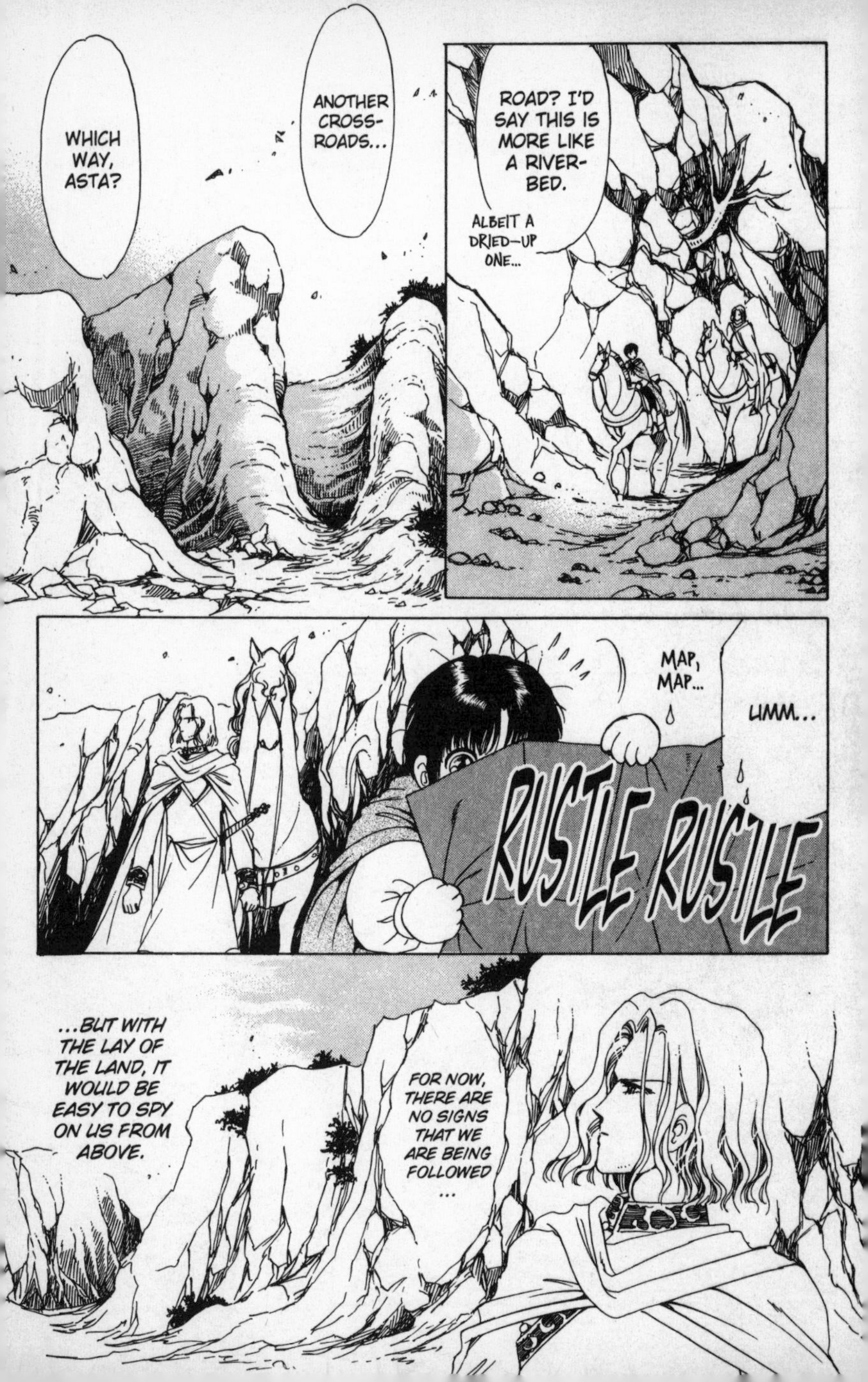
ROAD? I'D SAY THIS IS MORE LIKE A RIVER-BED.
ALBEIT A DRIED-UP ONE...
ANOTHER CROSS-ROADS...
WHICH WAY, ASTA?
UMM...
MAP, MAP...
RUSTLE RUSTLE
FOR NOW, THERE ARE NO SIGNS THAT WE ARE BEING FOLLOWED ...
...BUT WITH THE LAY OF THE LAND, IT WOULD BE EASY TO SPY ON US FROM ABOVE.

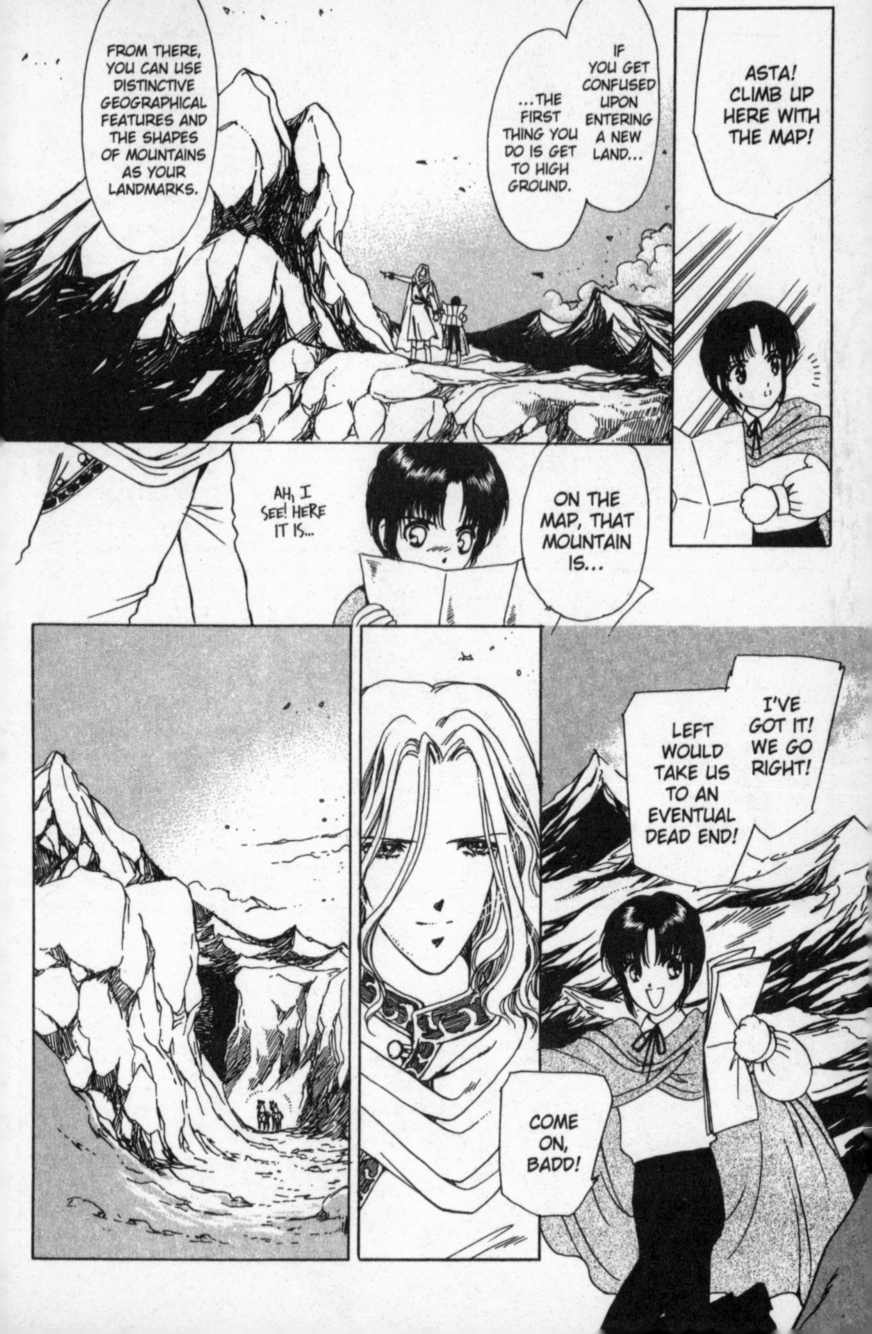
ASTA! CLIMB UP HERE WITH THE MAP!
IF YOU GET CONFUSED UPON ENTERING A NEW LAND...
...THE FIRST THING YOU DO IS GET TO HIGH GROUND.
FROM THERE, YOU CAN USE DISTINCTIVE GEOGRAPHICAL FEATURES AND THE SHAPES OF MOUNTAINS AS YOUR LANDMARKS.
ON THE MAP, THAT MOUNTAIN IS...
AH, I SEE! HERE IT IS...
I'VE GOT IT! WE GO RIGHT!
LEFT WOULD TAKE US TO AN EVENTUAL DEAD END!
COME ON, BADD!

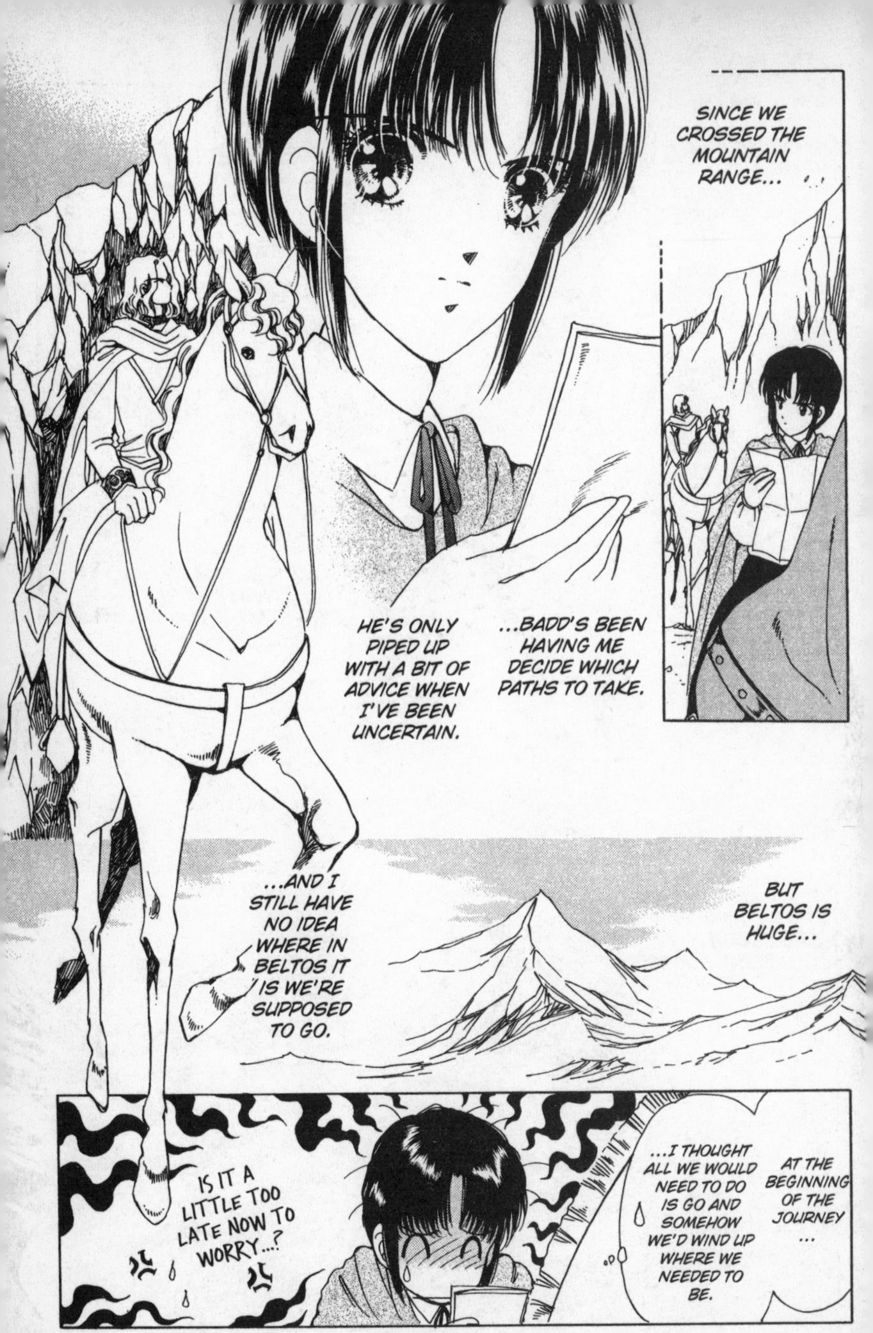
SINCE WE CROSSED THE MOUNTAIN RANGE...
...BADD'S BEEN HAVING ME DECIDE WHICH PATHS TO TAKE.
HE'S ONLY PIPED UP WITH A BIT OF ADVICE WHEN I'VE BEEN UNCERTAIN.
BUT BELTOS IS HUGE...
...AND I STILL HAVE NO IDEA WHERE IN BELTOS IT IS WE'RE SUPPOSED TO GO.
AT THE BEGINNING OF THE JOURNEY ...
...I THOUGHT ALL WE WOULD NEED TO DO IS GO AND SOMEHOW WE'D WIND UP WHERE WE NEEDED TO BE.
IS IT A LITTLE TOO LATE NOW TO WORRY...?

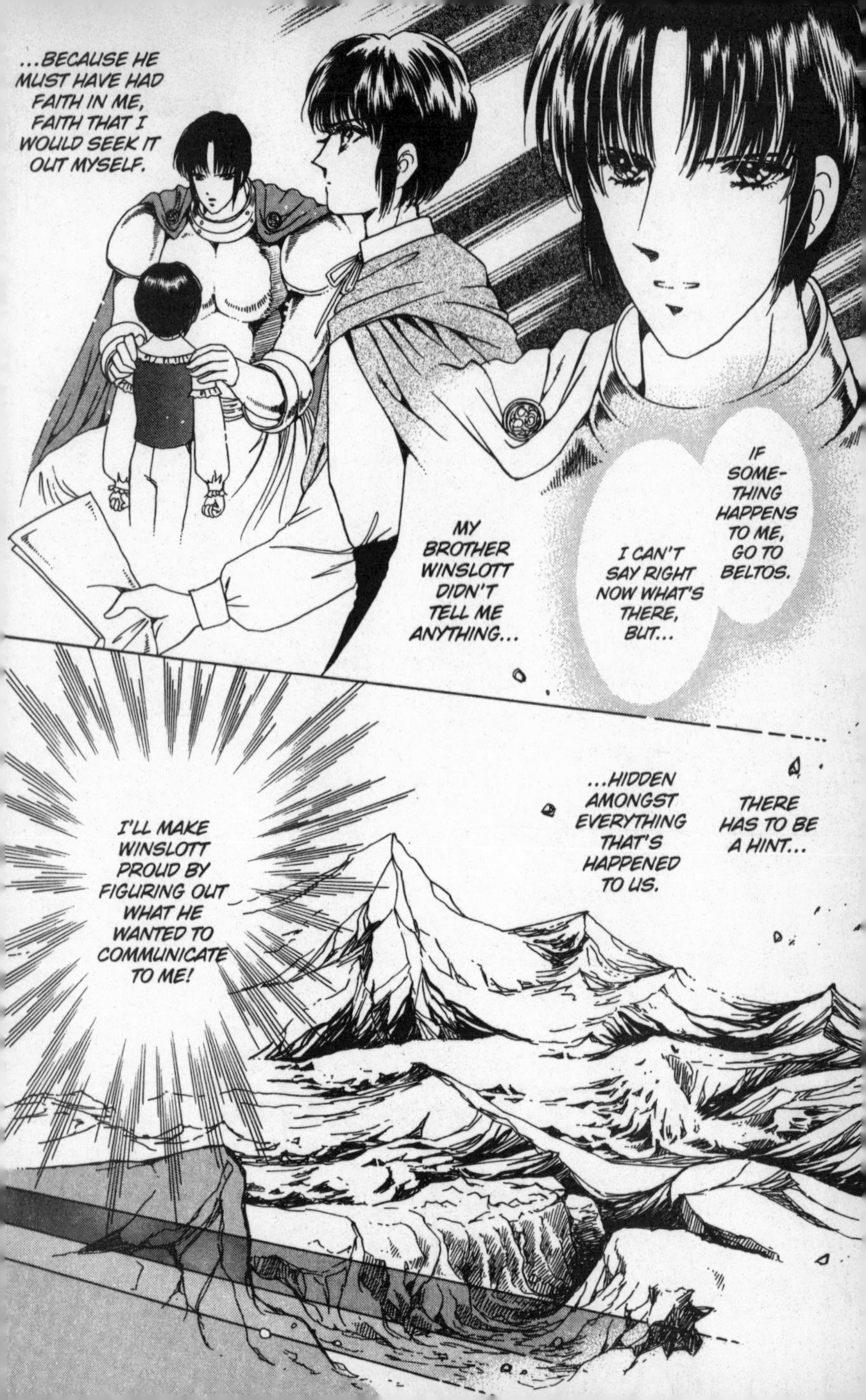
IF SOMETHING HAPPENS TO ME, GO TO BELTOS.
I CAN'T SAY RIGHT NOW WHAT'S THERE, BUT...
MY BROTHER WINSLOTT DIDN'T TELL ME ANYTHING...
...BECAUSE HE MUST HAVE HAD FAITH IN ME, FAITH THAT I WOULD SEEK IT OUT MYSELF.
THERE HAS TO BE A HINT...
...HIDDEN AMONGST EVERYTHING THAT'S HAPPENED TO US.
I'LL MAKE WINSLOTT PROUD BY FIGURING OUT WHAT HE WANTED TO COMMUNICATE TO ME!

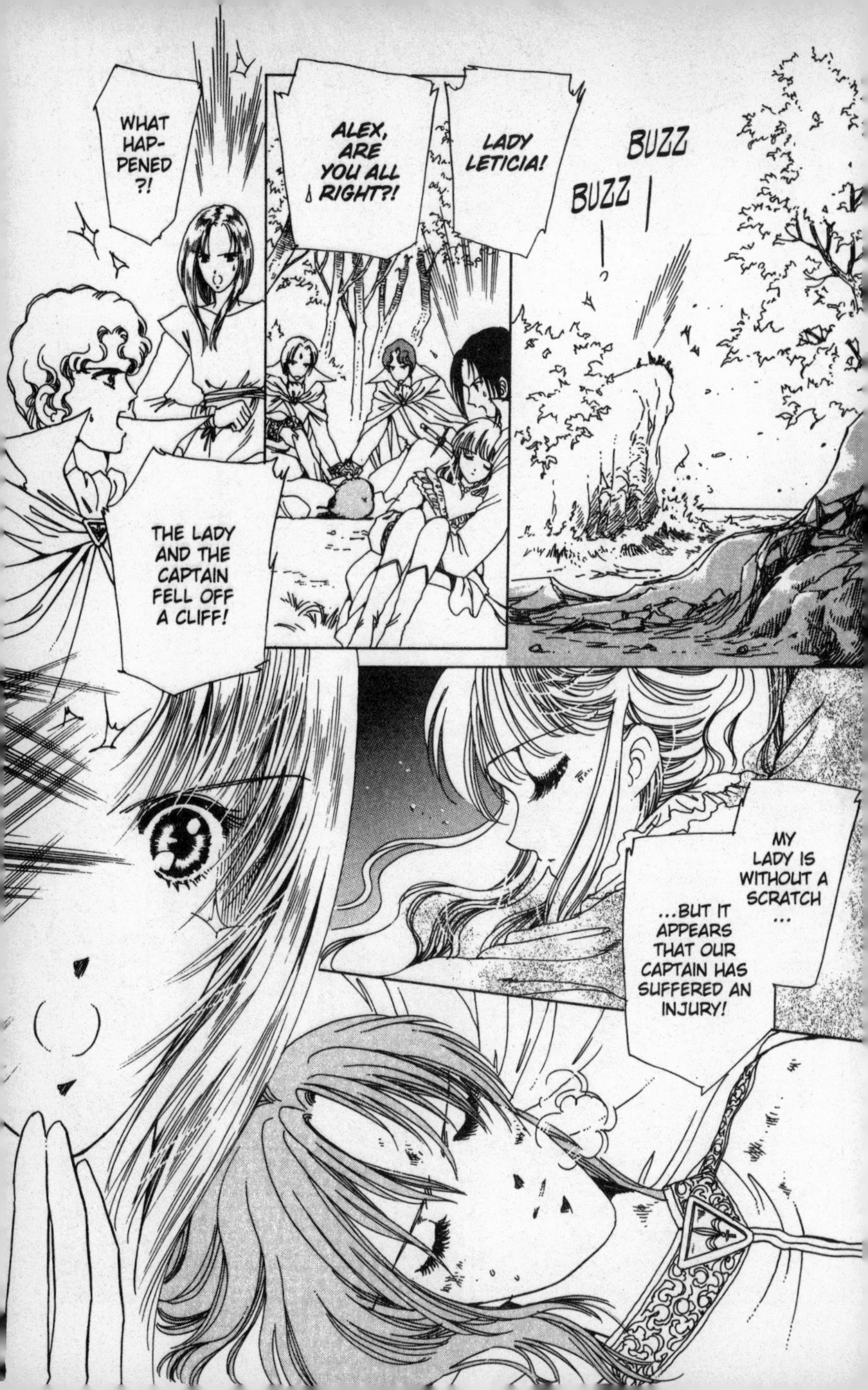
BUZZ
BUZZ
LADY LETICIA!
ALEX, ARE YOU ALL RIGHT?!
WHAT HAP-PENED?!
THE LADY AND THE CAPTAIN FELL OFF A CLIFF!
MY LADY IS WITHOUT A SCRATCH...
...BUT IT APPEARS THAT OUR CAPTAIN HAS SUFFERED AN INJURY!

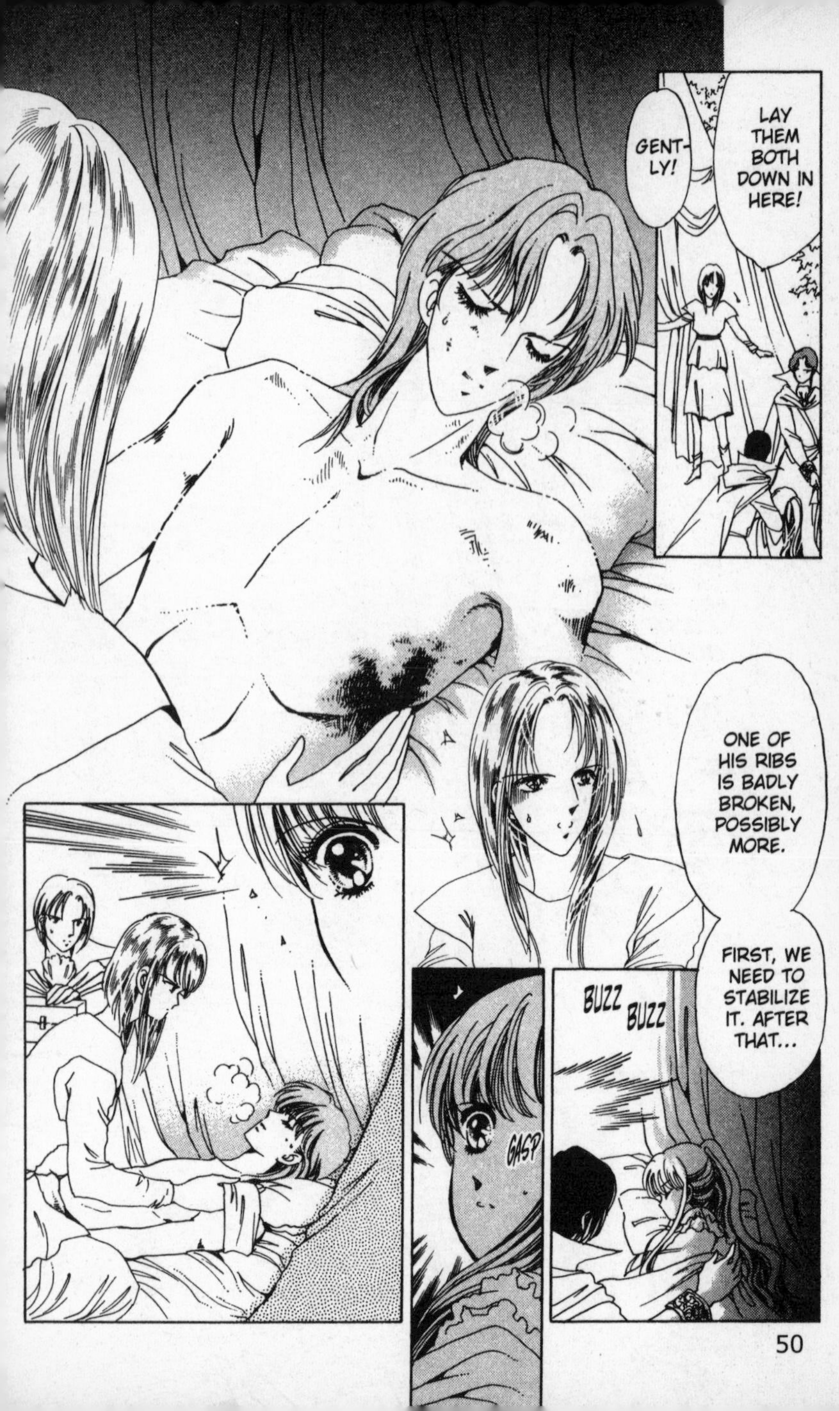
LAY THEM BOTH DOWN IN HERE!
GENT-LY!
ONE OF HIS RIBS IS BADLY BROKEN, POSSIBLY MORE.
FIRST, WE NEED TO STABILIZE IT. AFTER THAT...
BUZZ BUZZ
GASP

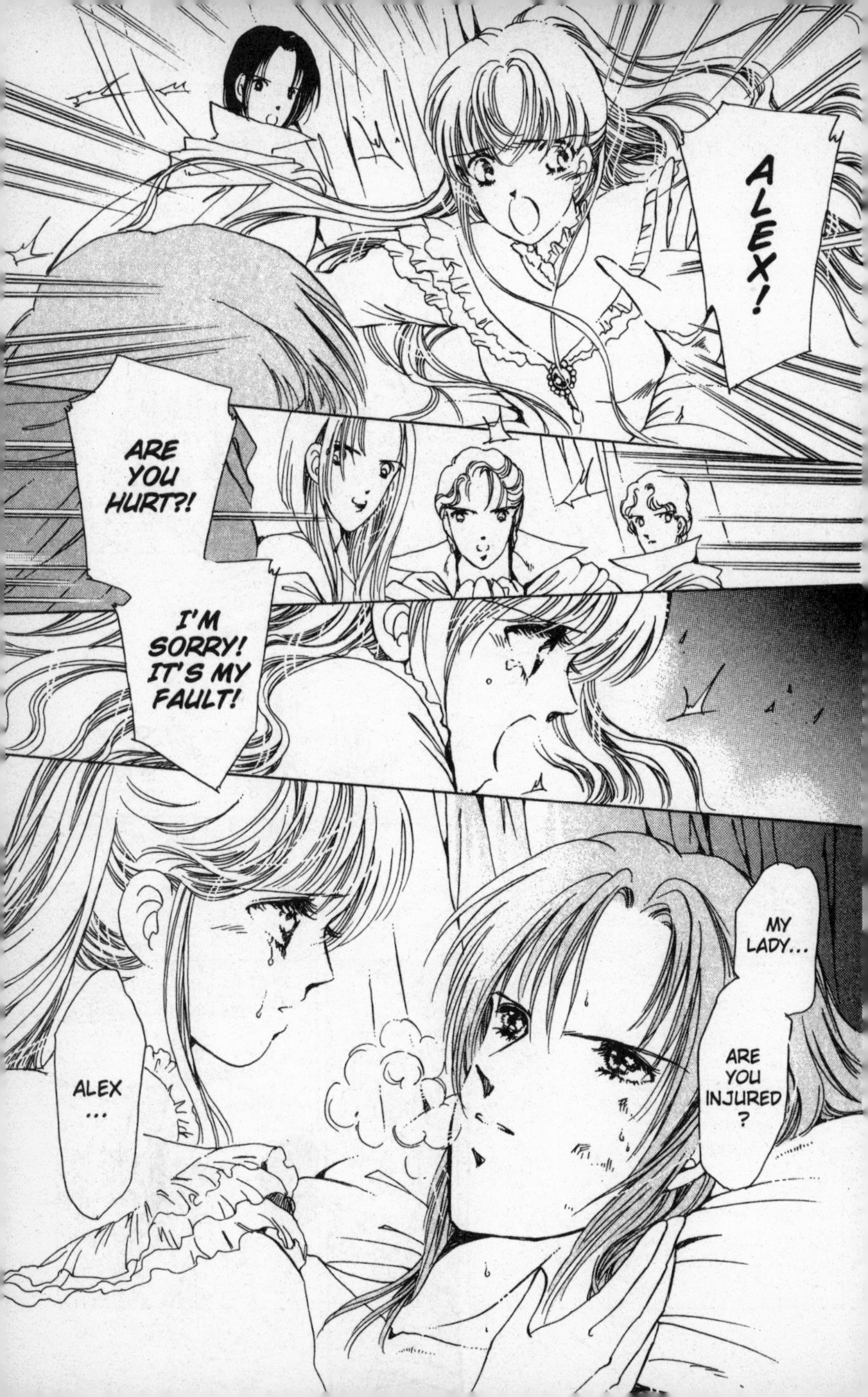
ALEX!
ARE YOU HURT?!
I'M SORRY! IT'S MY FAULT!
MY LADY...
ARE YOU INJURED?
ALEX...

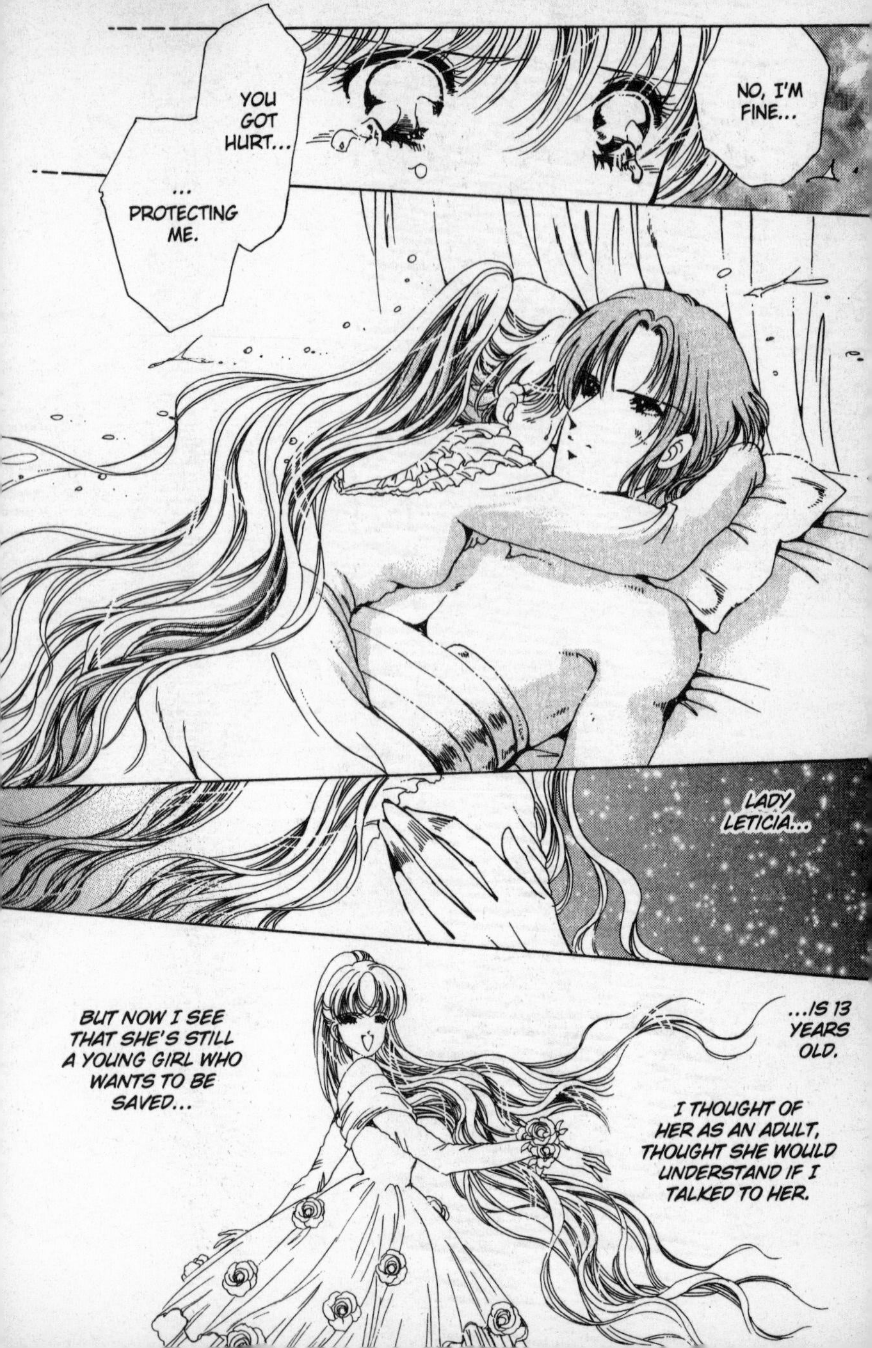

YOU GOT HURT...
... PROTECTING ME.
NO, I'M FINE...
LADY LETICIA...
...IS 13 YEARS OLD.
I THOUGHT OF HER AS AN ADULT, THOUGHT SHE WOULD UNDERSTAND IF I TALKED TO HER.
BUT NOW I SEE THAT SHE'S STILL A YOUNG GIRL WHO WANTS TO BE SAVED...

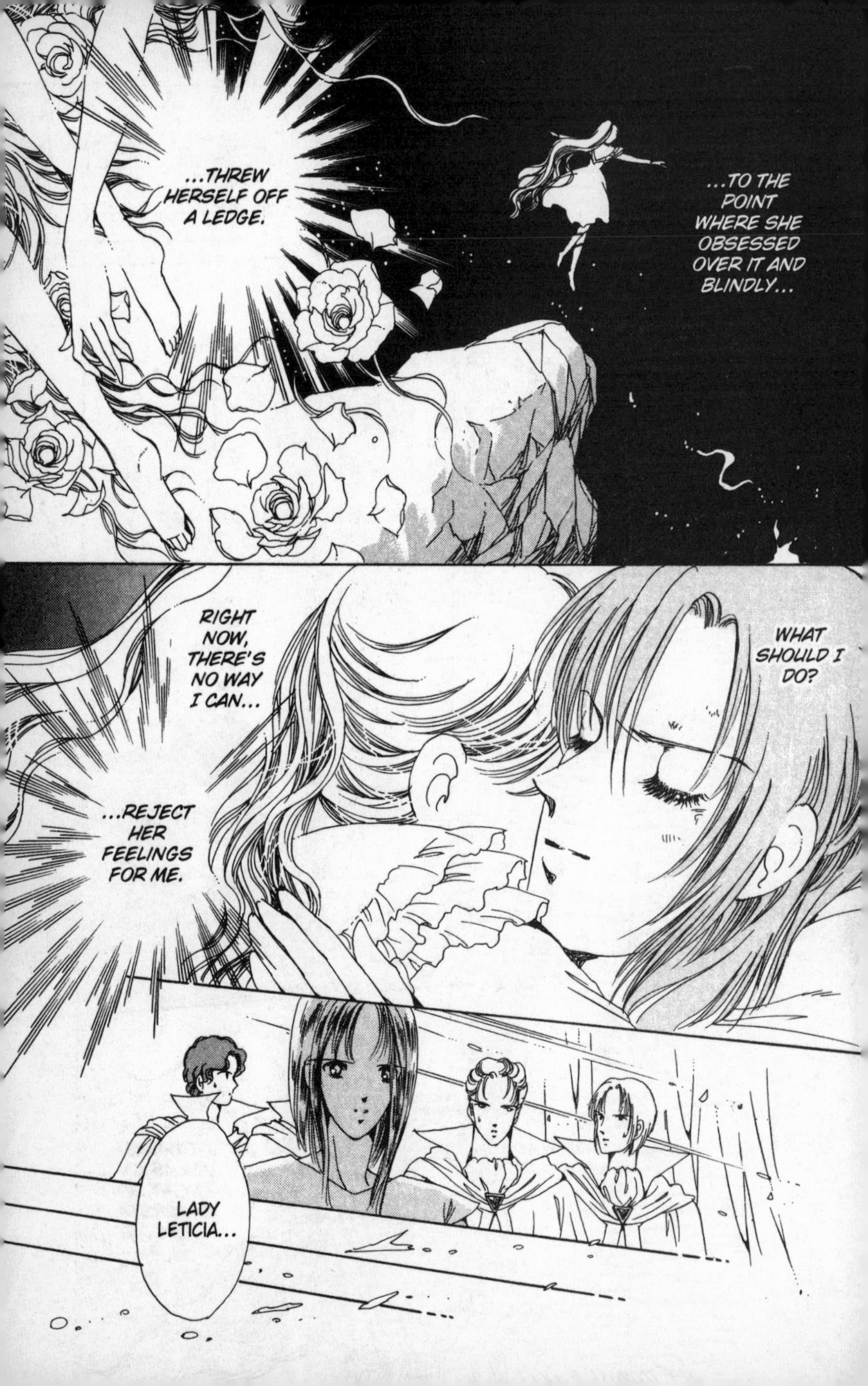
...TO THE POINT WHERE SHE OBSESSED OVER IT AND BLINDLY...
...THREW HERSELF OFF A LEDGE.
WHAT SHOULD I DO?
RIGHT NOW, THERE'S NO WAY I CAN...
...REJECT HER FEELINGS FOR ME.
LADY LETICIA...

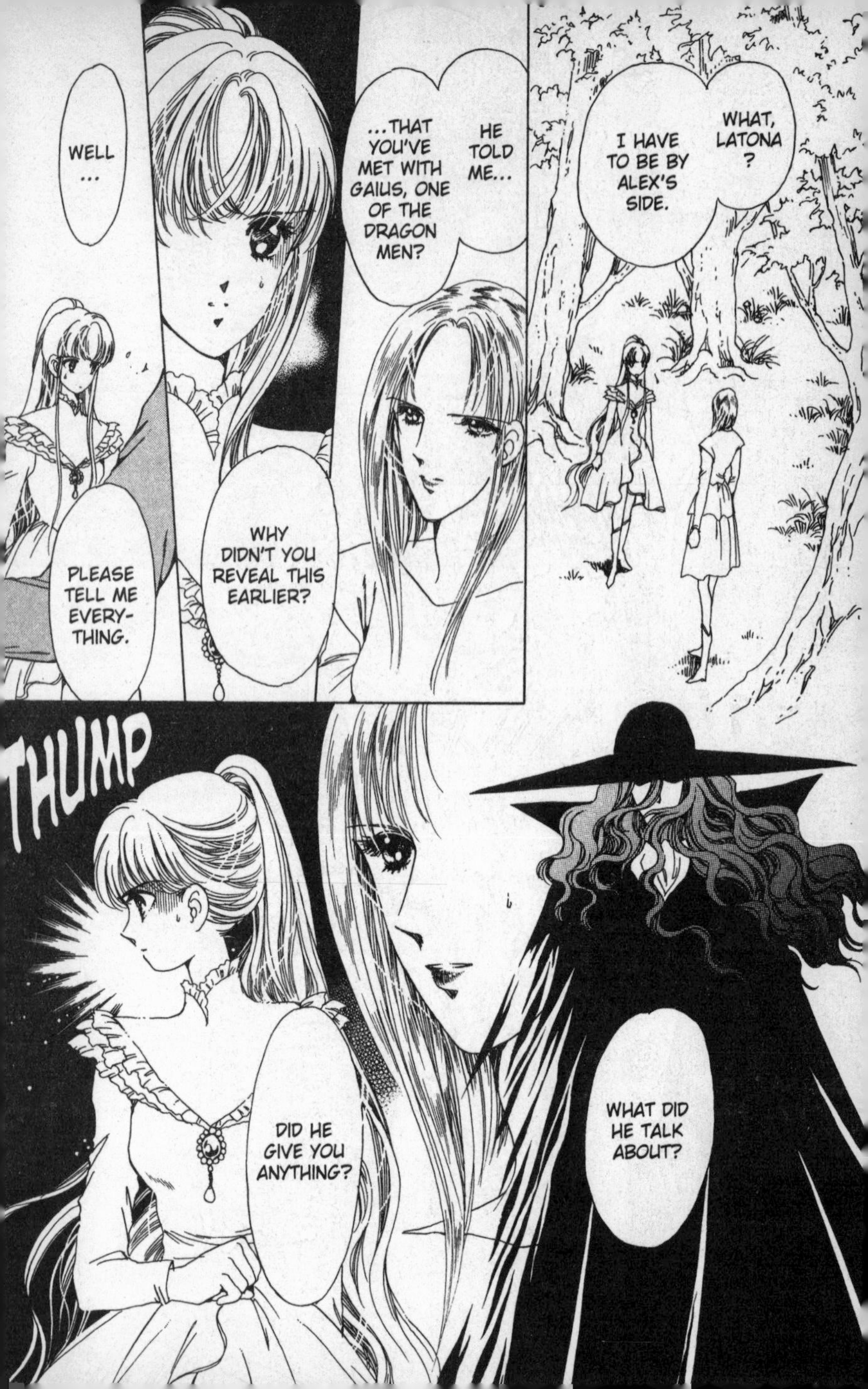
WHAT, LATONA ?
I HAVE TO BE BY ALEX'S SIDE.
HE TOLD ME...
...THAT YOU'VE MET WITH GAIUS, ONE OF THE DRAGON MEN?
WHY DIDN'T YOU REVEAL THIS EARLIER?
WELL ...
PLEASE TELL ME EVERY-THING.
WHAT DID HE TALK ABOUT?
DID HE GIVE YOU ANYTHING?
THUMP

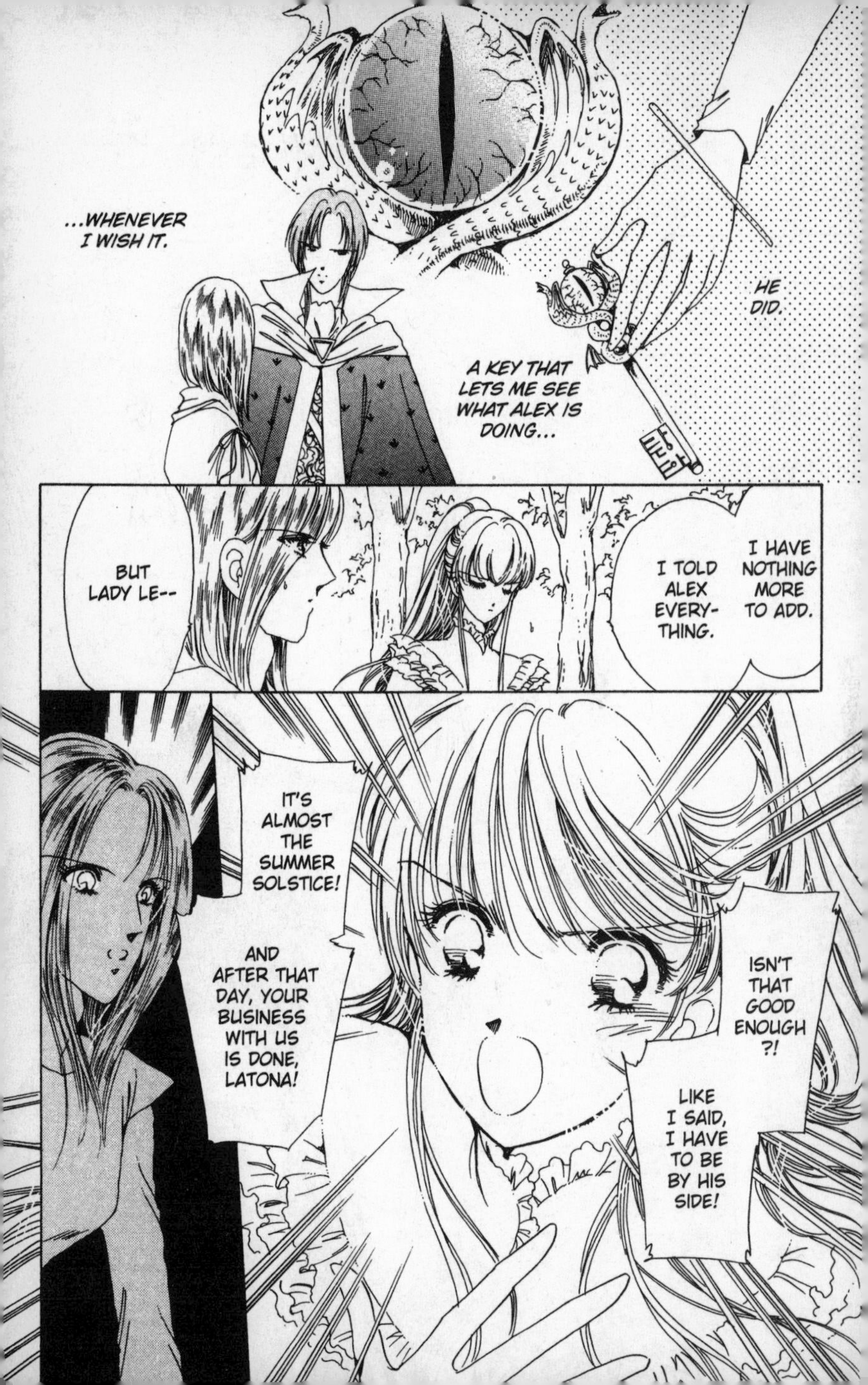

HE DID.
A KEY THAT LETS ME SEE WHAT ALEX IS DOING...
...WHENEVER I WISH IT.
I TOLD ALEX EVERY-THING. I HAVE NOTHING MORE TO ADD.
BUT LADY LE--
ISN'T THAT GOOD ENOUGH?!
LIKE I SAID, I HAVE TO BE BY HIS SIDE!
IT'S ALMOST THE SUMMER SOLSTICE!
AND AFTER THAT DAY, YOUR BUSINESS WITH US IS DONE, LATONA!

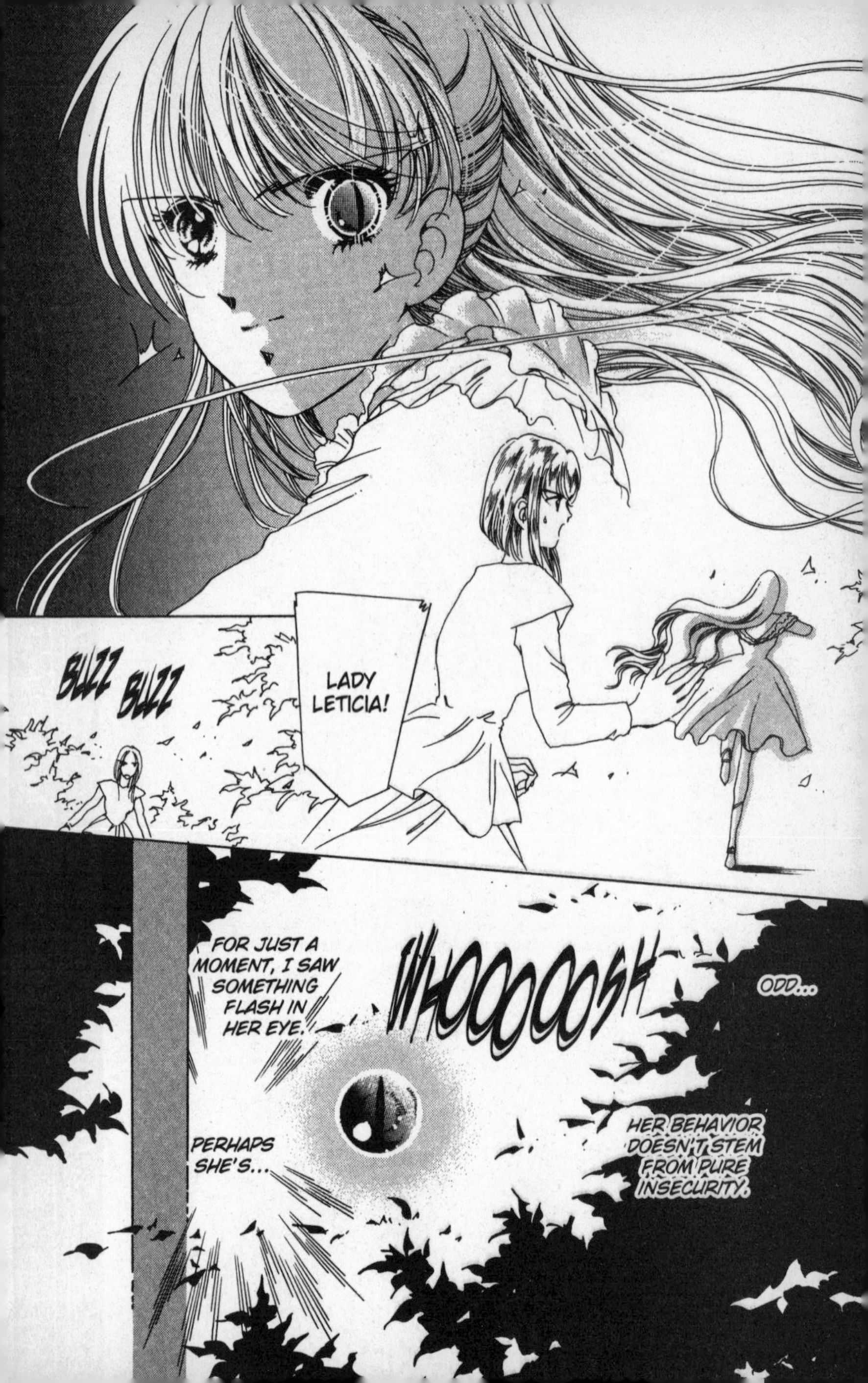
LADY LETICIA!
BUZZ BUZZ
ODD...
WHOOOOOSH
FOR JUST A MOMENT, I SAW SOMETHING FLASH IN HER EYE.
HER BEHAVIOR DOESN'T STEM FROM PURE INSECURITY.
PERHAPS SHE'S...

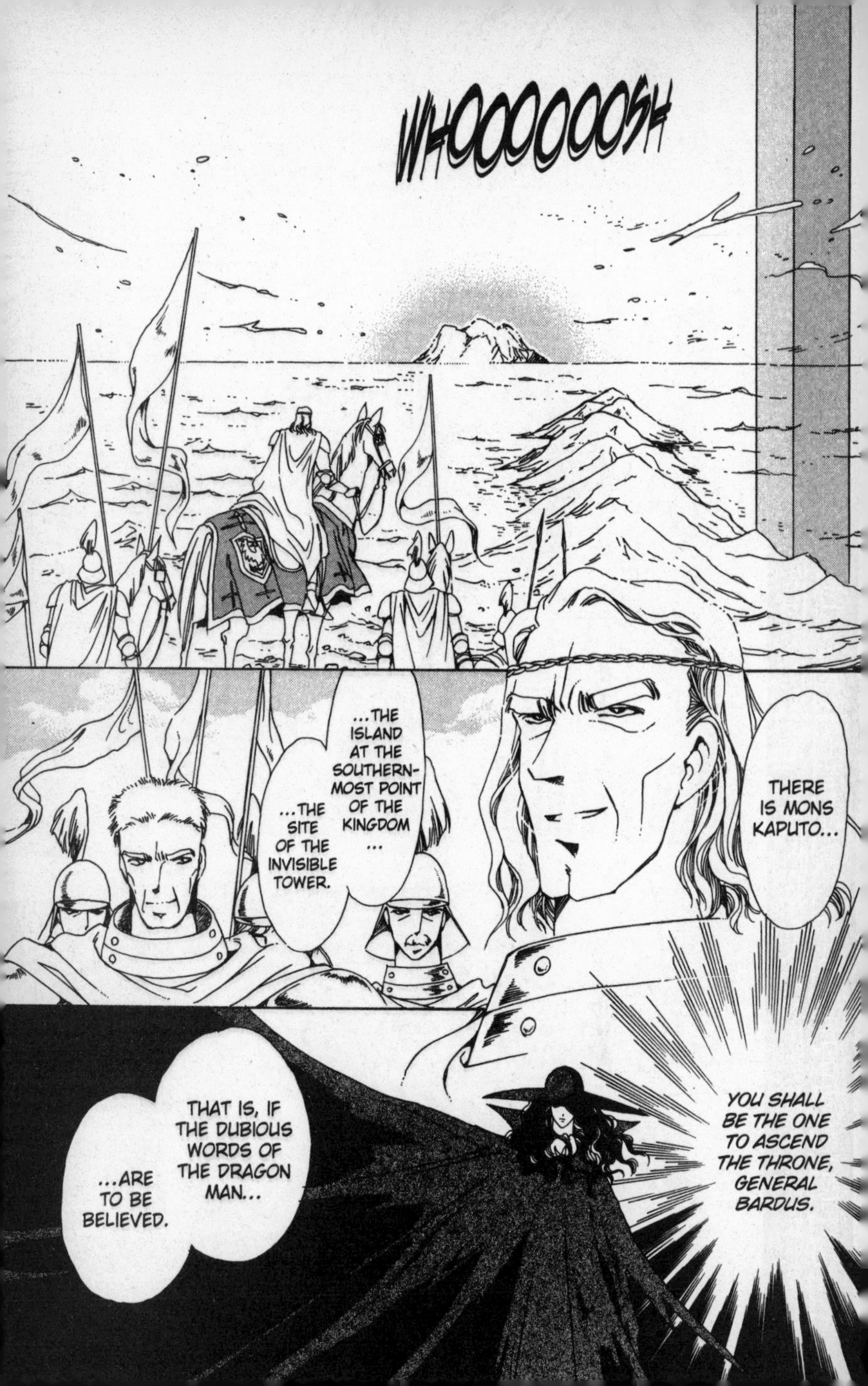
WHOOOOOOSH
THERE IS MONS KAPUTO...
...THE ISLAND AT THE SOUTHERN-MOST POINT OF THE KINGDOM...
...THE SITE OF THE INVISIBLE TOWER.
YOU SHALL BE THE ONE TO ASCEND THE THRONE, GENERAL BARDUS.
THAT IS, IF THE DUBIOUS WORDS OF THE DRAGON MAN...
...ARE TO BE BELIEVED.

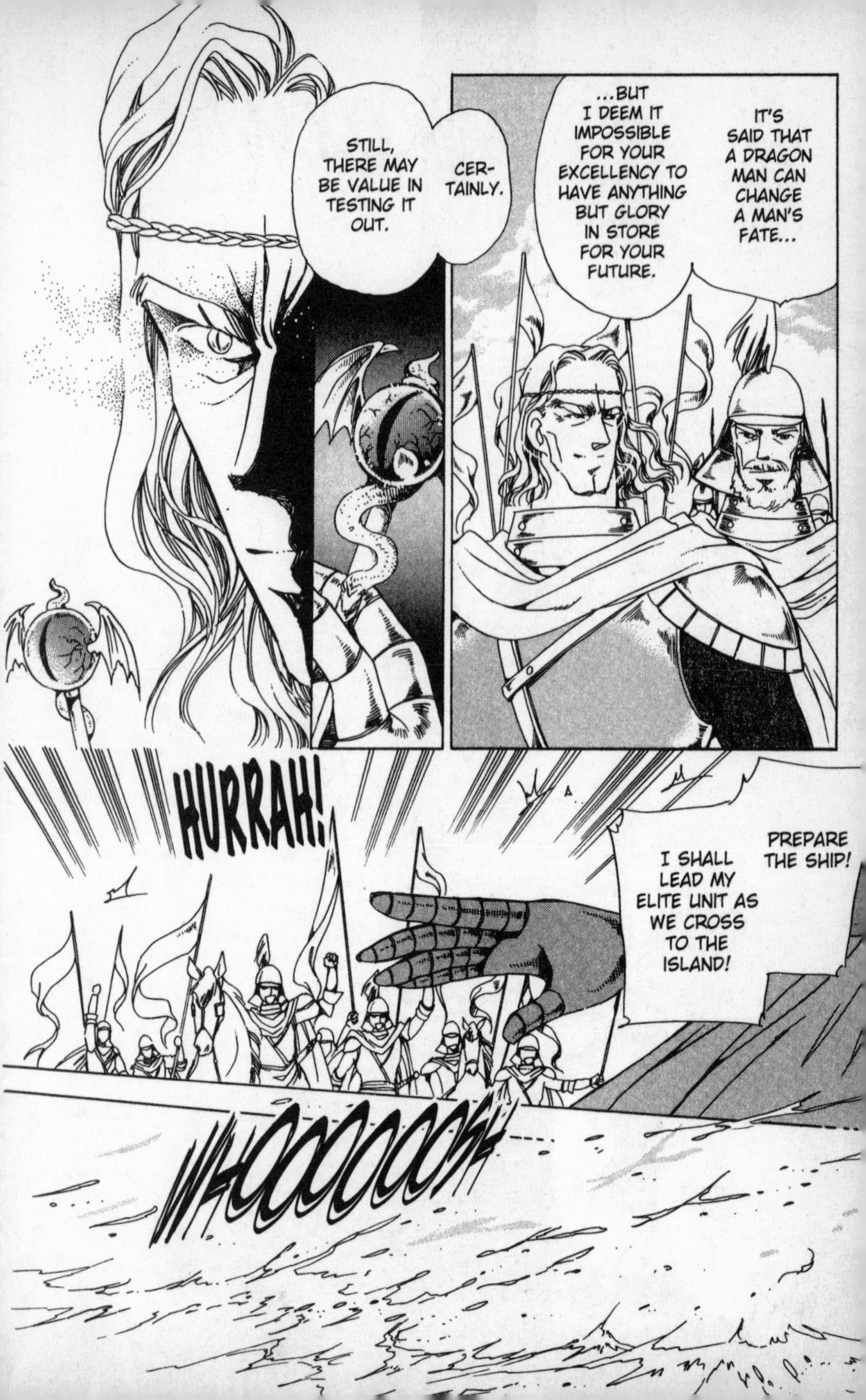
IT'S SAID THAT A DRAGON MAN CAN CHANGE A MAN'S FATE...
...BUT I DEEM IT IMPOSSIBLE FOR YOUR EXCELLENCY TO HAVE ANYTHING BUT GLORY IN STORE FOR YOUR FUTURE.
CER-TAINLY.
STILL, THERE MAY BE VALUE IN TESTING IT OUT.
PREPARE THE SHIP!
I SHALL LEAD MY ELITE UNIT AS WE CROSS TO THE ISLAND!
HURRAH!
WHOOOOOOH!

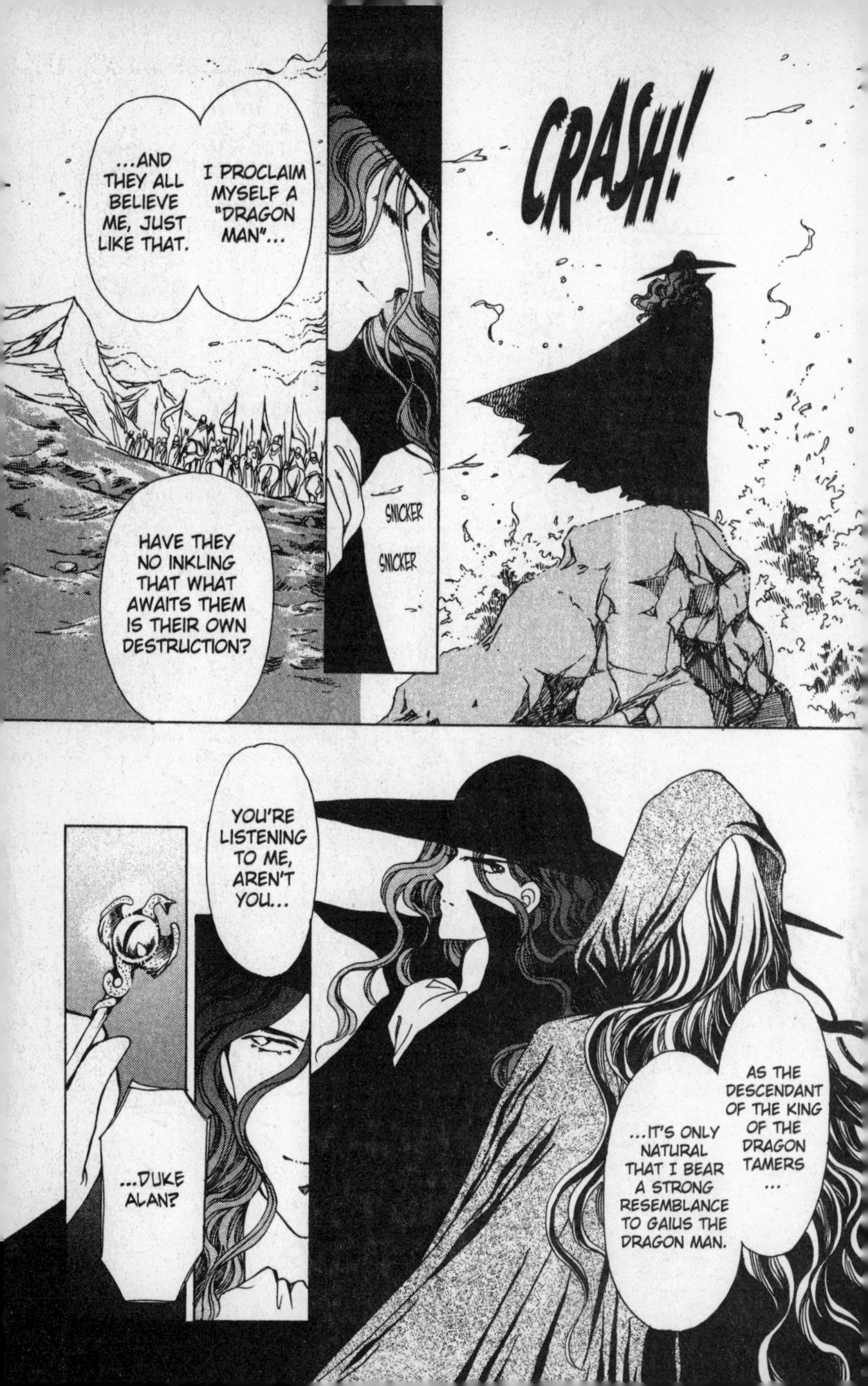
CRASH!
SNICKER
SNICKER
I PROCLAIM MYSELF A "DRAGON MAN"...
...AND THEY ALL BELIEVE ME, JUST LIKE THAT.
HAVE THEY NO INKLING THAT WHAT AWAITS THEM IS THEIR OWN DESTRUCTION?
AS THE DESCENDANT OF THE KING OF THE DRAGON TAMERS...
...IT'S ONLY NATURAL THAT I BEAR A STRONG RESEMBLANCE TO GAIUS THE DRAGON MAN.
YOU'RE LISTENING TO ME, AREN'T YOU...
...DUKE ALAN?

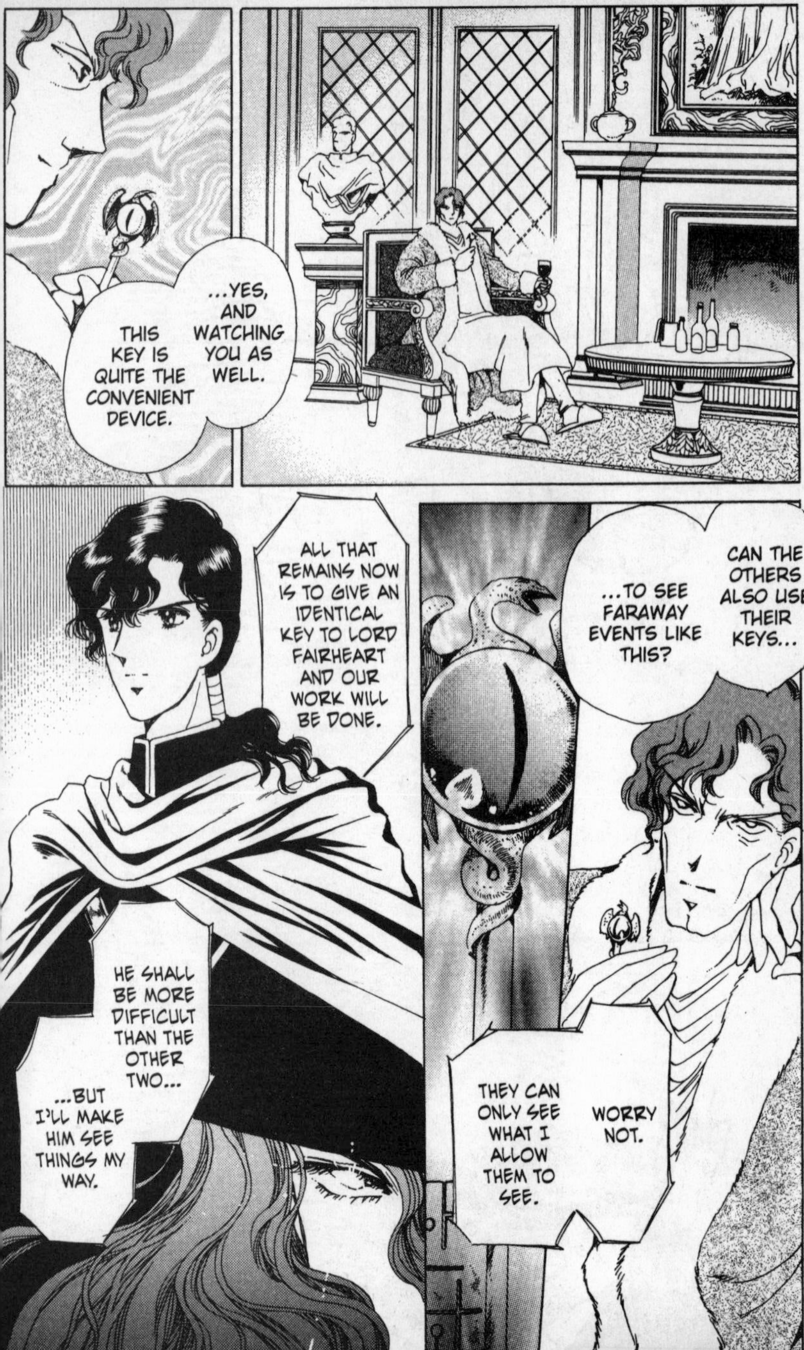
...YES, AND WATCHING YOU AS WELL.
THIS KEY IS QUITE THE CONVENIENT DEVICE.
CAN THE OTHERS ALSO USE THEIR KEYS...
...TO SEE FARAWAY EVENTS LIKE THIS?
WORRY NOT.
THEY CAN ONLY SEE WHAT I ALLOW THEM TO SEE.
ALL THAT REMAINS NOW IS TO GIVE AN IDENTICAL KEY TO LORD FAIRHEART AND OUR WORK WILL BE DONE.
HE SHALL BE MORE DIFFICULT THAN THE OTHER TWO...
...BUT I'LL MAKE HIM SEE THINGS MY WAY.

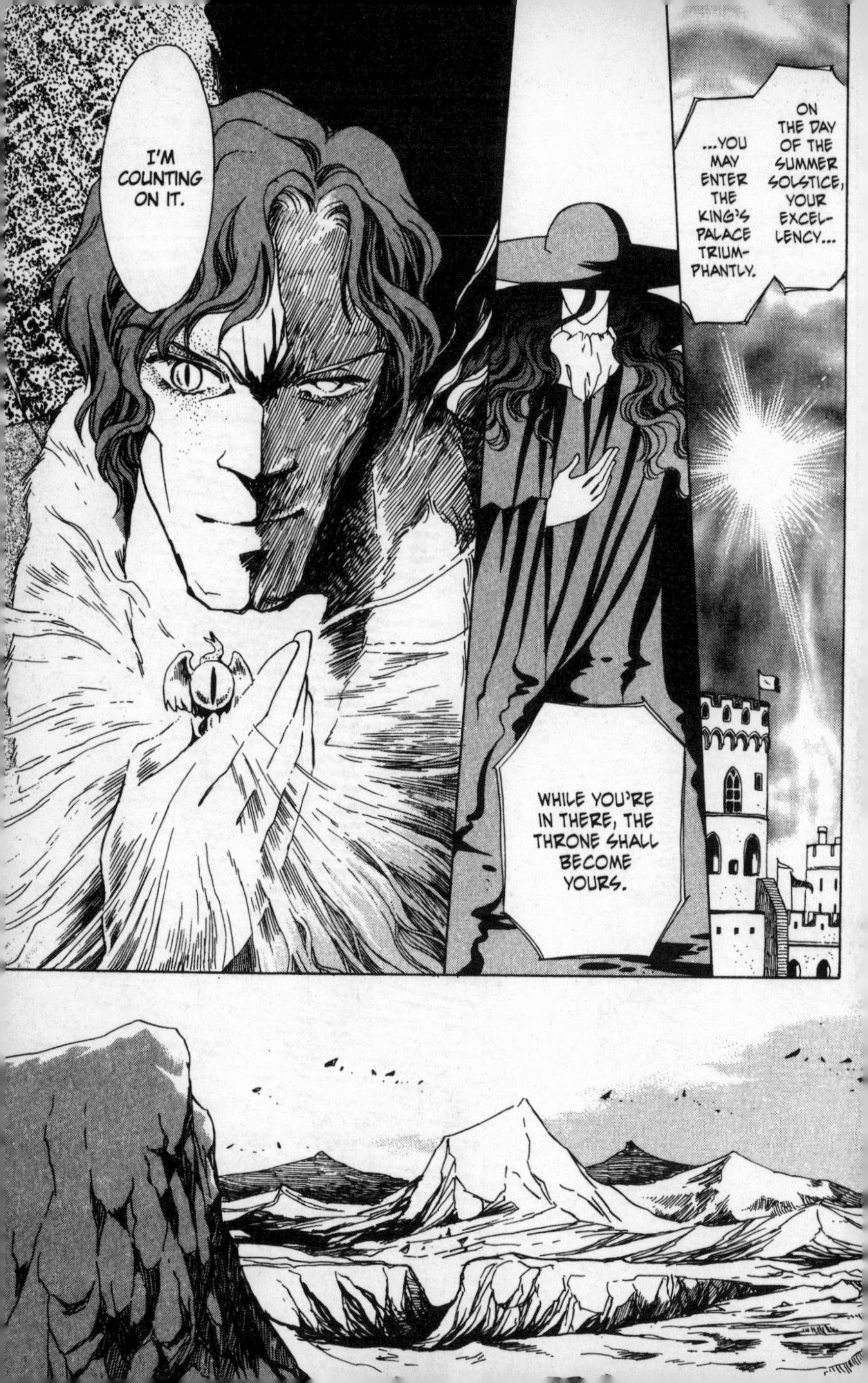
ON THE DAY OF THE SUMMER SOLSTICE, YOUR EXCELLENCY...
...YOU MAY ENTER THE KING'S PALACE TRIUMPHANTLY.
WHILE YOU'RE IN THERE, THE THRONE SHALL BECOME YOURS.
I'M COUNTING ON IT.

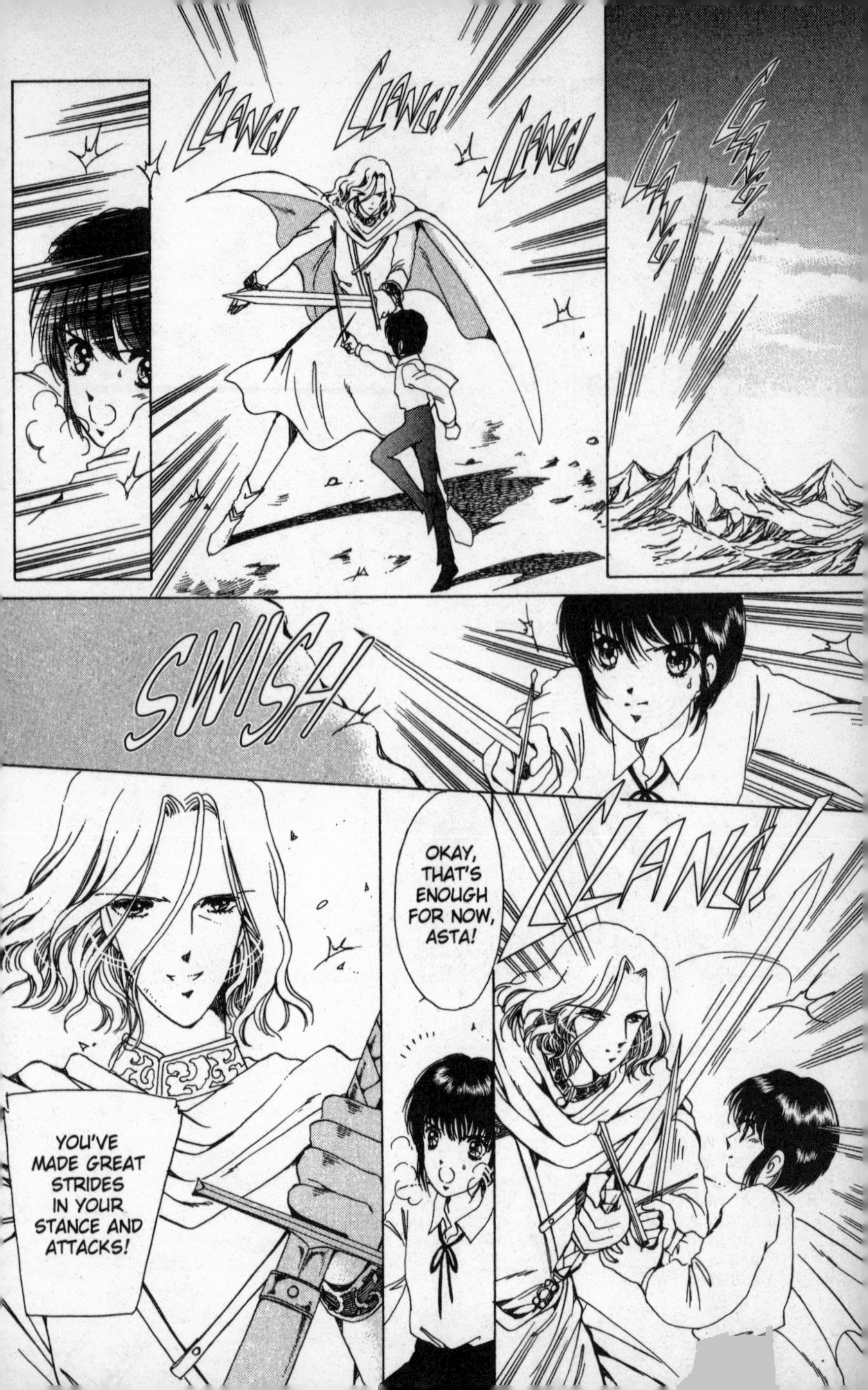

CLANG!
CLANG!
CLANG!
CLANG!
CLANG!
SWISH
CLANG!
OKAY, THAT'S ENOUGH FOR NOW, ASTA!
YOU'VE MADE GREAT STRIDES IN YOUR STANCE AND ATTACKS!

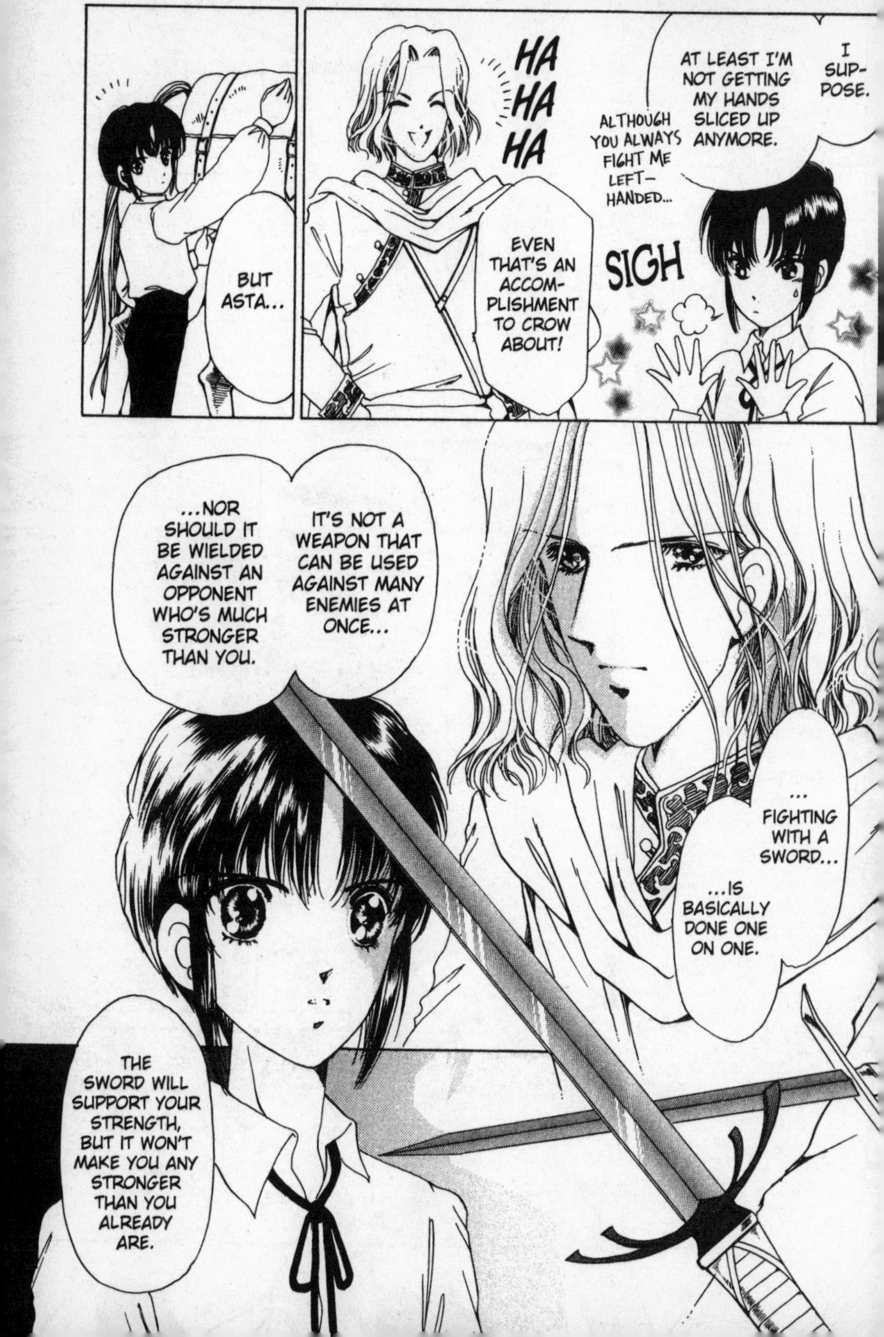
AT LEAST I'M NOT GETTING MY HANDS SLICED UP ANYMORE.
I SUP-POSE.
ALTHOUGH YOU ALWAYS FIGHT ME LEFT-HANDED...
SIGH
HA HA HA
EVEN THAT'S AN ACCOM-PLISHMENT TO CROW ABOUT!
BUT ASTA...
...FIGHTING WITH A SWORD...
...IS BASICALLY DONE ONE ON ONE.
IT'S NOT A WEAPON THAT CAN BE USED AGAINST MANY ENEMIES AT ONCE...
...NOR SHOULD IT BE WIELDED AGAINST AN OPPONENT WHO'S MUCH STRONGER THAN YOU.
THE SWORD WILL SUPPORT YOUR STRENGTH, BUT IT WON'T MAKE YOU ANY STRONGER THAN YOU ALREADY ARE.

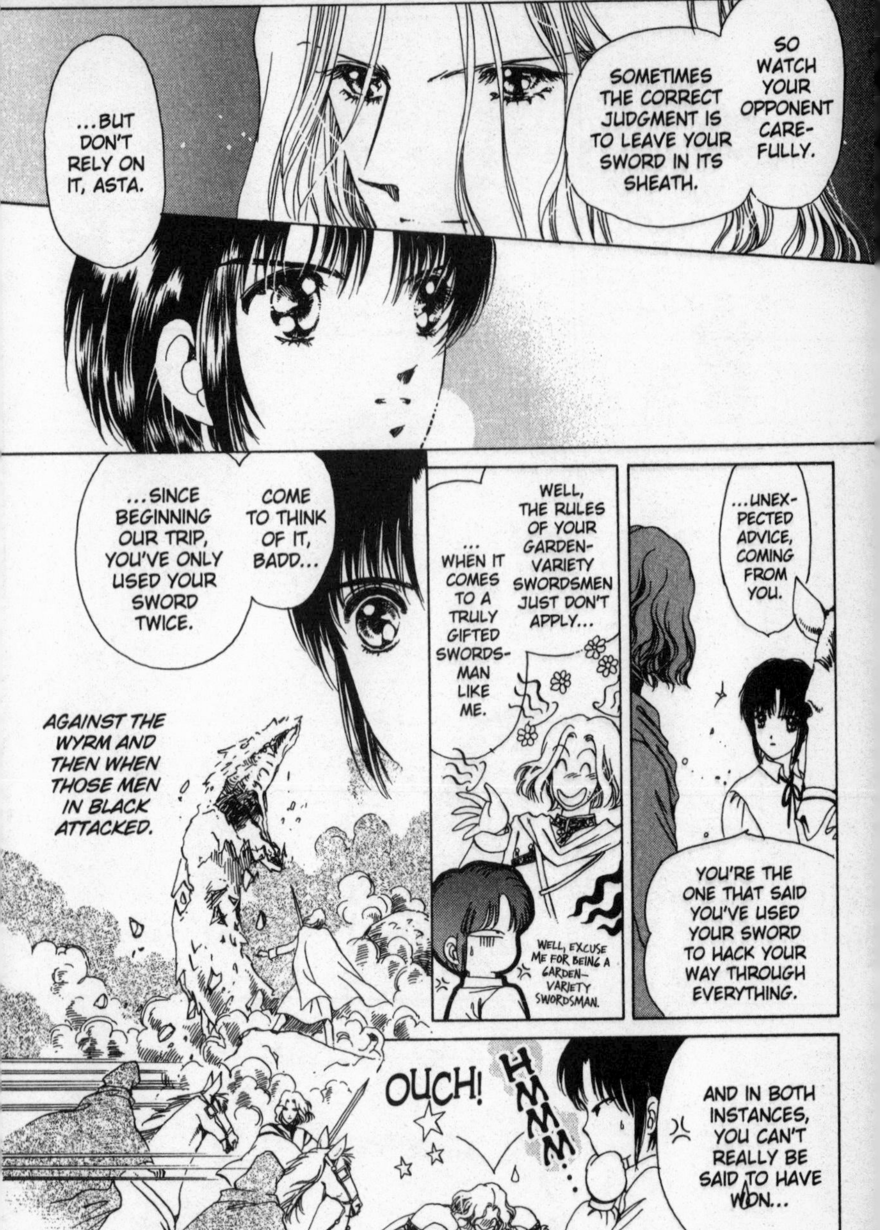

SO WATCH YOUR OPPONENT CAREFULLY.
SOMETIMES THE CORRECT JUDGMENT IS TO LEAVE YOUR SWORD IN ITS SHEATH.
...BUT DON'T RELY ON IT, ASTA.
...UNEXPECTED ADVICE, COMING FROM YOU.
YOU'RE THE ONE THAT SAID YOU'VE USED YOUR SWORD TO HACK YOUR WAY THROUGH EVERYTHING.
WELL, THE RULES OF YOUR GARDEN-VARIETY SWORDSMEN JUST DON'T APPLY...
...WHEN IT COMES TO A TRULY GIFTED SWORDSMAN LIKE ME.
WELL, EXCUSE ME FOR BEING A GARDEN-VARIETY SWORDSMAN.
COME TO THINK OF IT, BADD...
...SINCE BEGINNING OUR TRIP, YOU'VE ONLY USED YOUR SWORD TWICE.
AGAINST THE WYRM AND THEN WHEN THOSE MEN IN BLACK ATTACKED.
AND IN BOTH INSTANCES, YOU CAN'T REALLY BE SAID TO HAVE WON...
HMMM...
OUCH!

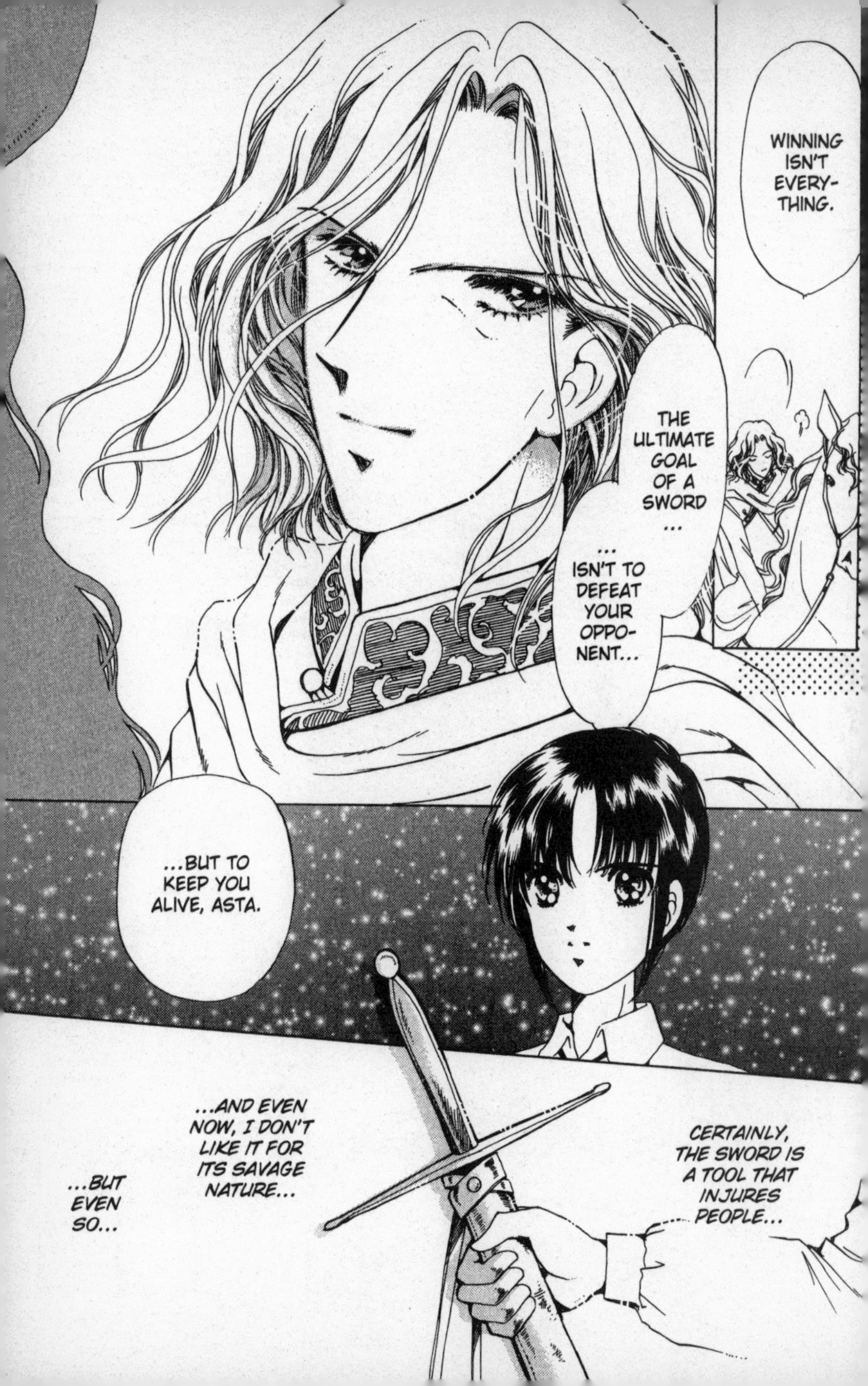
WINNING ISN'T EVERY-THING.
THE ULTIMATE GOAL OF A SWORD ...
... ISN'T TO DEFEAT YOUR OPPO-NENT...
...BUT TO KEEP YOU ALIVE, ASTA.
CERTAINLY, THE SWORD IS A TOOL THAT INJURES PEOPLE...
...AND EVEN NOW, I DON'T LIKE IT FOR ITS SAVAGE NATURE...
...BUT EVEN SO...

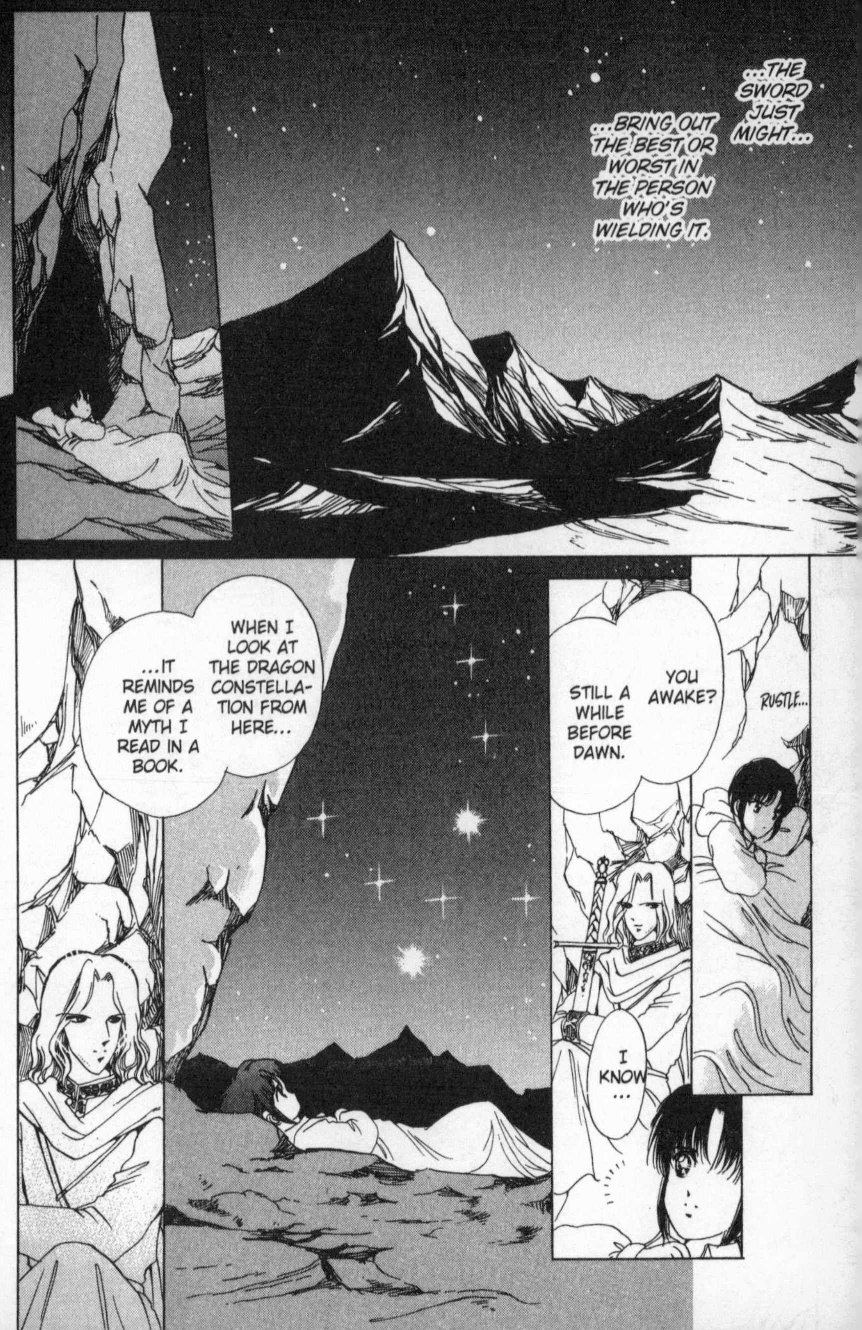
...THE SWORD JUST MIGHT...
...BRING OUT THE BEST OR WORST IN THE PERSON WHO'S WIELDING IT.
RUSTLE...
YOU AWAKE?
STILL A WHILE BEFORE DAWN.
I KNOW...
WHEN I LOOK AT THE DRAGON CONSTELLATION FROM HERE...
...IT REMINDS ME OF A MYTH I READ IN A BOOK.

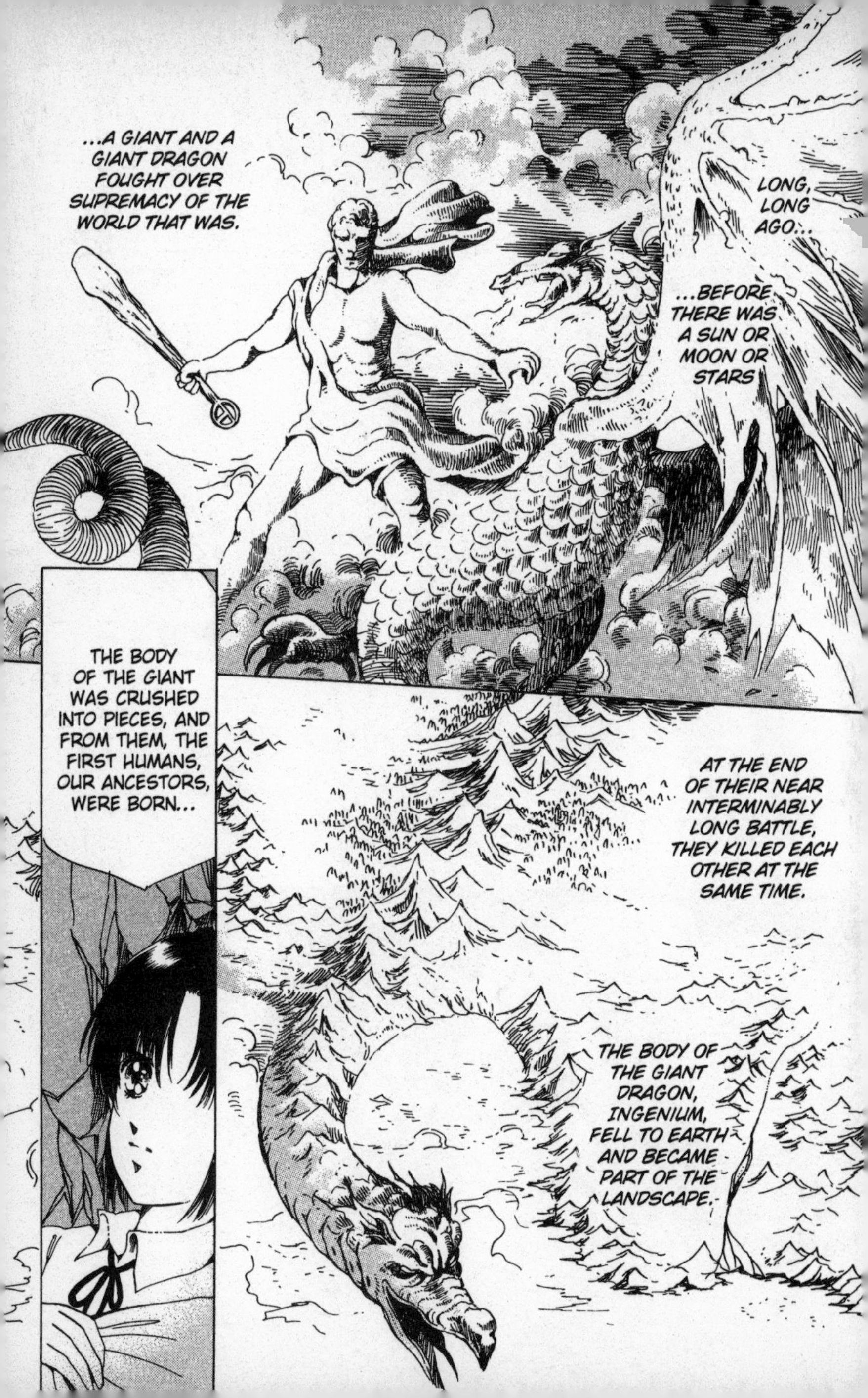
LONG, LONG AGO...
...BEFORE THERE WAS A SUN OR MOON OR STARS
...A GIANT AND A GIANT DRAGON FOUGHT OVER SUPREMACY OF THE WORLD THAT WAS.
AT THE END OF THEIR NEAR INTERMINABLY LONG BATTLE, THEY KILLED EACH OTHER AT THE SAME TIME.
THE BODY OF THE GIANT DRAGON, INGENIUM, FELL TO EARTH AND BECAME PART OF THE LANDSCAPE.
THE BODY OF THE GIANT WAS CRUSHED INTO PIECES, AND FROM THEM, THE FIRST HUMANS, OUR ANCESTORS, WERE BORN...

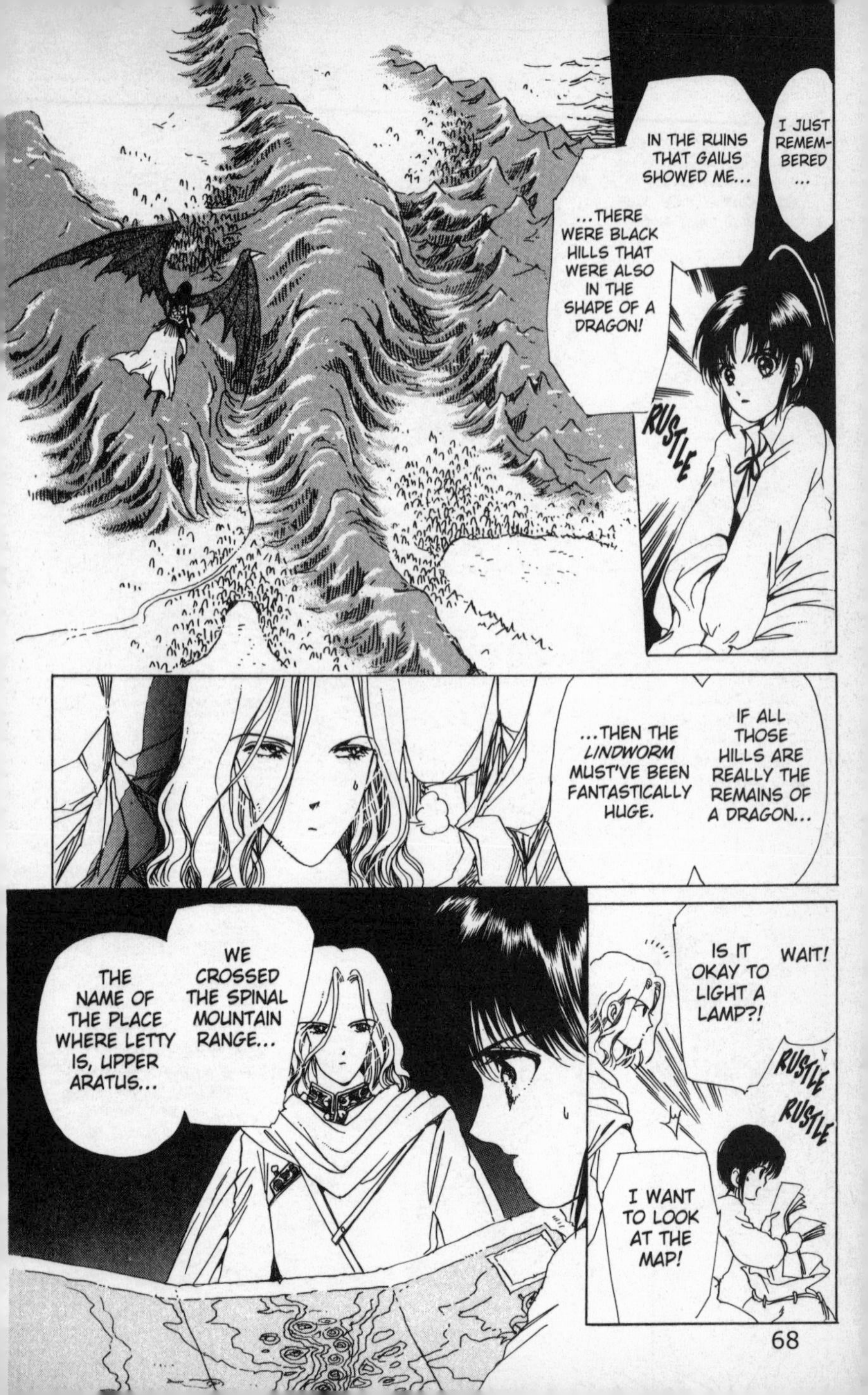
I JUST REMEMBERED...
IN THE RUINS THAT GAIUS SHOWED ME...
...THERE WERE BLACK HILLS THAT WERE ALSO IN THE SHAPE OF A DRAGON!
RUSTLE
IF ALL THOSE HILLS ARE REALLY THE REMAINS OF A DRAGON...
...THEN THE *LINDWORM* MUST'VE BEEN FANTASTICALLY HUGE.
WAIT!
IS IT OKAY TO LIGHT A LAMP?!
RUSTLE
RUSTLE
I WANT TO LOOK AT THE MAP!
WE CROSSED THE SPINAL MOUNTAIN RANGE...
THE NAME OF THE PLACE WHERE LETTY IS, UPPER ARATUS...

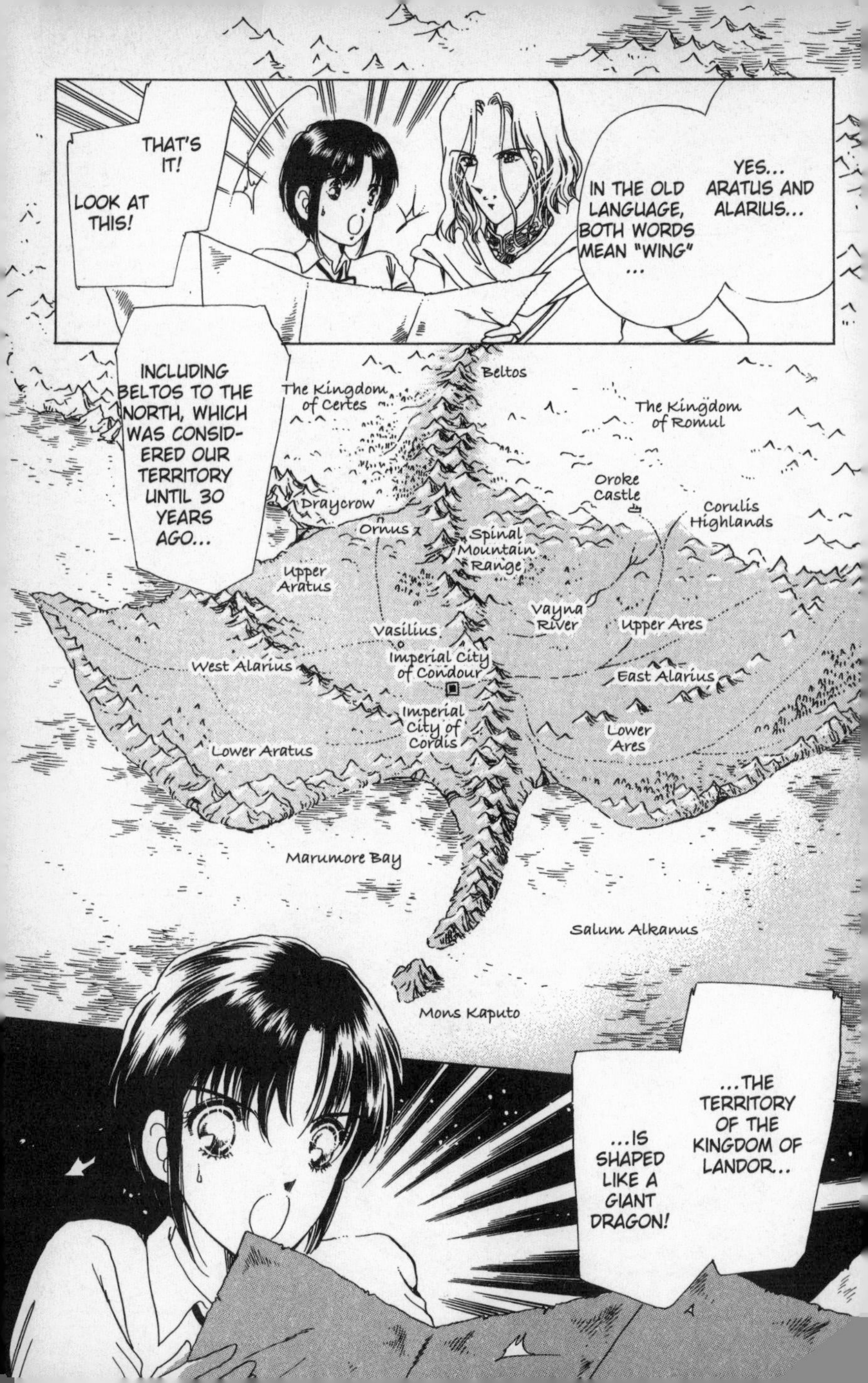
YES... ARATUS AND ALARIUS...
IN THE OLD LANGUAGE, BOTH WORDS MEAN "WING" ...
THAT'S IT!
LOOK AT THIS!
INCLUDING BELTOS TO THE NORTH, WHICH WAS CONSIDERED OUR TERRITORY UNTIL 30 YEARS AGO...
Beltos
The Kingdom of Romul
The Kingdom of Certes
Oroke Castle
Corulis Highlands
Draycrow
Ornus
Spinal Mountain Range
Upper Aratus
Vayna River
Upper Ares
Vasilius
Imperial City of Condour
West Alarius
East Alarius
Imperial City of Cordis
Lower Ares
Lower Aratus
Marumore Bay
Salum Alkanus
Mons Kaputo
...THE TERRITORY OF THE KINGDOM OF LANDOR...
...IS SHAPED LIKE A GIANT DRAGON!

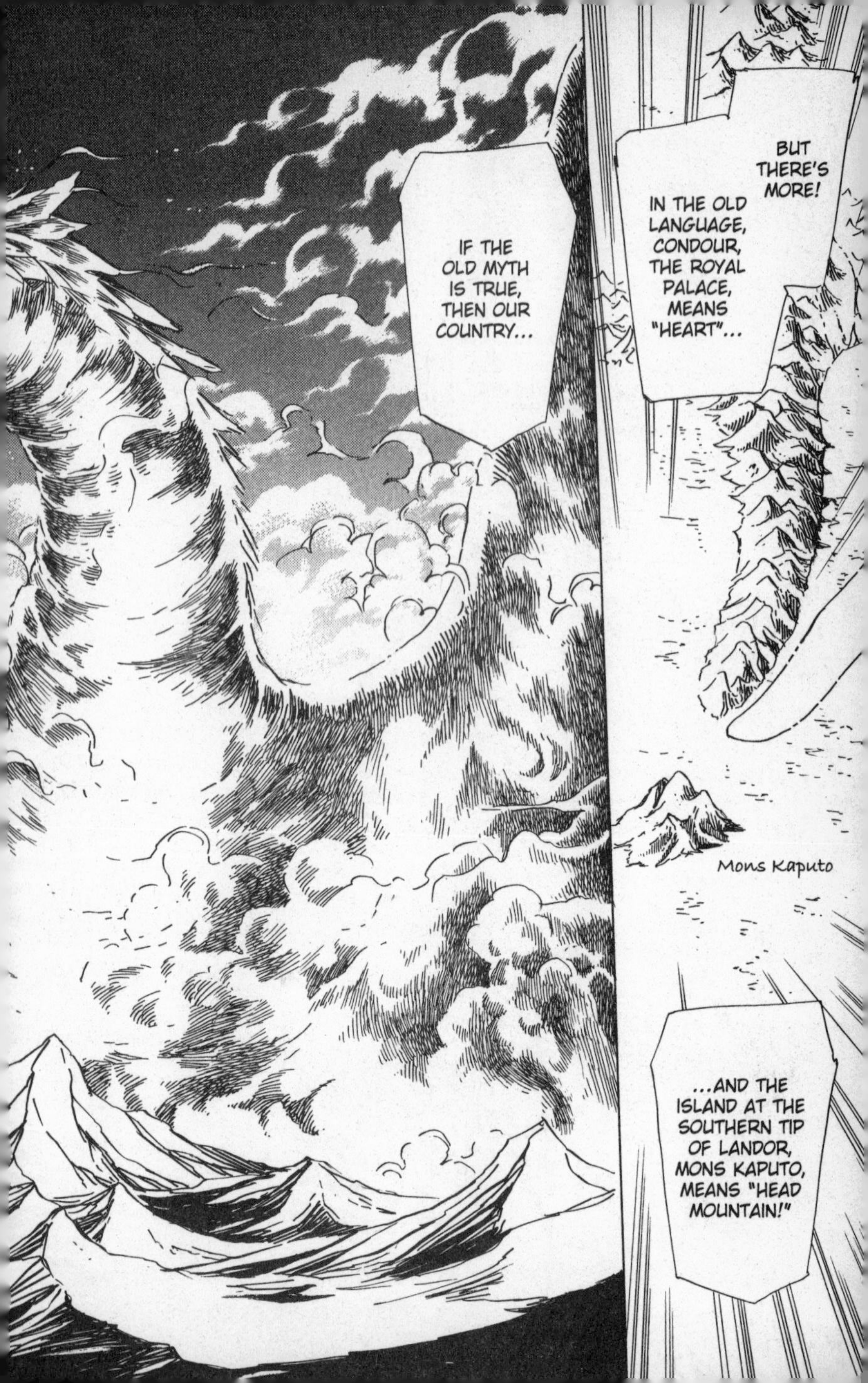
BUT THERE'S MORE!
IN THE OLD LANGUAGE, CONDOUR, THE ROYAL PALACE, MEANS "HEART"...
Mons Kaputo
...AND THE ISLAND AT THE SOUTHERN TIP OF LANDOR, MONS KAPUTO, MEANS "HEAD MOUNTAIN!"
IF THE OLD MYTH IS TRUE, THEN OUR COUNTRY...

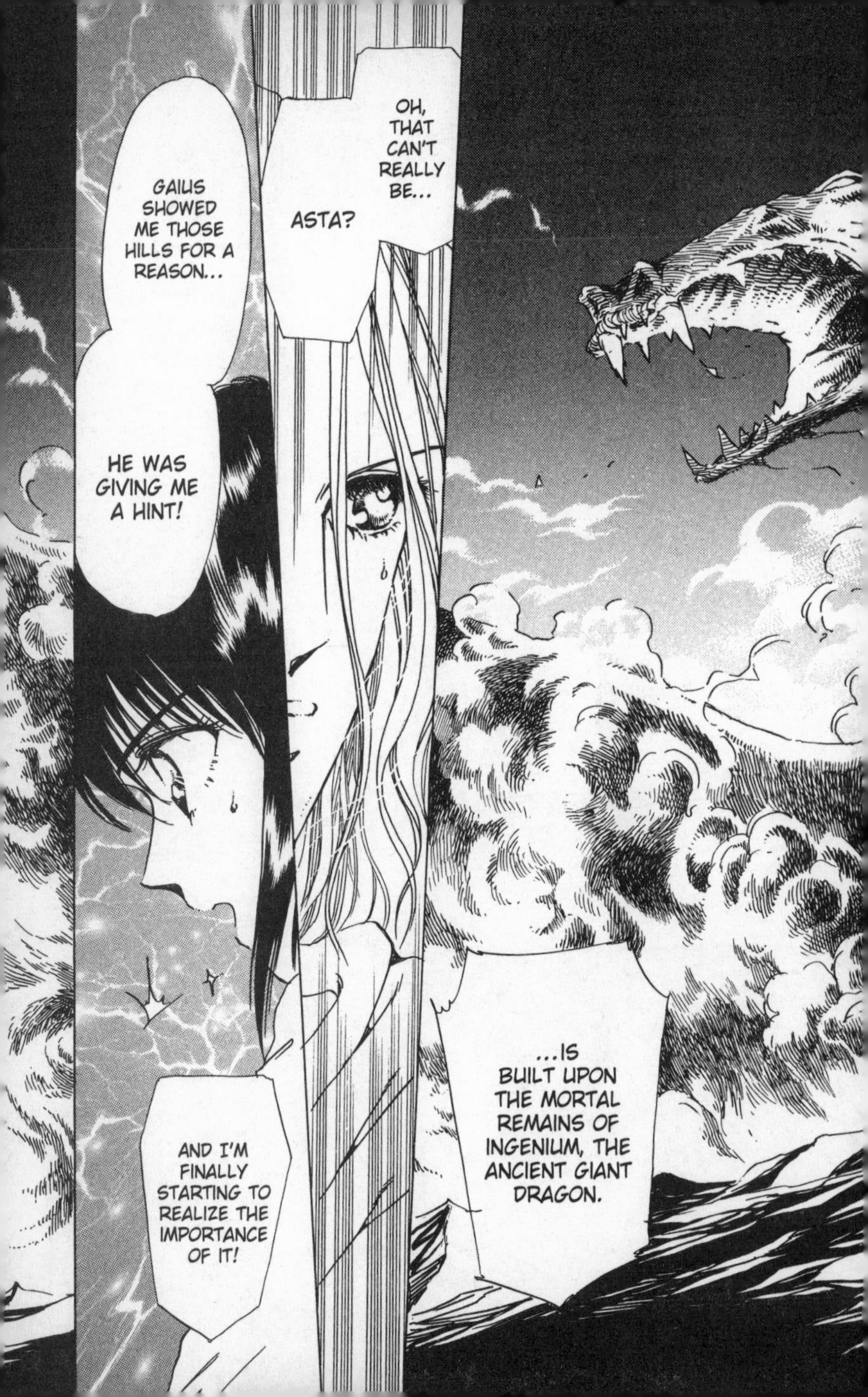
...IS BUILT UPON THE MORTAL REMAINS OF INGENIUM, THE ANCIENT GIANT DRAGON.
OH, THAT CAN'T REALLY BE...
ASTA?
GAIUS SHOWED ME THOSE HILLS FOR A REASON...
HE WAS GIVING ME A HINT!
AND I'M FINALLY STARTING TO REALIZE THE IMPORTANCE OF IT!

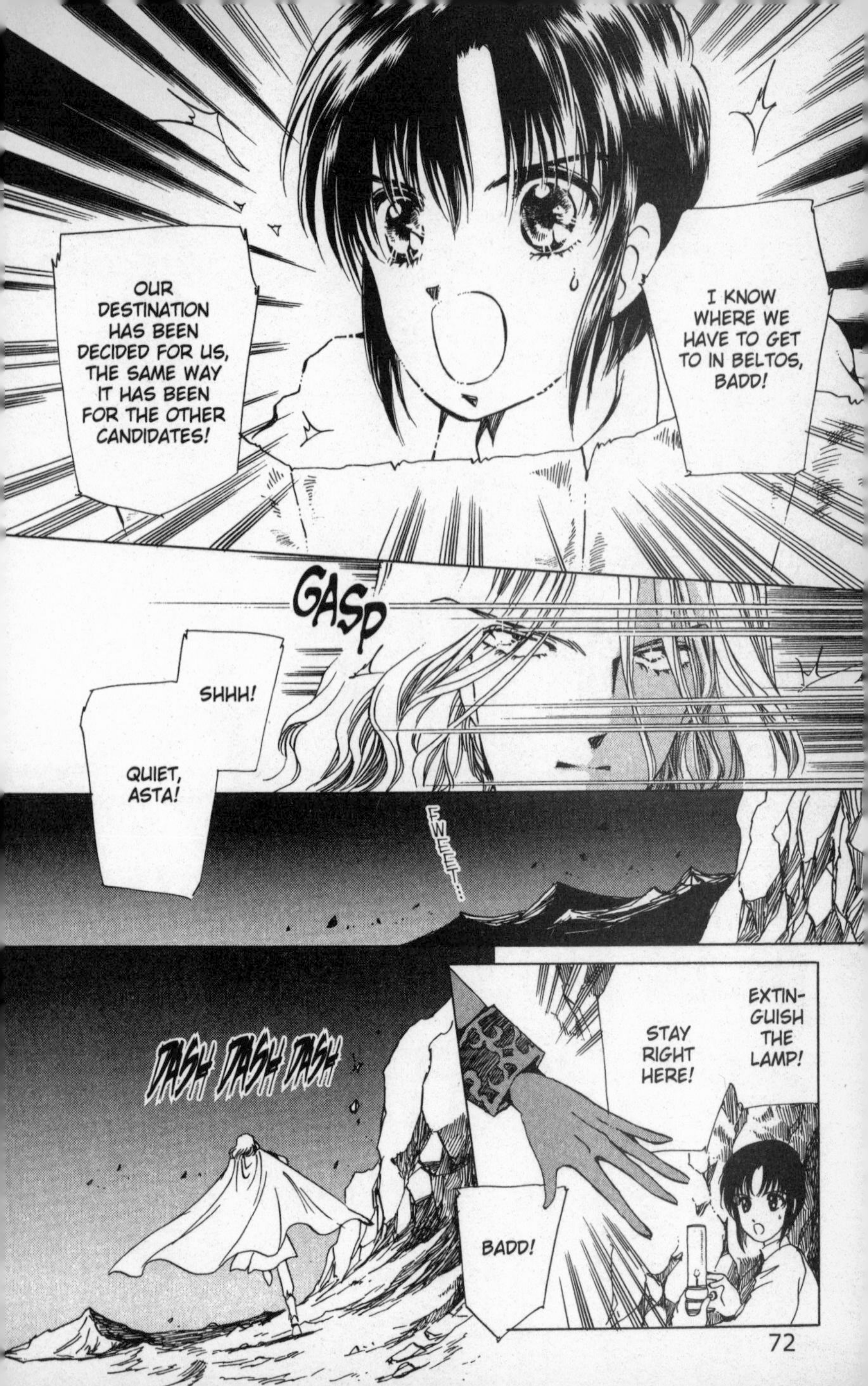
I KNOW WHERE WE HAVE TO GET TO IN BELTOS, BADD!
OUR DESTINATION HAS BEEN DECIDED FOR US, THE SAME WAY IT HAS BEEN FOR THE OTHER CANDIDATES!
GASP
SHHH!
QUIET, ASTA!
FWEET...
EXTIN-GUISH THE LAMP!
STAY RIGHT HERE!
BADD!
DASH DASH DASH

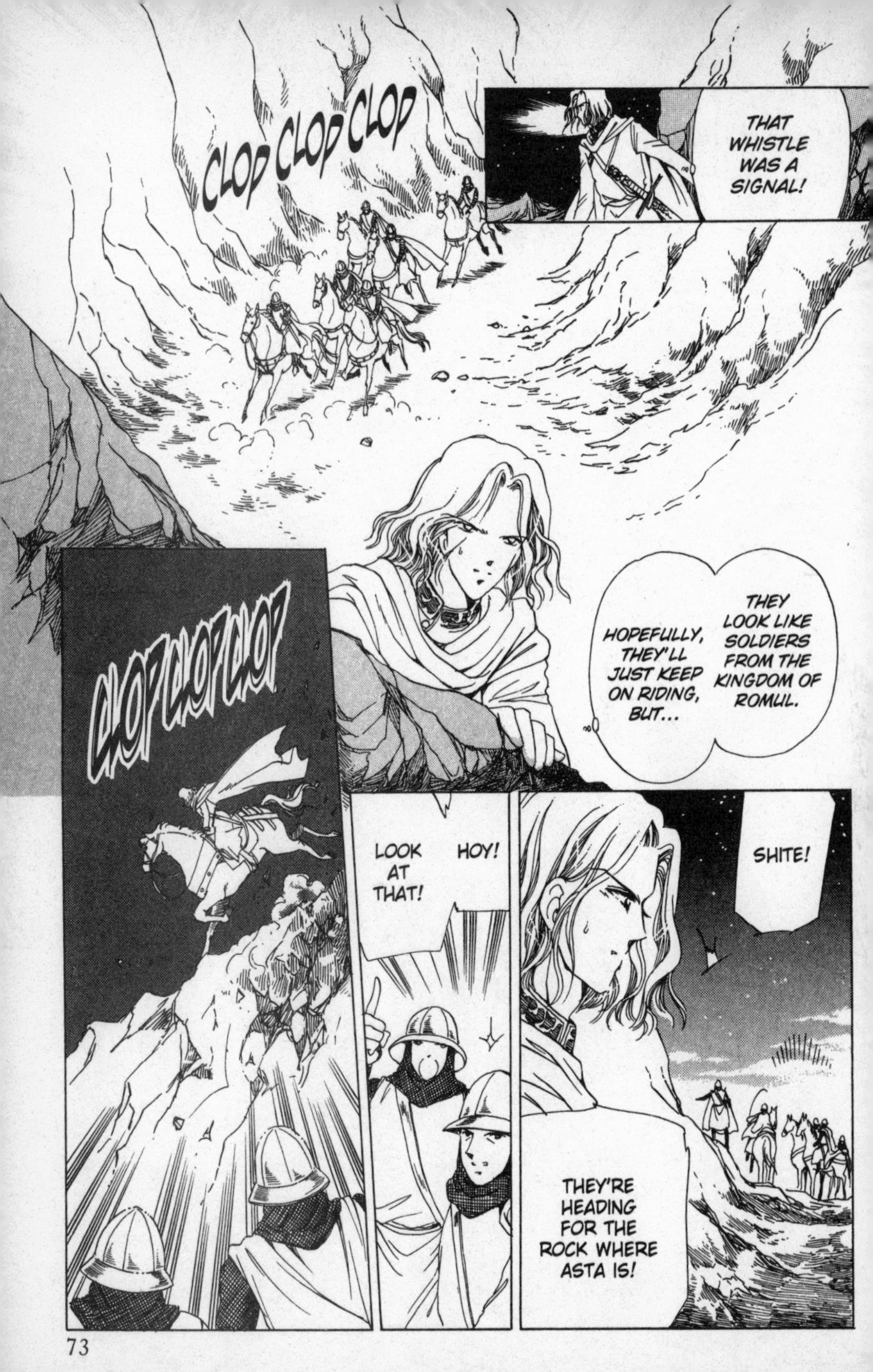
THAT WHISTLE WAS A SIGNAL!
CLOP CLOP CLOP
THEY LOOK LIKE SOLDIERS FROM THE KINGDOM OF ROMUL.
HOPEFULLY, THEY'LL JUST KEEP ON RIDING, BUT...
SHITE!
THEY'RE HEADING FOR THE ROCK WHERE ASTA IS!
HOY!
LOOK AT THAT!
CLOP CLOP CLOP

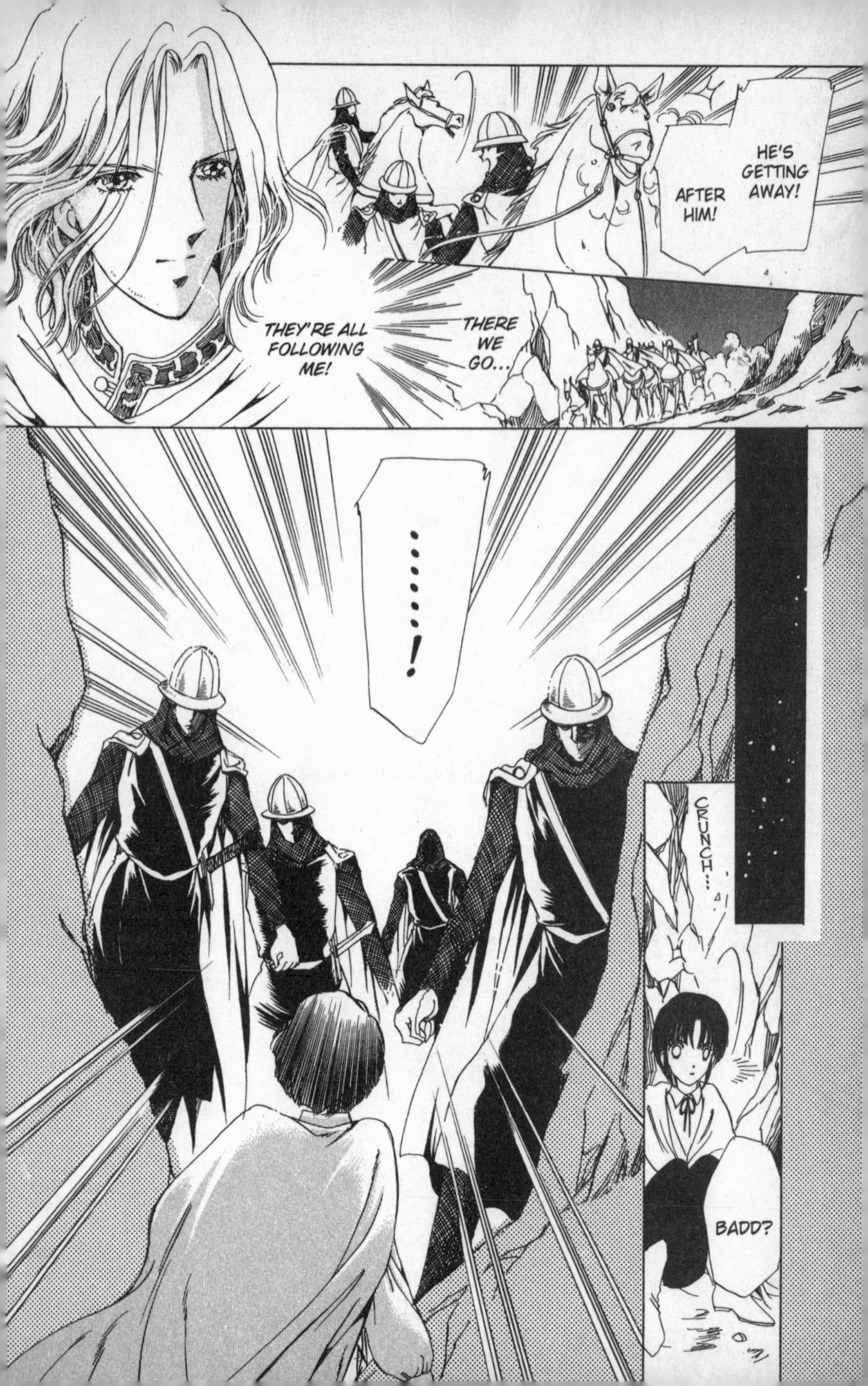

HE'S GETTING AWAY!
AFTER HIM!
THERE WE GO...
THEY'RE ALL FOLLOWING ME!
CRUNCH...
BADD?
......!

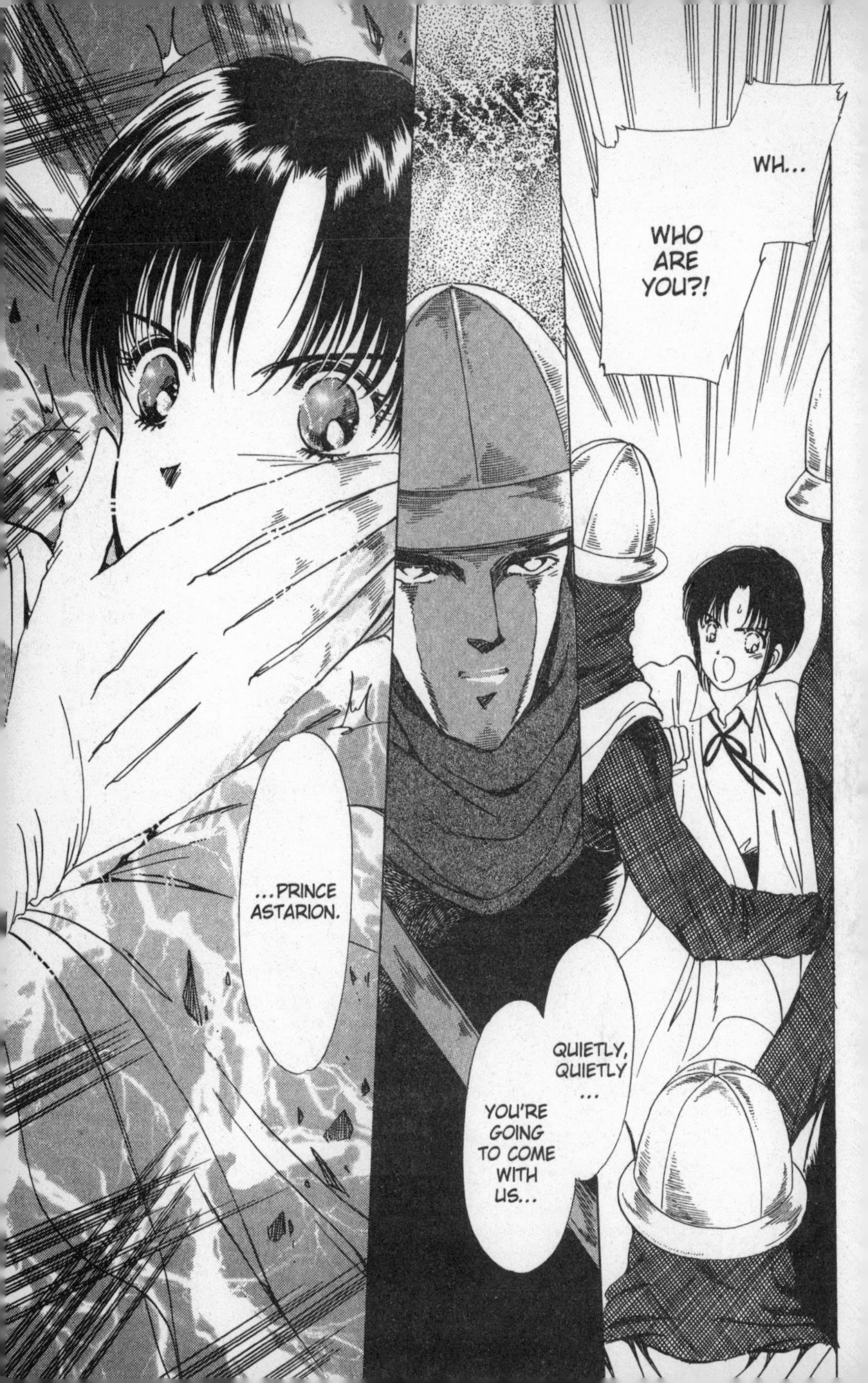
WH...
WHO ARE YOU?!
QUIETLY, QUIETLY ...
YOU'RE GOING TO COME WITH US...
...PRINCE ASTARION.

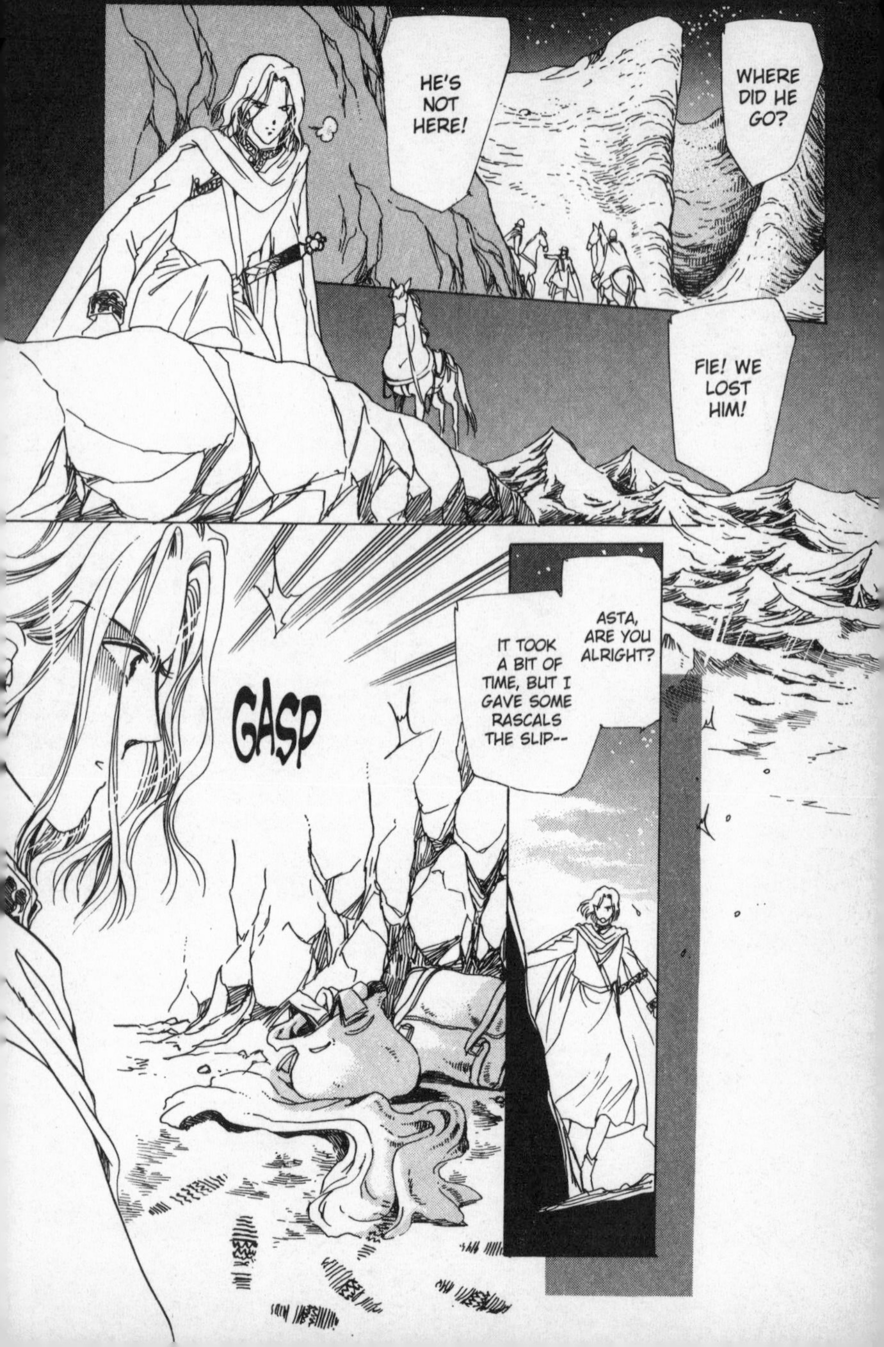
WHERE DID HE GO?
HE'S NOT HERE!
FIE! WE LOST HIM!
ASTA, ARE YOU ALRIGHT?
IT TOOK A BIT OF TIME, BUT I GAVE SOME RASCALS THE SLIP--
GASP

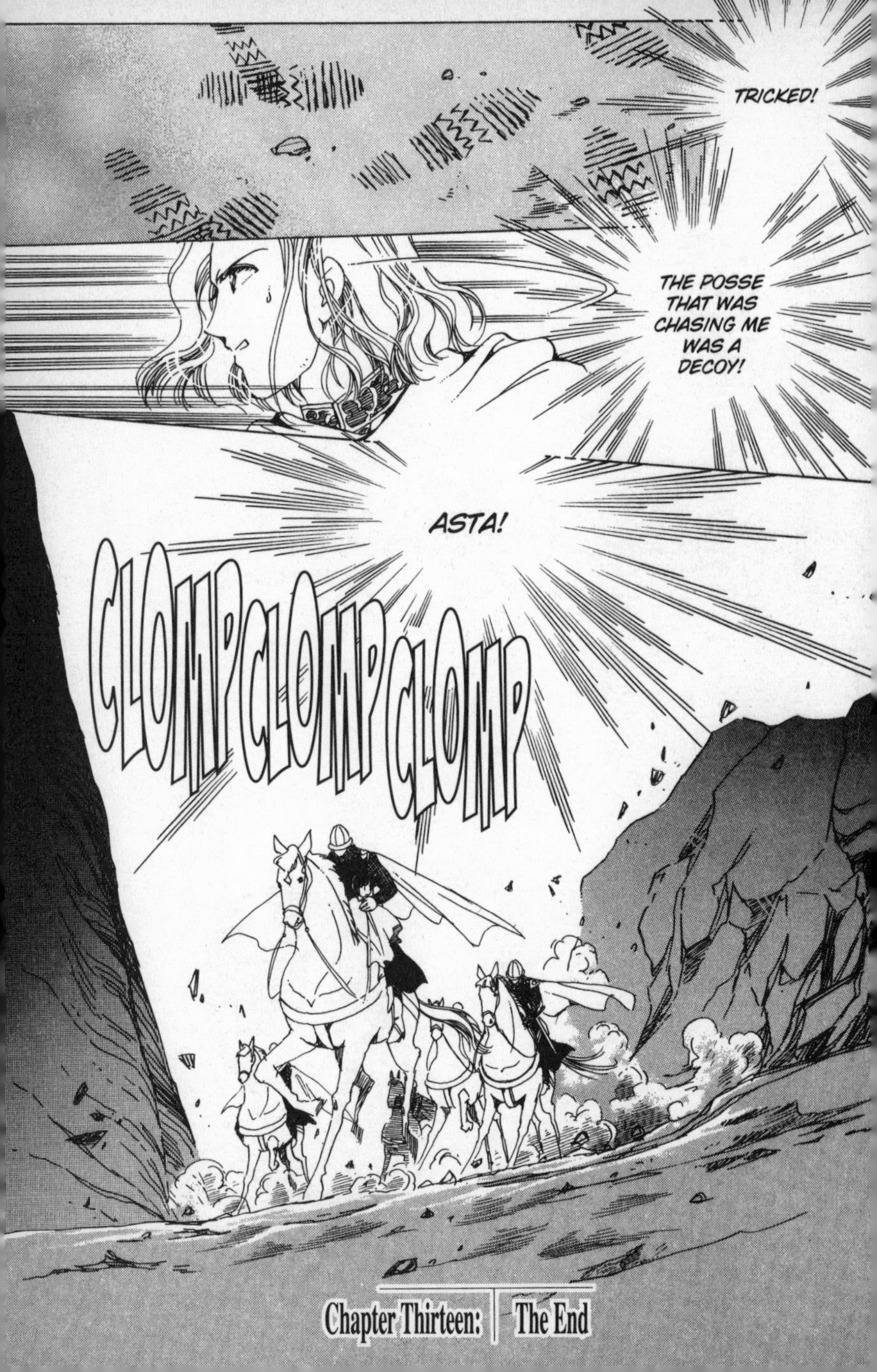
TRICKED!
THE POSSE THAT WAS CHASING ME WAS A DECOY!
ASTA!
CLOMP CLOMP CLOMP
Chapter Thirteen: The End

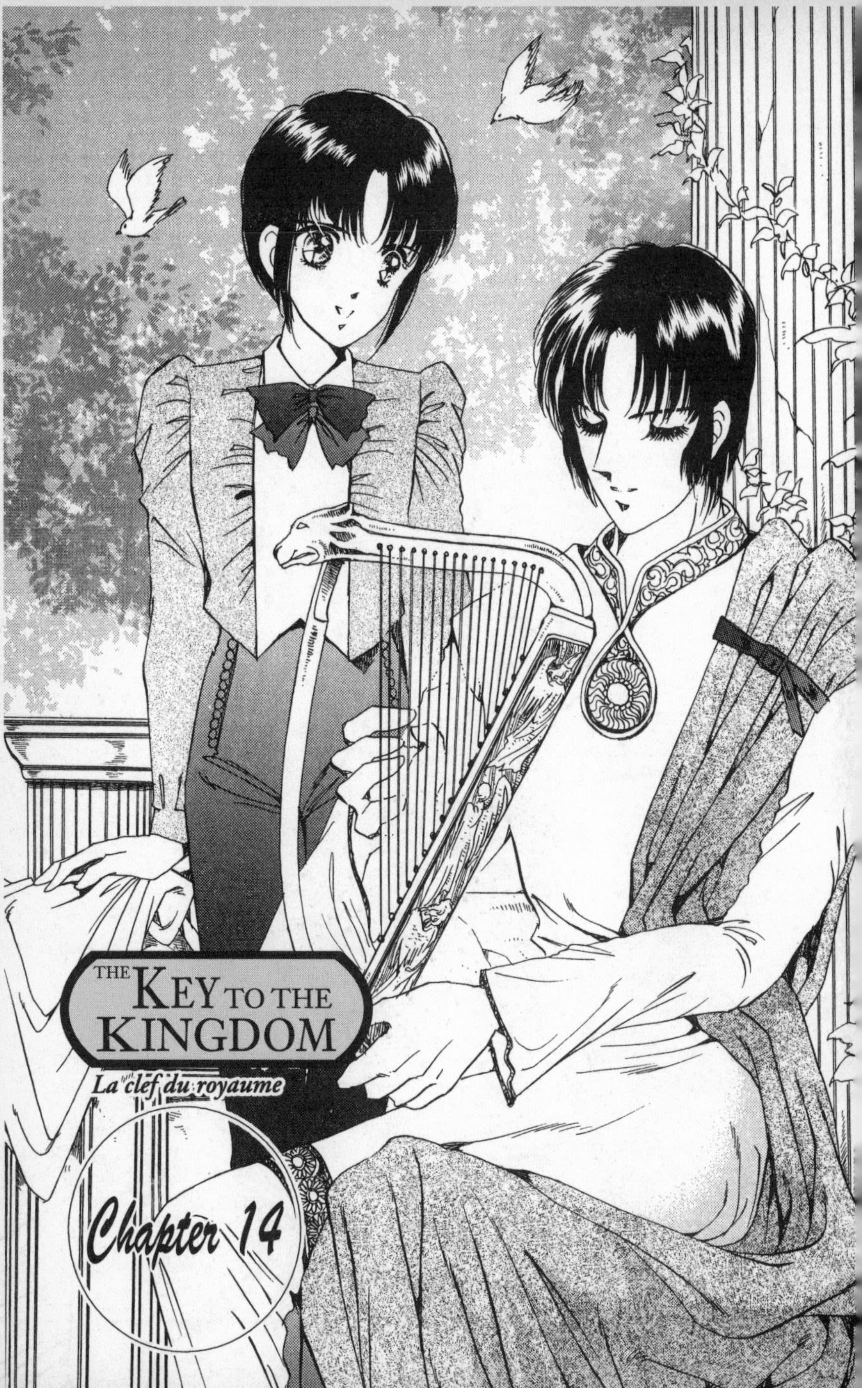
THE KEY TO THE KINGDOM
La clef du royaume
Chapter 14

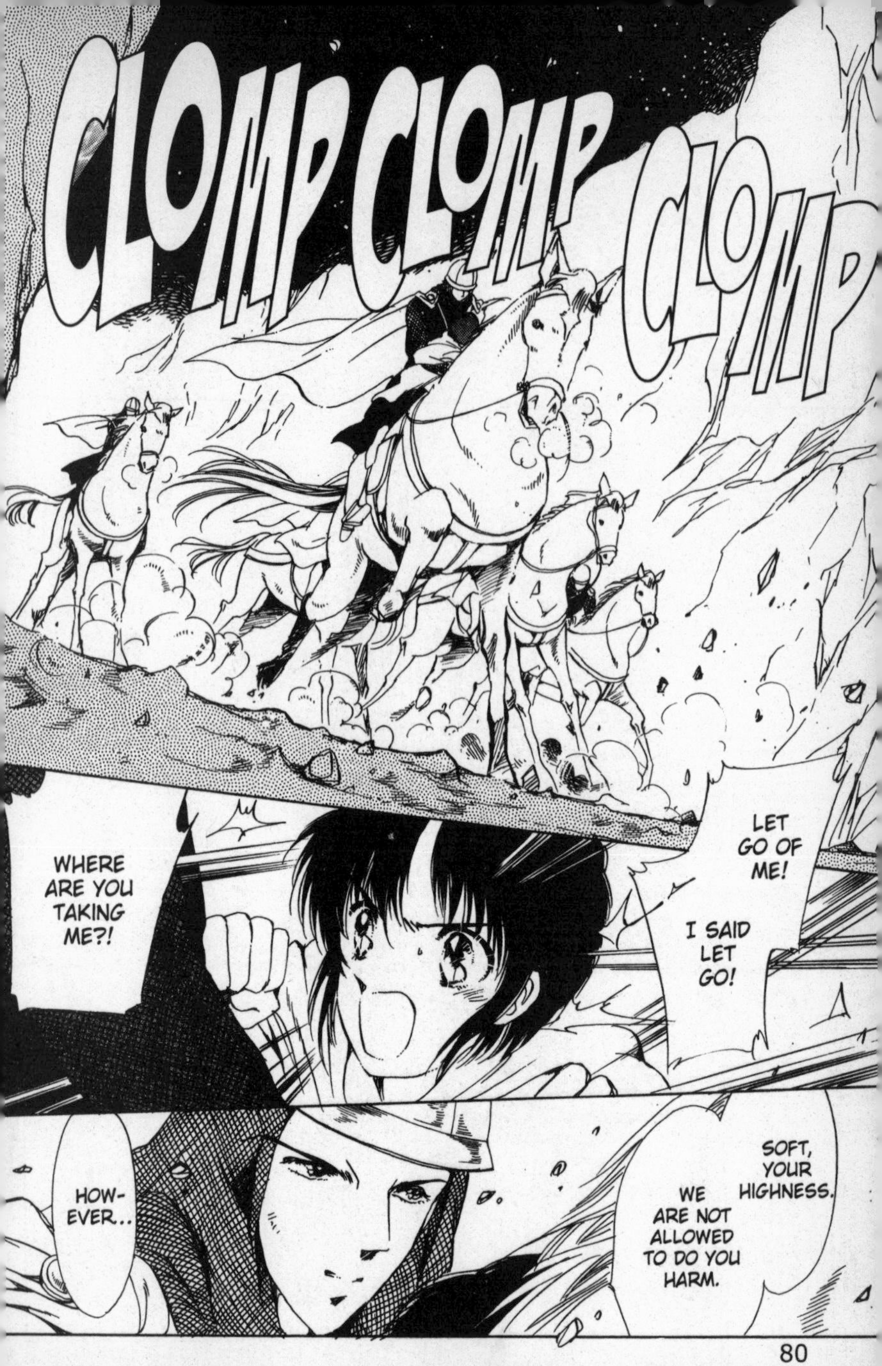
CLOMP CLOMP
CLOMP
LET GO OF ME!
I SAID LET GO!
WHERE ARE YOU TAKING ME?!
SOFT, YOUR HIGHNESS.
WE ARE NOT ALLOWED TO DO YOU HARM.
HOW-EVER...

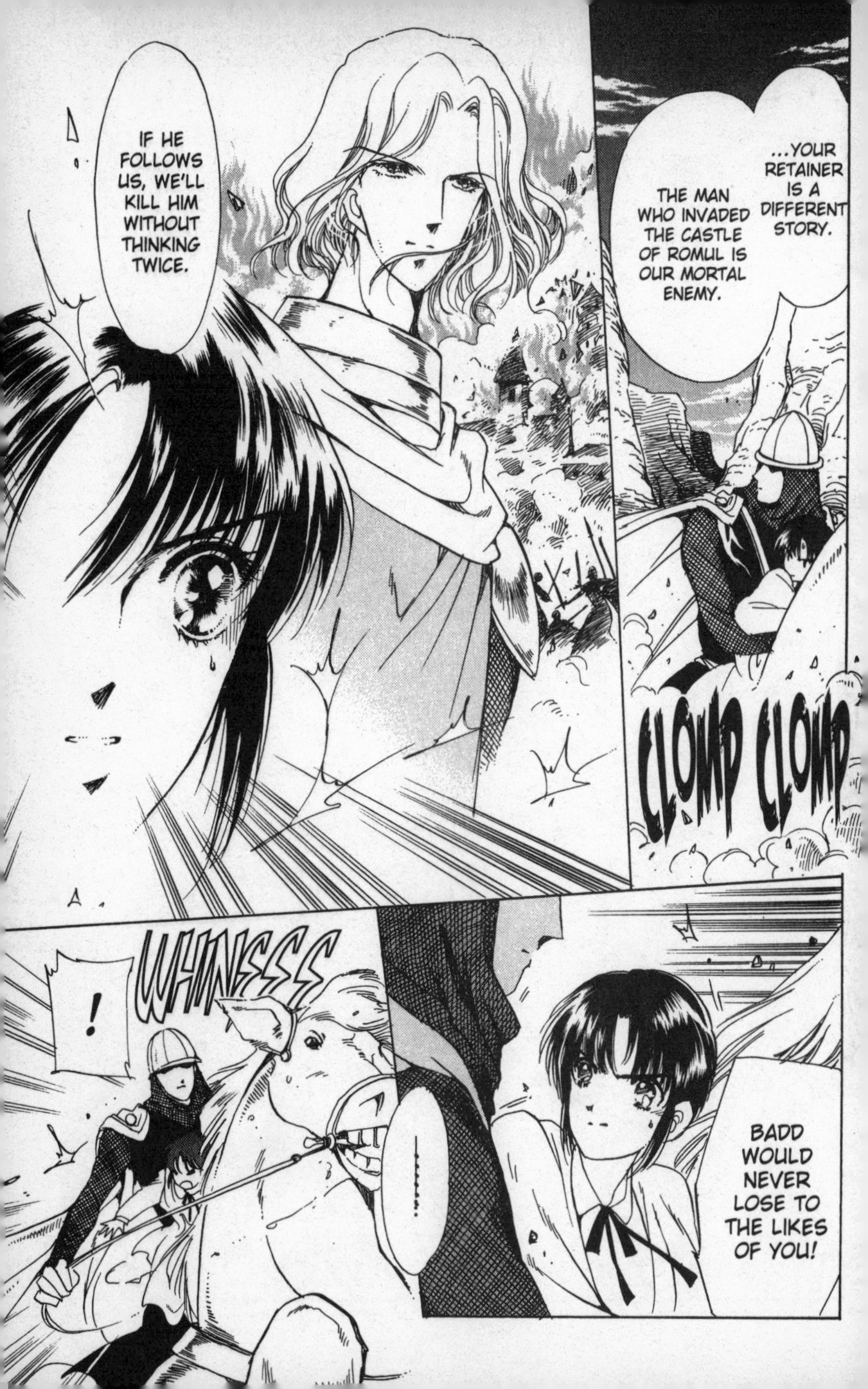
...YOUR RETAINER IS A DIFFERENT STORY.
THE MAN WHO INVADED THE CASTLE OF ROMUL IS OUR MORTAL ENEMY.
CLOMP CLOMP
IF HE FOLLOWS US, WE'LL KILL HIM WITHOUT THINKING TWICE.
BADD WOULD NEVER LOSE TO THE LIKES OF YOU!
......
WHINEEE
!

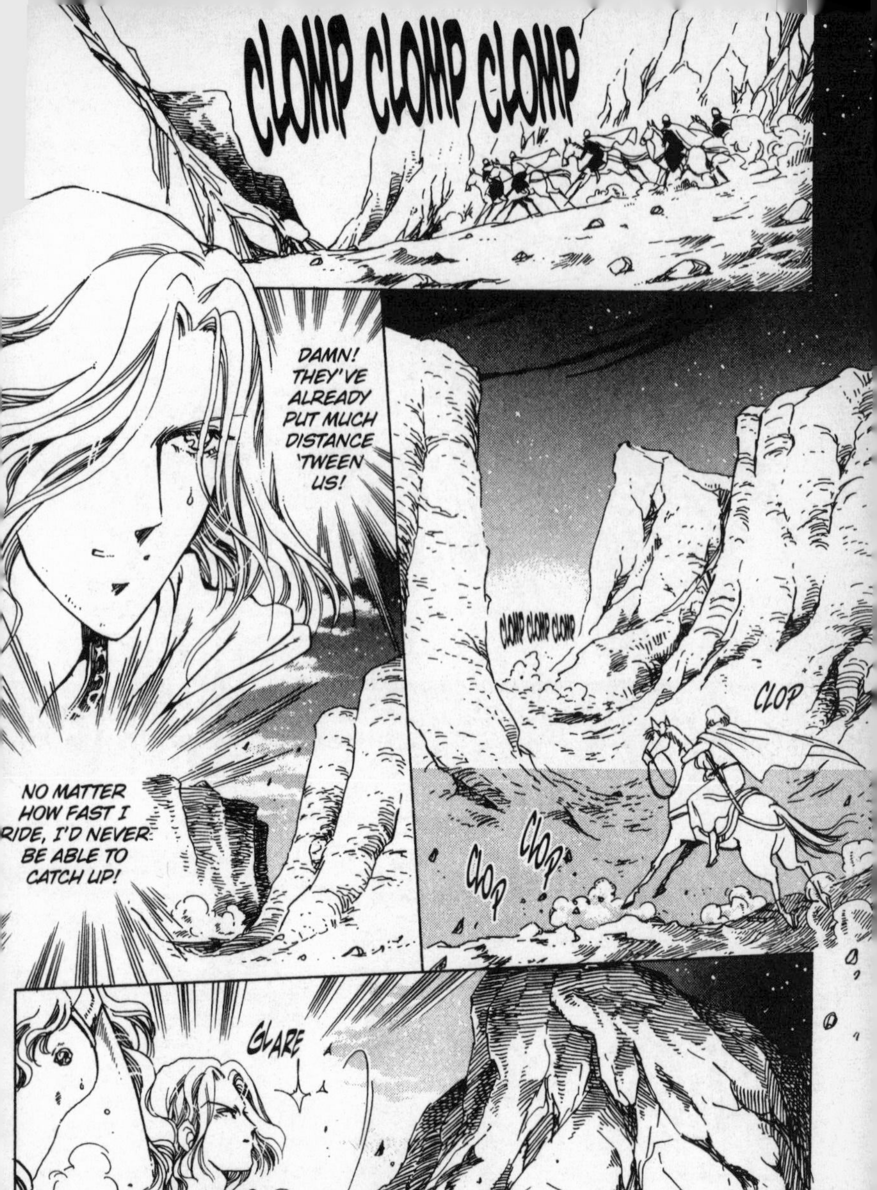
CLOMP CLOMP CLOMP
CLOMP CLOMP CLOMP
CLOP
CLOP
CLOP
DAMN! THEY'VE ALREADY PUT MUCH DISTANCE 'TWEEN US!
NO MATTER HOW FAST I RIDE, I'D NEVER BE ABLE TO CATCH UP!
GLARE

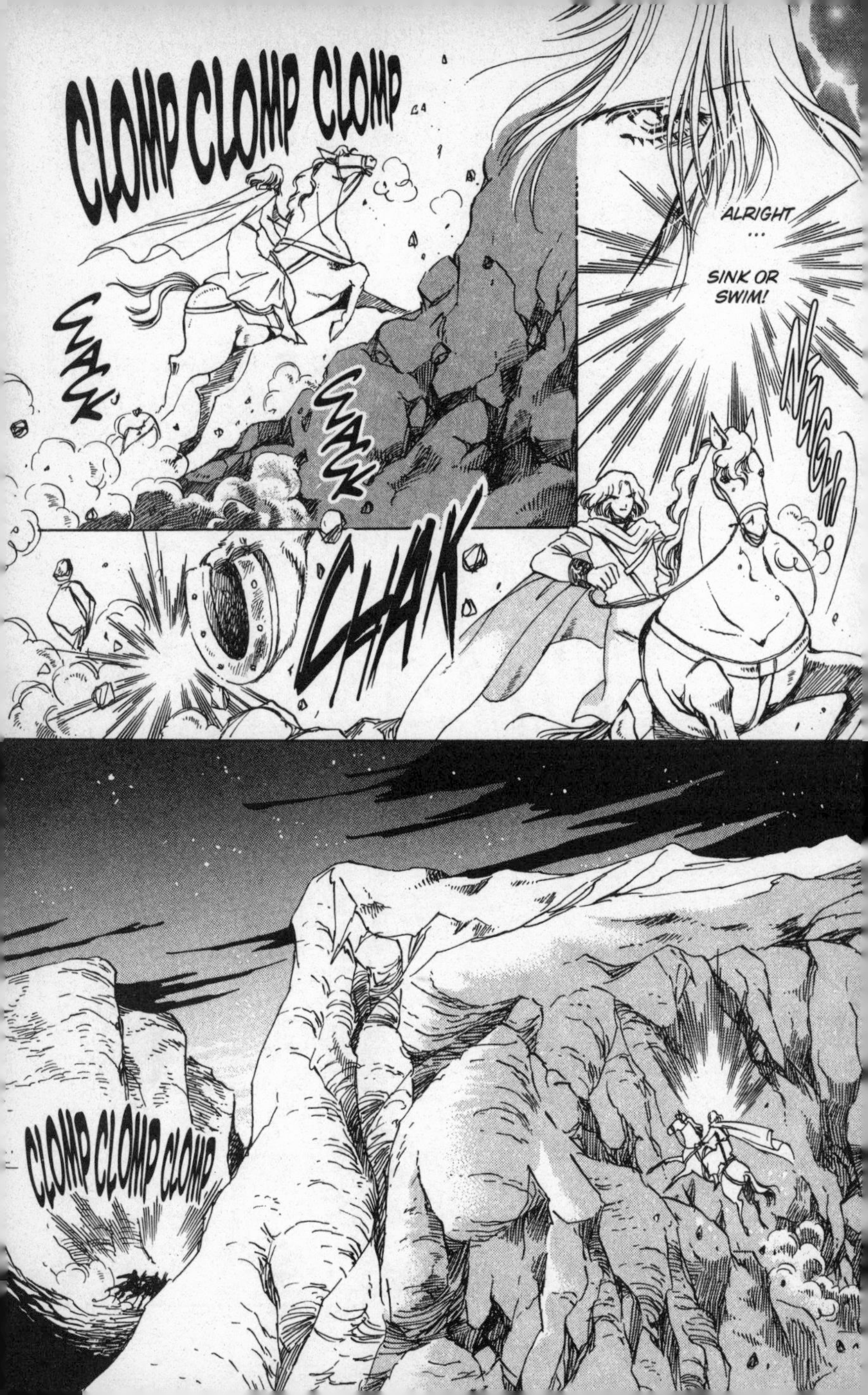
ALRIGHT ...
SINK OR SWIM!
NEIGH!
CLOMP CLOMP CLOMP
WACK
WACK
CHAK
CLOMP CLOMP CLOMP

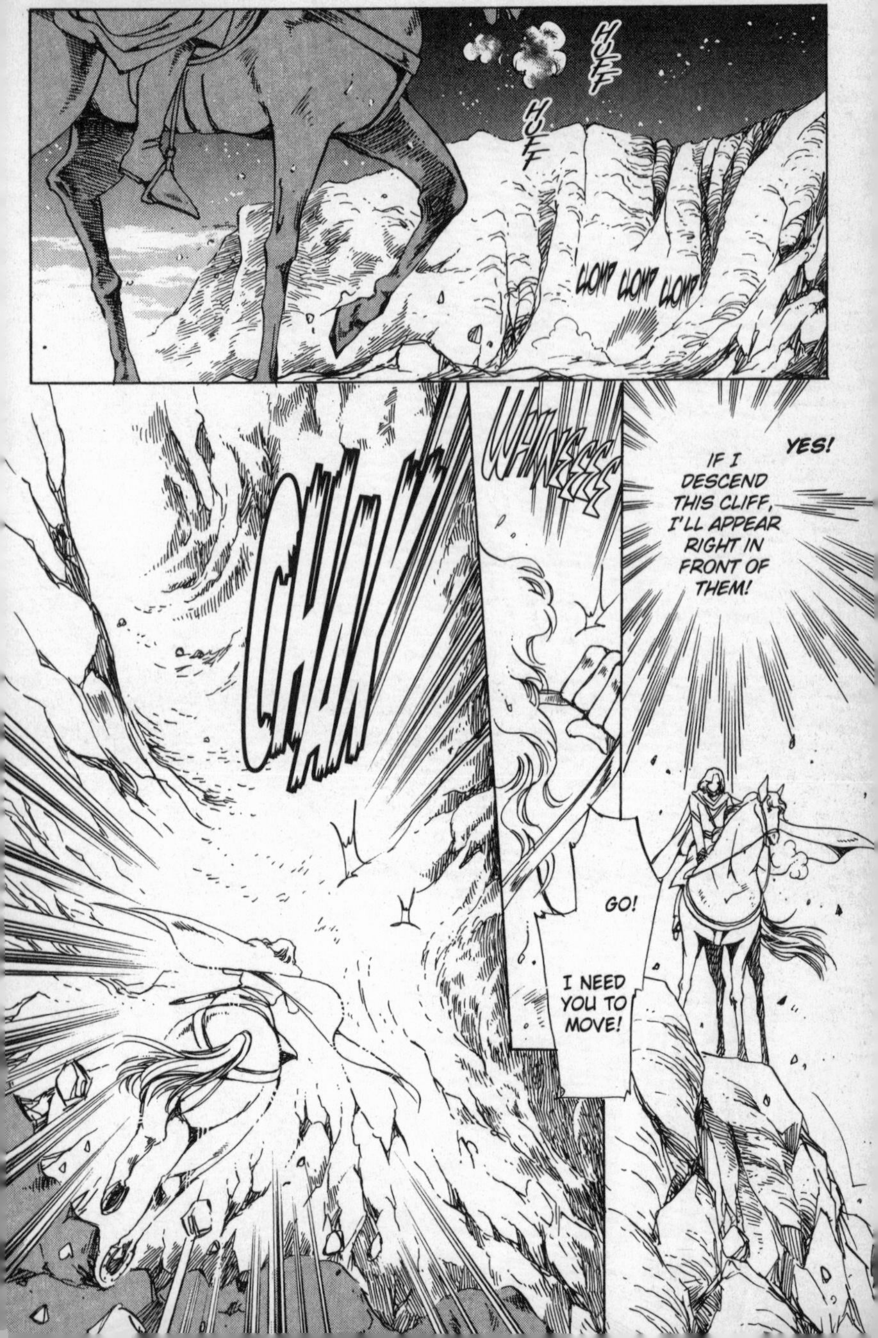
HUFF
HUFF
CLOMP CLOMP CLOMP
YES!
IF I DESCEND THIS CLIFF, I'LL APPEAR RIGHT IN FRONT OF THEM!
GO!
I NEED YOU TO MOVE!

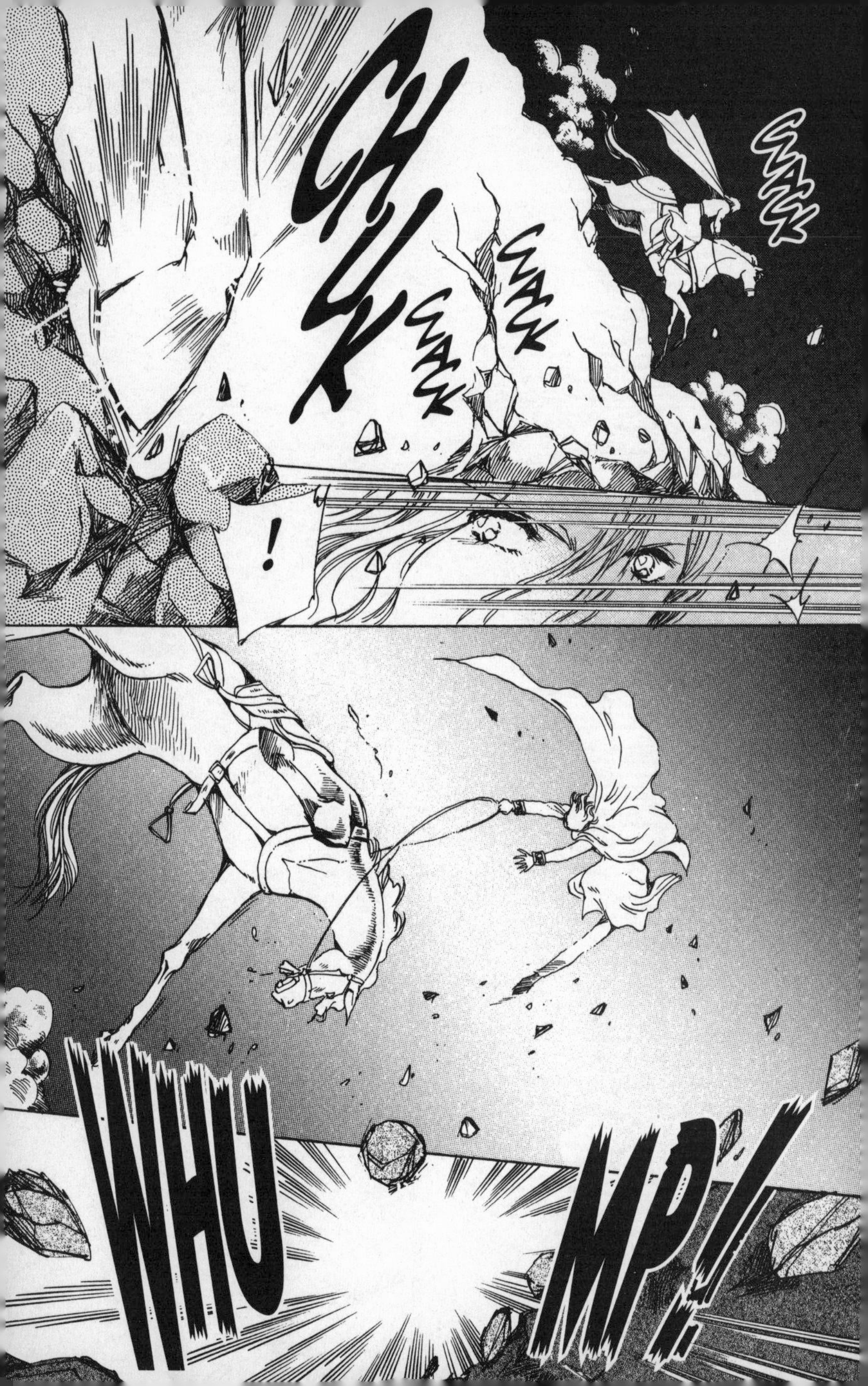
CLACK
CLACK
CLACK
CHUK
!
WHUMP!

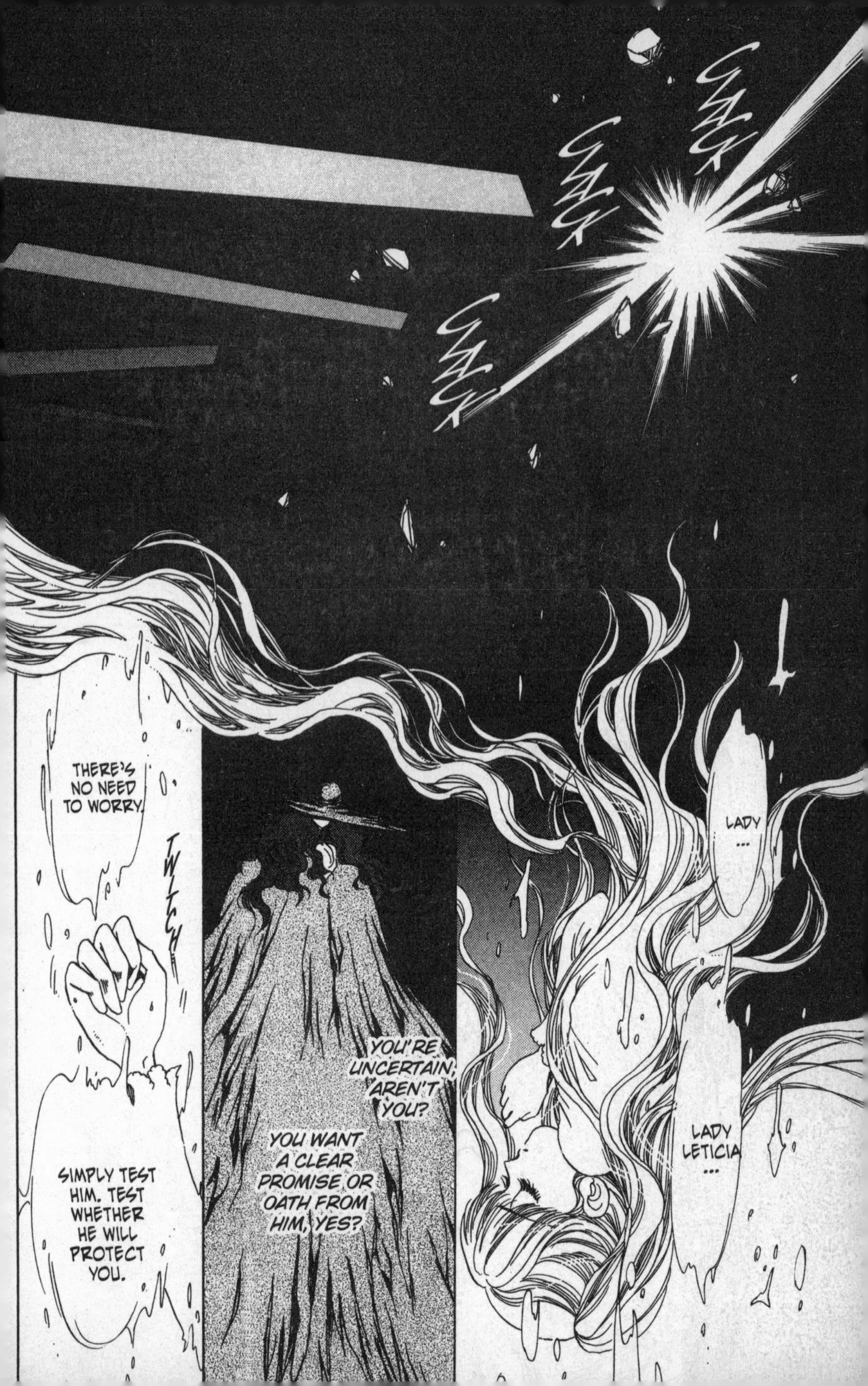
CLACK
CLACK
CLACK
LADY ...
LADY LETICIA ...
YOU'RE UNCERTAIN, AREN'T YOU?
YOU WANT A CLEAR PROMISE OR OATH FROM HIM, YES?
THERE'S NO NEED TO WORRY.
TWITCH
SIMPLY TEST HIM. TEST WHETHER HE WILL PROTECT YOU.

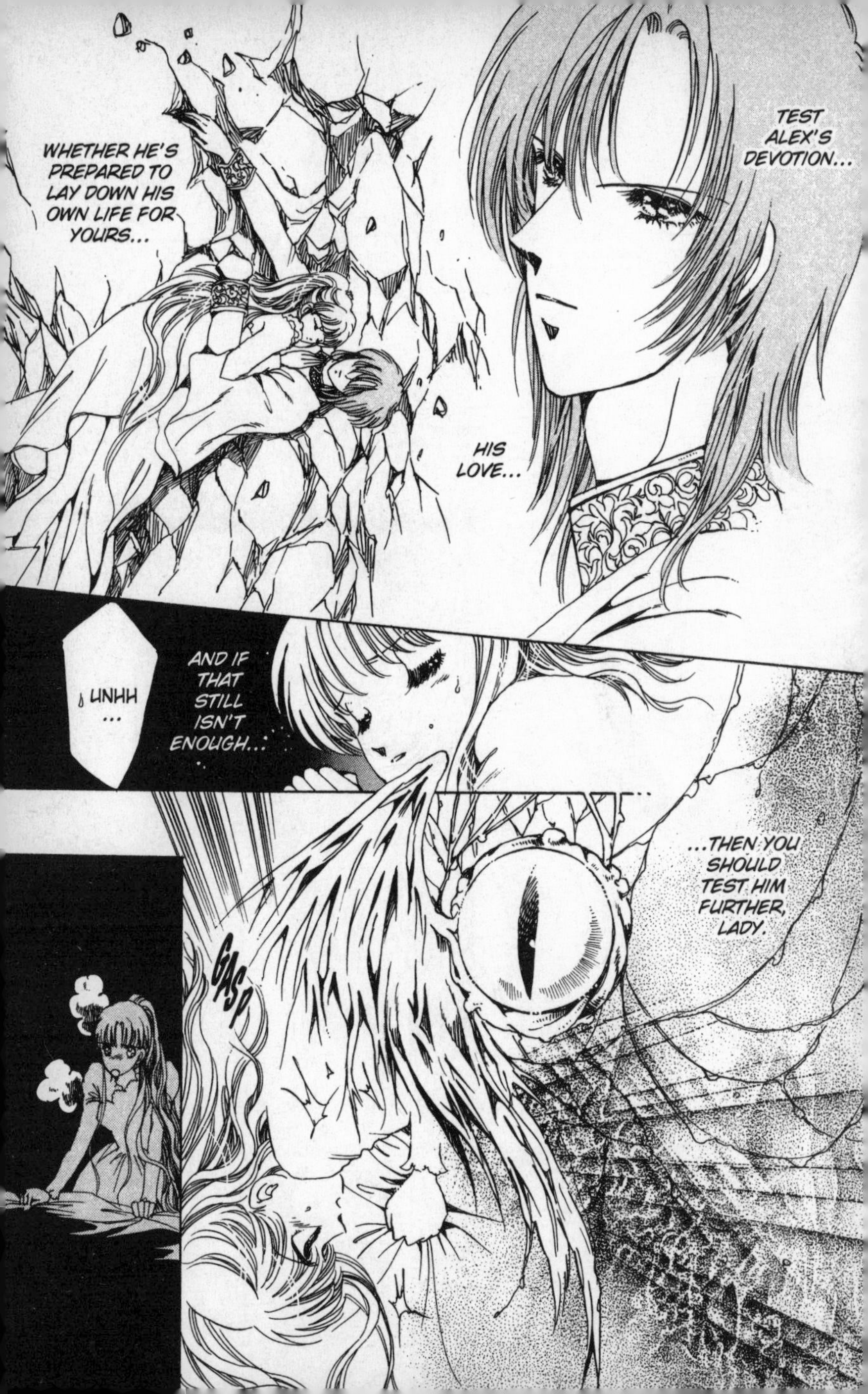
TEST ALEX'S DEVOTION...
HIS LOVE...
WHETHER HE'S PREPARED TO LAY DOWN HIS OWN LIFE FOR YOURS...
AND IF THAT STILL ISN'T ENOUGH...
UNHH ...
...THEN YOU SHOULD TEST HIM FURTHER, LADY.
GASP

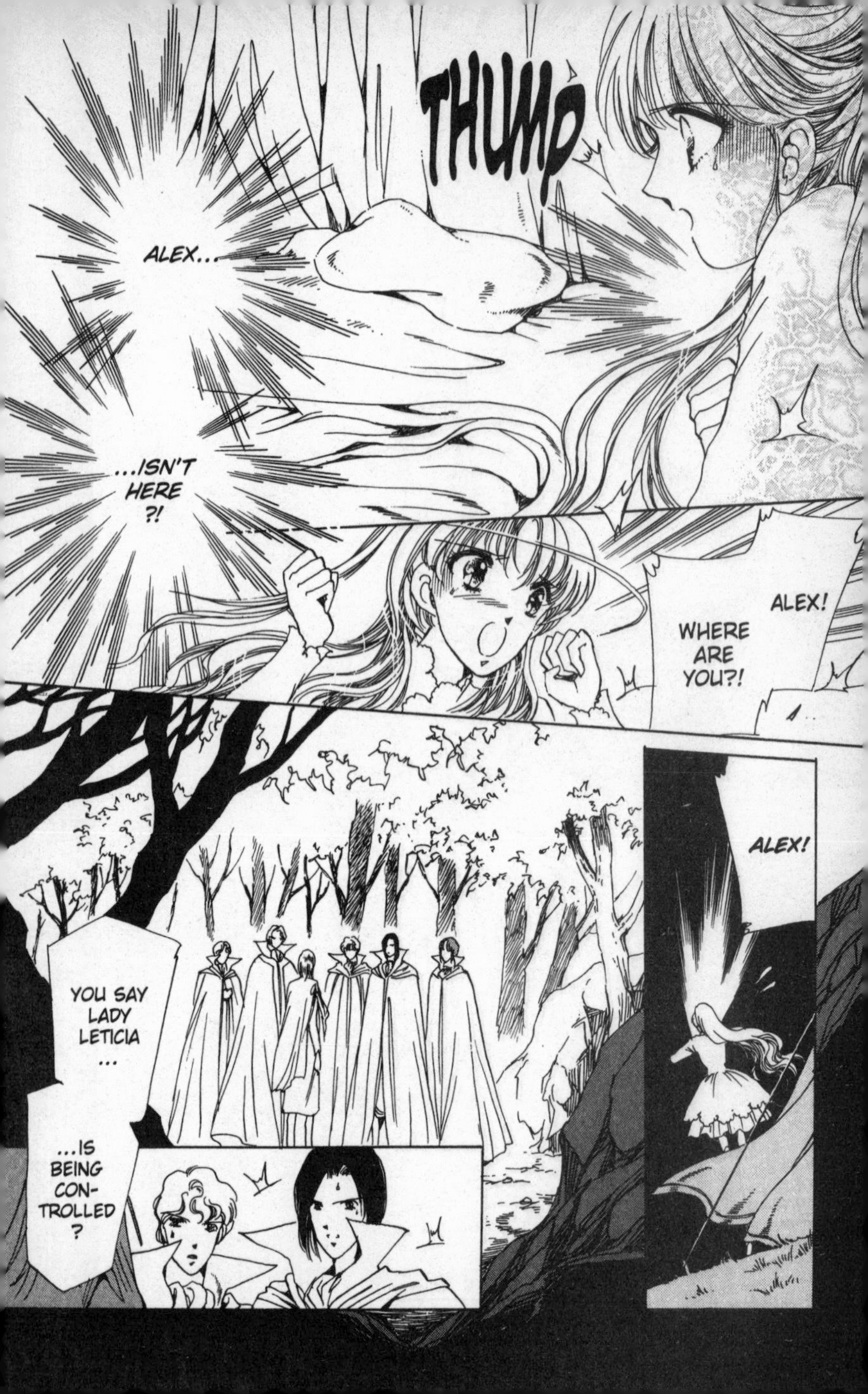
THUMP
ALEX...
...ISN'T HERE ?!
ALEX!
WHERE ARE YOU?!
ALEX!
YOU SAY LADY LETICIA ...
...IS BEING CON-TROLLED ?

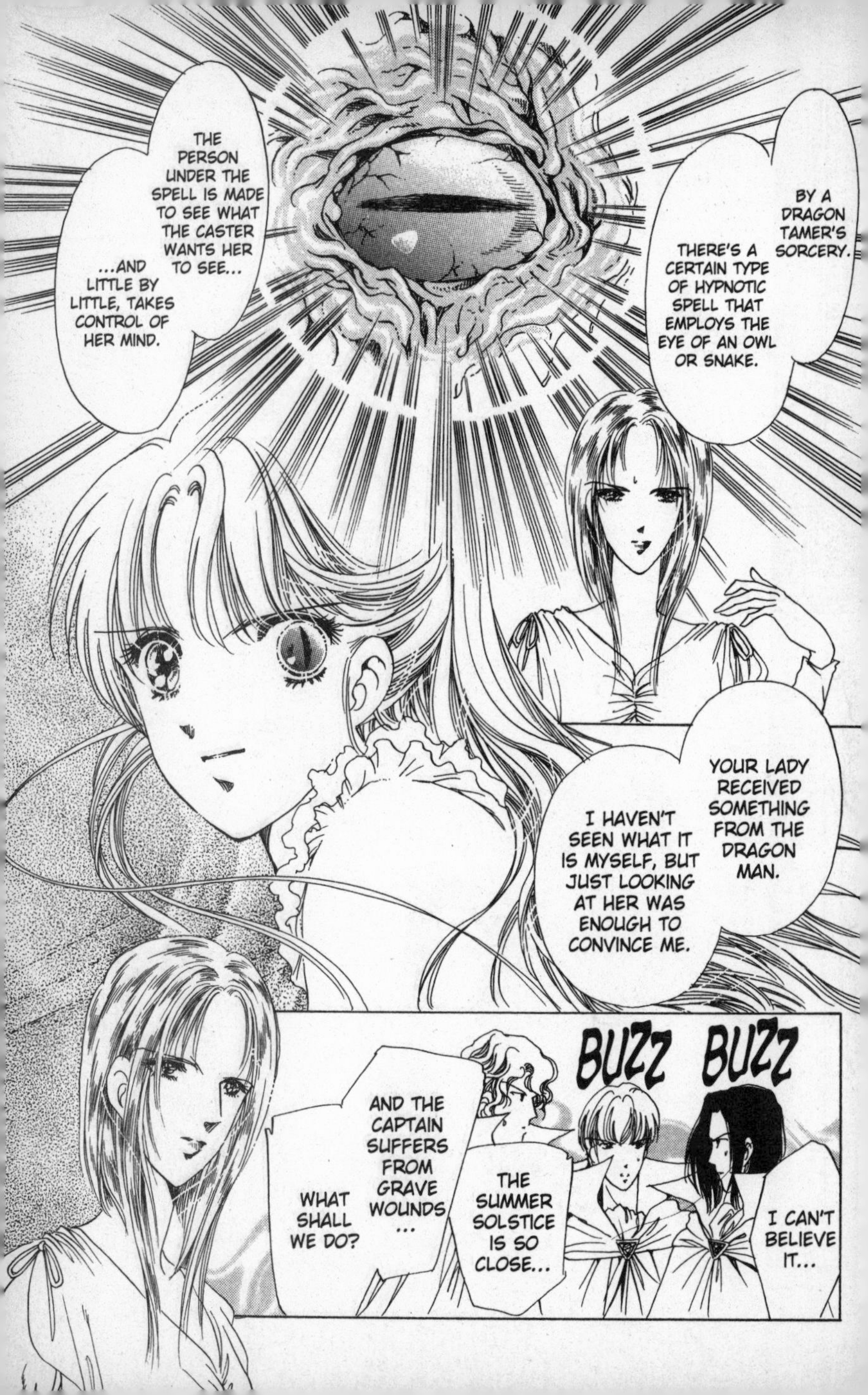
BY A DRAGON TAMER'S SORCERY.
THERE'S A CERTAIN TYPE OF HYPNOTIC SPELL THAT EMPLOYS THE EYE OF AN OWL OR SNAKE.
THE PERSON UNDER THE SPELL IS MADE TO SEE WHAT THE CASTER WANTS HER TO SEE...
...AND LITTLE BY LITTLE, TAKES CONTROL OF HER MIND.
YOUR LADY RECEIVED SOMETHING FROM THE DRAGON MAN.
I HAVEN'T SEEN WHAT IT IS MYSELF, BUT JUST LOOKING AT HER WAS ENOUGH TO CONVINCE ME.
BUZZ BUZZ
I CAN'T BELIEVE IT...
THE SUMMER SOLSTICE IS SO CLOSE...
AND THE CAPTAIN SUFFERS FROM GRAVE WOUNDS...
WHAT SHALL WE DO?

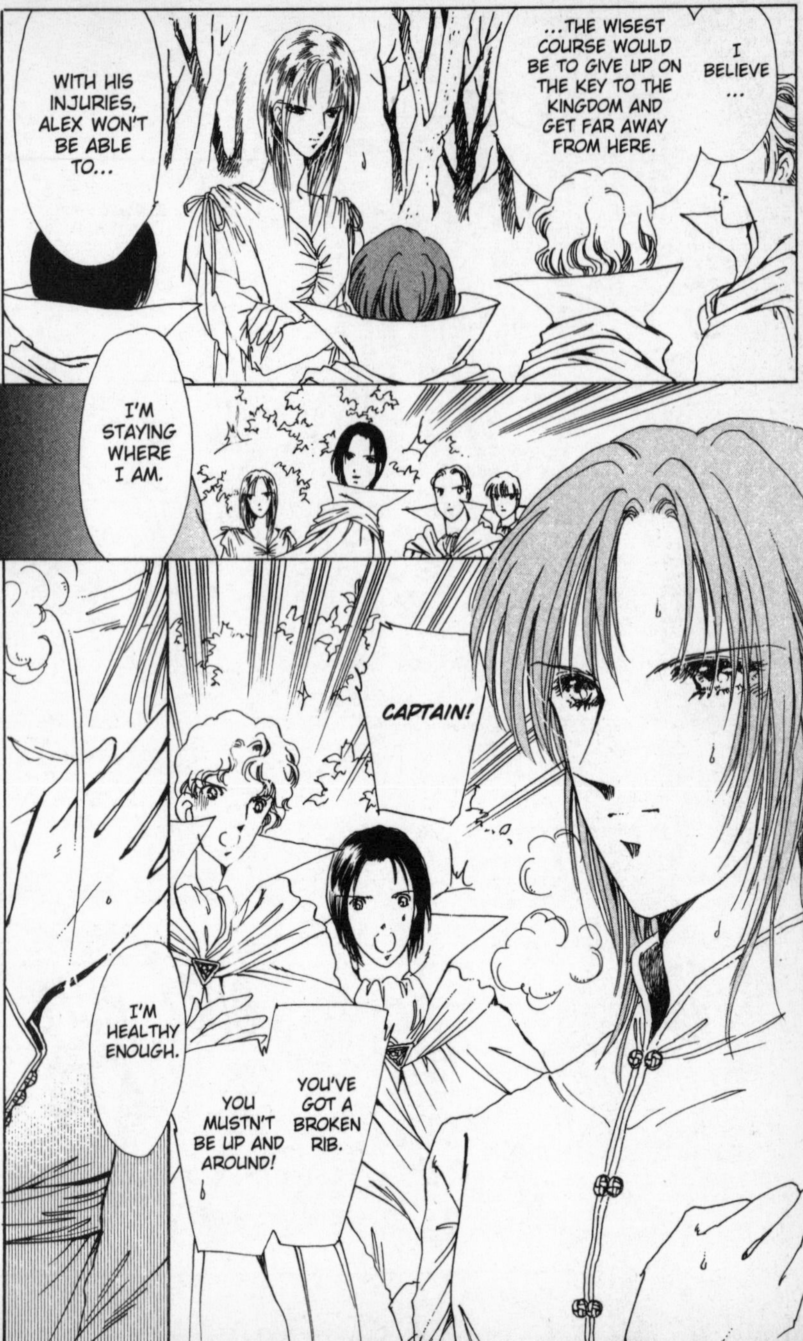
I BELIEVE ...
...THE WISEST COURSE WOULD BE TO GIVE UP ON THE KEY TO THE KINGDOM AND GET FAR AWAY FROM HERE.
WITH HIS INJURIES, ALEX WON'T BE ABLE TO...
I'M STAYING WHERE I AM.
CAPTAIN!
YOU'VE GOT A BROKEN RIB.
YOU MUSTN'T BE UP AND AROUND!
I'M HEALTHY ENOUGH.

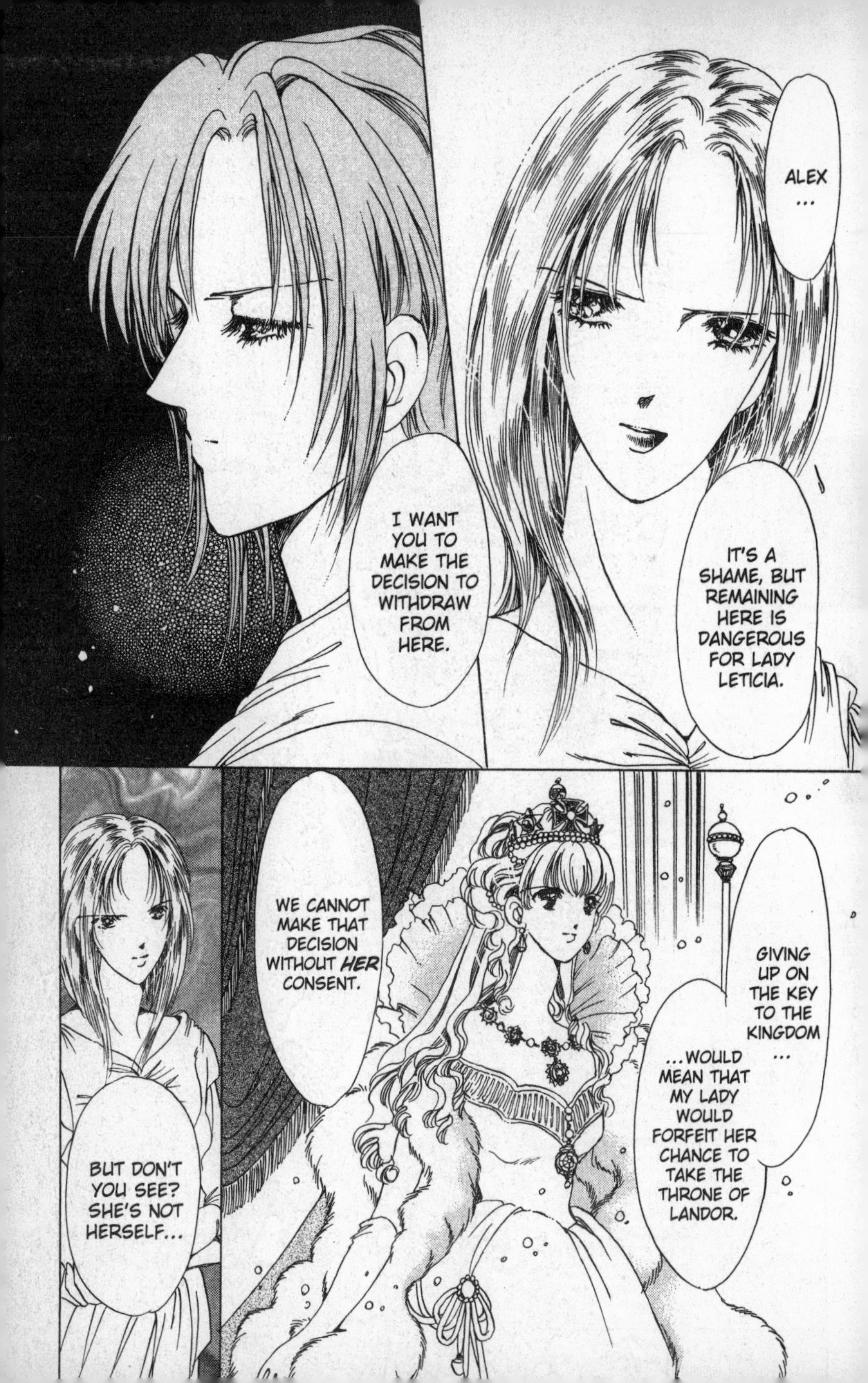
ALEX ...
IT'S A SHAME, BUT REMAINING HERE IS DANGEROUS FOR LADY LETICIA.
I WANT YOU TO MAKE THE DECISION TO WITHDRAW FROM HERE.
GIVING UP ON THE KEY TO THE KINGDOM ...
...WOULD MEAN THAT MY LADY WOULD FORFEIT HER CHANCE TO TAKE THE THRONE OF LANDOR.
WE CANNOT MAKE THAT DECISION WITHOUT *HER* CONSENT.
BUT DON'T YOU SEE? SHE'S NOT HERSELF...

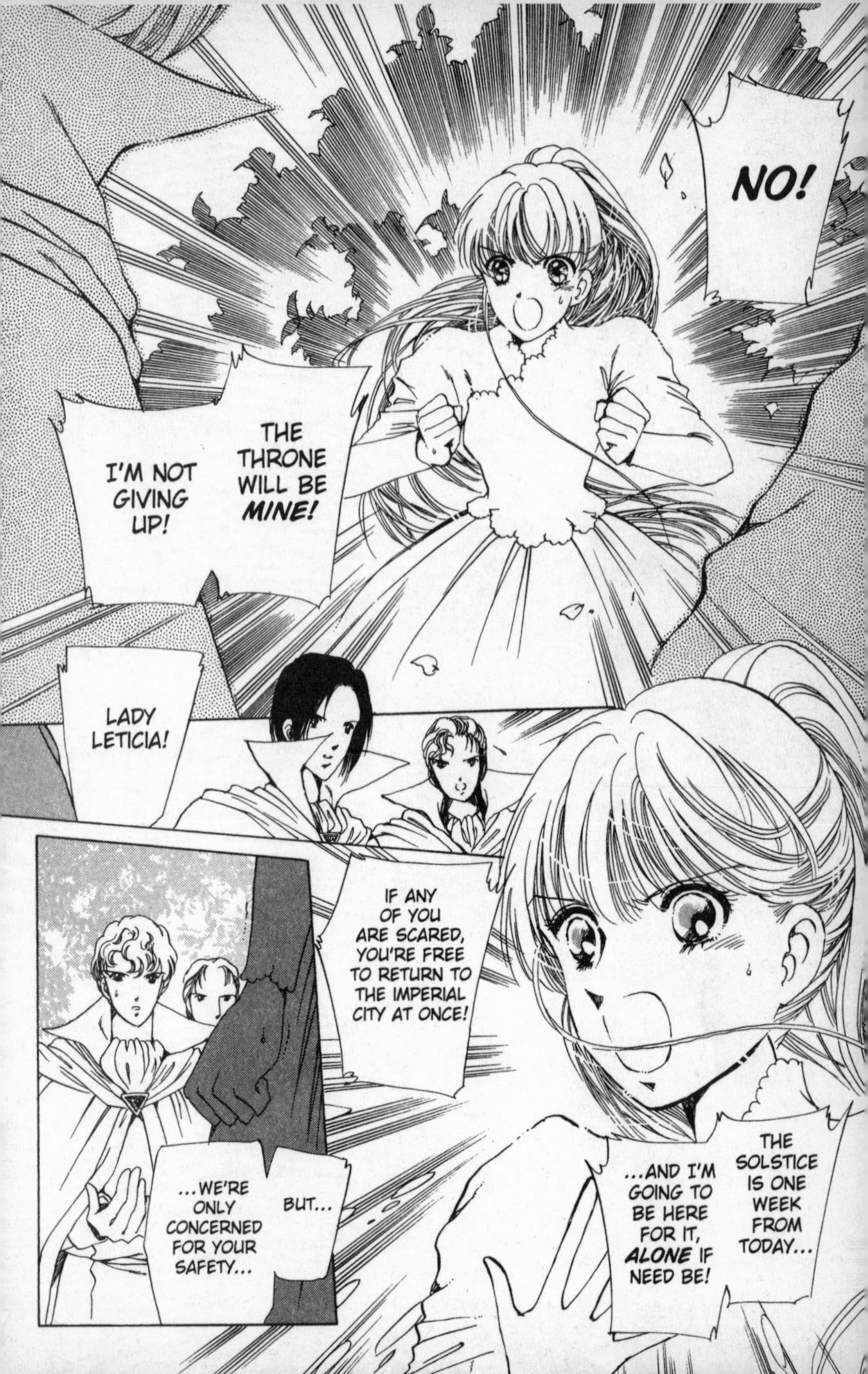
NO!
THE THRONE WILL BE *MINE!*
I'M NOT GIVING UP!
LADY LETICIA!
IF ANY OF YOU ARE SCARED, YOU'RE FREE TO RETURN TO THE IMPERIAL CITY AT ONCE!
THE SOLSTICE IS ONE WEEK FROM TODAY...
...AND I'M GOING TO BE HERE FOR IT, *ALONE* IF NEED BE!
BUT...
...WE'RE ONLY CONCERNED FOR YOUR SAFETY...

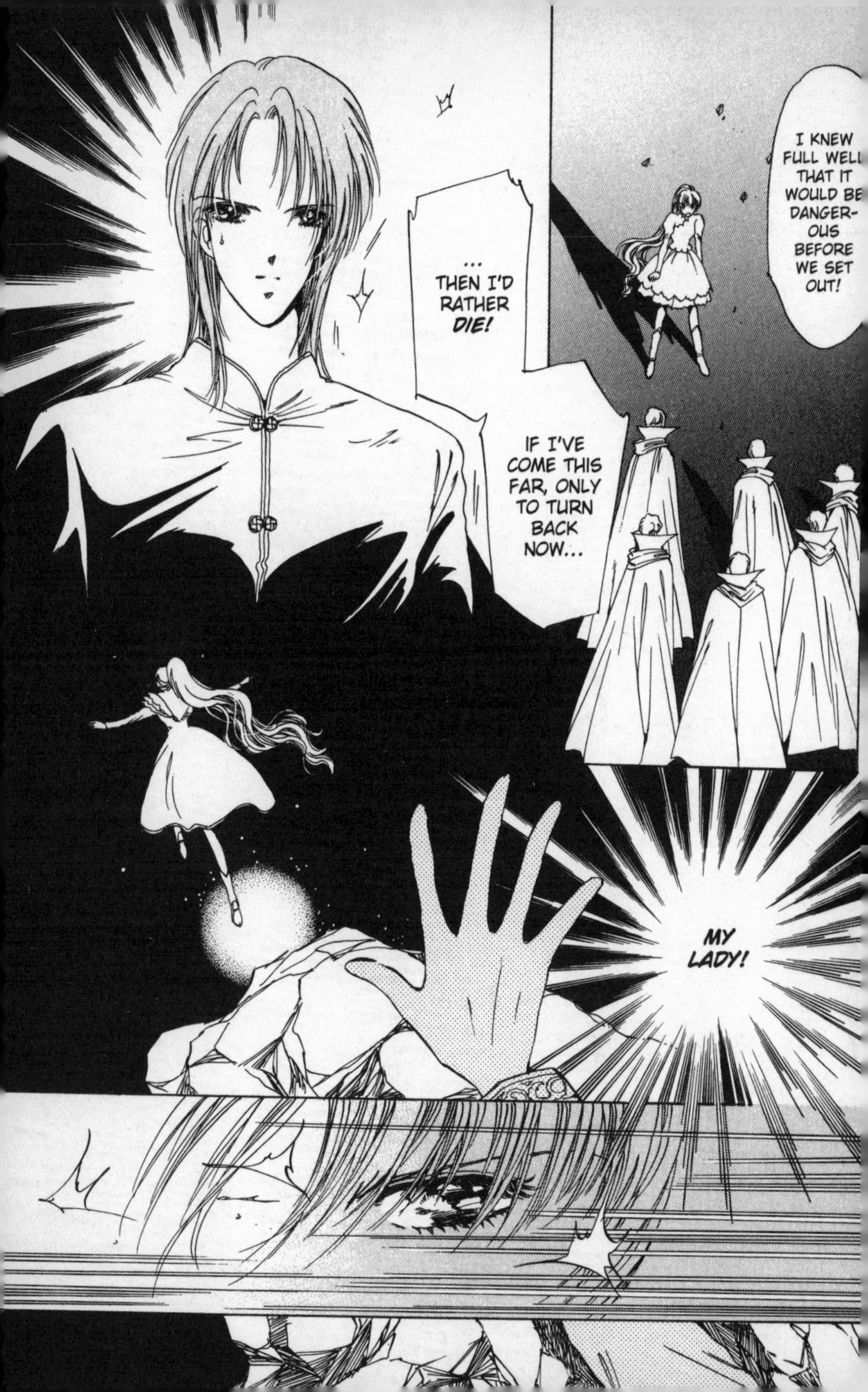
I KNEW FULL WELL THAT IT WOULD BE DANGER-OUS BEFORE WE SET OUT!
IF I'VE COME THIS FAR, ONLY TO TURN BACK NOW...
... THEN I'D RATHER DIE!
MY LADY!

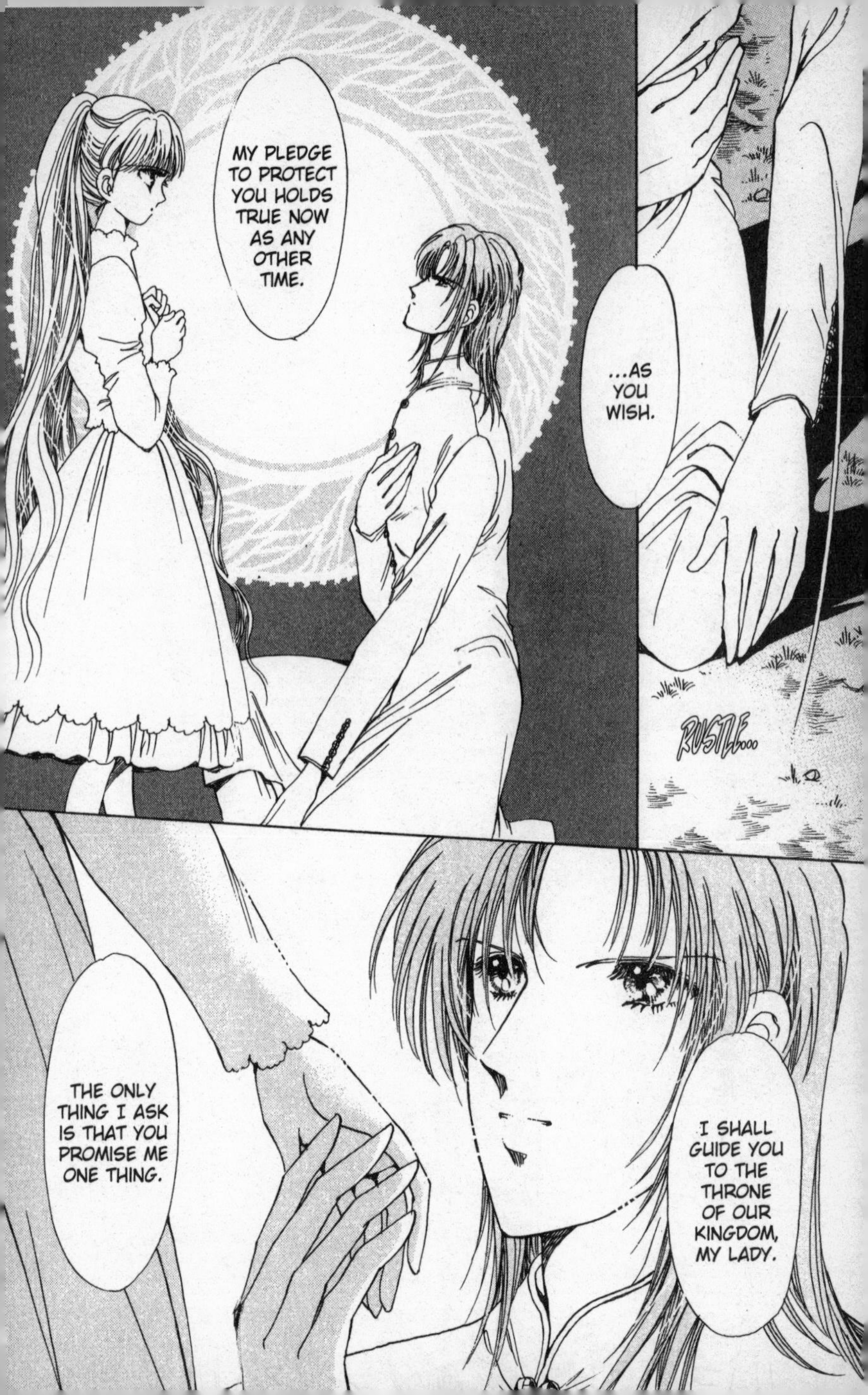
...AS YOU WISH.
RUSTLE...
MY PLEDGE TO PROTECT YOU HOLDS TRUE NOW AS ANY OTHER TIME.
I SHALL GUIDE YOU TO THE THRONE OF OUR KINGDOM, MY LADY.
THE ONLY THING I ASK IS THAT YOU PROMISE ME ONE THING.

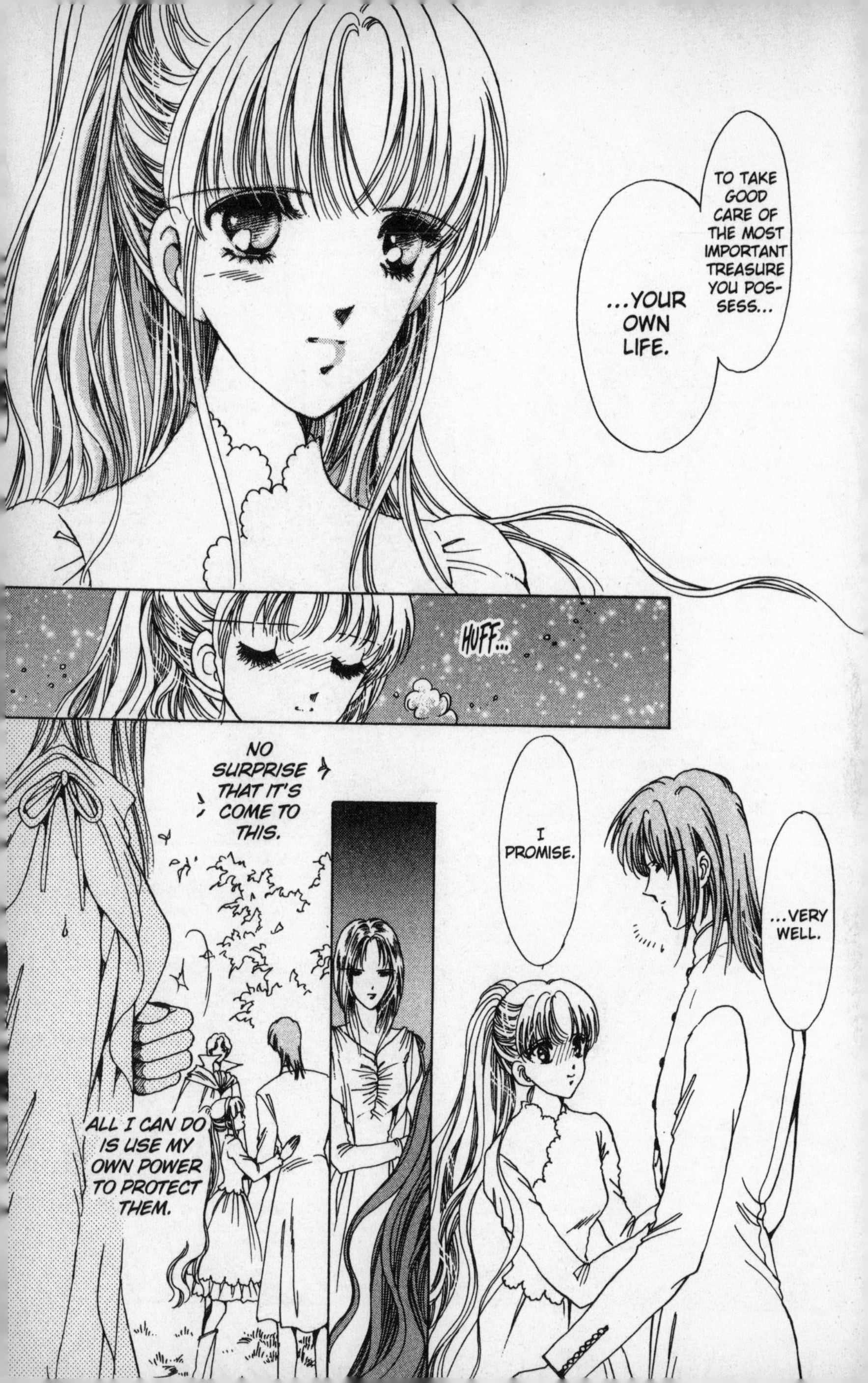
TO TAKE GOOD CARE OF THE MOST IMPORTANT TREASURE YOU POS-SESS...
...YOUR OWN LIFE.
HUFF...
...VERY WELL.
I PROMISE.
NO SURPRISE THAT IT'S COME TO THIS.
ALL I CAN DO IS USE MY OWN POWER TO PROTECT THEM.

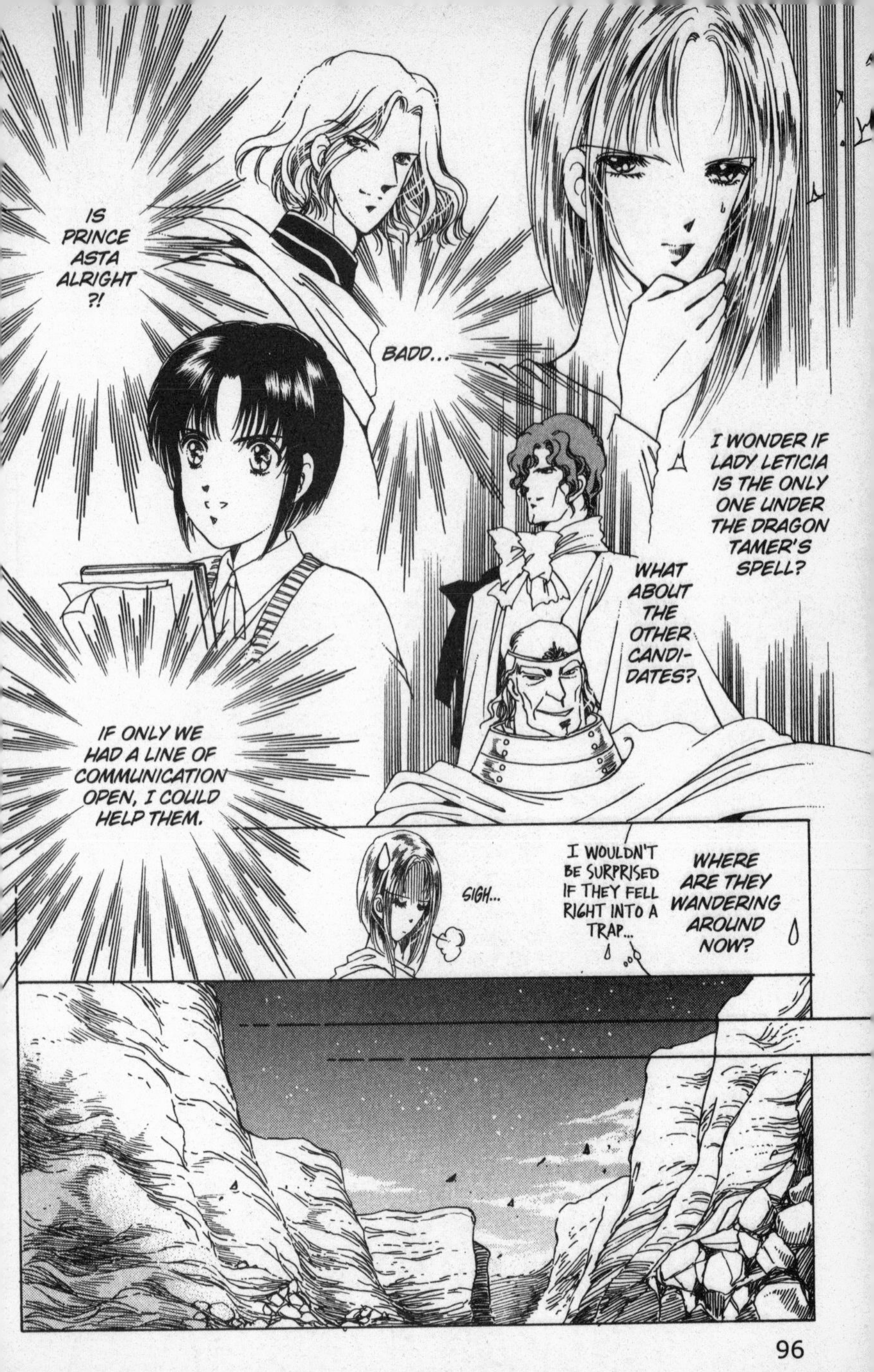
IS PRINCE ASTA ALRIGHT ?!
BADD...
I WONDER IF LADY LETICIA IS THE ONLY ONE UNDER THE DRAGON TAMER'S SPELL?
WHAT ABOUT THE OTHER CANDI-DATES?
IF ONLY WE HAD A LINE OF COMMUNICATION OPEN, I COULD HELP THEM.
WHERE ARE THEY WANDERING AROUND NOW?
I WOULDN'T BE SURPRISED IF THEY FELL RIGHT INTO A TRAP...
SIGH...

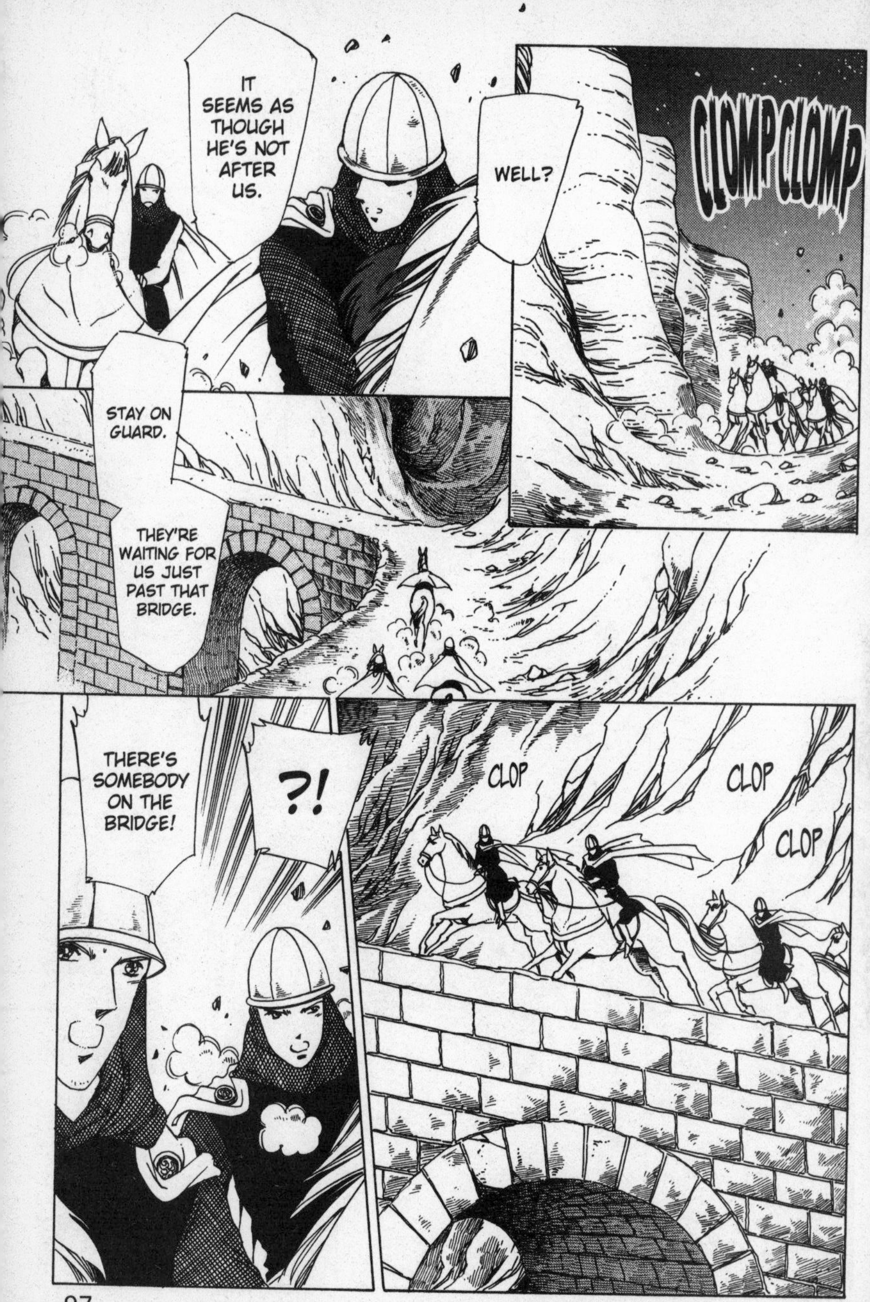
CLOMP CLOMP
WELL?
IT SEEMS AS THOUGH HE'S NOT AFTER US.
STAY ON GUARD.
THEY'RE WAITING FOR US JUST PAST THAT BRIDGE.
CLOP
CLOP
CLOP
?!
THERE'S SOMEBODY ON THE BRIDGE!

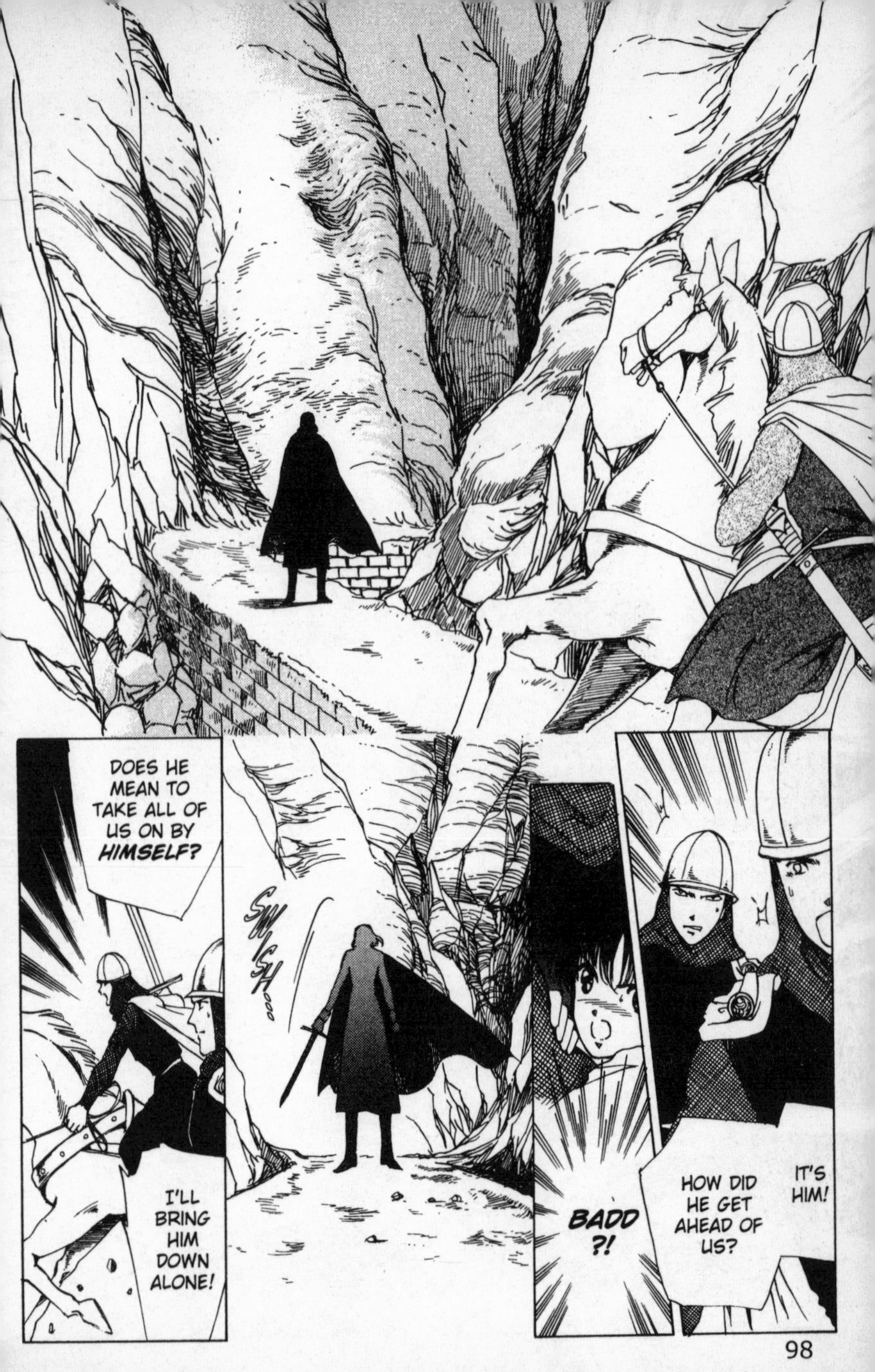
IT'S HIM!
HOW DID HE GET AHEAD OF US?
BADD ?!
SWISH...
DOES HE MEAN TO TAKE ALL OF US ON BY *HIMSELF?*
I'LL BRING HIM DOWN ALONE!

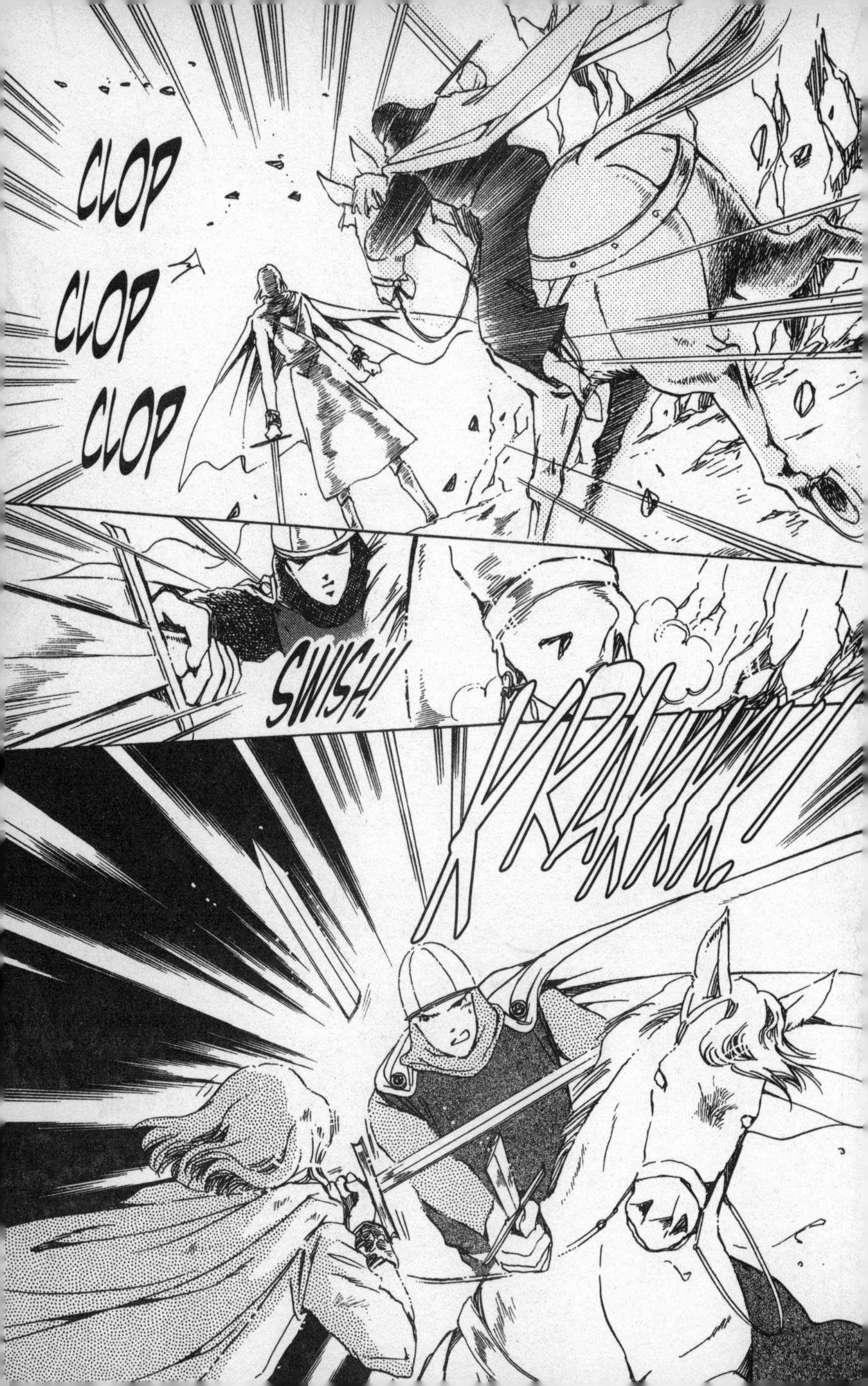
CLOP
CLOP
CLOP
SWISH!
KRAKKK!

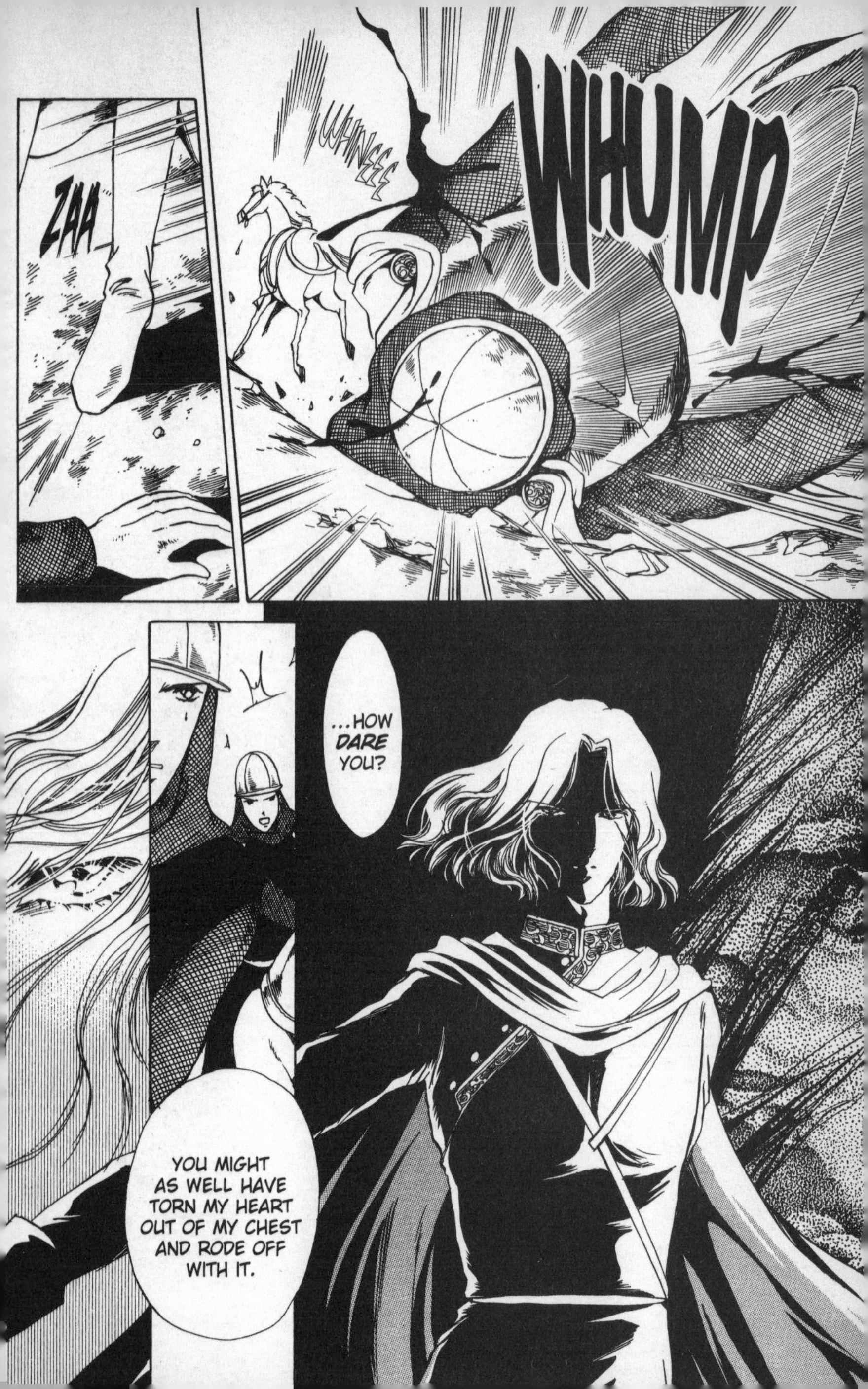
WHUMP
WHINEEE
ZAA
...HOW DARE YOU?
YOU MIGHT AS WELL HAVE TORN MY HEART OUT OF MY CHEST AND RODE OFF WITH IT.

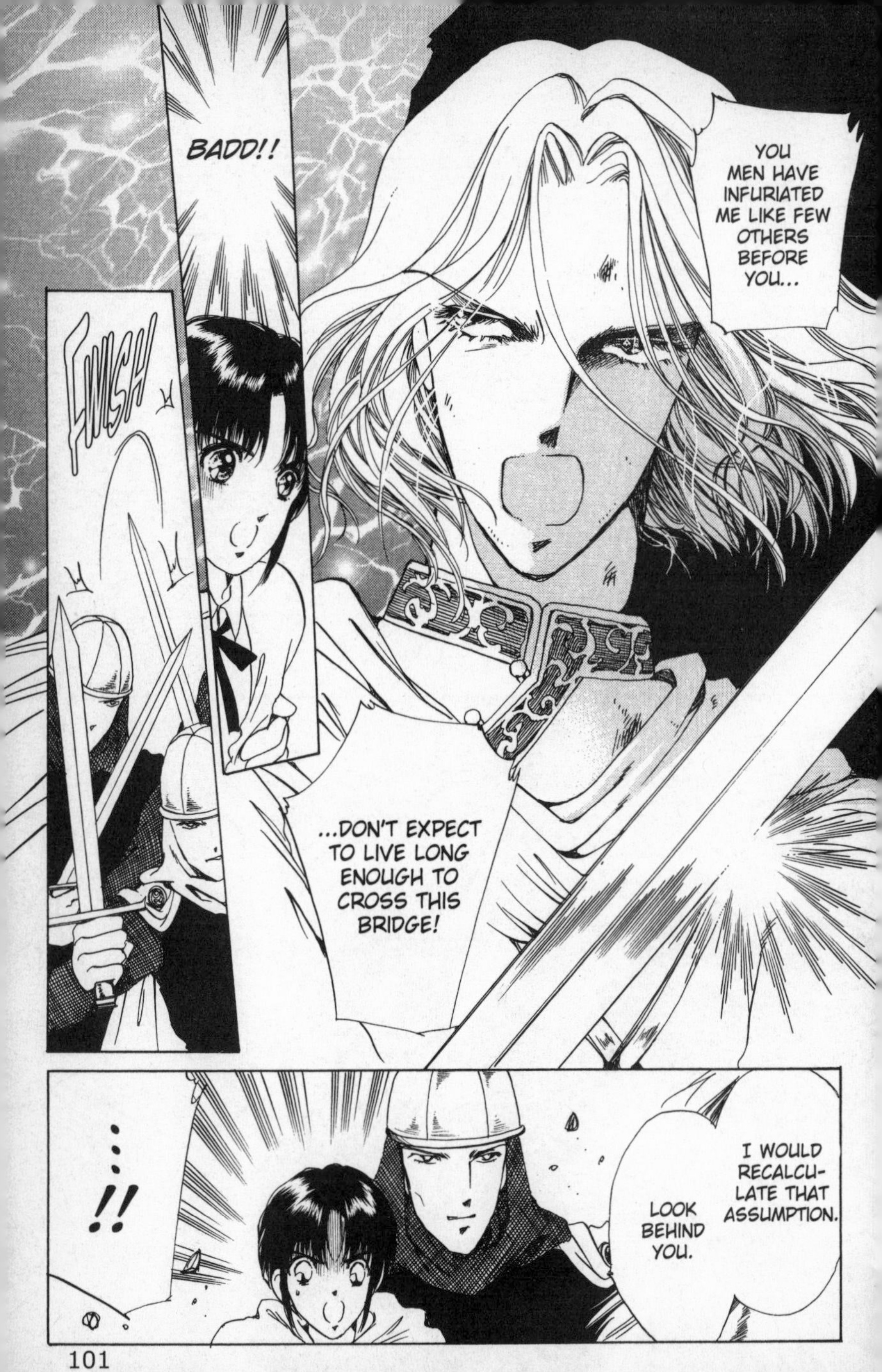
YOU MEN HAVE INFURIATED ME LIKE FEW OTHERS BEFORE YOU...
...DON'T EXPECT TO LIVE LONG ENOUGH TO CROSS THIS BRIDGE!
BADD!!
FWISH
I WOULD RECALCU-LATE THAT ASSUMPTION.
LOOK BEHIND YOU.
...!!

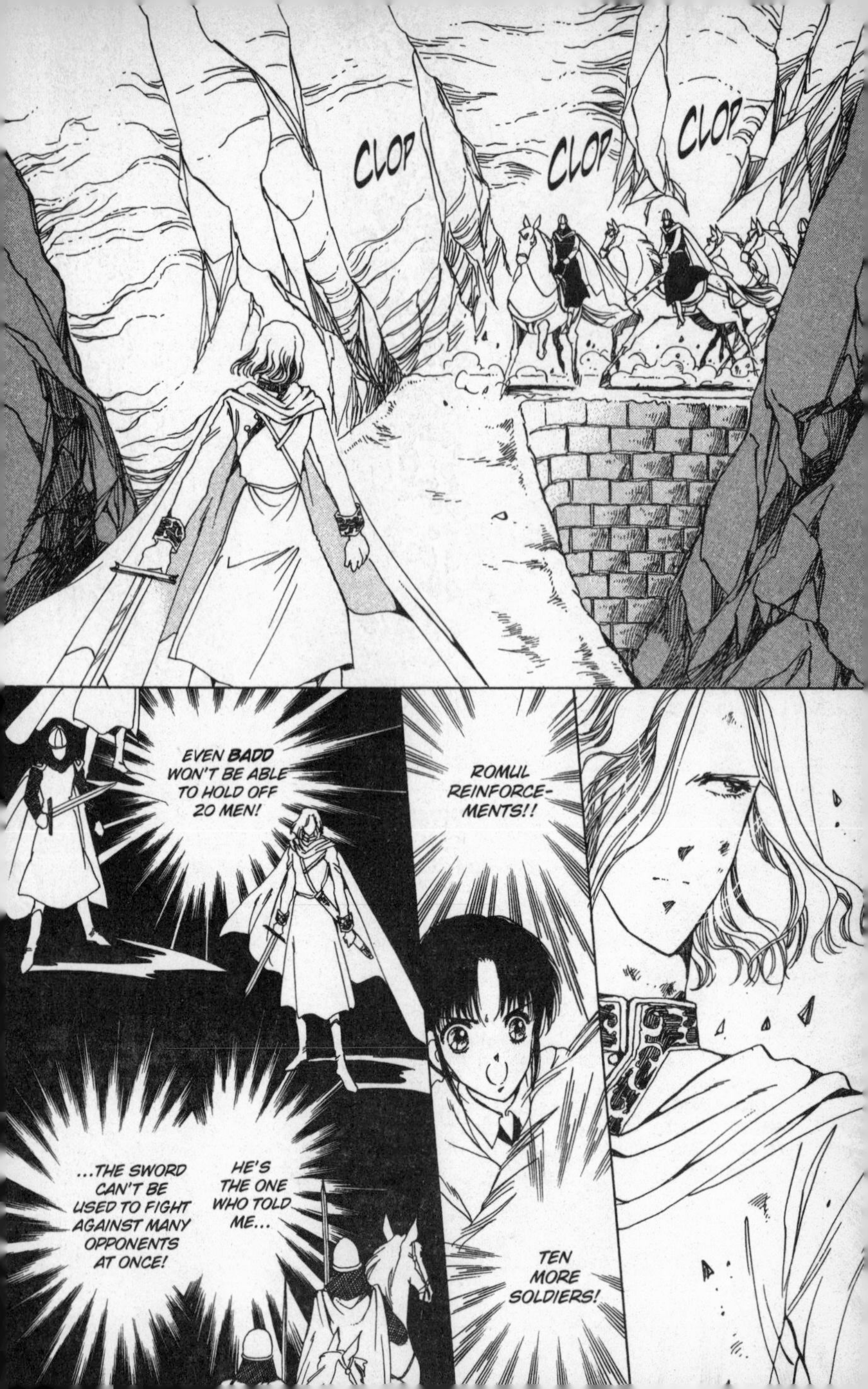
CLOP
CLOP
CLOP
ROMUL REINFORCE-MENTS!!
TEN MORE SOLDIERS!
EVEN BADD WON'T BE ABLE TO HOLD OFF 20 MEN!
HE'S THE ONE WHO TOLD ME...
...THE SWORD CAN'T BE USED TO FIGHT AGAINST MANY OPPONENTS AT ONCE!

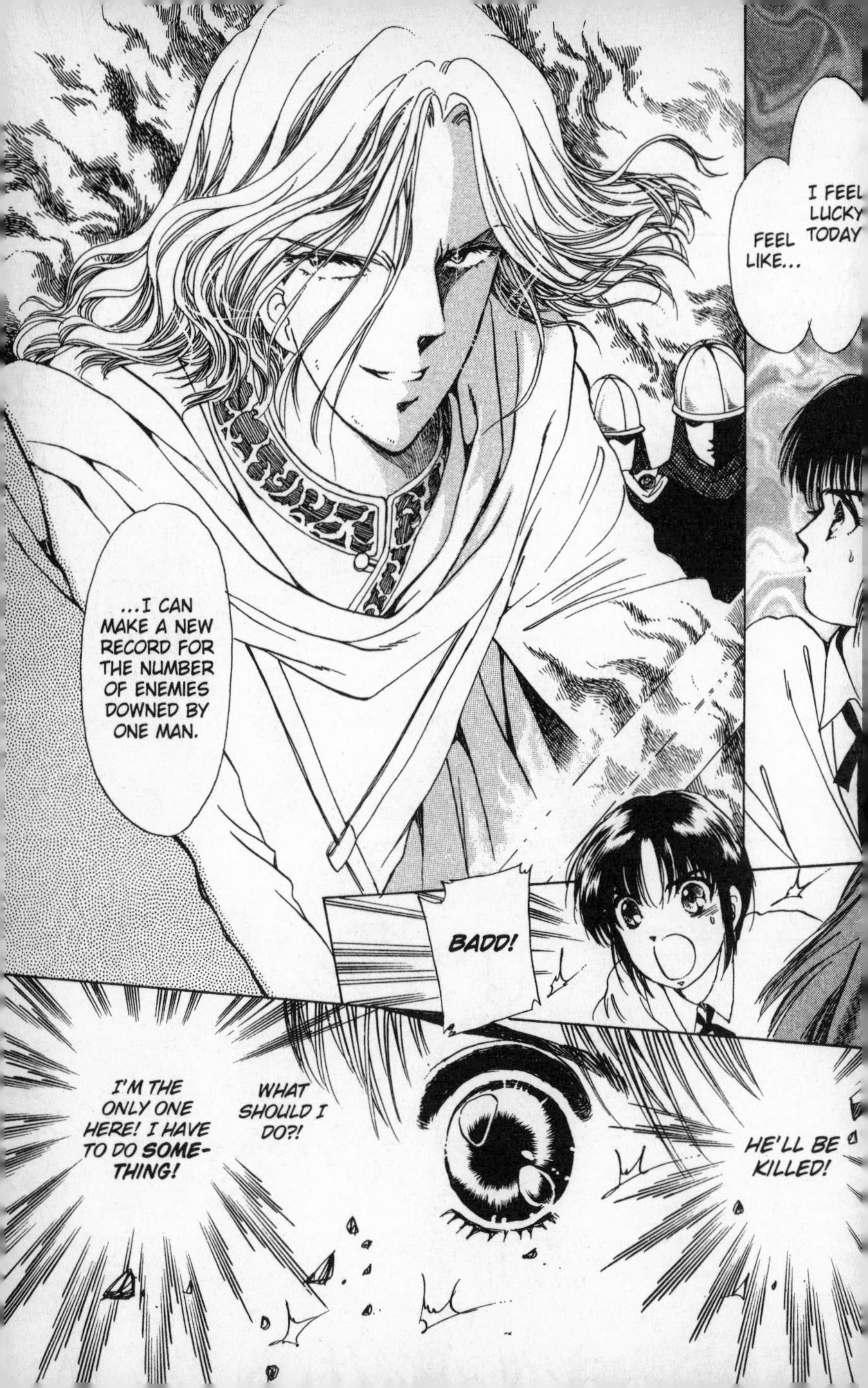
I FEEL LUCKY TODAY
FEEL LIKE...
...I CAN MAKE A NEW RECORD FOR THE NUMBER OF ENEMIES DOWNED BY ONE MAN.
BADD!
HE'LL BE KILLED!
WHAT SHOULD I DO?!
I'M THE ONLY ONE HERE! I HAVE TO DO SOME-THING!

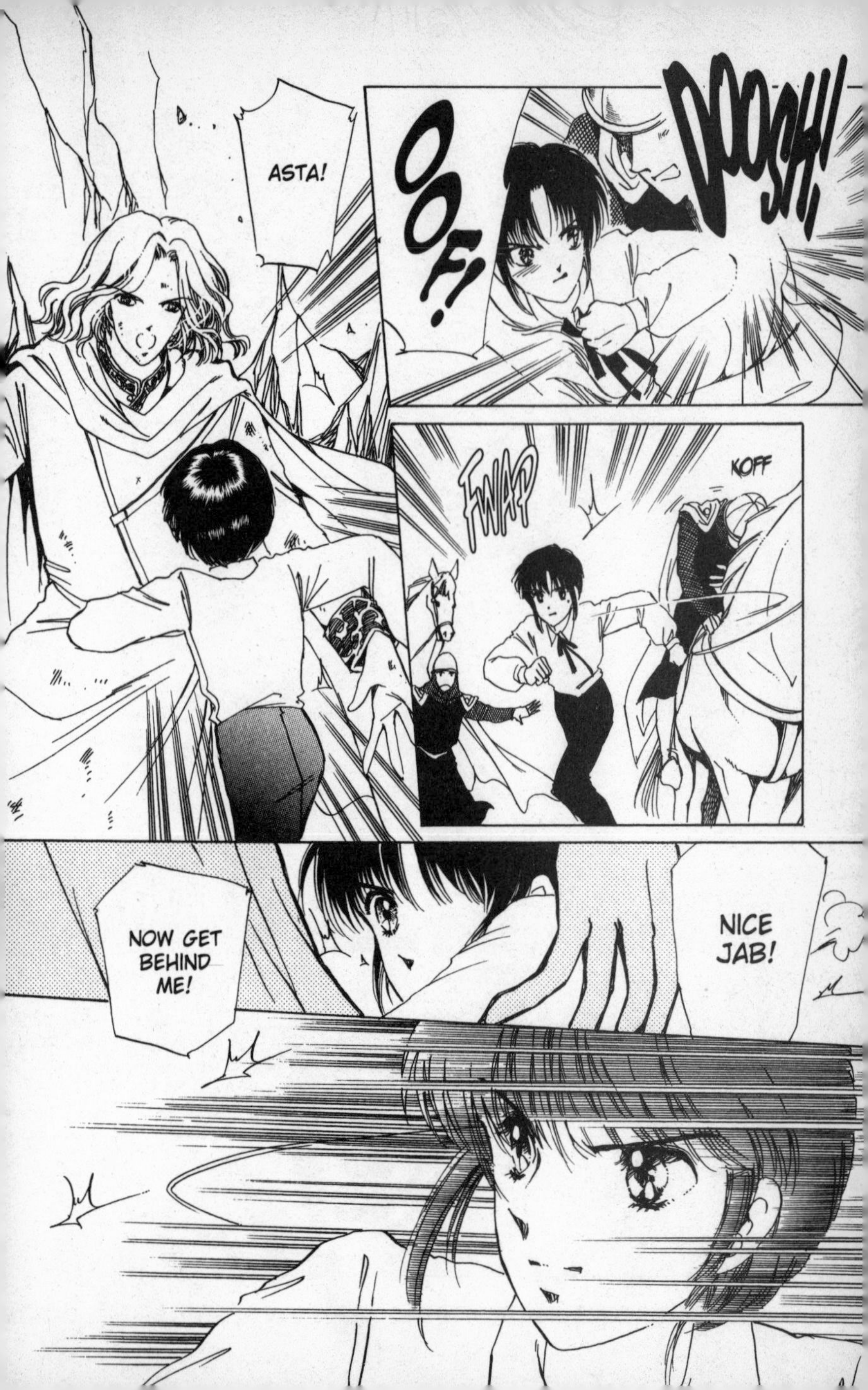
DOOSH!!
OOF!!
KOFF
FWAP
ASTA!
D...
NICE JAB!
NOW GET BEHIND ME!

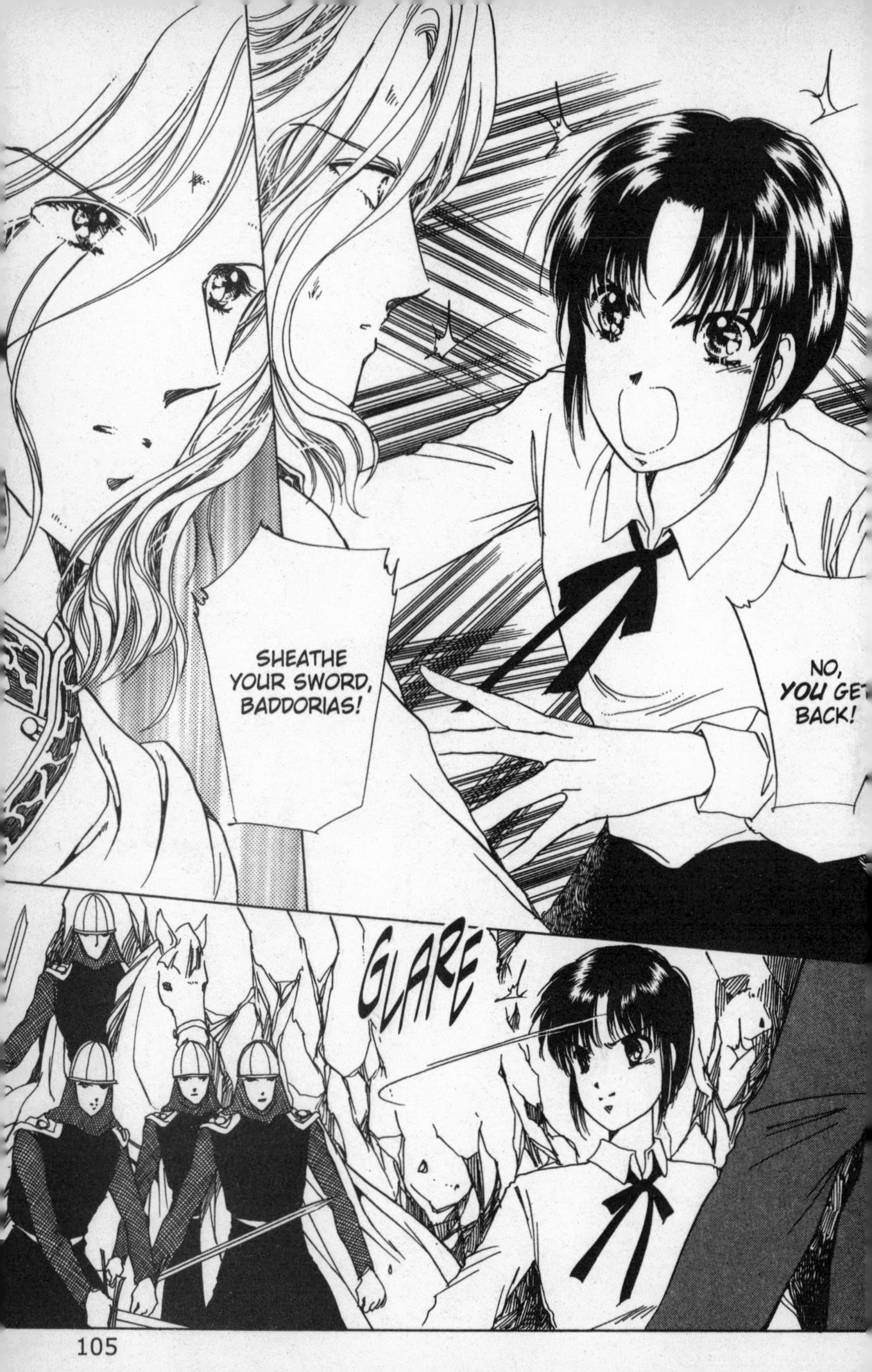
NO, YOU GET BACK!
SHEATHE YOUR SWORD, BADDORIAS!
GLARE

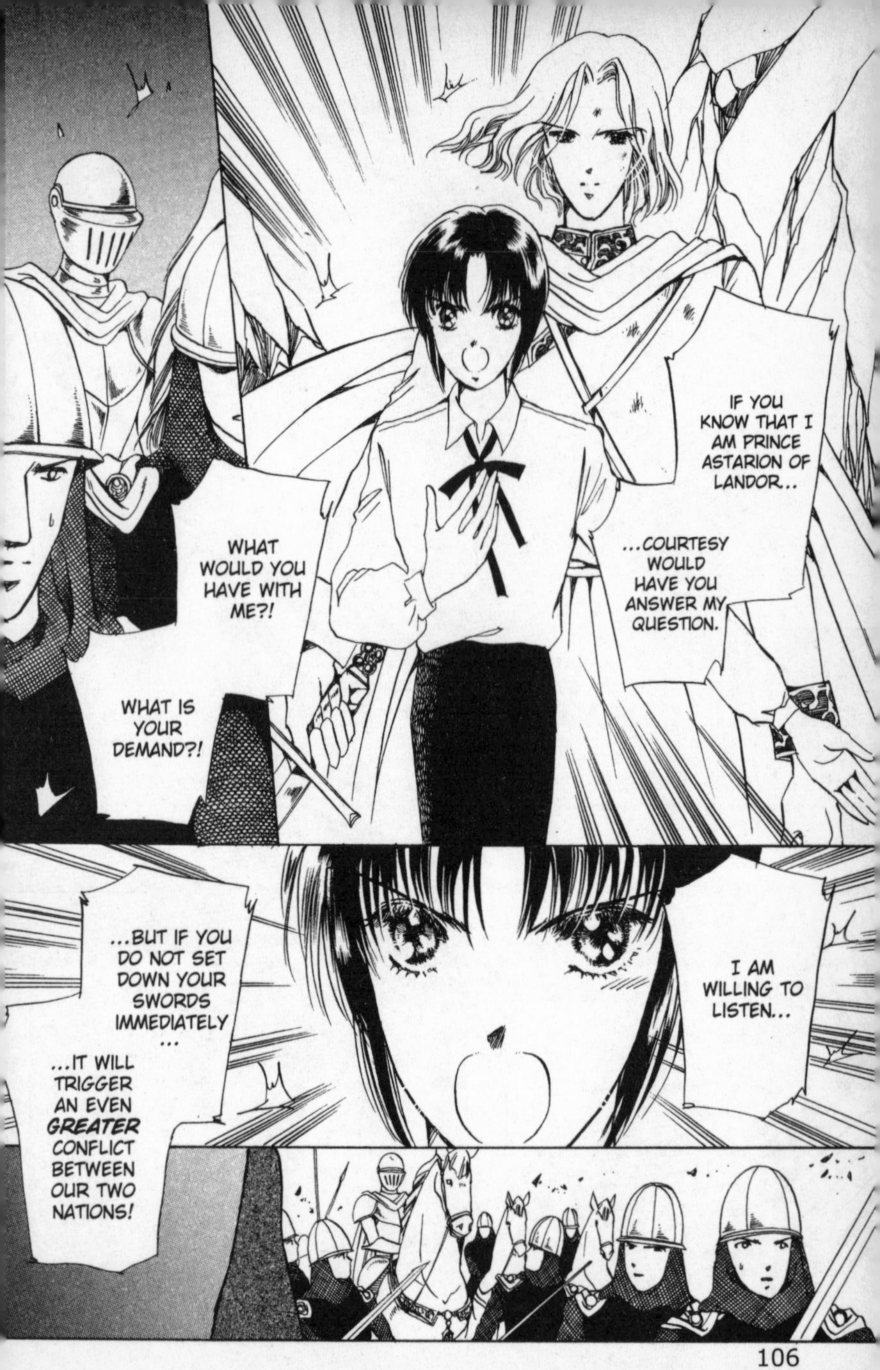
IF YOU KNOW THAT I AM PRINCE ASTARION OF LANDOR...
...COURTESY WOULD HAVE YOU ANSWER MY QUESTION.
WHAT WOULD YOU HAVE WITH ME?!
WHAT IS YOUR DEMAND?!
I AM WILLING TO LISTEN...
...BUT IF YOU DO NOT SET DOWN YOUR SWORDS IMMEDIATELY ...
...IT WILL TRIGGER AN EVEN GREATER CONFLICT BETWEEN OUR TWO NATIONS!

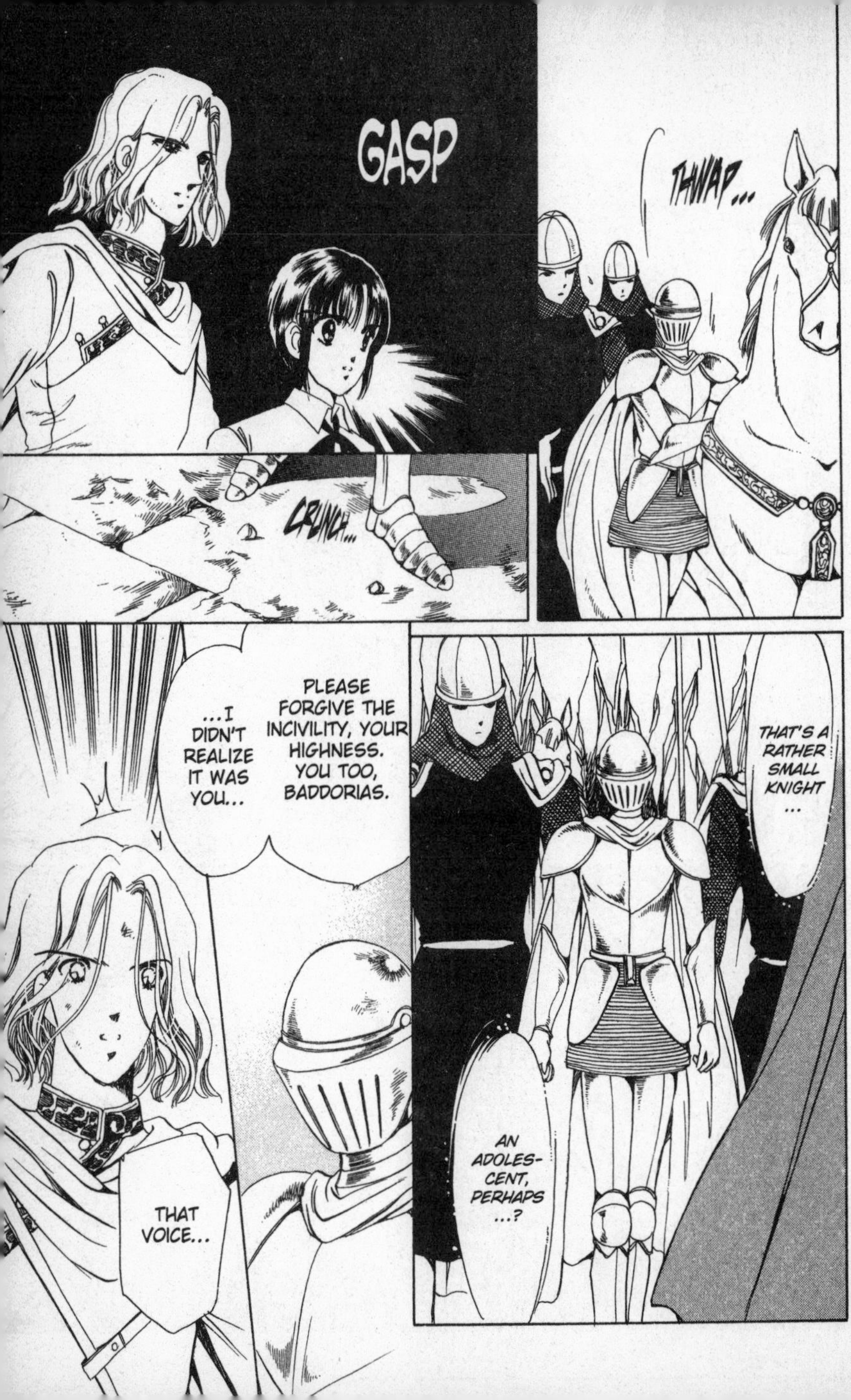
THWAP...
GASP
CRUNCH...
THAT'S A RATHER SMALL KNIGHT...
AN ADOLES-CENT, PERHAPS...?
PLEASE FORGIVE THE INCIVILITY, YOUR HIGHNESS. YOU TOO, BADDORIAS.
...I DIDN'T REALIZE IT WAS YOU...
THAT VOICE...

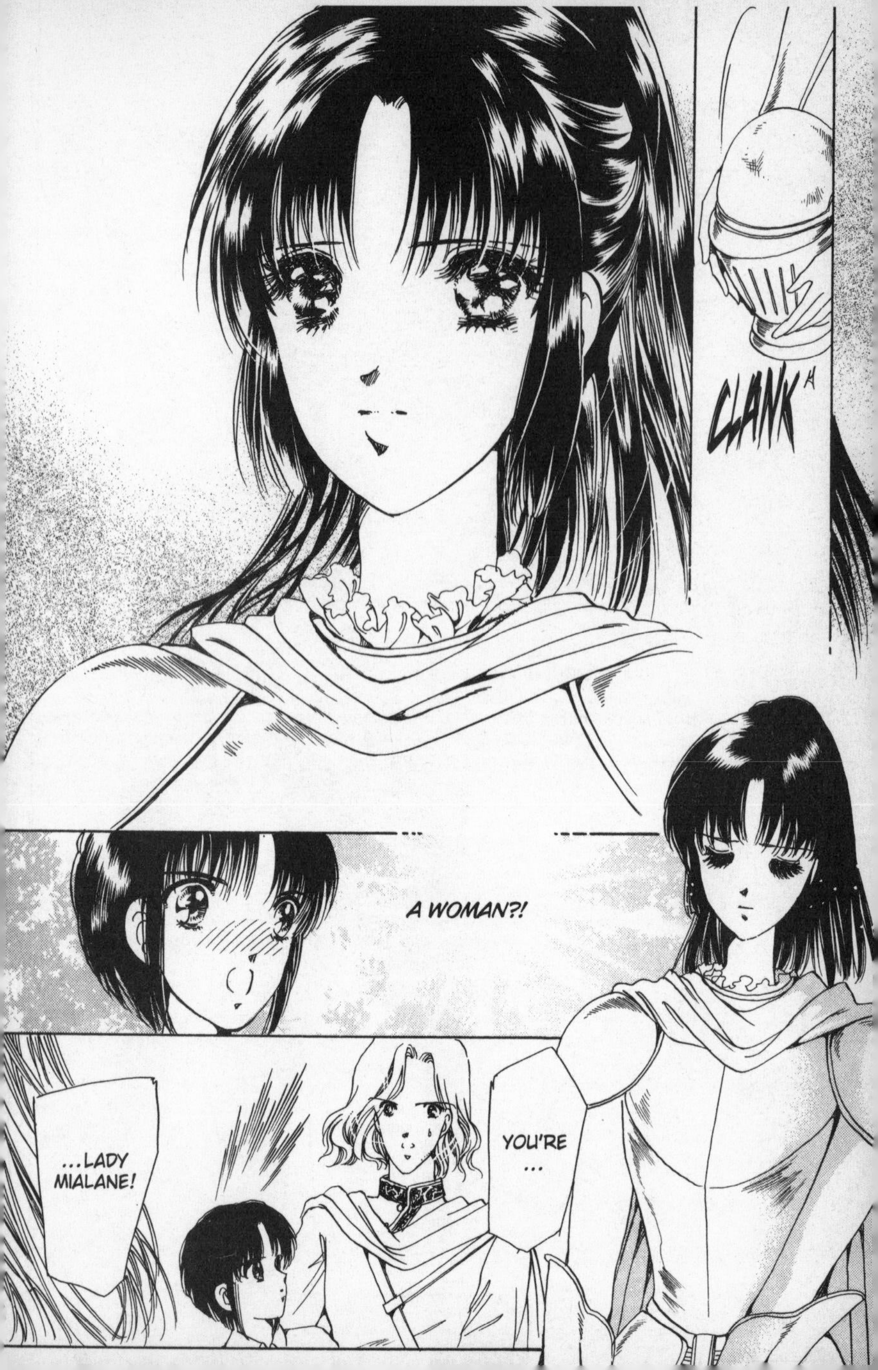
CLANK
A WOMAN?!
YOU'RE ...
...LADY MIALANE!

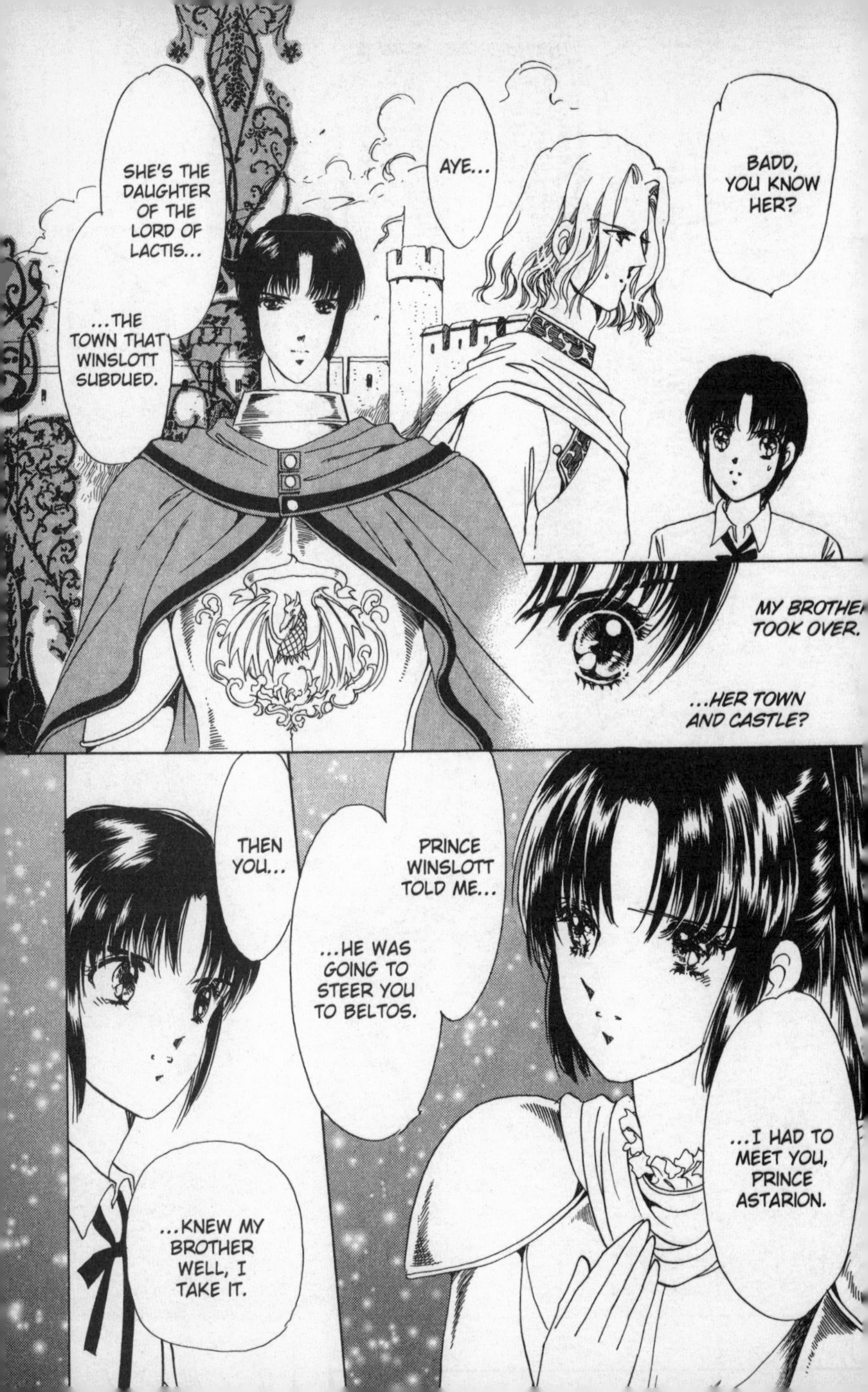
BADD, YOU KNOW HER?
AYE...
SHE'S THE DAUGHTER OF THE LORD OF LACTIS...
...THE TOWN THAT WINSLOTT SUBDUED.
MY BROTHE TOOK OVER.
...HER TOWN AND CASTLE?
PRINCE WINSLOTT TOLD ME...
...HE WAS GOING TO STEER YOU TO BELTOS.
...I HAD TO MEET YOU, PRINCE ASTARION.
THEN YOU...
...KNEW MY BROTHER WELL, I TAKE IT.

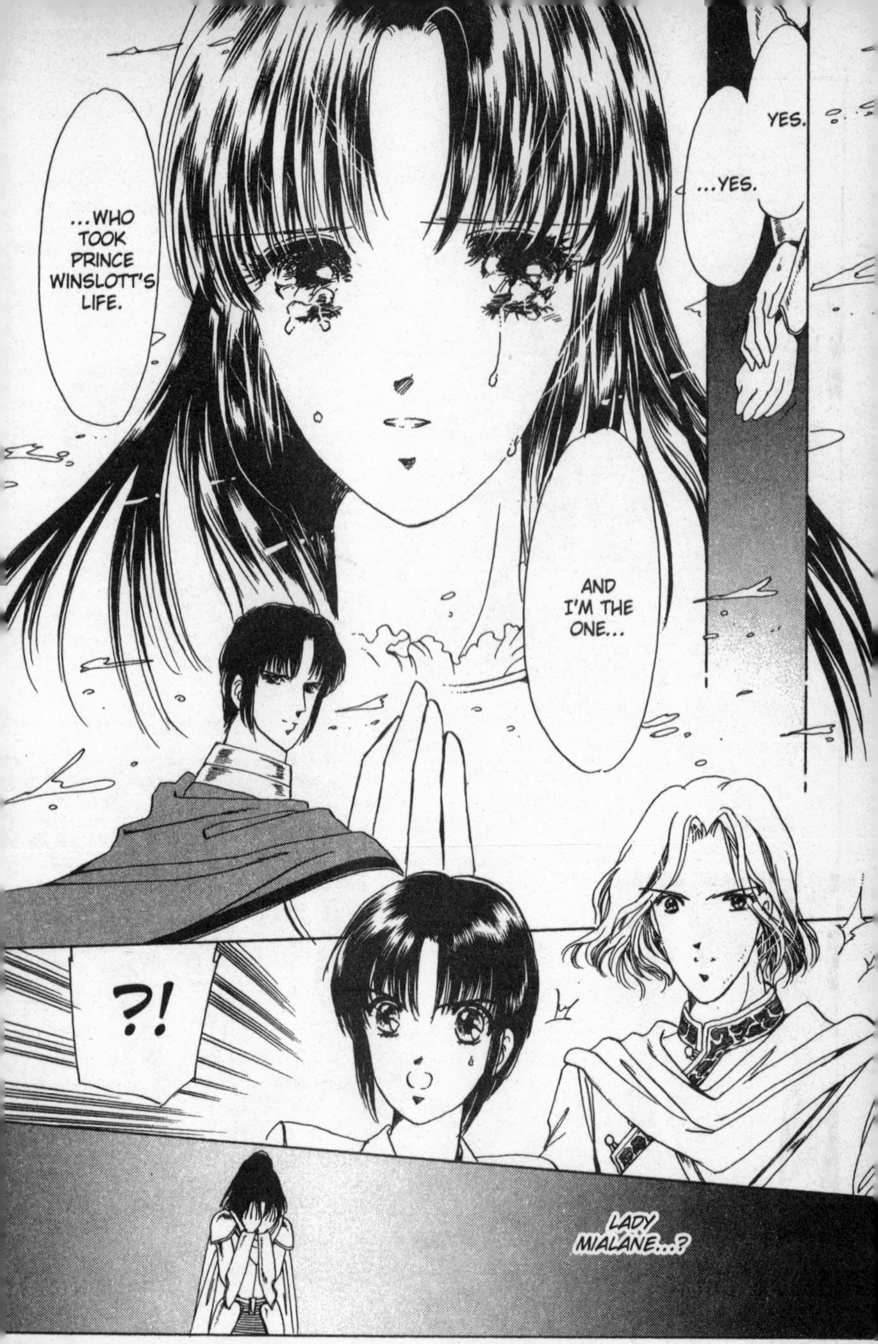
YES.
...YES.
AND I'M THE ONE...
...WHO TOOK PRINCE WINSLOTT'S LIFE.
?!
LADY MIALANE...?

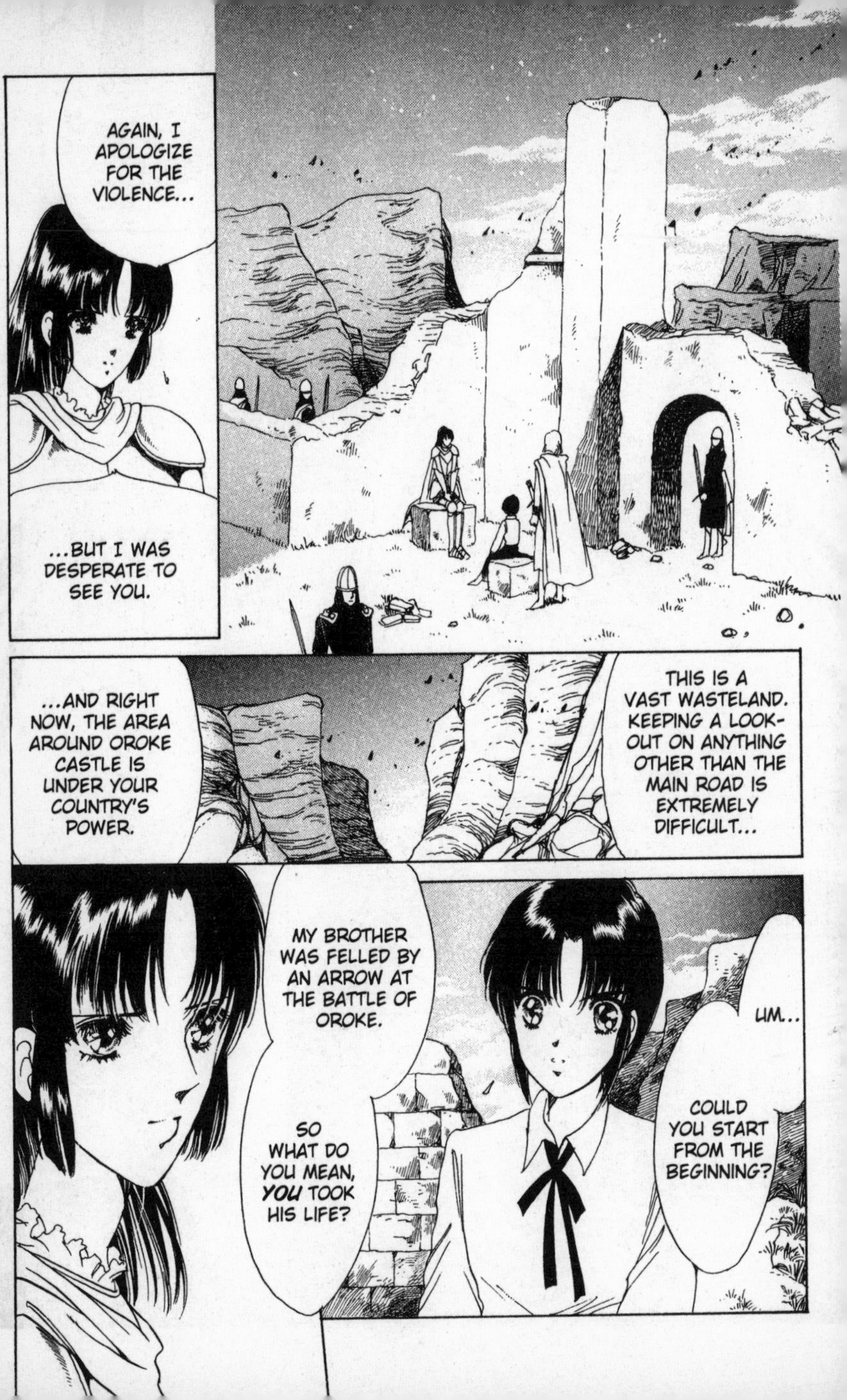
AGAIN, I APOLOGIZE FOR THE VIOLENCE...
...BUT I WAS DESPERATE TO SEE YOU.
THIS IS A VAST WASTELAND. KEEPING A LOOK-OUT ON ANYTHING OTHER THAN THE MAIN ROAD IS EXTREMELY DIFFICULT...
...AND RIGHT NOW, THE AREA AROUND OROKE CASTLE IS UNDER YOUR COUNTRY'S POWER.
UM...
COULD YOU START FROM THE BEGINNING?
MY BROTHER WAS FELLED BY AN ARROW AT THE BATTLE OF OROKE.
SO WHAT DO YOU MEAN, *YOU* TOOK HIS LIFE?

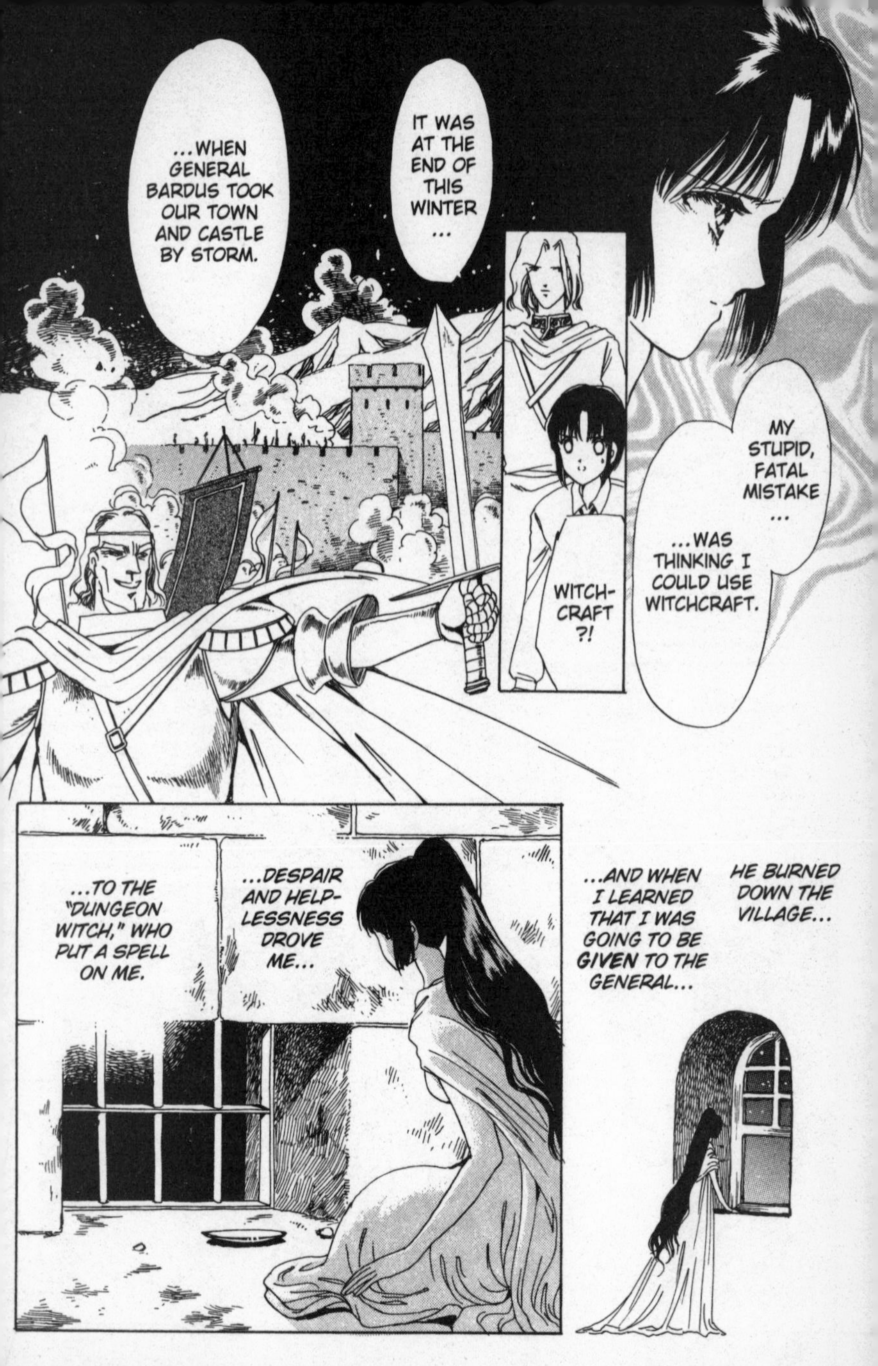
MY STUPID, FATAL MISTAKE...
...WAS THINKING I COULD USE WITCHCRAFT.
WITCH-CRAFT?!
IT WAS AT THE END OF THIS WINTER...
...WHEN GENERAL BARDUS TOOK OUR TOWN AND CASTLE BY STORM.
HE BURNED DOWN THE VILLAGE...
...AND WHEN I LEARNED THAT I WAS GOING TO BE **GIVEN** TO THE GENERAL...
...DESPAIR AND HELP-LESSNESS DROVE ME...
...TO THE "DUNGEON WITCH," WHO PUT A SPELL ON ME.

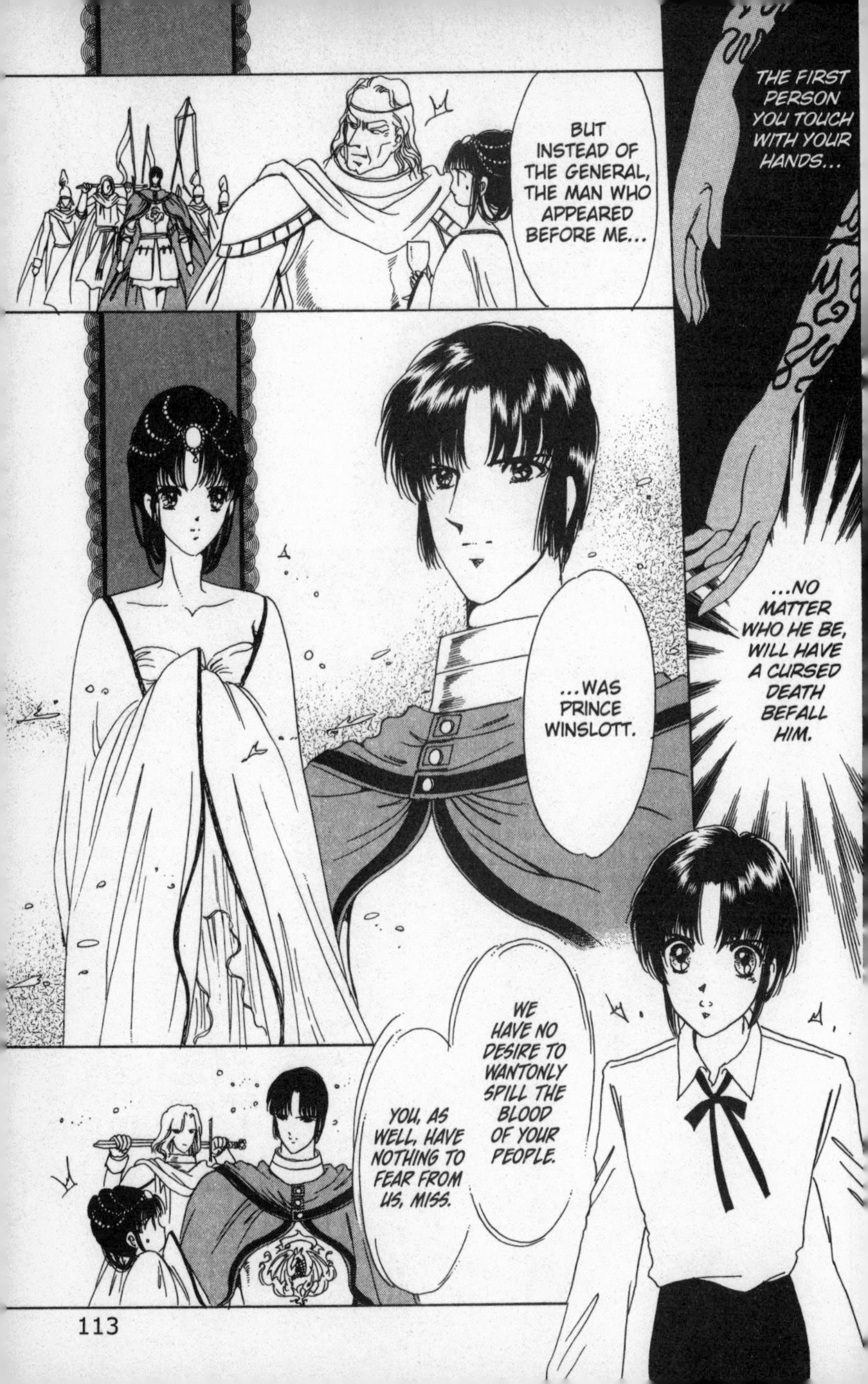
THE FIRST PERSON YOU TOUCH WITH YOUR HANDS...
...NO MATTER WHO HE BE, WILL HAVE A CURSED DEATH BEFALL HIM.
BUT INSTEAD OF THE GENERAL, THE MAN WHO APPEARED BEFORE ME...
...WAS PRINCE WINSLOTT.
WE HAVE NO DESIRE TO WANTONLY SPILL THE BLOOD OF YOUR PEOPLE.
YOU, AS WELL, HAVE NOTHING TO FEAR FROM US, MISS.

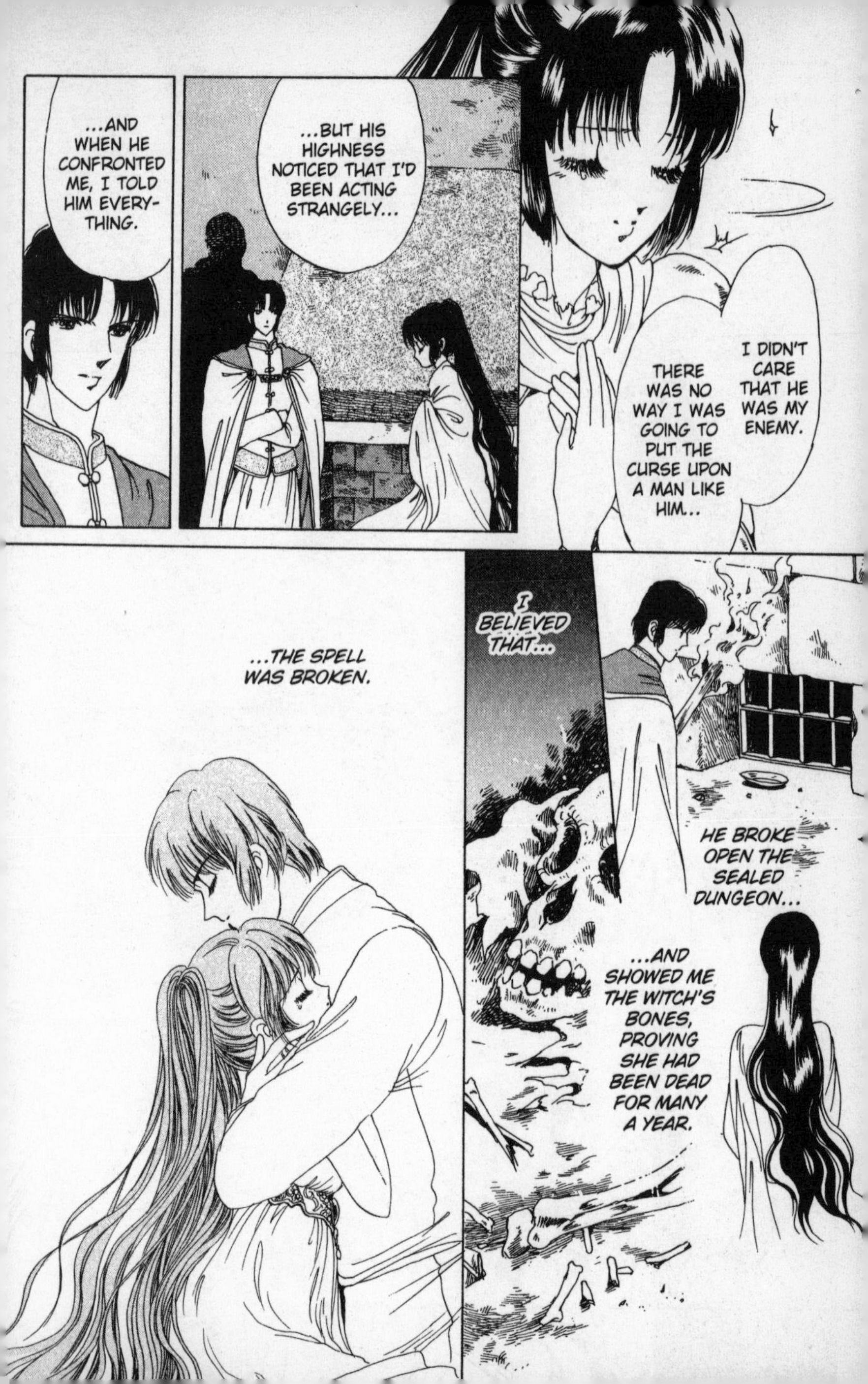
I DIDN'T CARE THAT HE WAS MY ENEMY.
THERE WAS NO WAY I WAS GOING TO PUT THE CURSE UPON A MAN LIKE HIM...
...BUT HIS HIGHNESS NOTICED THAT I'D BEEN ACTING STRANGELY...
...AND WHEN HE CONFRONTED ME, I TOLD HIM EVERY-THING.
HE BROKE OPEN THE SEALED DUNGEON...
...AND SHOWED ME THE WITCH'S BONES, PROVING SHE HAD BEEN DEAD FOR MANY A YEAR.
I BELIEVED THAT...
...THE SPELL WAS BROKEN.

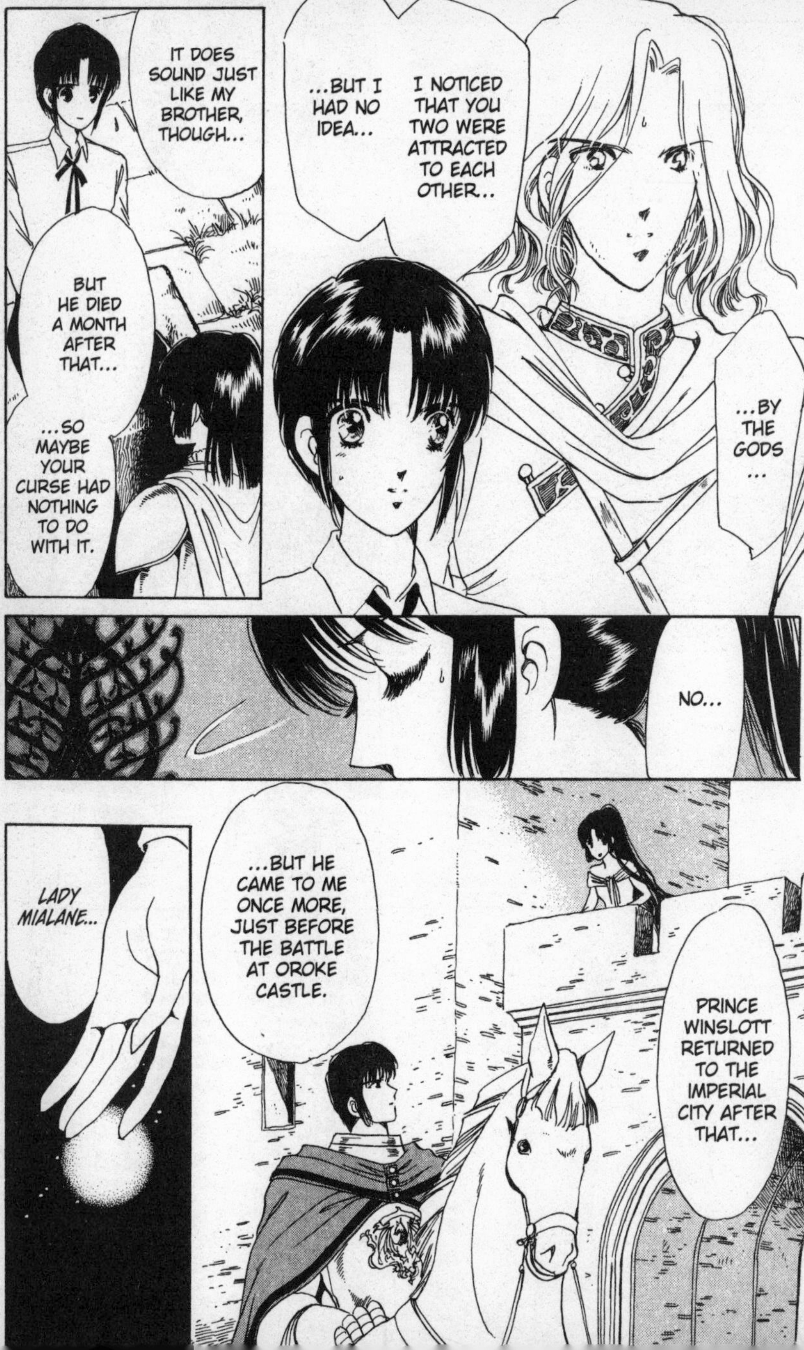
I NOTICED THAT YOU TWO WERE ATTRACTED TO EACH OTHER...
...BUT I HAD NO IDEA...
...BY THE GODS...
IT DOES SOUND JUST LIKE MY BROTHER, THOUGH...
BUT HE DIED A MONTH AFTER THAT...
...SO MAYBE YOUR CURSE HAD NOTHING TO DO WITH IT.
NO...
PRINCE WINSLOTT RETURNED TO THE IMPERIAL CITY AFTER THAT...
...BUT HE CAME TO ME ONCE MORE, JUST BEFORE THE BATTLE AT OROKE CASTLE.
LADY MIALANE...

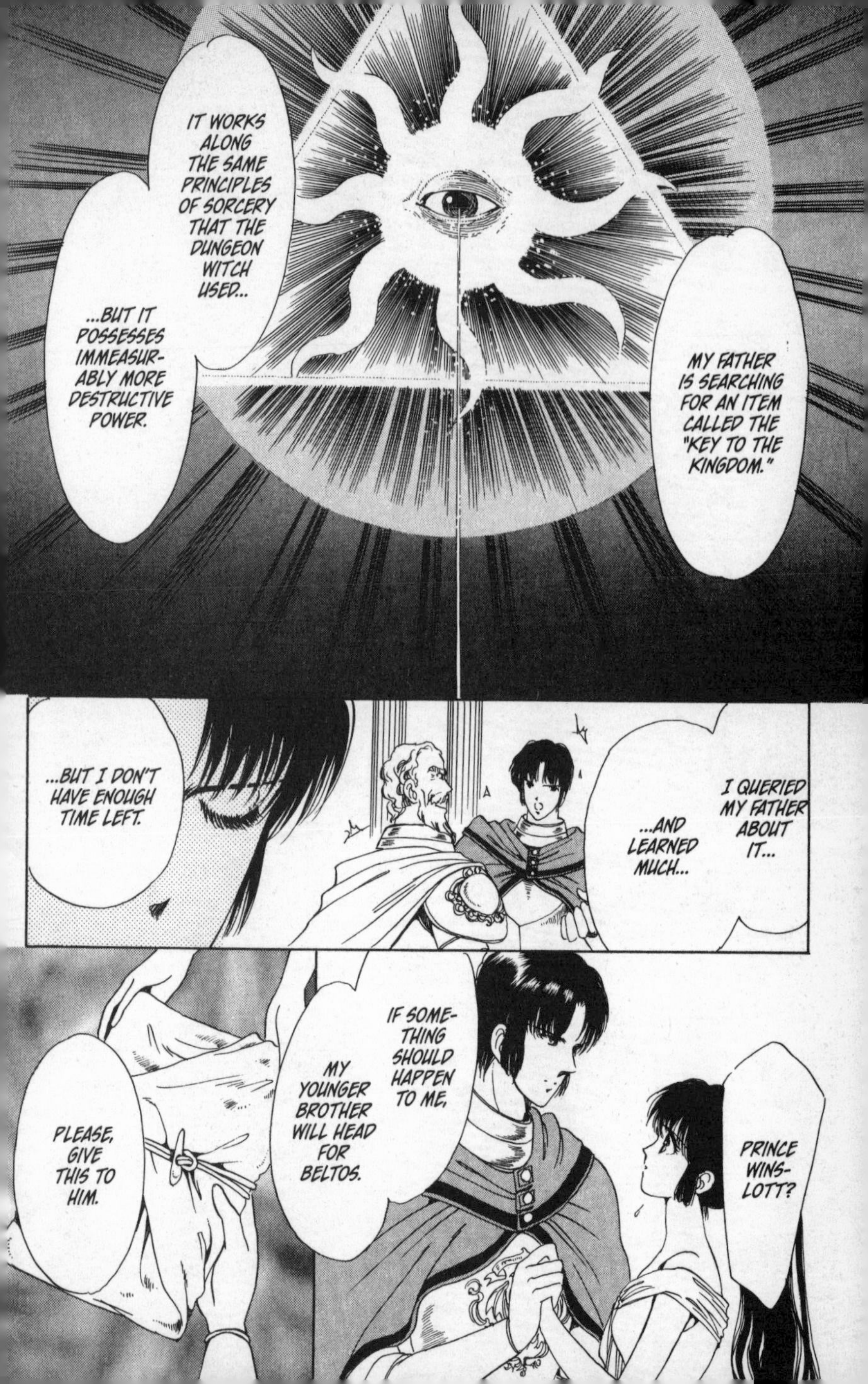
MY FATHER IS SEARCHING FOR AN ITEM CALLED THE "KEY TO THE KINGDOM."
IT WORKS ALONG THE SAME PRINCIPLES OF SORCERY THAT THE DUNGEON WITCH USED...
...BUT IT POSSESSES IMMEASUR-ABLY MORE DESTRUCTIVE POWER.
I QUERIED MY FATHER ABOUT IT...
...AND LEARNED MUCH...
...BUT I DON'T HAVE ENOUGH TIME LEFT.
PRINCE WINS-LOTT?
IF SOME-THING SHOULD HAPPEN TO ME,
MY YOUNGER BROTHER WILL HEAD FOR BELTOS.
PLEASE, GIVE THIS TO HIM.

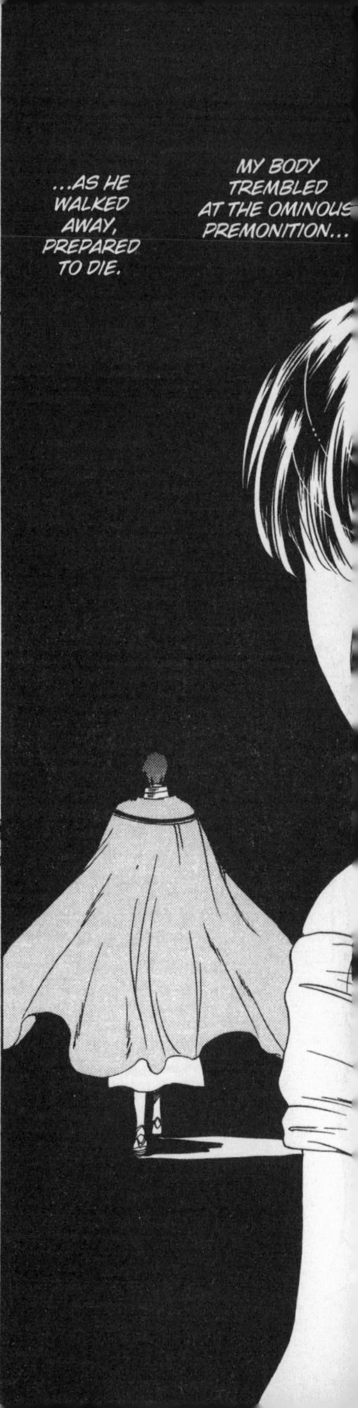
MY BODY TREMBLED AT THE OMINOUS PREMONITION...
...AS HE WALKED AWAY, PREPARED TO DIE.

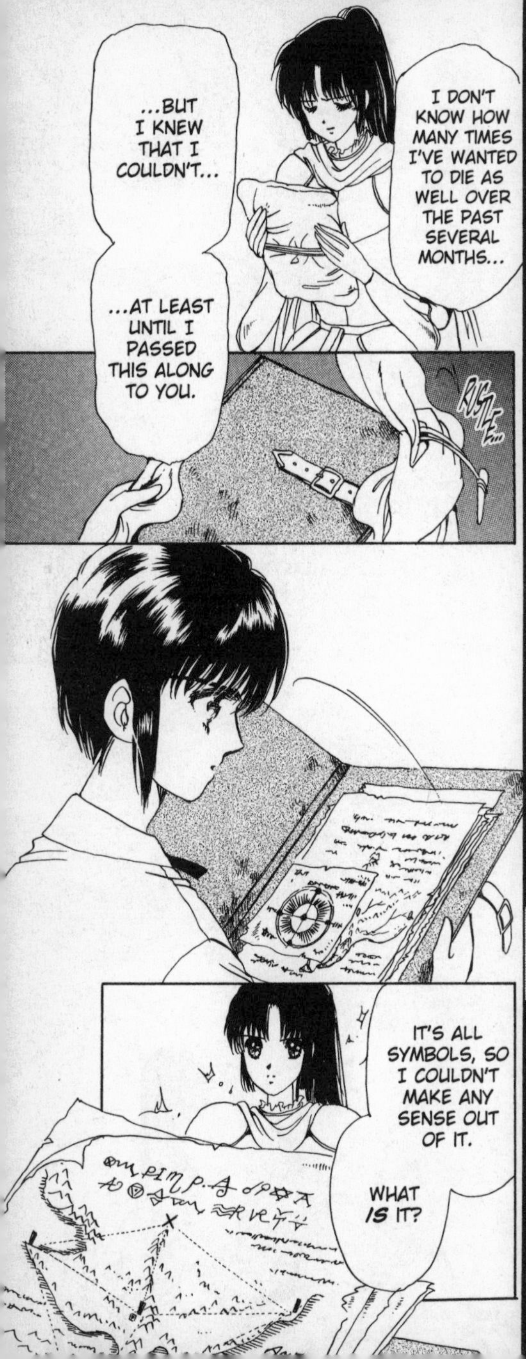
I DON'T KNOW HOW MANY TIMES I'VE WANTED TO DIE AS WELL OVER THE PAST SEVERAL MONTHS...
...BUT I KNEW THAT I COULDN'T...
...AT LEAST UNTIL I PASSED THIS ALONG TO YOU.
RUSTLE...
IT'S ALL SYMBOLS, SO I COULDN'T MAKE ANY SENSE OUT OF IT.
WHAT *IS* IT?

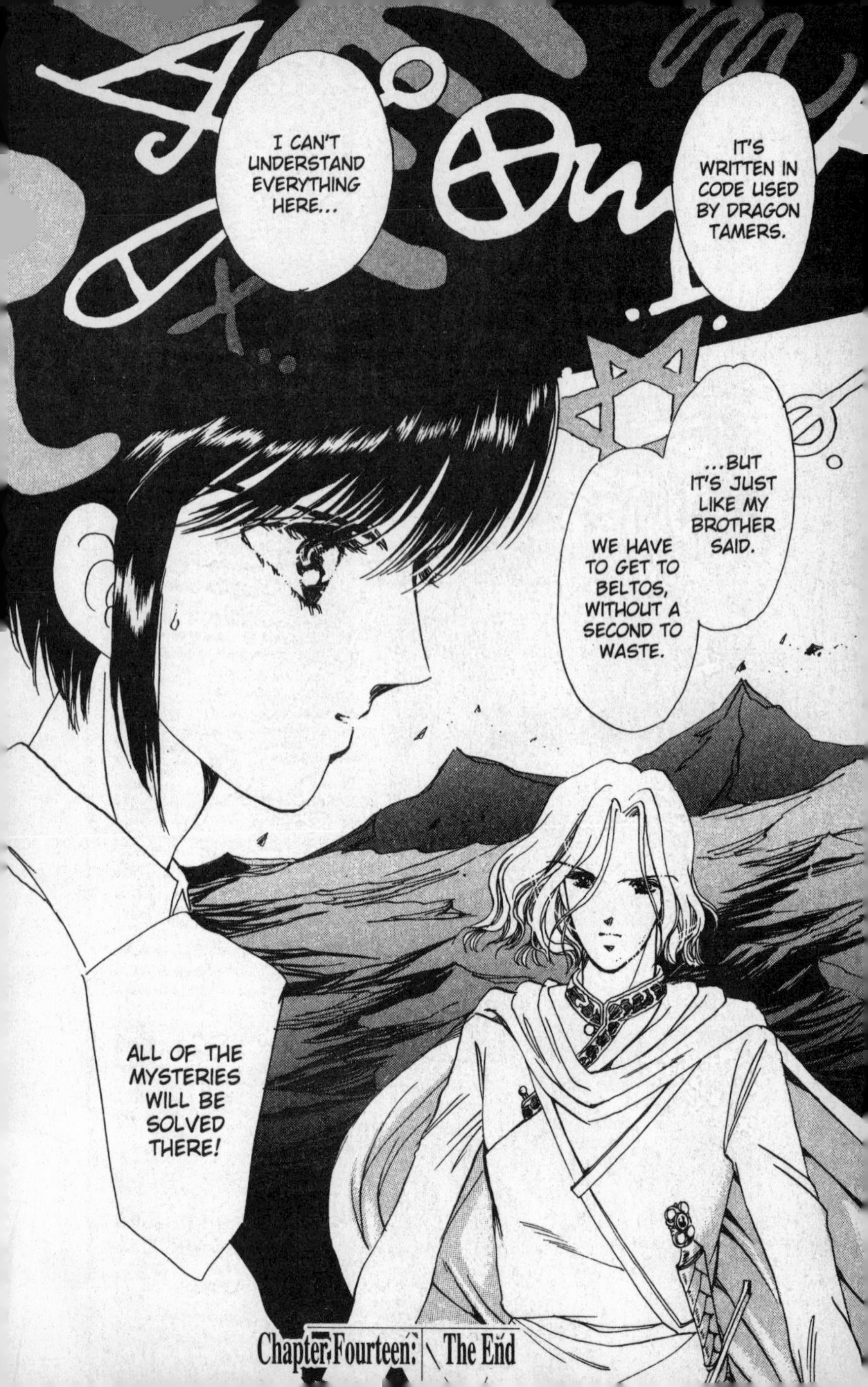
IT'S WRITTEN IN CODE USED BY DRAGON TAMERS.
I CAN'T UNDERSTAND EVERYTHING HERE...
...BUT IT'S JUST LIKE MY BROTHER SAID.
WE HAVE TO GET TO BELTOS, WITHOUT A SECOND TO WASTE.
ALL OF THE MYSTERIES WILL BE SOLVED THERE!
Chapter Fourteen: The End

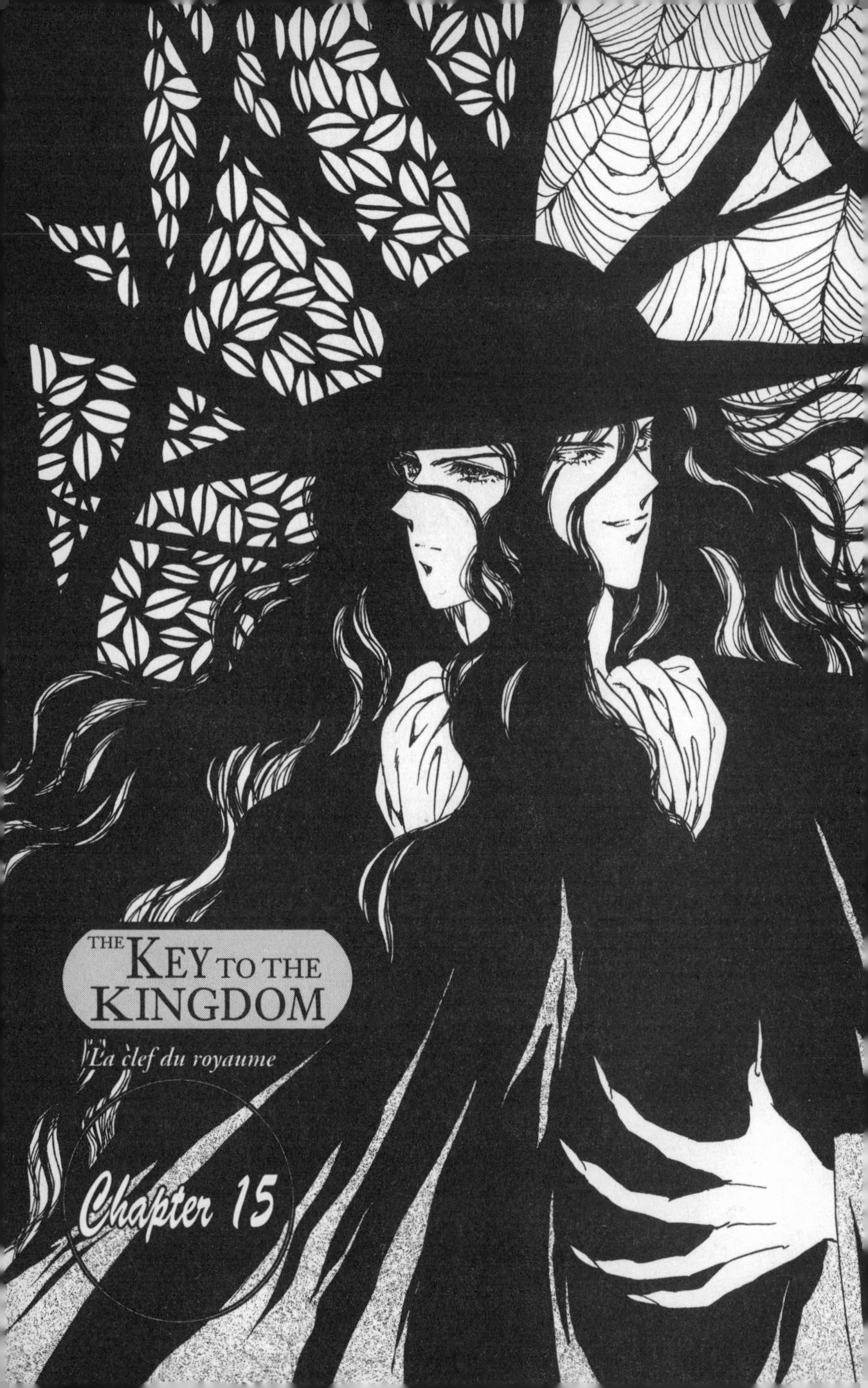
THE KEY TO THE KINGDOM
La clef du royaume
Chapter 15

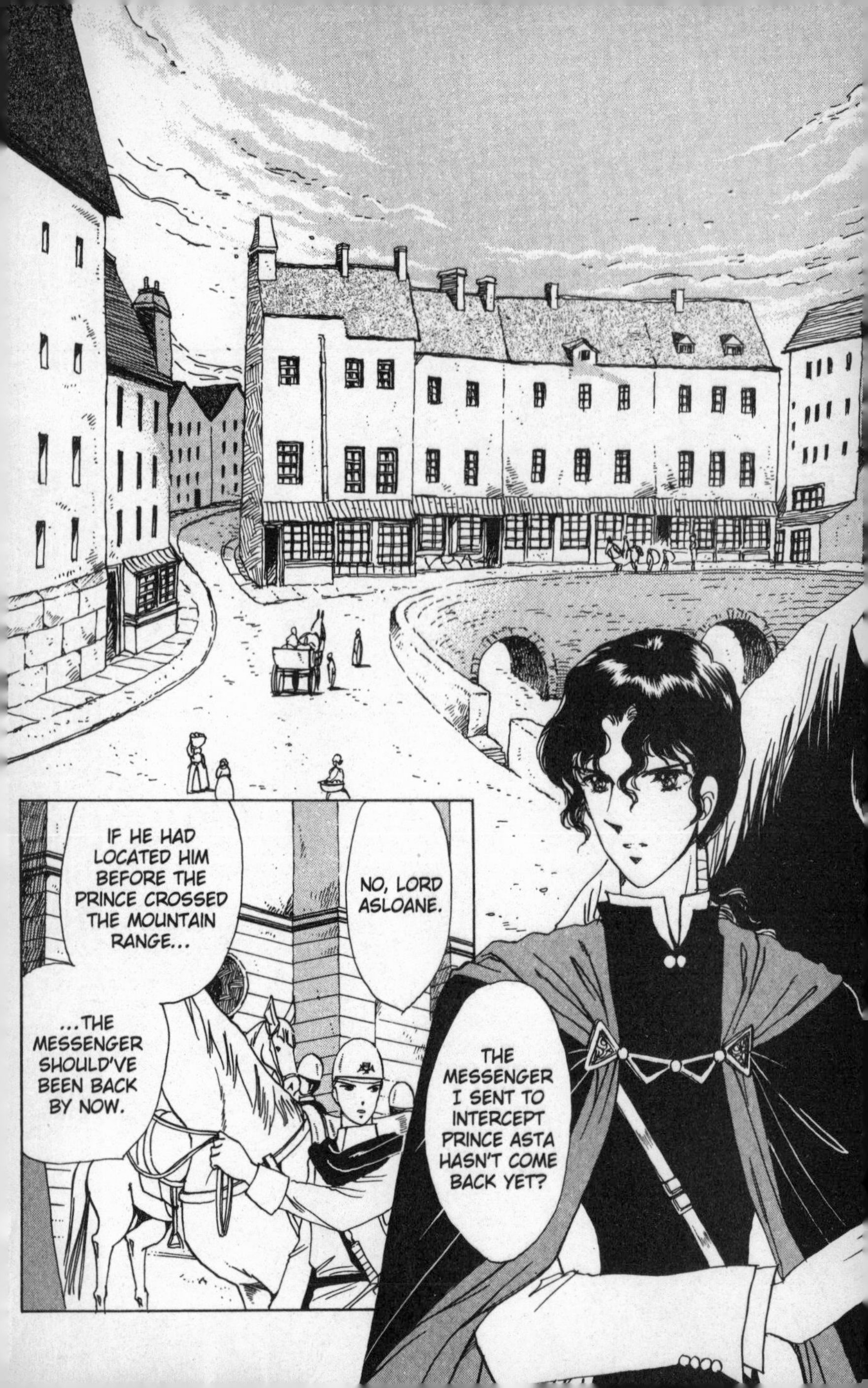
THE MESSENGER I SENT TO INTERCEPT PRINCE ASTA HASN'T COME BACK YET?
NO, LORD ASLOANE.
IF HE HAD LOCATED HIM BEFORE THE PRINCE CROSSED THE MOUNTAIN RANGE...
...THE MESSENGER SHOULD'VE BEEN BACK BY NOW.

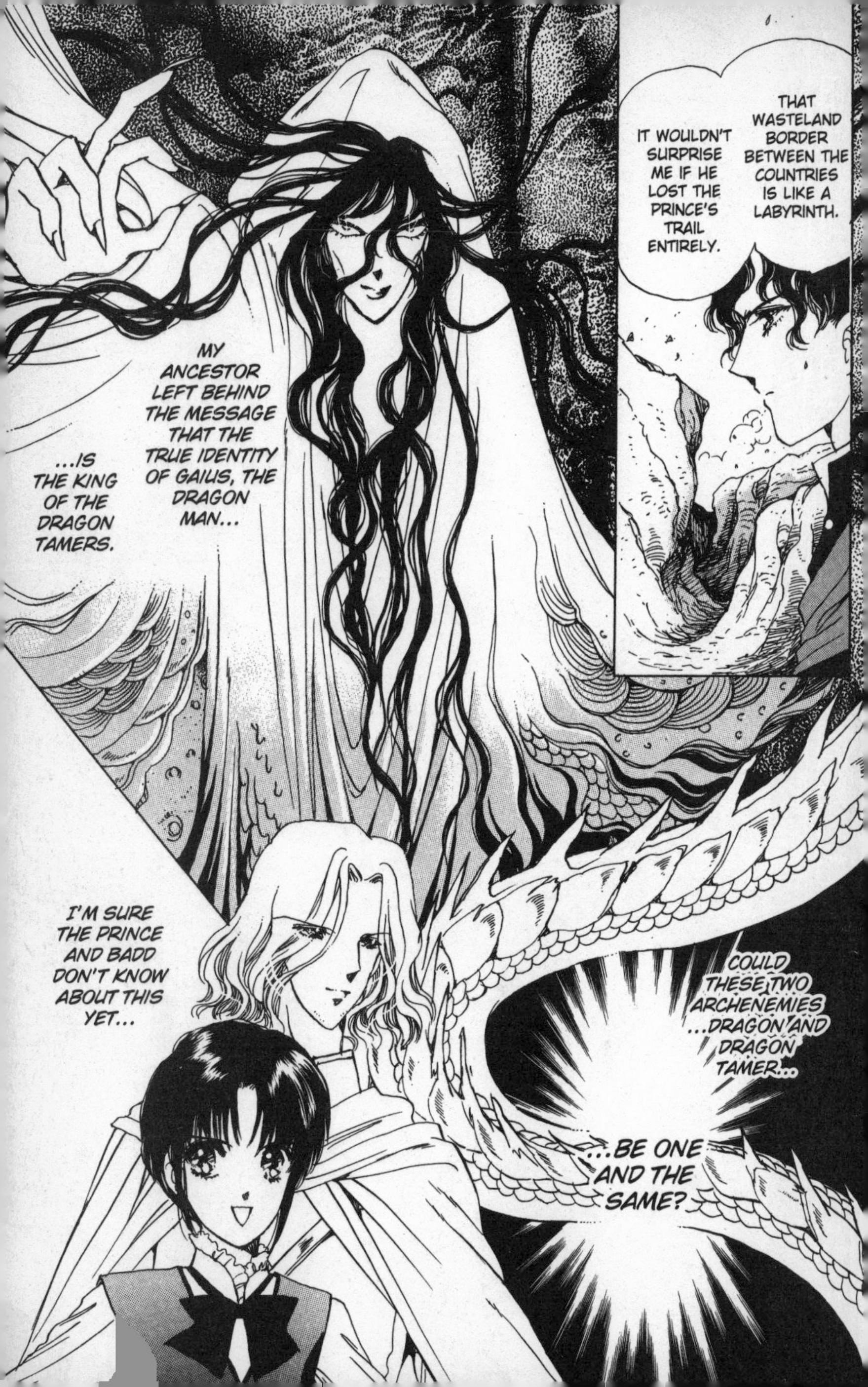
THAT WASTELAND BORDER BETWEEN THE COUNTRIES IS LIKE A LABYRINTH.
IT WOULDN'T SURPRISE ME IF HE LOST THE PRINCE'S TRAIL ENTIRELY.
MY ANCESTOR LEFT BEHIND THE MESSAGE THAT THE TRUE IDENTITY OF GAIUS, THE DRAGON MAN...
...IS THE KING OF THE DRAGON TAMERS.
COULD THESE TWO ARCHENEMIES ...DRAGON AND DRAGON TAMER...
...BE ONE AND THE SAME?
I'M SURE THE PRINCE AND BADD DON'T KNOW ABOUT THIS YET...

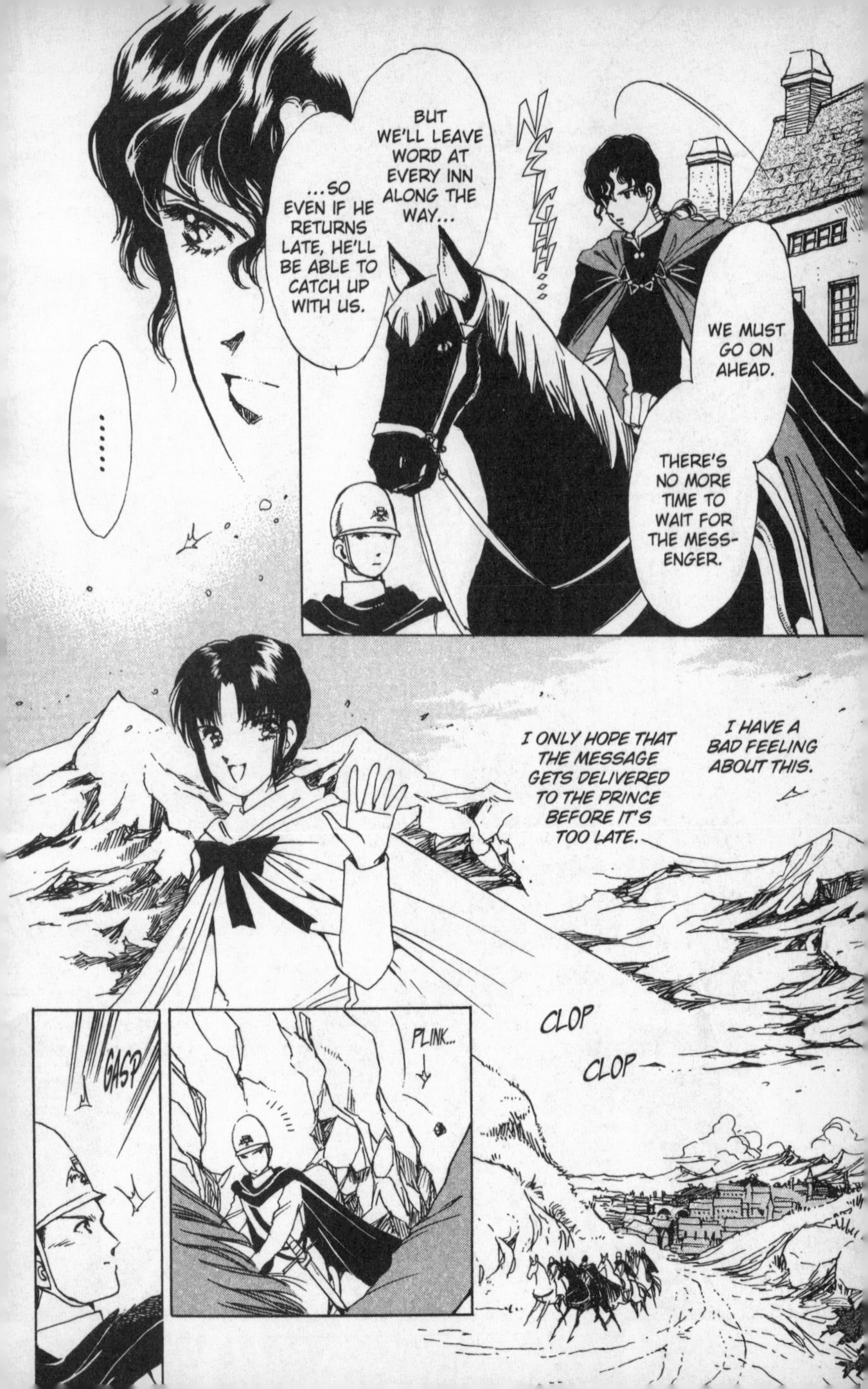
NEIGH...
WE MUST GO ON AHEAD.
THERE'S NO MORE TIME TO WAIT FOR THE MESS-ENGER.
BUT WE'LL LEAVE WORD AT EVERY INN ALONG THE WAY...
...SO EVEN IF HE RETURNS LATE, HE'LL BE ABLE TO CATCH UP WITH US.
......
I HAVE A BAD FEELING ABOUT THIS.
I ONLY HOPE THAT THE MESSAGE GETS DELIVERED TO THE PRINCE BEFORE IT'S TOO LATE.
CLOP
CLOP
PLINK...
GASP

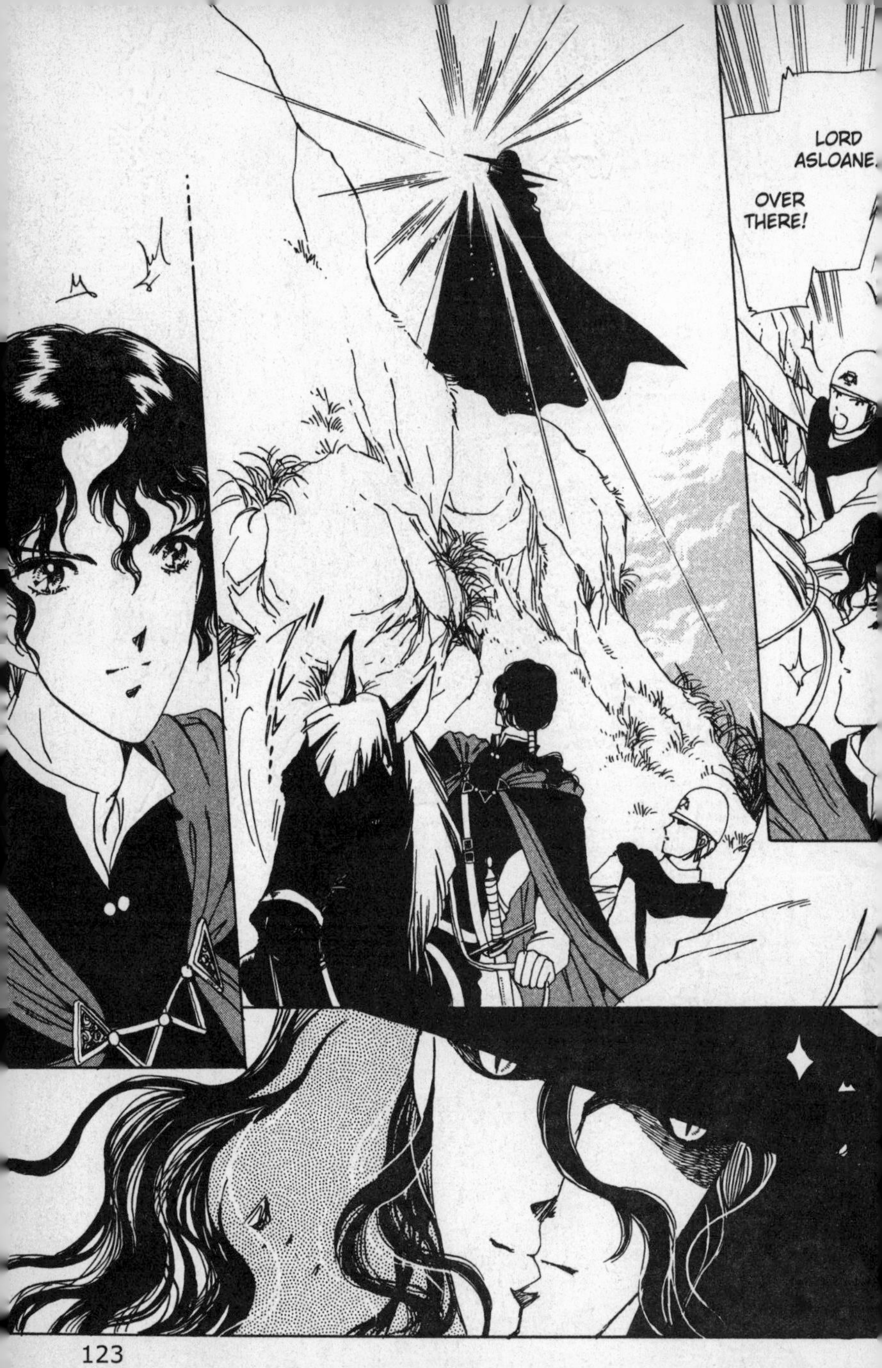
LORD ASLOANE.
OVER THERE!

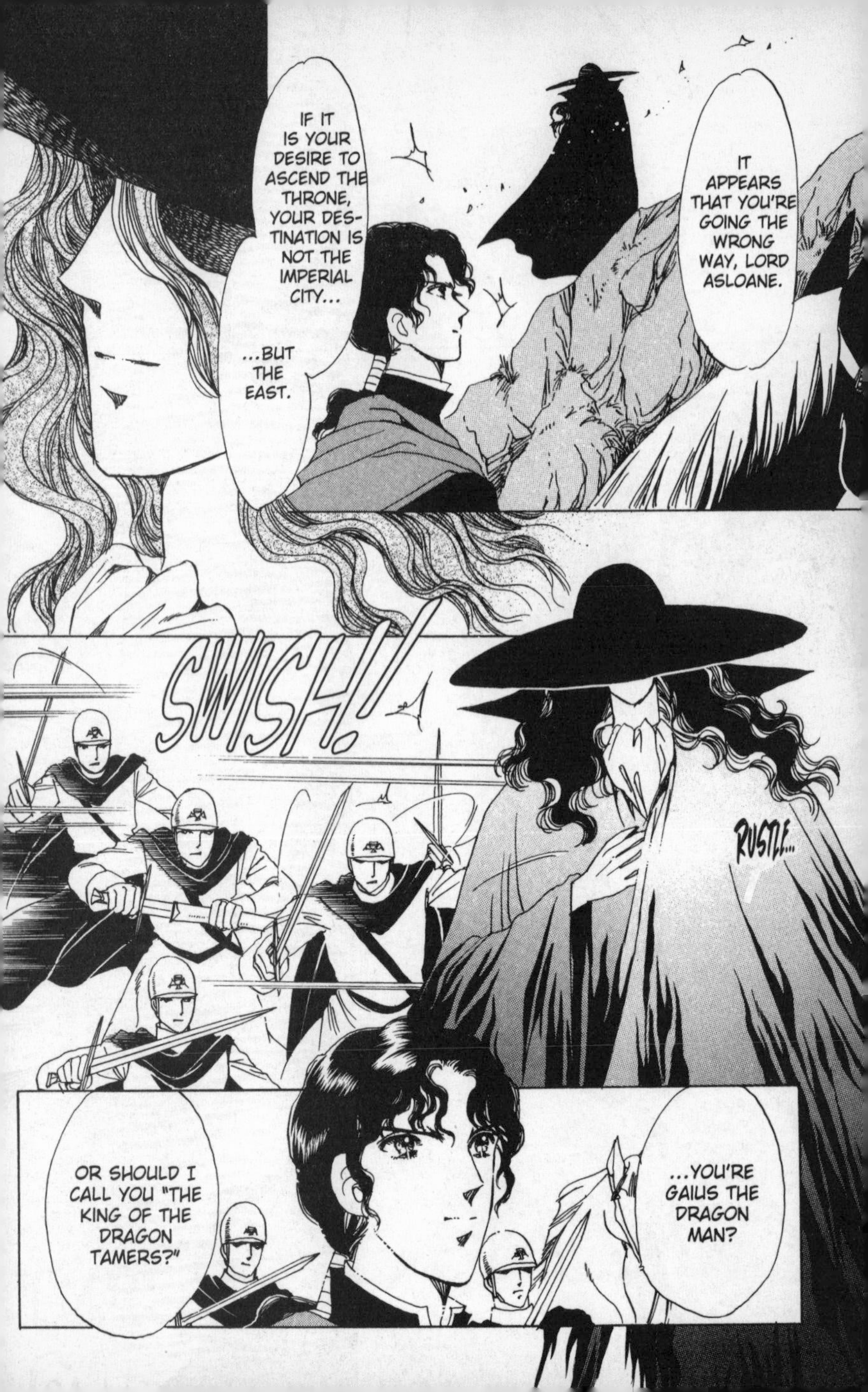
IT APPEARS THAT YOU'RE GOING THE WRONG WAY, LORD ASLOANE.
IF IT IS YOUR DESIRE TO ASCEND THE THRONE, YOUR DES-TINATION IS NOT THE IMPERIAL CITY...
...BUT THE EAST.
RUSTLE...
SWISH!!
...YOU'RE GAIUS THE DRAGON MAN?
OR SHOULD I CALL YOU "THE KING OF THE DRAGON TAMERS?"

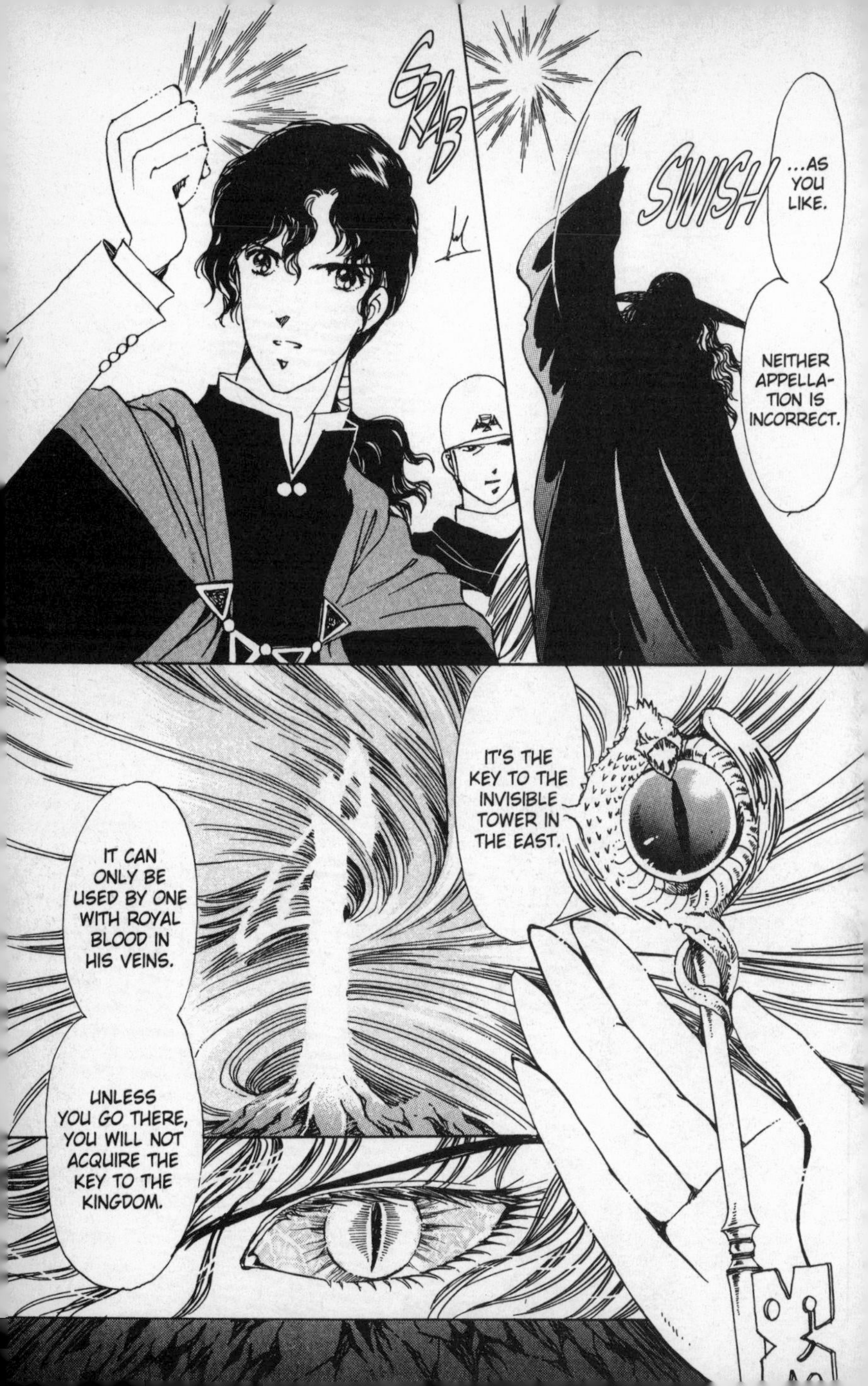
...AS YOU LIKE.
SWISH
NEITHER APPELLATION IS INCORRECT.
GRAB
IT'S THE KEY TO THE INVISIBLE TOWER IN THE EAST.
IT CAN ONLY BE USED BY ONE WITH ROYAL BLOOD IN HIS VEINS.
UNLESS YOU GO THERE, YOU WILL NOT ACQUIRE THE KEY TO THE KINGDOM.

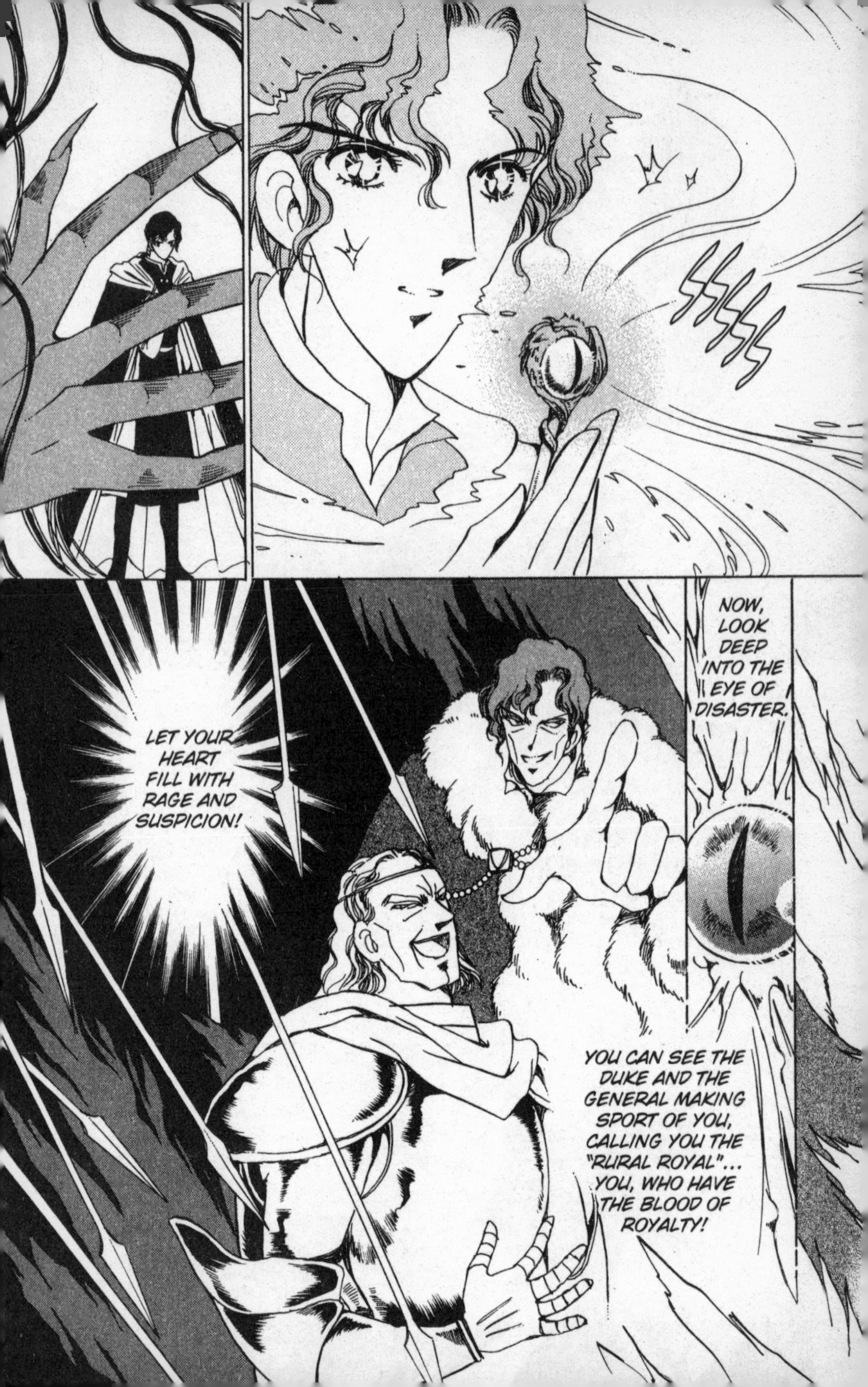
NOW, LOOK DEEP INTO THE EYE OF DISASTER.
YOU CAN SEE THE DUKE AND THE GENERAL MAKING SPORT OF YOU, CALLING YOU THE "RURAL ROYAL"... YOU, WHO HAVE THE BLOOD OF ROYALTY!
LET YOUR HEART FILL WITH RAGE AND SUSPICION!

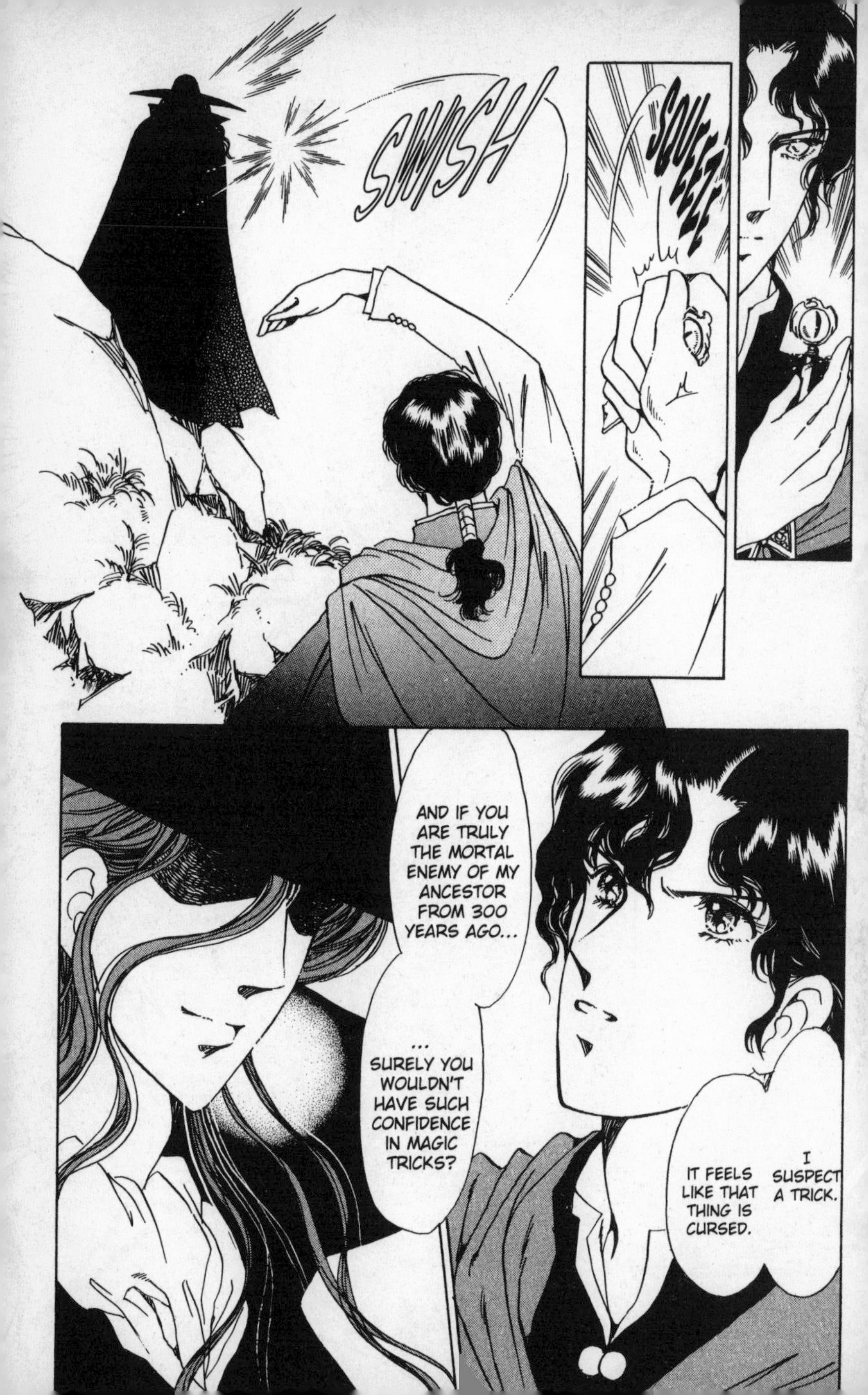
SQUEEZE
SWISH
I SUSPECT A TRICK.
IT FEELS LIKE THAT THING IS CURSED.
AND IF YOU ARE TRULY THE MORTAL ENEMY OF MY ANCESTOR FROM 300 YEARS AGO...
... SURELY YOU WOULDN'T HAVE SUCH CONFIDENCE IN MAGIC TRICKS?

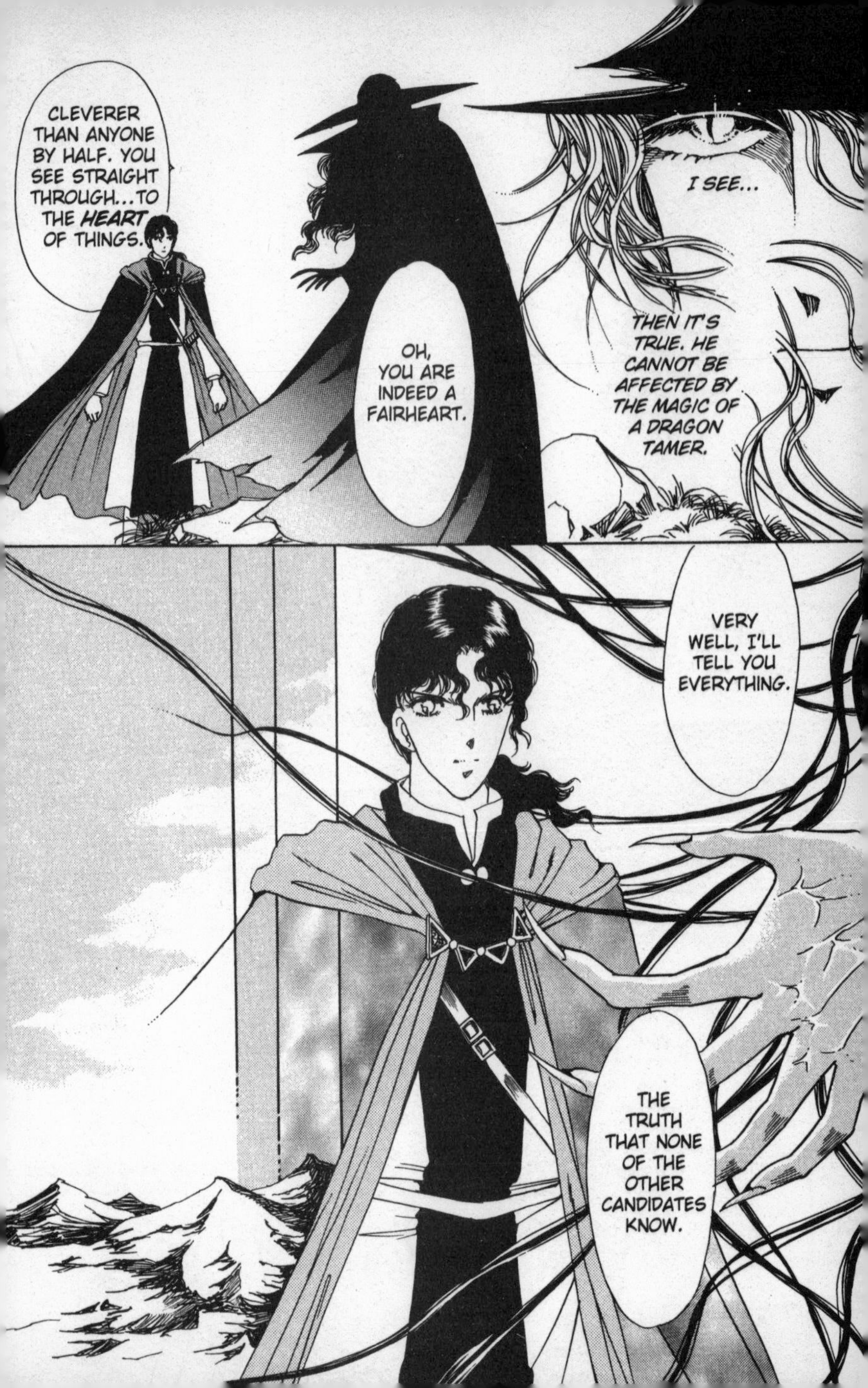
I SEE...
THEN IT'S TRUE. HE CANNOT BE AFFECTED BY THE MAGIC OF A DRAGON TAMER.
OH, YOU ARE INDEED A FAIRHEART.
CLEVERER THAN ANYONE BY HALF. YOU SEE STRAIGHT THROUGH...TO THE **HEART** OF THINGS.
VERY WELL, I'LL TELL YOU EVERYTHING.
THE TRUTH THAT NONE OF THE OTHER CANDIDATES KNOW.

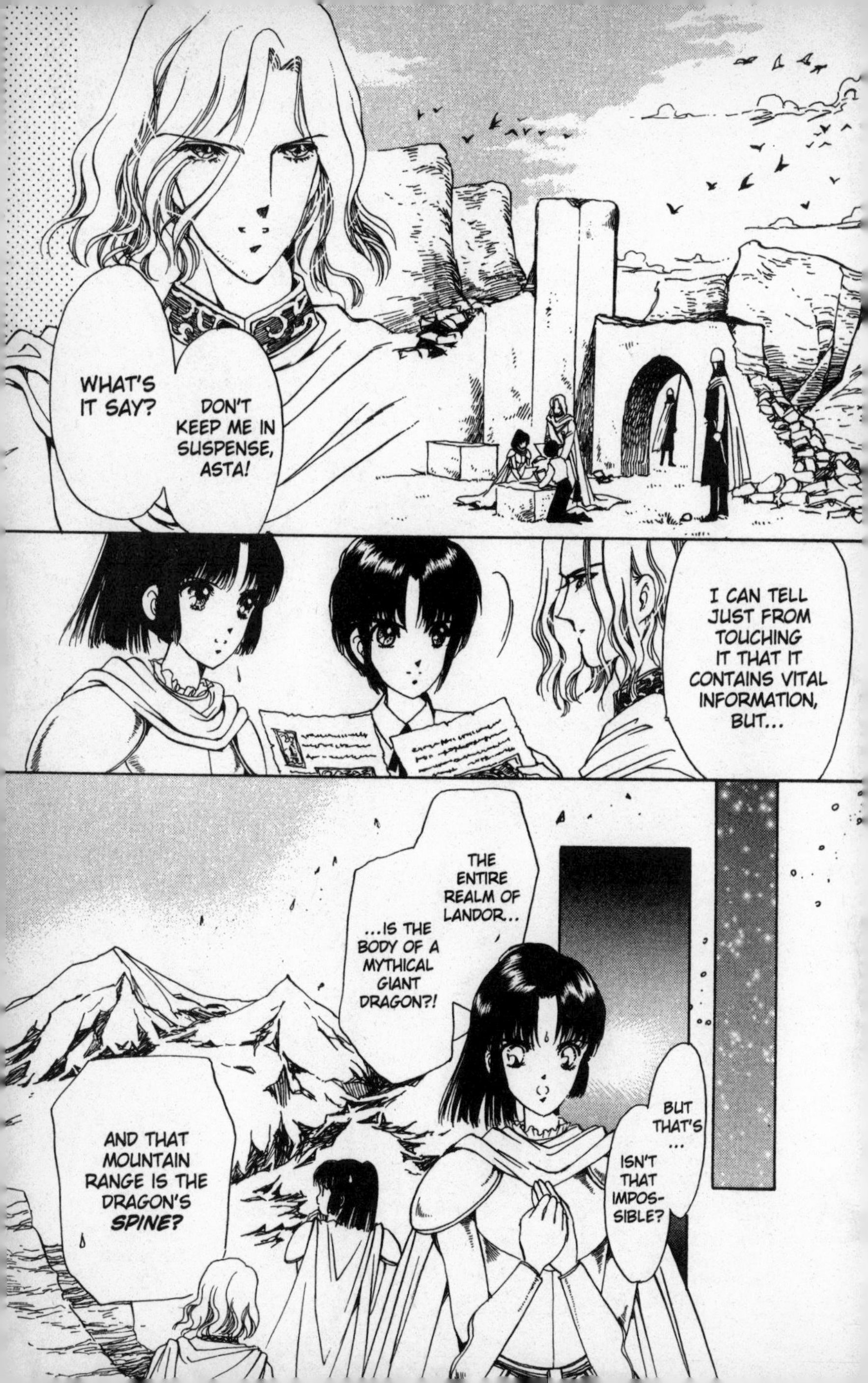
WHAT'S IT SAY?
DON'T KEEP ME IN SUSPENSE, ASTA!
I CAN TELL JUST FROM TOUCHING IT THAT IT CONTAINS VITAL INFORMATION, BUT...
THE ENTIRE REALM OF LANDOR...
...IS THE BODY OF A MYTHICAL GIANT DRAGON?!
BUT THAT'S ...
ISN'T THAT IMPOSSIBLE?
AND THAT MOUNTAIN RANGE IS THE DRAGON'S *SPINE*?

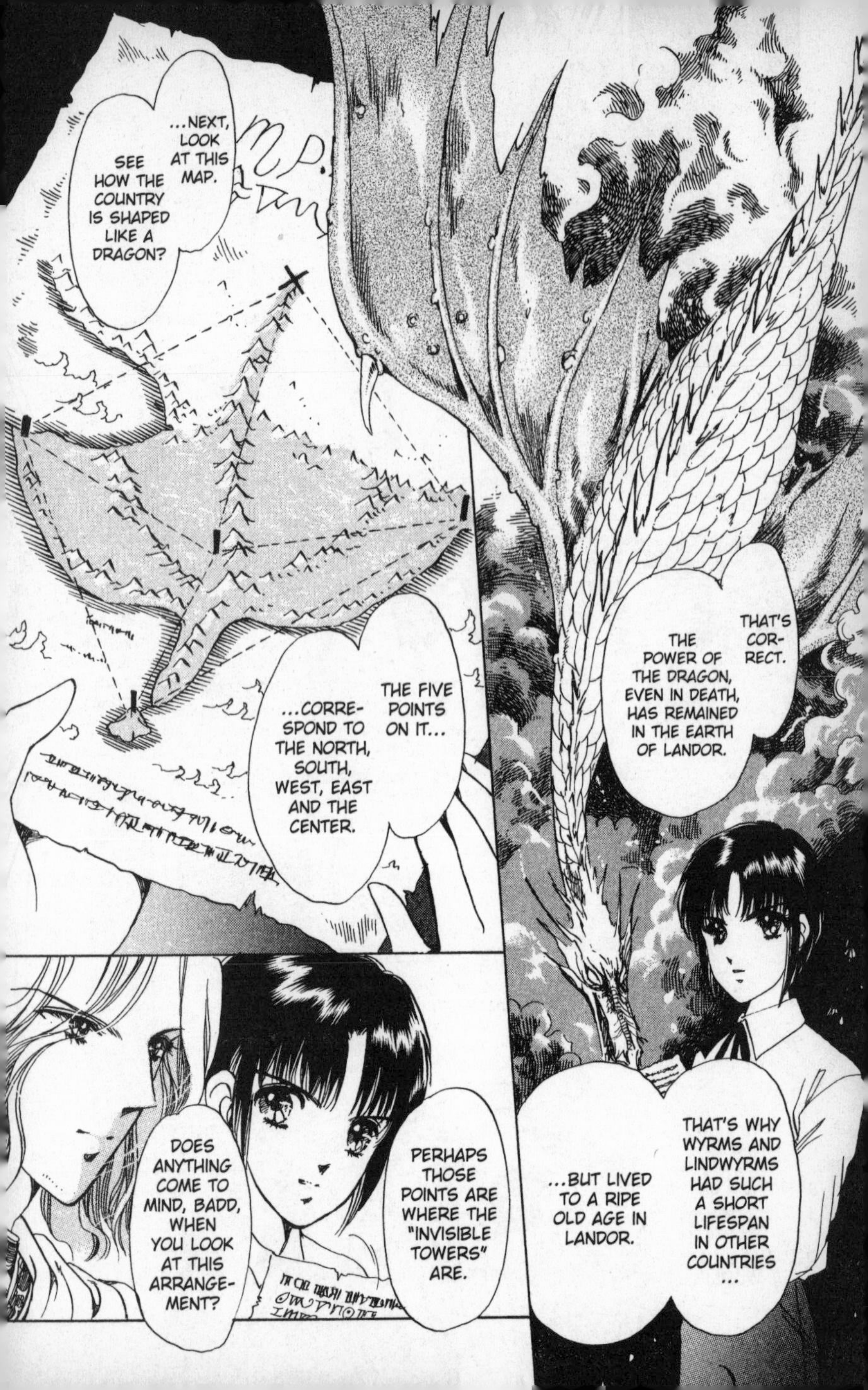
...NEXT, LOOK AT THIS MAP.
SEE HOW THE COUNTRY IS SHAPED LIKE A DRAGON?
THE FIVE POINTS ON IT...
...CORRESPOND TO THE NORTH, SOUTH, WEST, EAST AND THE CENTER.
PERHAPS THOSE POINTS ARE WHERE THE "INVISIBLE TOWERS" ARE.
DOES ANYTHING COME TO MIND, BADD, WHEN YOU LOOK AT THIS ARRANGEMENT?
THAT'S CORRECT.
THE POWER OF THE DRAGON, EVEN IN DEATH, HAS REMAINED IN THE EARTH OF LANDOR.
THAT'S WHY WYRMS AND LINDWYRMS HAD SUCH A SHORT LIFESPAN IN OTHER COUNTRIES...
...BUT LIVED TO A RIPE OLD AGE IN LANDOR.

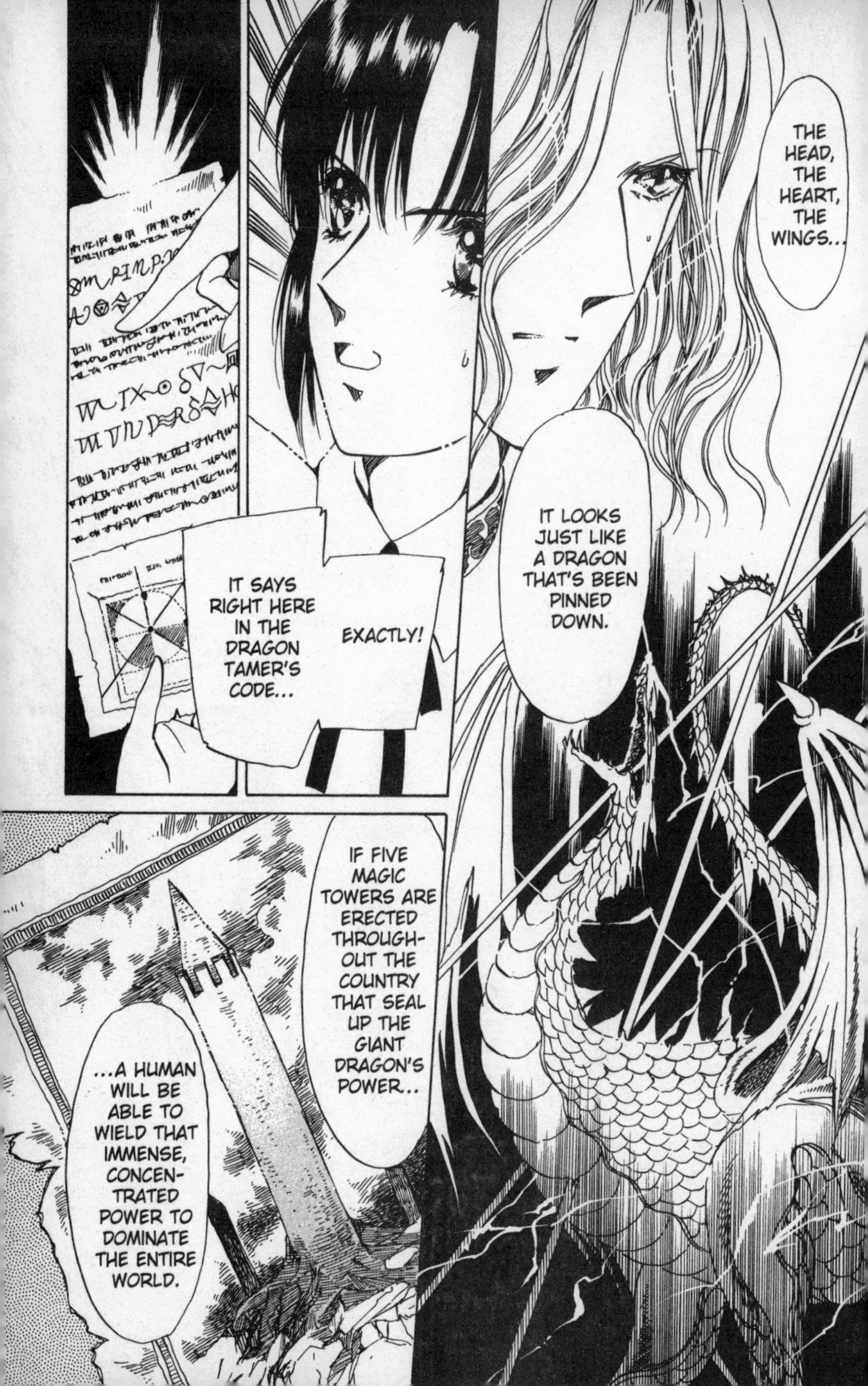
THE HEAD, THE HEART, THE WINGS...
IT LOOKS JUST LIKE A DRAGON THAT'S BEEN PINNED DOWN.
EXACTLY!
IT SAYS RIGHT HERE IN THE DRAGON TAMER'S CODE...
IF FIVE MAGIC TOWERS ARE ERECTED THROUGH-OUT THE COUNTRY THAT SEAL UP THE GIANT DRAGON'S POWER...
...A HUMAN WILL BE ABLE TO WIELD THAT IMMENSE, CONCEN-TRATED POWER TO DOMINATE THE ENTIRE WORLD.

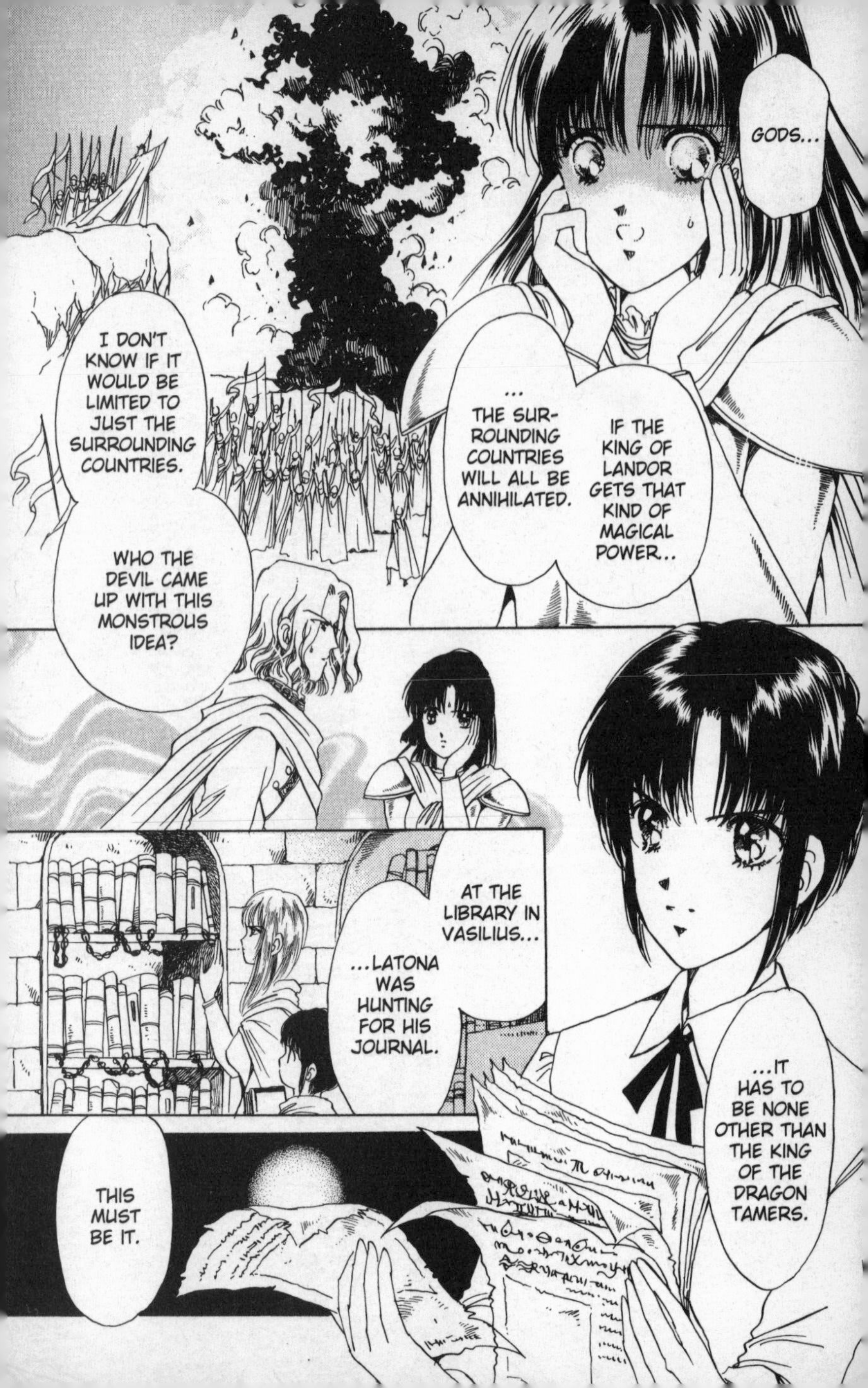
GODS...
IF THE KING OF LANDOR GETS THAT KIND OF MAGICAL POWER...
... THE SUR-ROUNDING COUNTRIES WILL ALL BE ANNIHILATED.
I DON'T KNOW IF IT WOULD BE LIMITED TO JUST THE SURROUNDING COUNTRIES.
WHO THE DEVIL CAME UP WITH THIS MONSTROUS IDEA?
...IT HAS TO BE NONE OTHER THAN THE KING OF THE DRAGON TAMERS.
AT THE LIBRARY IN VASILIUS...
...LATONA WAS HUNTING FOR HIS JOURNAL.
THIS MUST BE IT.

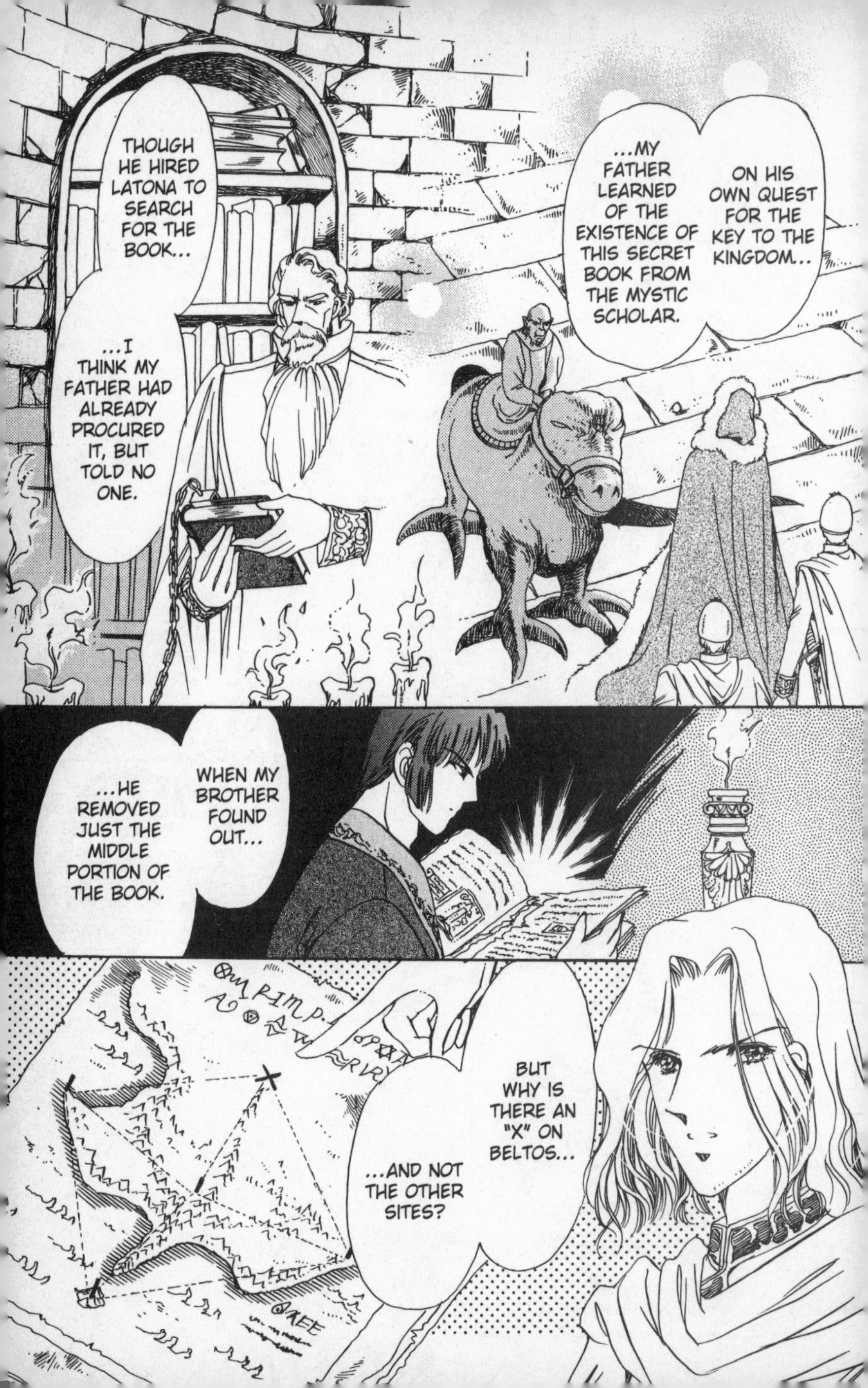
ON HIS OWN QUEST FOR THE KEY TO THE KINGDOM...
...MY FATHER LEARNED OF THE EXISTENCE OF THIS SECRET BOOK FROM THE MYSTIC SCHOLAR.
THOUGH HE HIRED LATONA TO SEARCH FOR THE BOOK...
...I THINK MY FATHER HAD ALREADY PROCURED IT, BUT TOLD NO ONE.
WHEN MY BROTHER FOUND OUT...
...HE REMOVED JUST THE MIDDLE PORTION OF THE BOOK.
BUT WHY IS THERE AN "X" ON BELTOS...
...AND NOT THE OTHER SITES?

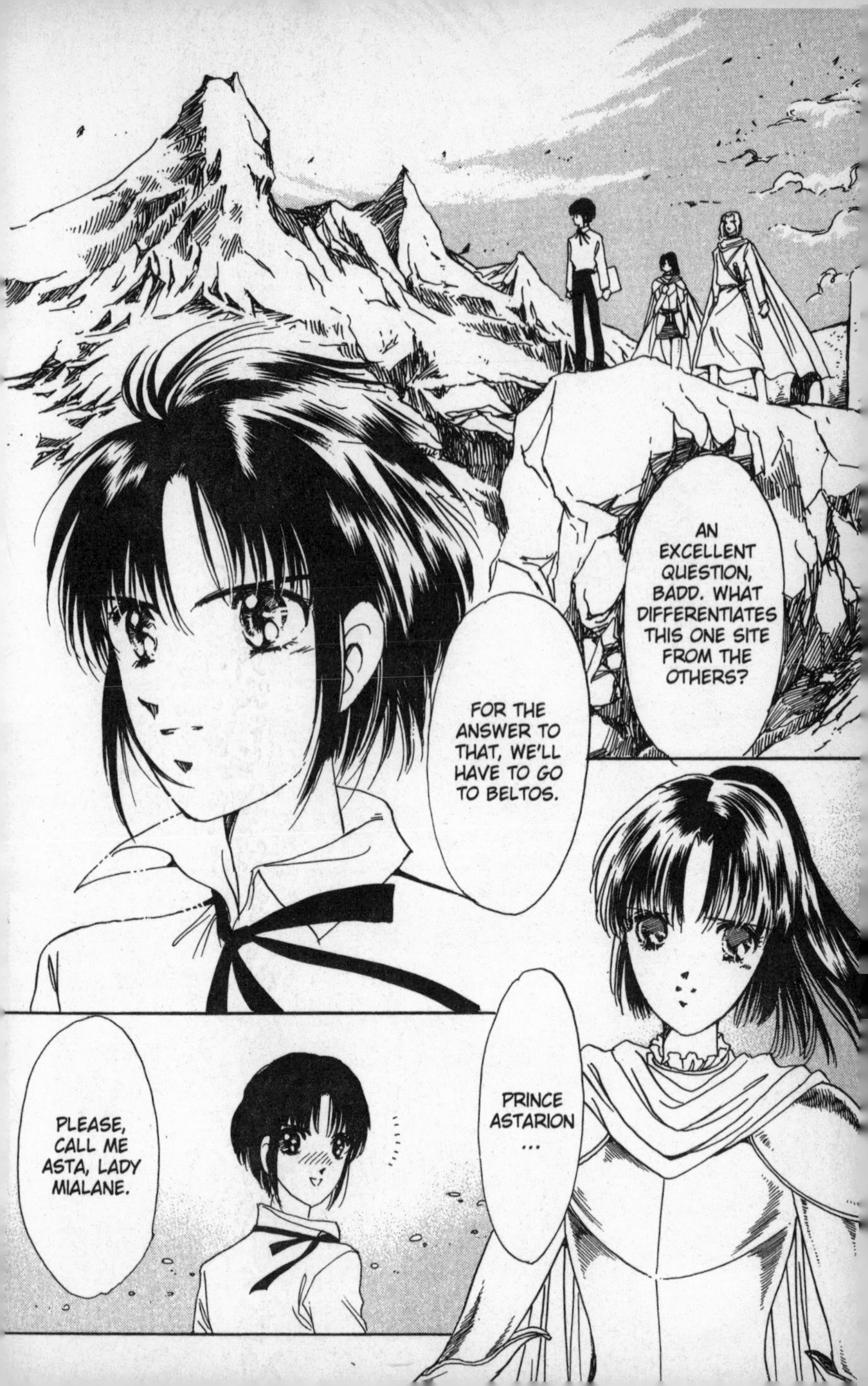
AN EXCELLENT QUESTION, BADD. WHAT DIFFERENTIATES THIS ONE SITE FROM THE OTHERS?
FOR THE ANSWER TO THAT, WE'LL HAVE TO GO TO BELTOS.
PRINCE ASTARION ...
PLEASE, CALL ME ASTA, LADY MIALANE.

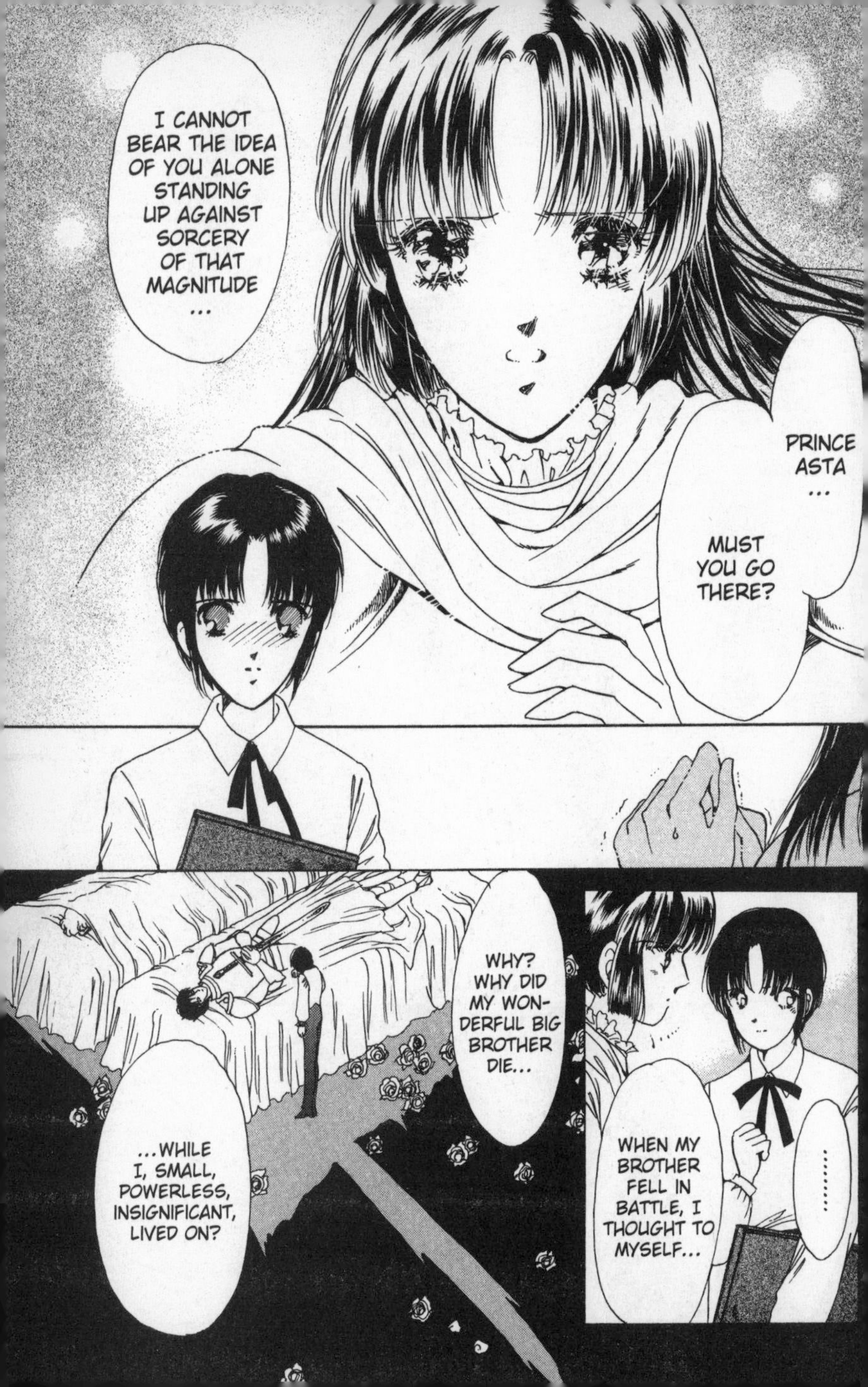
PRINCE ASTA ... MUST YOU GO THERE?
I CANNOT BEAR THE IDEA OF YOU ALONE STANDING UP AGAINST SORCERY OF THAT MAGNITUDE ...
......
WHEN MY BROTHER FELL IN BATTLE, I THOUGHT TO MYSELF...
WHY? WHY DID MY WON-DERFUL BIG BROTHER DIE...
...WHILE I, SMALL, POWERLESS, INSIGNIFICANT, LIVED ON?

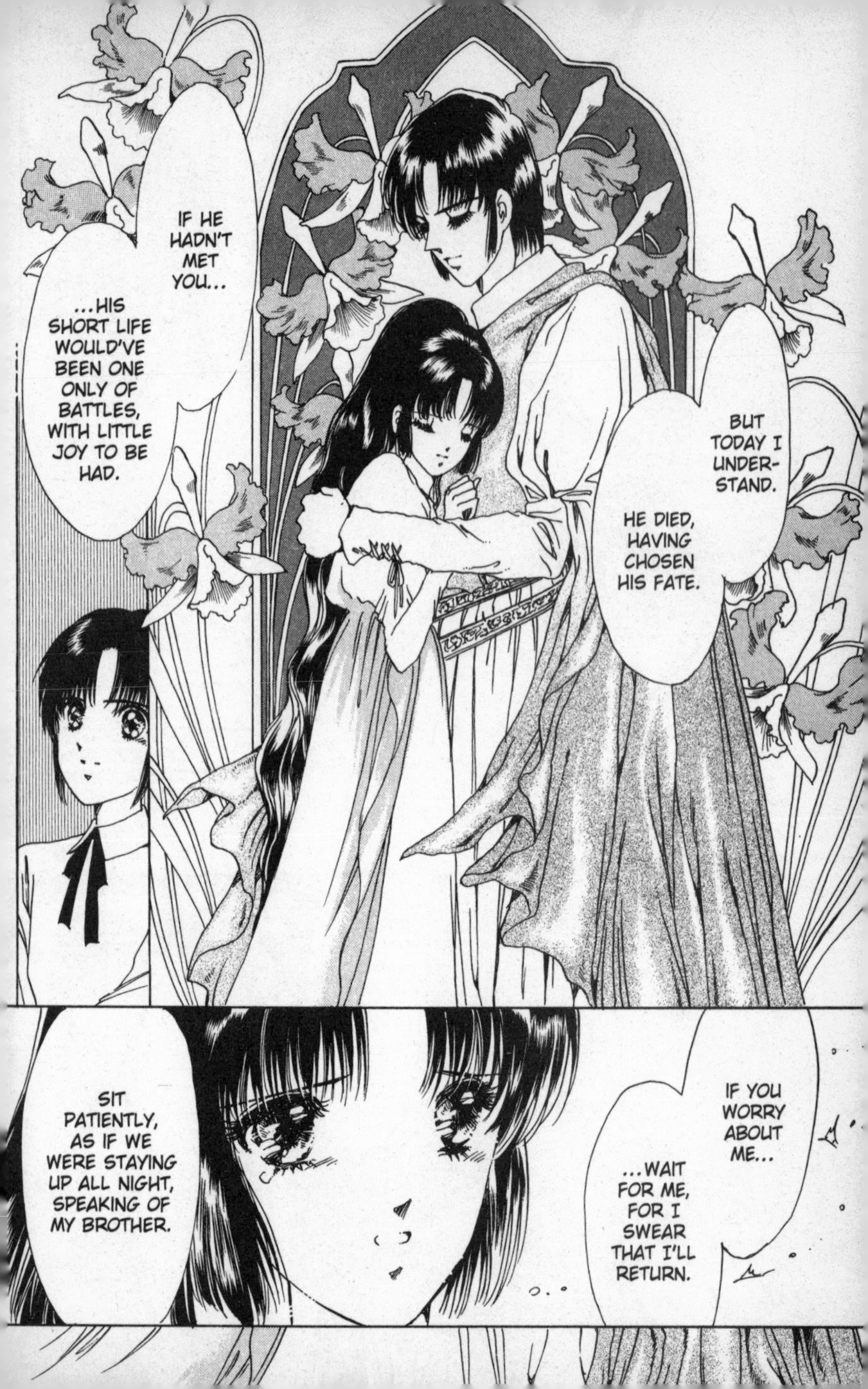
IF HE HADN'T MET YOU...
...HIS SHORT LIFE WOULD'VE BEEN ONE ONLY OF BATTLES, WITH LITTLE JOY TO BE HAD.
BUT TODAY I UNDERSTAND.
HE DIED, HAVING CHOSEN HIS FATE.
IF YOU WORRY ABOUT ME...
...WAIT FOR ME, FOR I SWEAR THAT I'LL RETURN.
SIT PATIENTLY, AS IF WE WERE STAYING UP ALL NIGHT, SPEAKING OF MY BROTHER.

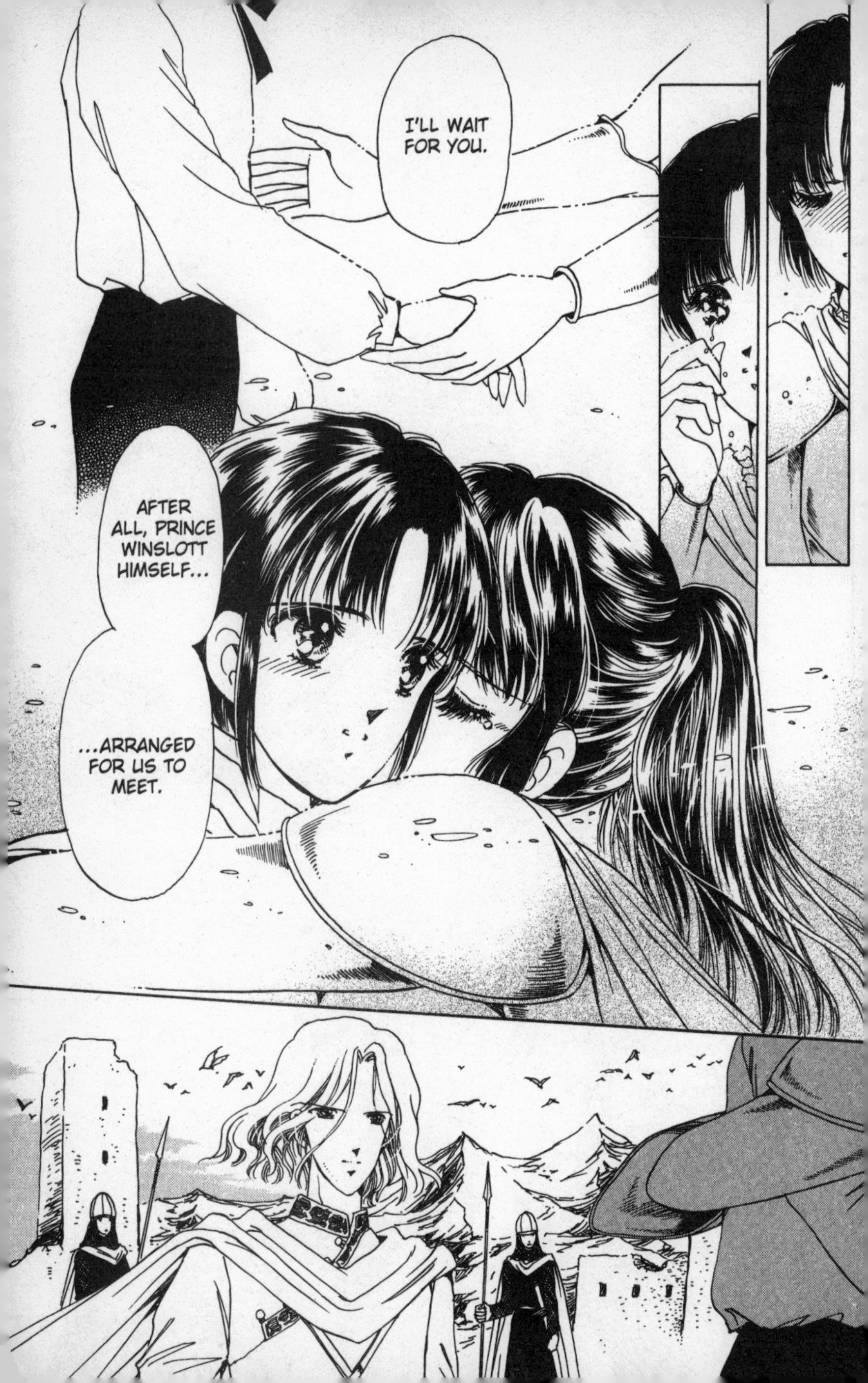
I'LL WAIT FOR YOU.
AFTER ALL, PRINCE WINSLOTT HIMSELF...
...ARRANGED FOR US TO MEET.

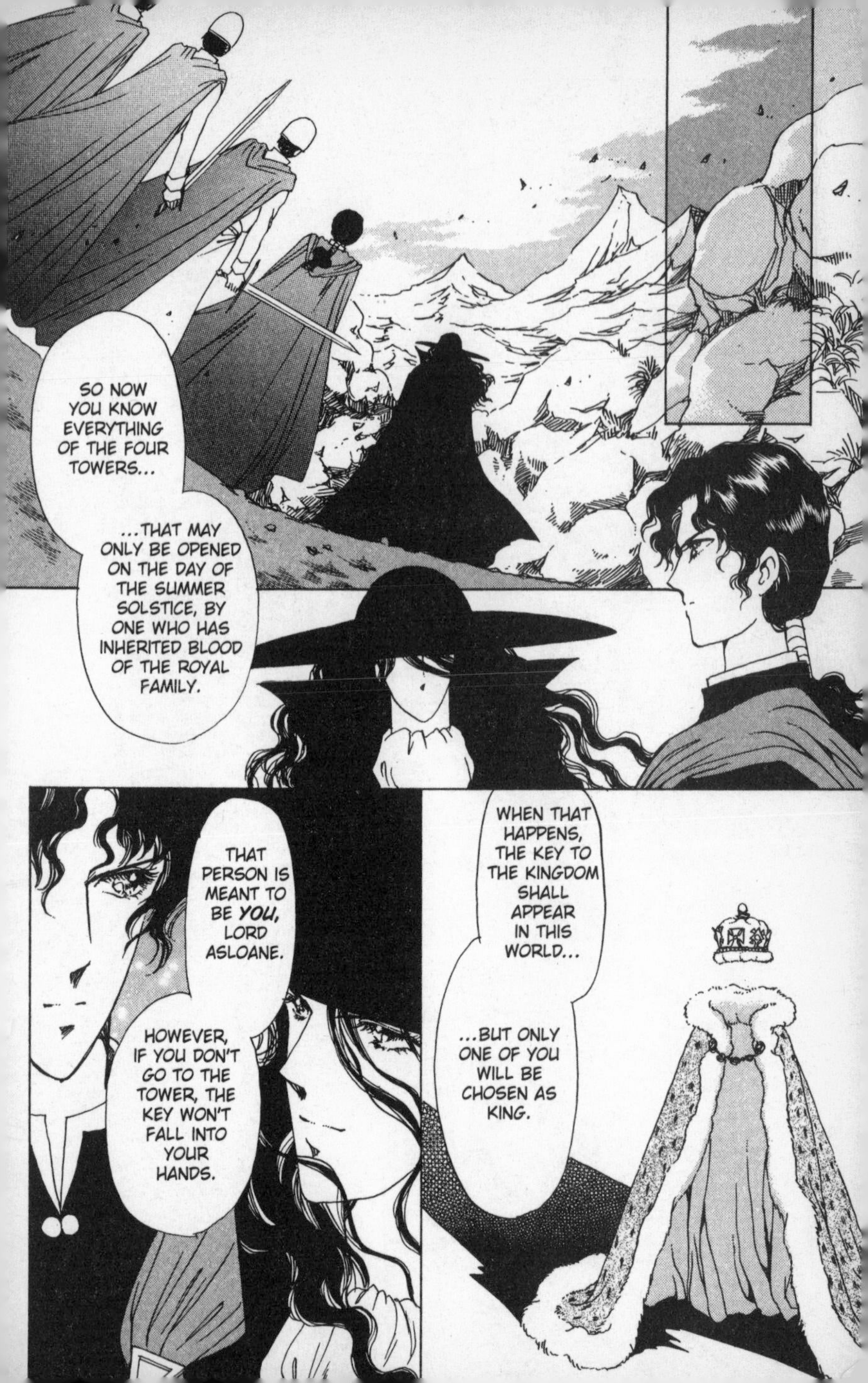
SO NOW YOU KNOW EVERYTHING OF THE FOUR TOWERS...
...THAT MAY ONLY BE OPENED ON THE DAY OF THE SUMMER SOLSTICE, BY ONE WHO HAS INHERITED BLOOD OF THE ROYAL FAMILY.
WHEN THAT HAPPENS, THE KEY TO THE KINGDOM SHALL APPEAR IN THIS WORLD...
...BUT ONLY ONE OF YOU WILL BE CHOSEN AS KING.
THAT PERSON IS MEANT TO BE *YOU,* LORD ASLOANE.
HOWEVER, IF YOU DON'T GO TO THE TOWER, THE KEY WON'T FALL INTO YOUR HANDS.

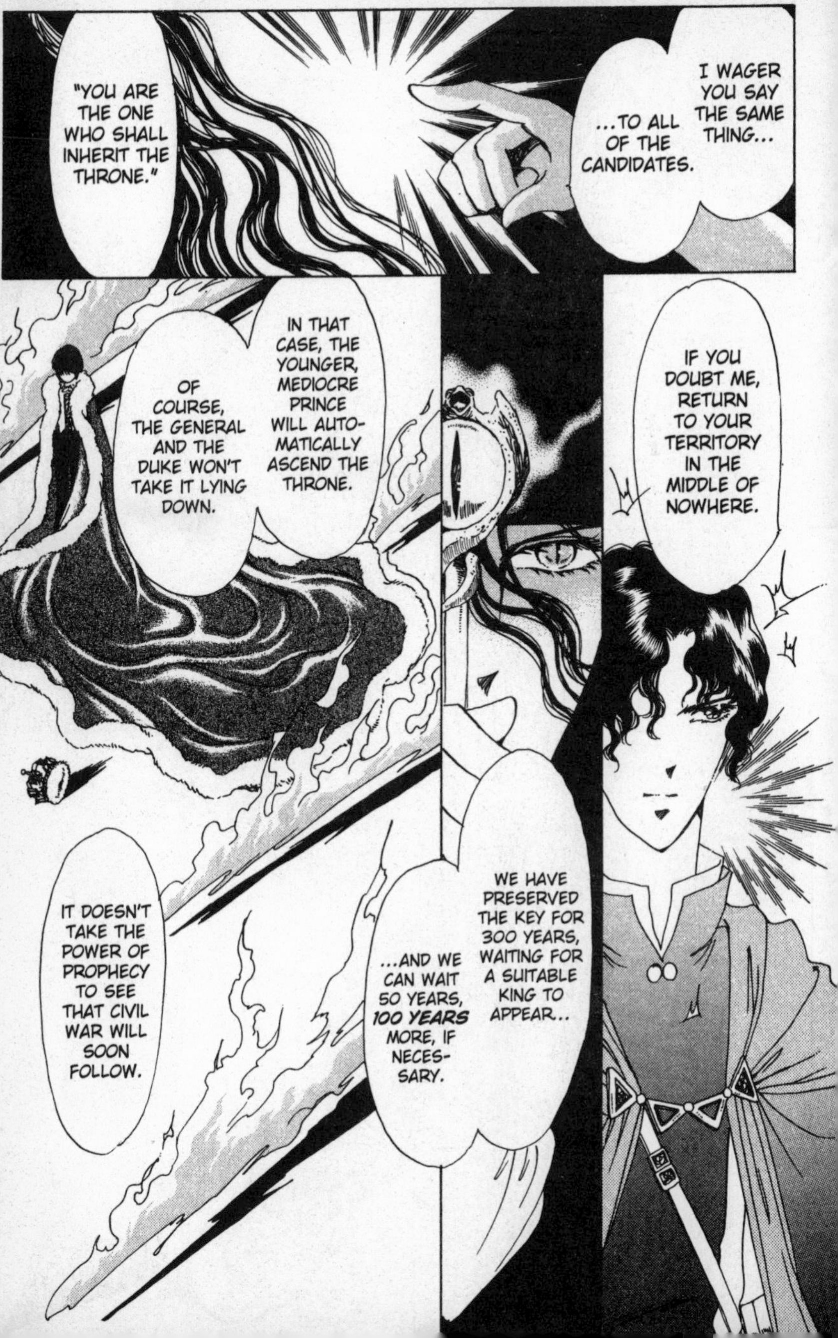
I WAGER YOU SAY THE SAME THING... ...TO ALL OF THE CANDIDATES.
"YOU ARE THE ONE WHO SHALL INHERIT THE THRONE."
IF YOU DOUBT ME, RETURN TO YOUR TERRITORY IN THE MIDDLE OF NOWHERE.
WE HAVE PRESERVED THE KEY FOR 300 YEARS, WAITING FOR A SUITABLE KING TO APPEAR...
...AND WE CAN WAIT 50 YEARS, **100 YEARS** MORE, IF NECES-SARY.
IN THAT CASE, THE YOUNGER, MEDIOCRE PRINCE WILL AUTO-MATICALLY ASCEND THE THRONE.
OF COURSE, THE GENERAL AND THE DUKE WON'T TAKE IT LYING DOWN.
IT DOESN'T TAKE THE POWER OF PROPHECY TO SEE THAT CIVIL WAR WILL SOON FOLLOW.

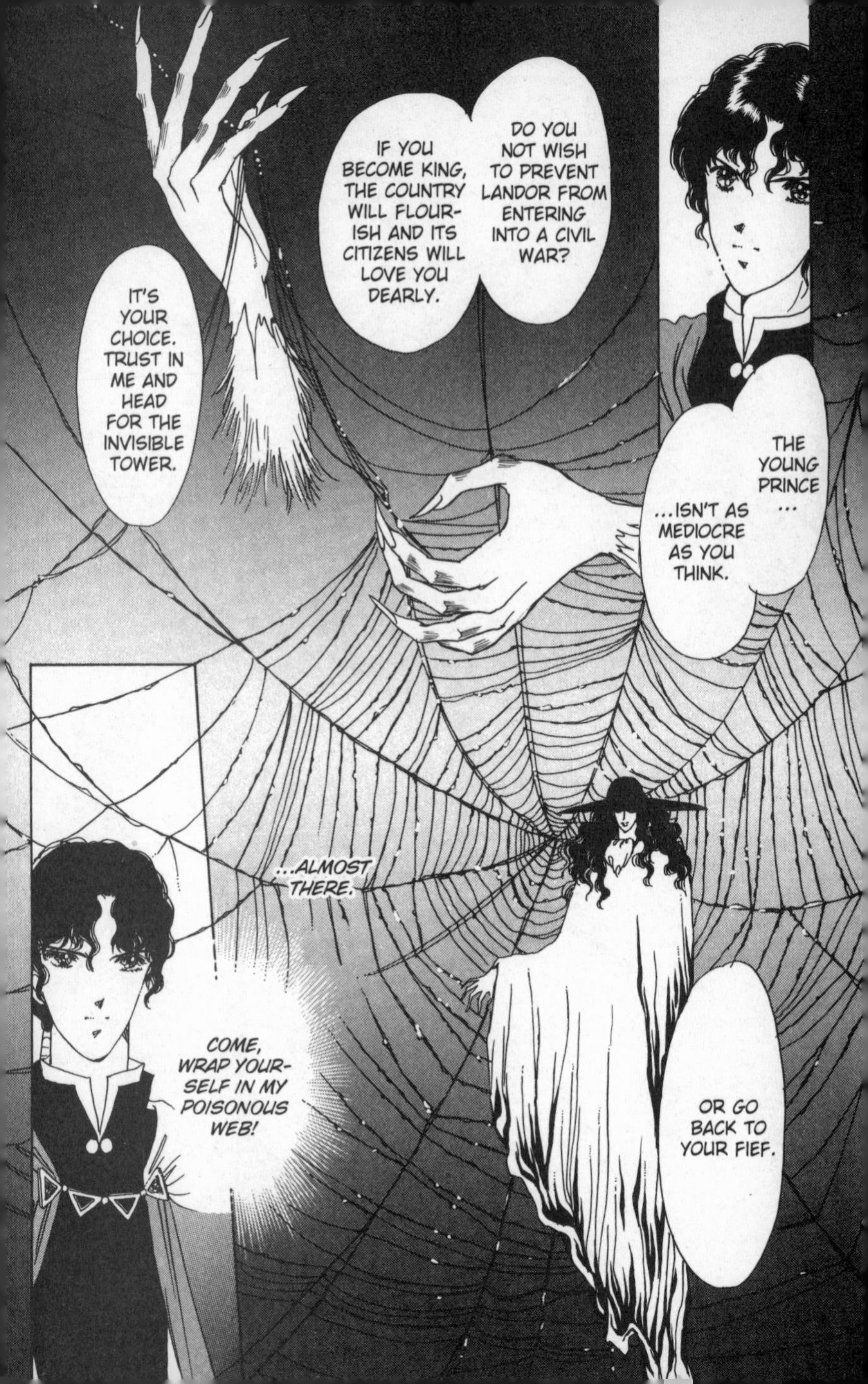
DO YOU NOT WISH TO PREVENT LANDOR FROM ENTERING INTO A CIVIL WAR?
IF YOU BECOME KING, THE COUNTRY WILL FLOUR-ISH AND ITS CITIZENS WILL LOVE YOU DEARLY.
THE YOUNG PRINCE ...
...ISN'T AS MEDIOCRE AS YOU THINK.
IT'S YOUR CHOICE. TRUST IN ME AND HEAD FOR THE INVISIBLE TOWER.
OR GO BACK TO YOUR FIEF.
...ALMOST THERE.
COME, WRAP YOUR-SELF IN MY POISONOUS WEB!

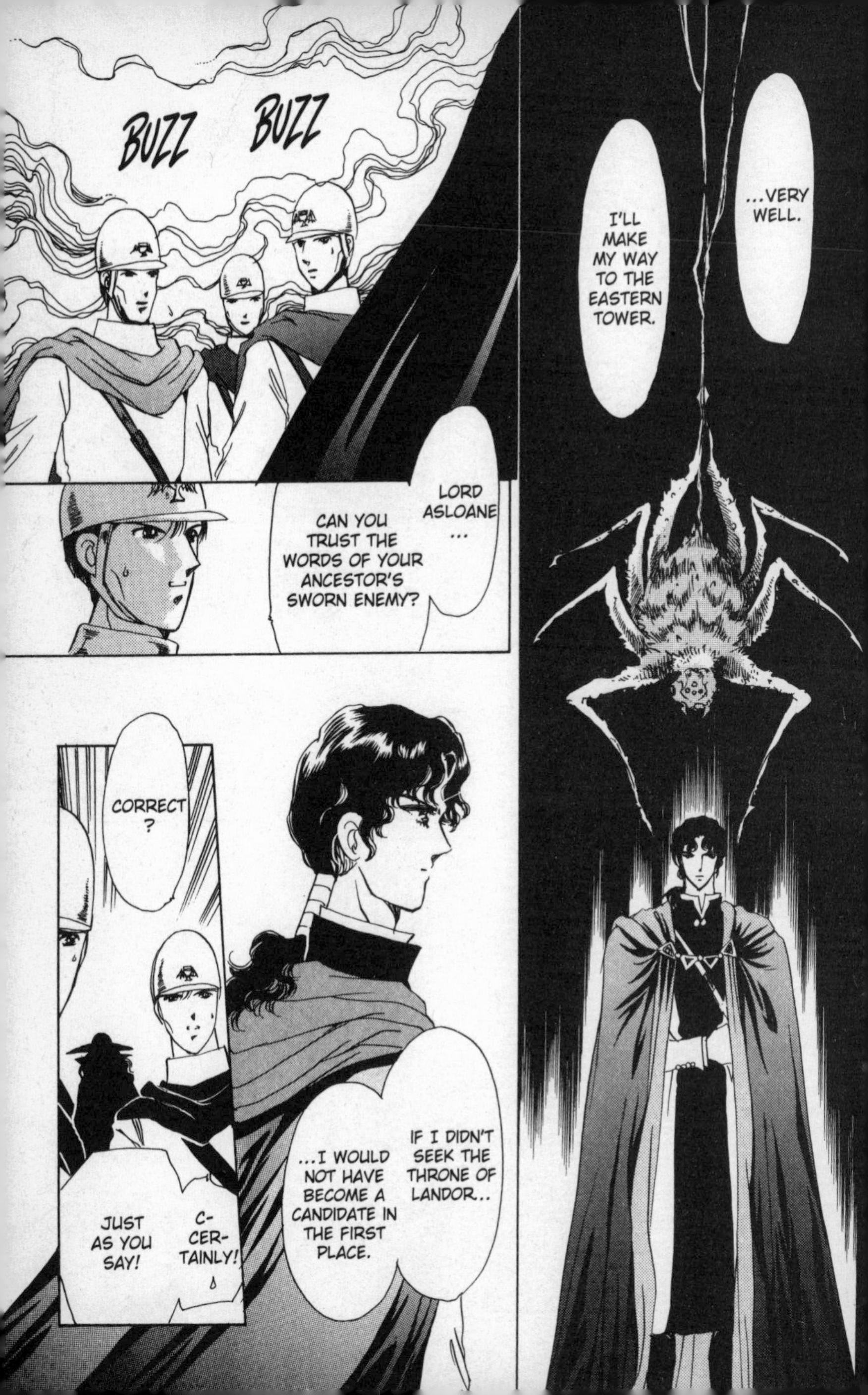
...VERY WELL.
I'LL MAKE MY WAY TO THE EASTERN TOWER.
BUZZ BUZZ
LORD ASLOANE...
CAN YOU TRUST THE WORDS OF YOUR ANCESTOR'S SWORN ENEMY?
IF I DIDN'T SEEK THE THRONE OF LANDOR...
...I WOULD NOT HAVE BECOME A CANDIDATE IN THE FIRST PLACE.
CORRECT?
C-CER-TAINLY!
JUST AS YOU SAY!

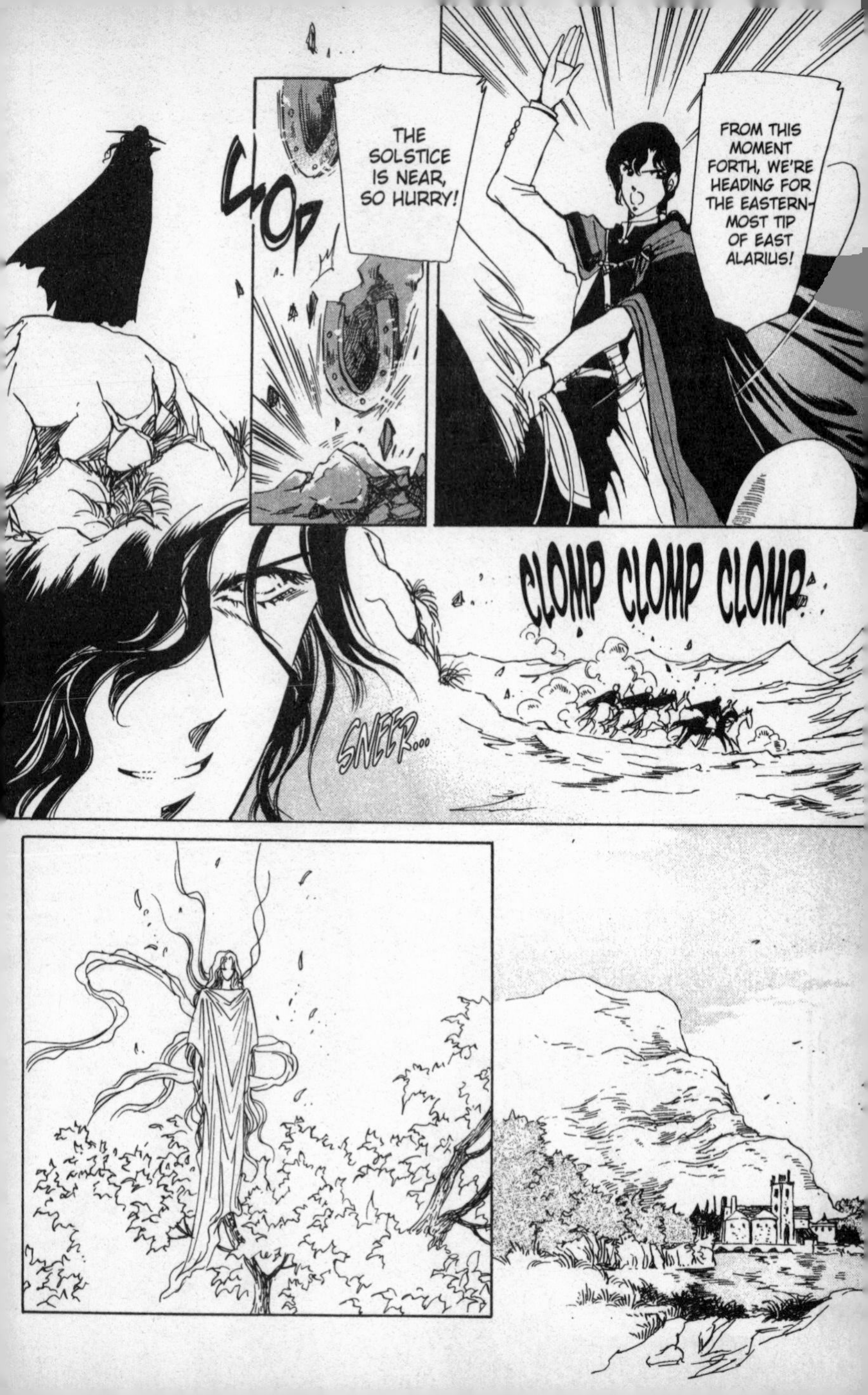
FROM THIS MOMENT FORTH, WE'RE HEADING FOR THE EASTERN-MOST TIP OF EAST ALARIUS!
THE SOLSTICE IS NEAR, SO HURRY!
CHOP
CLOMP CLOMP CLOMP
SNEER...

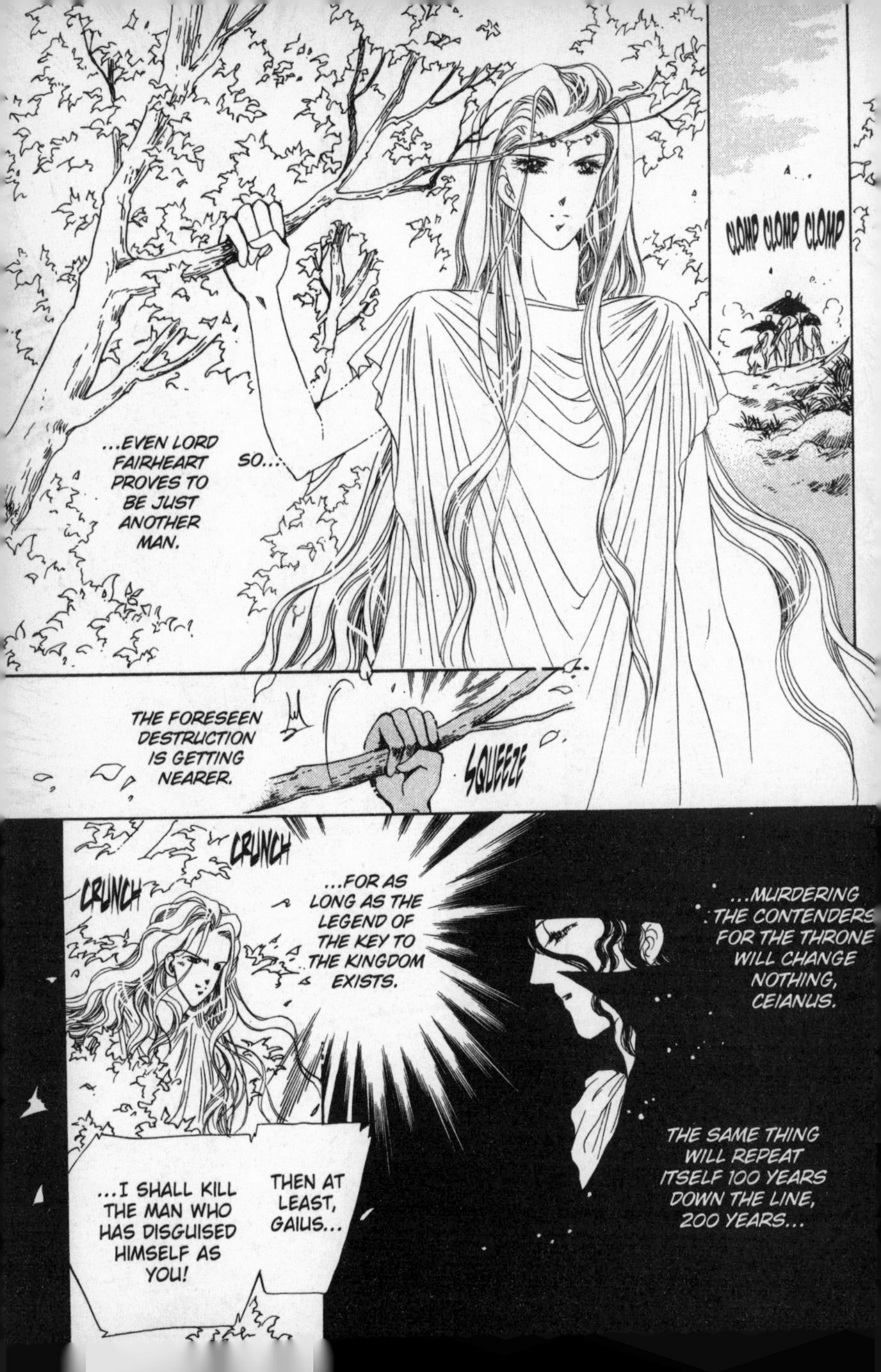
CLOMP CLOMP CLOMP
SO...
...EVEN LORD FAIRHEART PROVES TO BE JUST ANOTHER MAN.
THE FORESEEN DESTRUCTION IS GETTING NEARER.
SQUEEZE
...MURDERING THE CONTENDERS FOR THE THRONE WILL CHANGE NOTHING, CEIANUS.
THE SAME THING WILL REPEAT ITSELF 100 YEARS DOWN THE LINE, 200 YEARS...
...FOR AS LONG AS THE LEGEND OF THE KEY TO THE KINGDOM EXISTS.
CRUNCH
CRUNCH
THEN AT LEAST, GAIUS...
...I SHALL KILL THE MAN WHO HAS DISGUISED HIMSELF AS YOU!

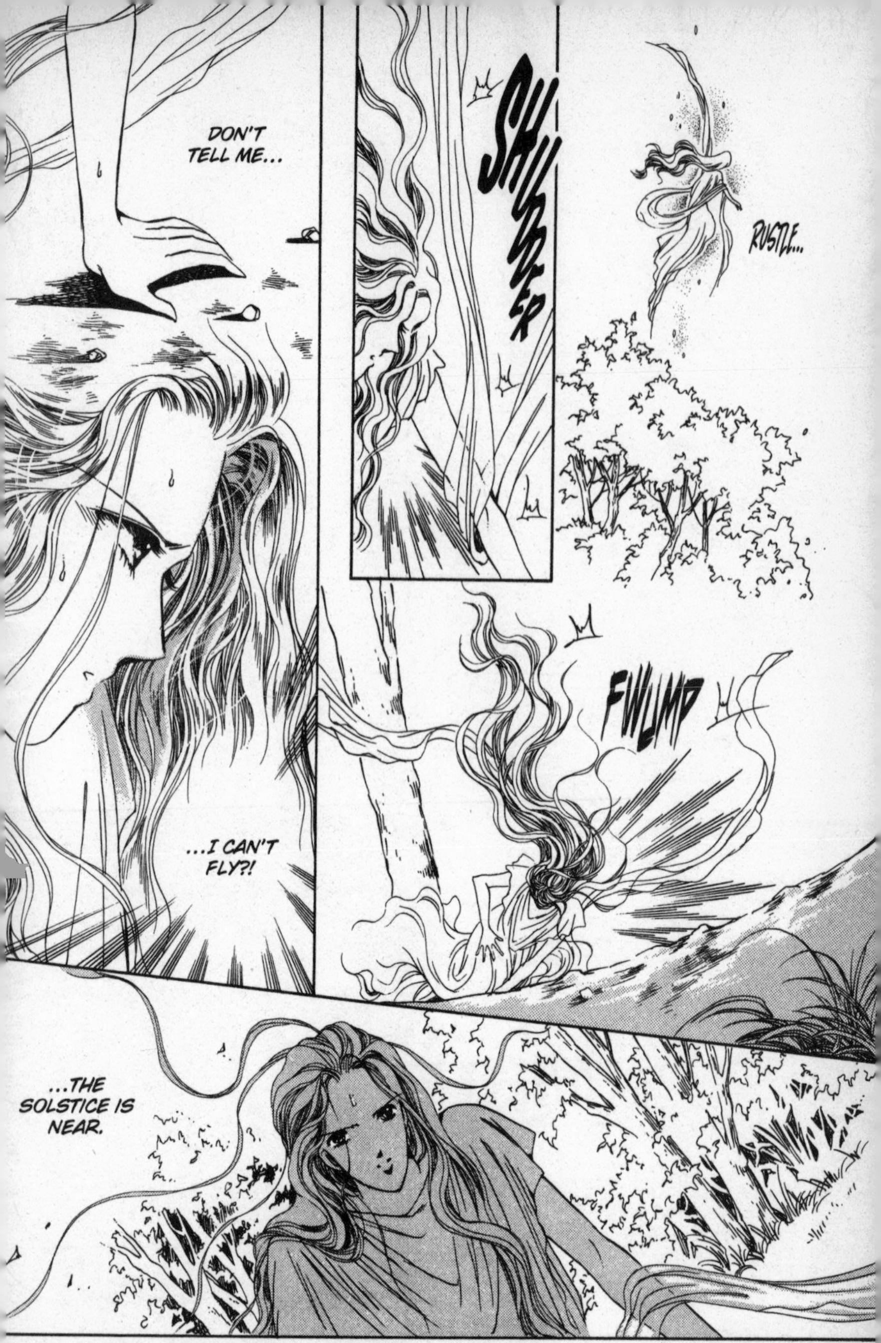
RUSTLE...
SHUDDER
FWUMP
DON'T TELL ME...
...I CAN'T FLY?!
...THE SOLSTICE IS NEAR.

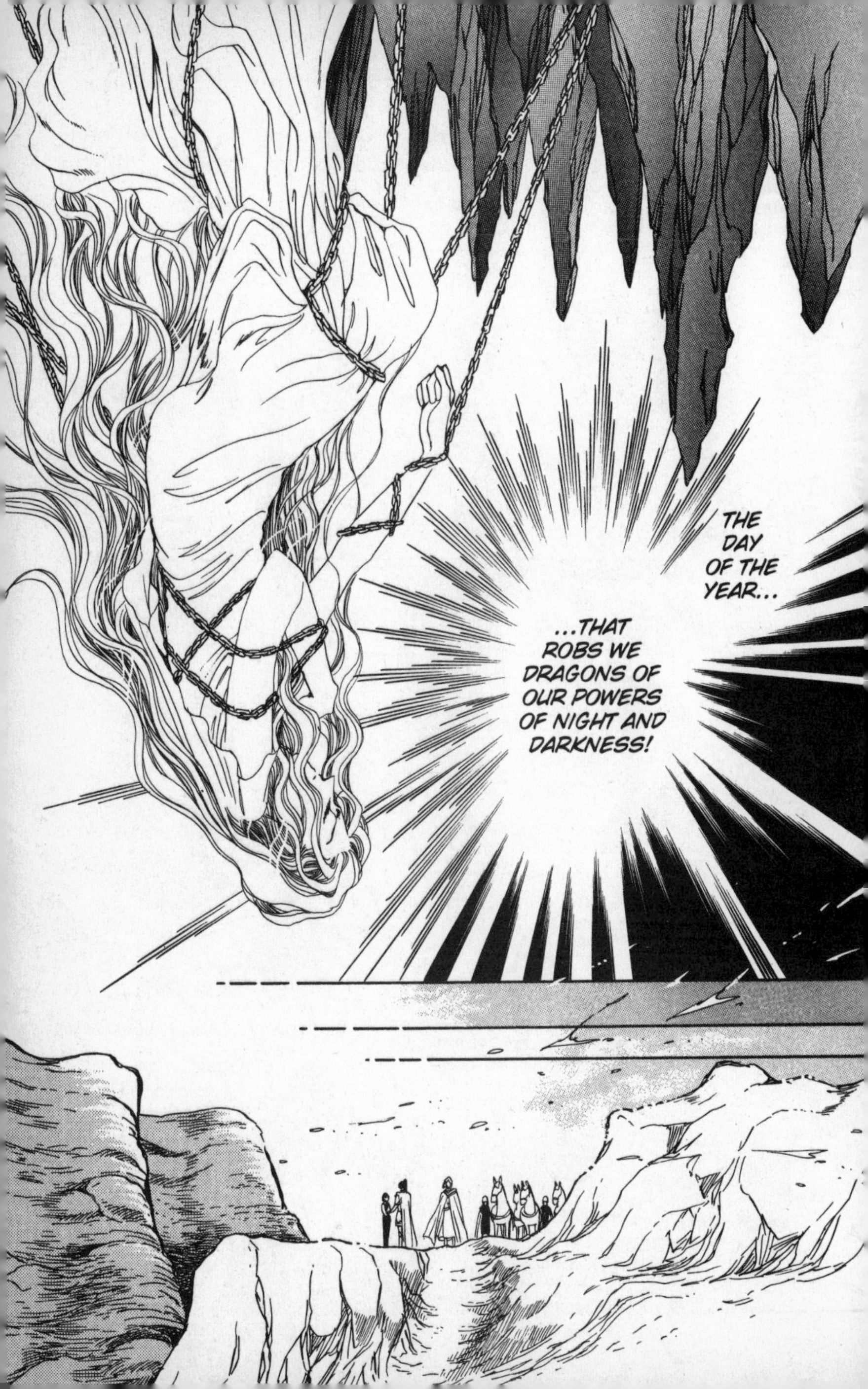
THE DAY OF THE YEAR...
...THAT ROBS WE DRAGONS OF OUR POWERS OF NIGHT AND DARKNESS!

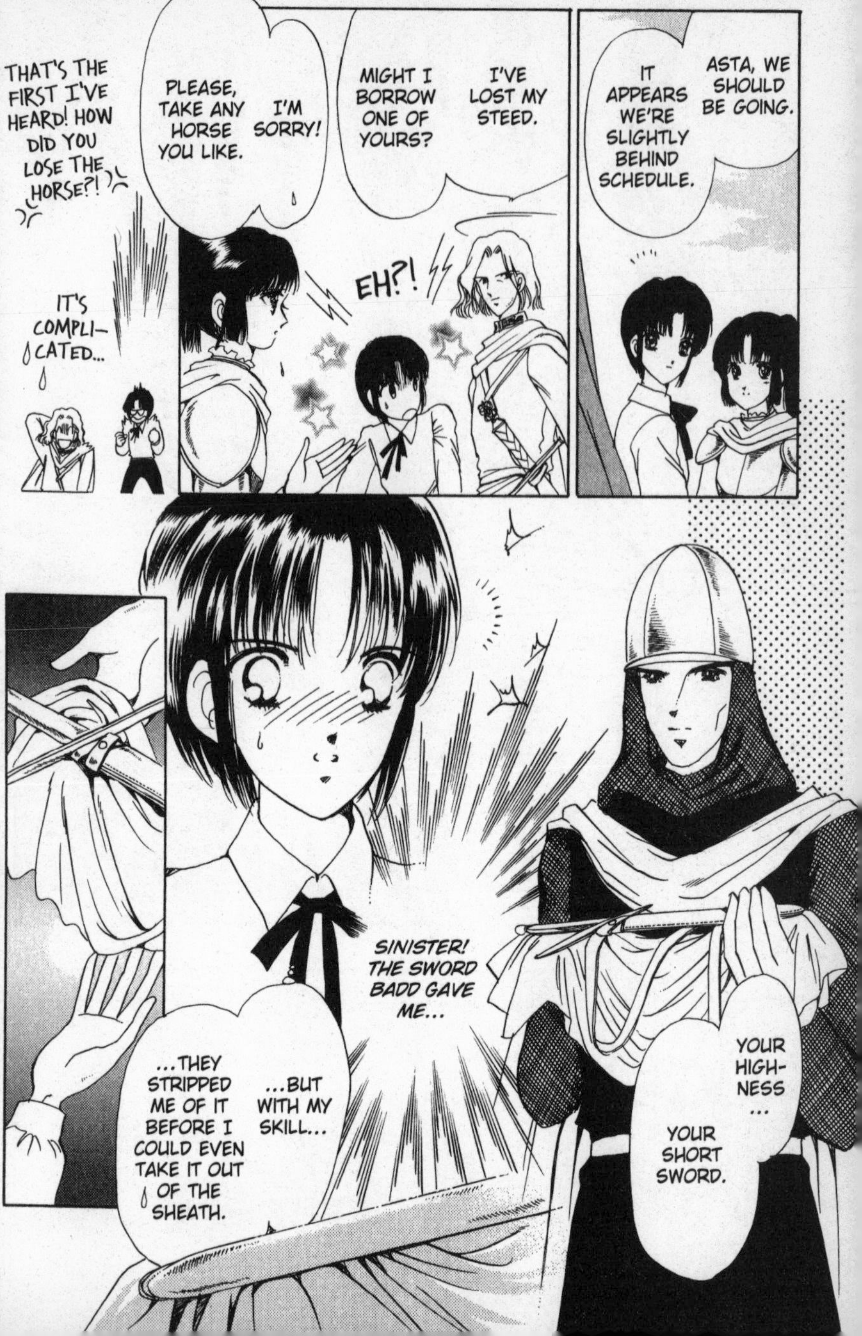
ASTA, WE SHOULD BE GOING.
IT APPEARS WE'RE SLIGHTLY BEHIND SCHEDULE.
I'VE LOST MY STEED.
MIGHT I BORROW ONE OF YOURS?
I'M SORRY!
PLEASE, TAKE ANY HORSE YOU LIKE.
EH?!
THAT'S THE FIRST I'VE HEARD! HOW DID YOU LOSE THE HORSE?!
IT'S COMPLI-CATED...
YOUR HIGH-NESS...
YOUR SHORT SWORD.
SINISTER! THE SWORD BADD GAVE ME...
...BUT WITH MY SKILL...
...THEY STRIPPED ME OF IT BEFORE I COULD EVEN TAKE IT OUT OF THE SHEATH.

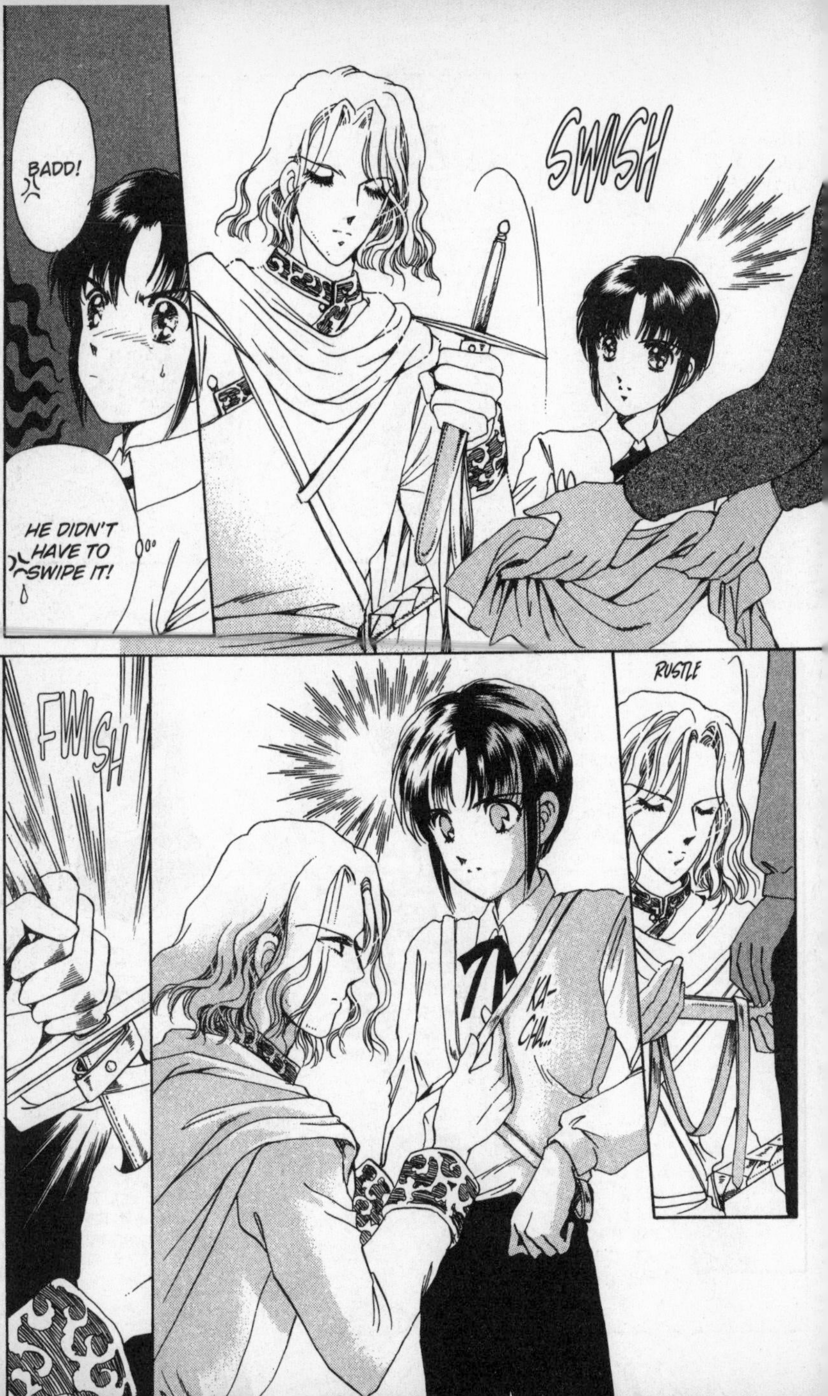
SWISH
BADD!
HE DIDN'T HAVE TO SWIPE IT!
RUSTLE
KA-CHA...
FWISH

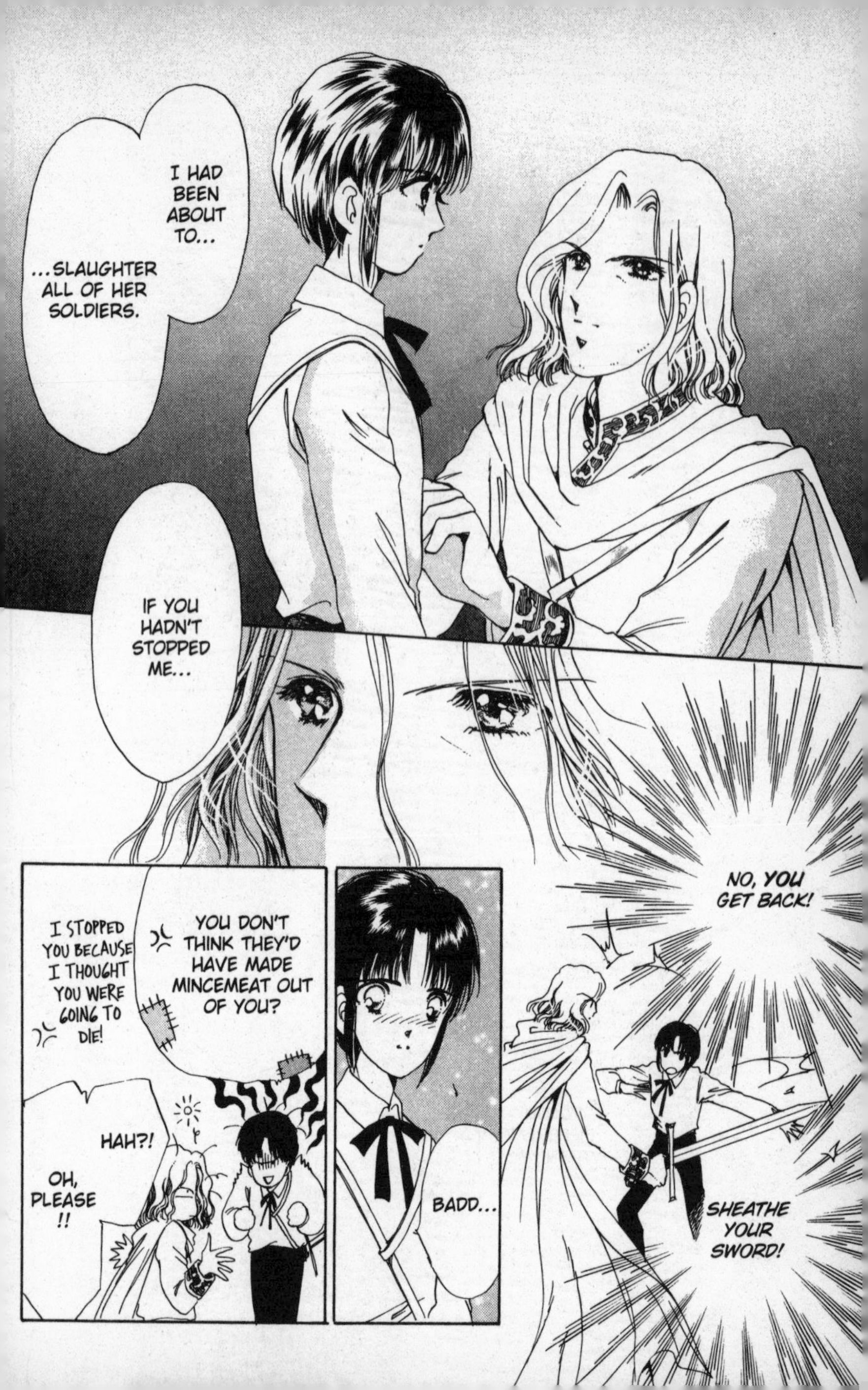
I HAD BEEN ABOUT TO...
...SLAUGHTER ALL OF HER SOLDIERS.
IF YOU HADN'T STOPPED ME...
NO, YOU GET BACK!
SHEATHE YOUR SWORD!
BADD...
YOU DON'T THINK THEY'D HAVE MADE MINCEMEAT OUT OF YOU?
I STOPPED YOU BECAUSE I THOUGHT YOU WERE GOING TO DIE!
HAH?!
OH, PLEASE !!

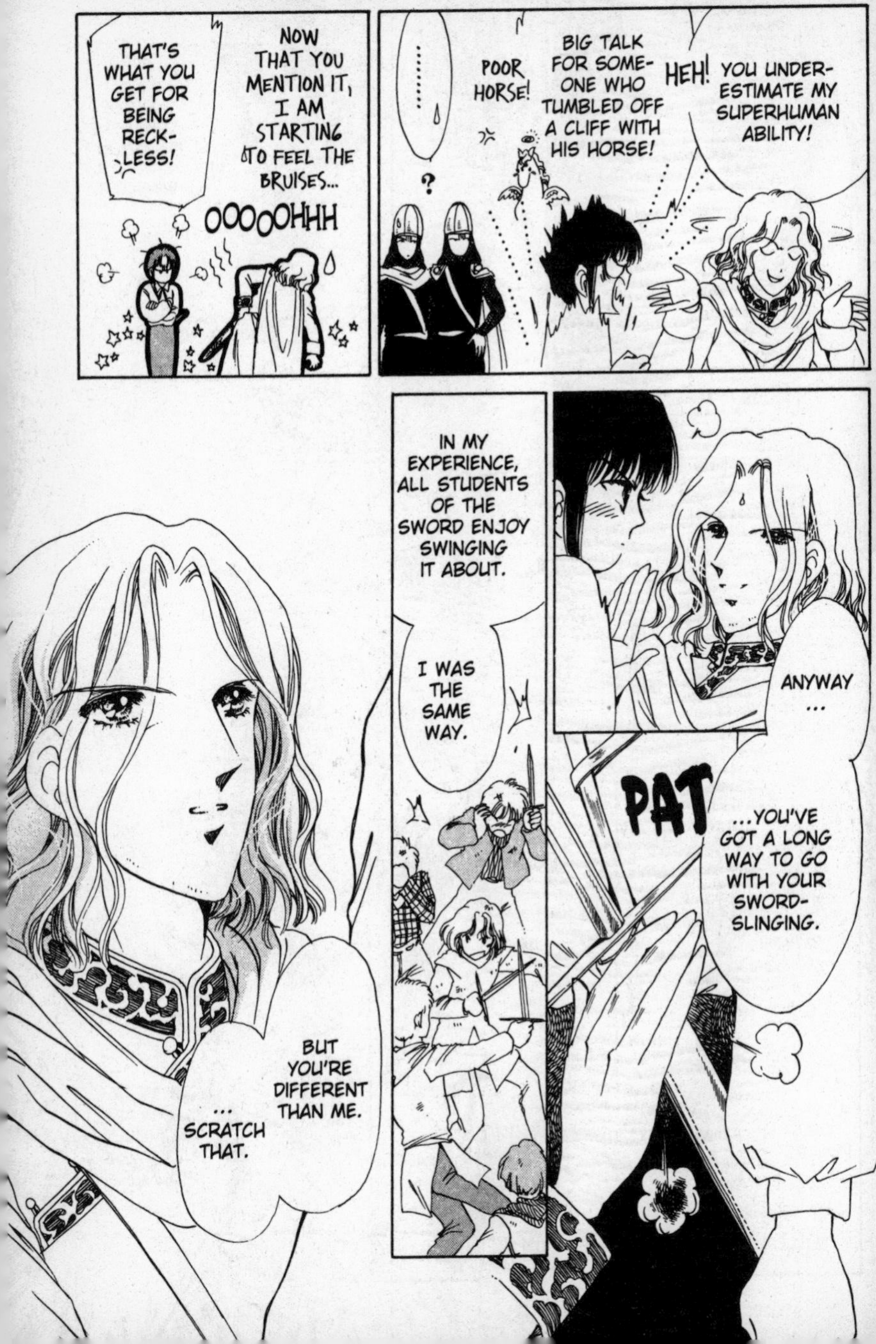
YOU UNDER-ESTIMATE MY SUPERHUMAN ABILITY!
HEH!
BIG TALK FOR SOME-ONE WHO TUMBLED OFF A CLIFF WITH HIS HORSE!
POOR HORSE!
......
?
NOW THAT YOU MENTION IT, I AM STARTING TO FEEL THE BRUISES...
OOOOOHHH
THAT'S WHAT YOU GET FOR BEING RECK-LESS!
ANYWAY ...
PAT
...YOU'VE GOT A LONG WAY TO GO WITH YOUR SWORD-SLINGING.
IN MY EXPERIENCE, ALL STUDENTS OF THE SWORD ENJOY SWINGING IT ABOUT.
I WAS THE SAME WAY.
BUT YOU'RE DIFFERENT THAN ME.
... SCRATCH THAT.

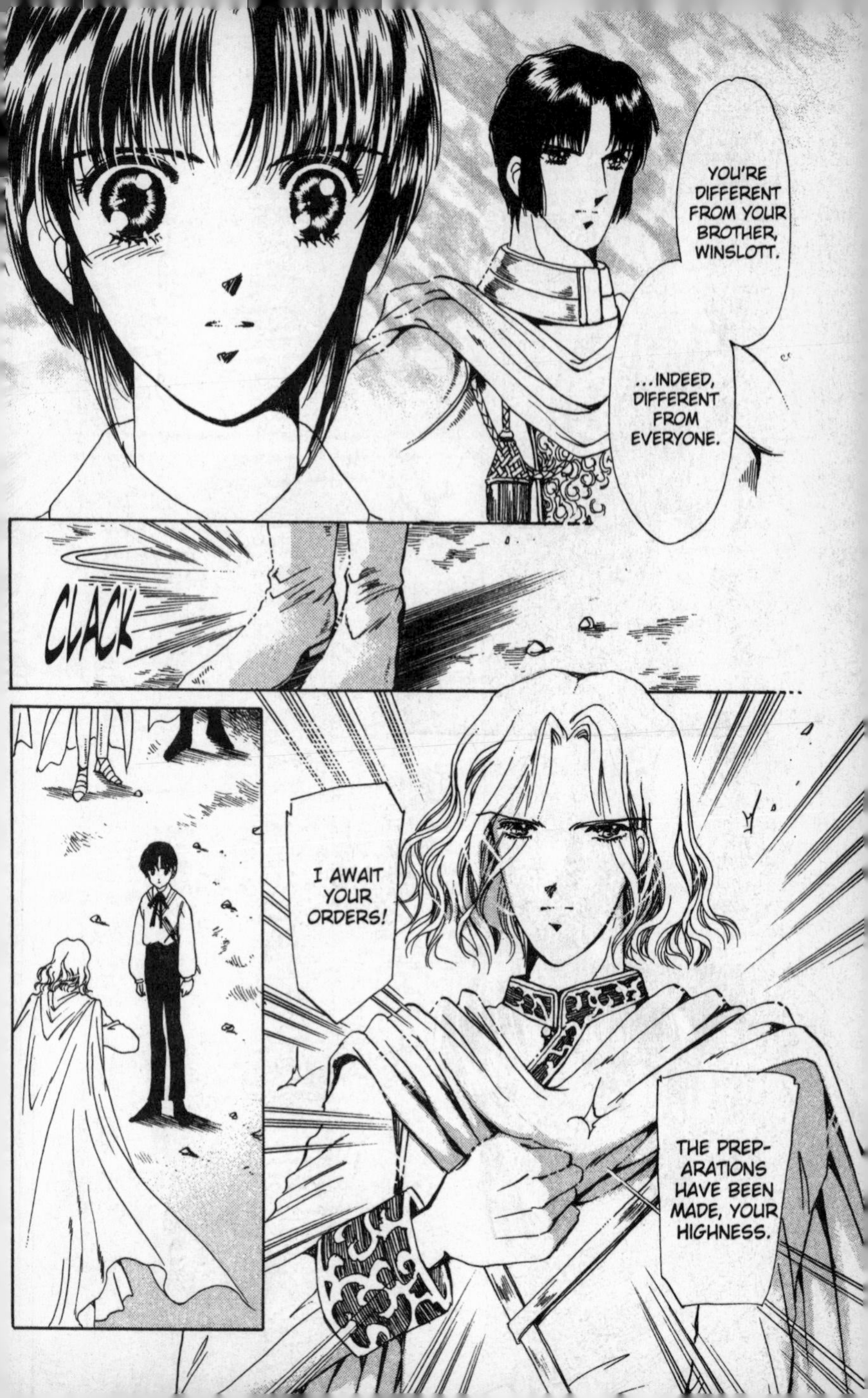
YOU'RE DIFFERENT FROM YOUR BROTHER, WINSLOTT.
...INDEED, DIFFERENT FROM EVERYONE.
CLACK
I AWAIT YOUR ORDERS!
THE PREPARATIONS HAVE BEEN MADE, YOUR HIGHNESS.

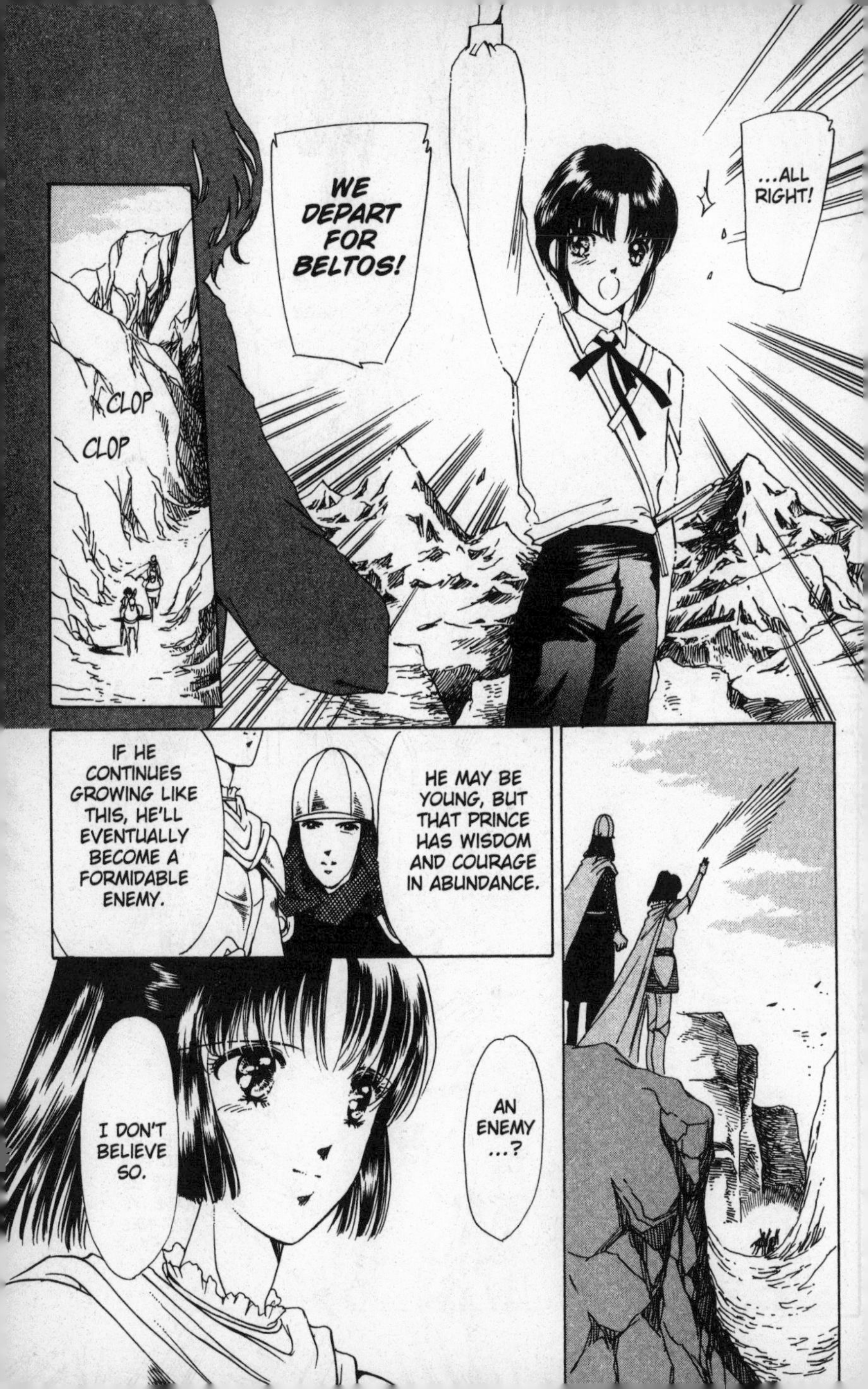
...ALL RIGHT!
WE DEPART FOR BELTOS!
CLOP
CLOP
HE MAY BE YOUNG, BUT THAT PRINCE HAS WISDOM AND COURAGE IN ABUNDANCE.
IF HE CONTINUES GROWING LIKE THIS, HE'LL EVENTUALLY BECOME A FORMIDABLE ENEMY.
AN ENEMY ...?
I DON'T BELIEVE SO.

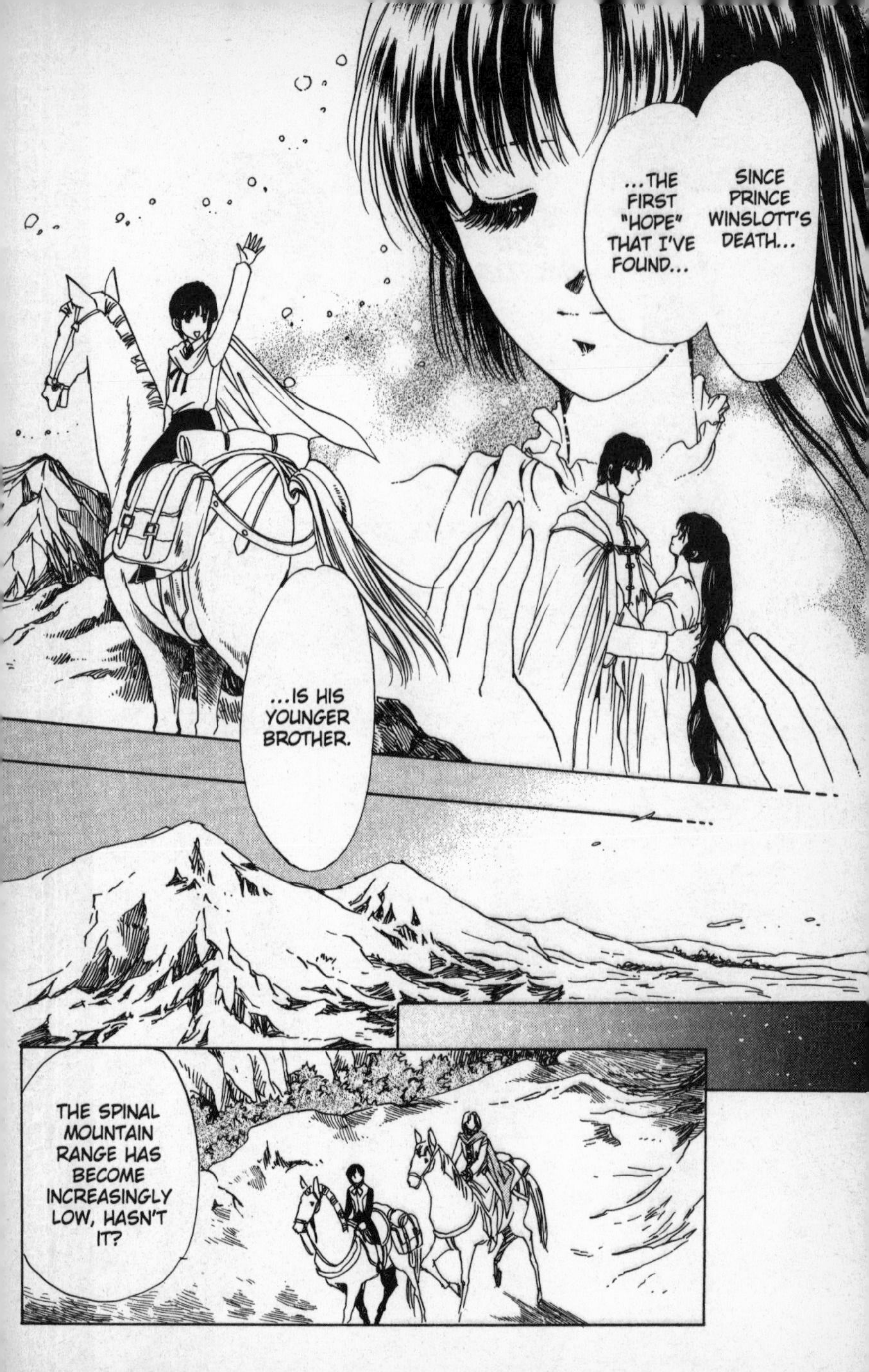
SINCE PRINCE WINSLOTT'S DEATH...
...THE FIRST "HOPE" THAT I'VE FOUND...
...IS HIS YOUNGER BROTHER.
THE SPINAL MOUNTAIN RANGE HAS BECOME INCREASINGLY LOW, HASN'T IT?

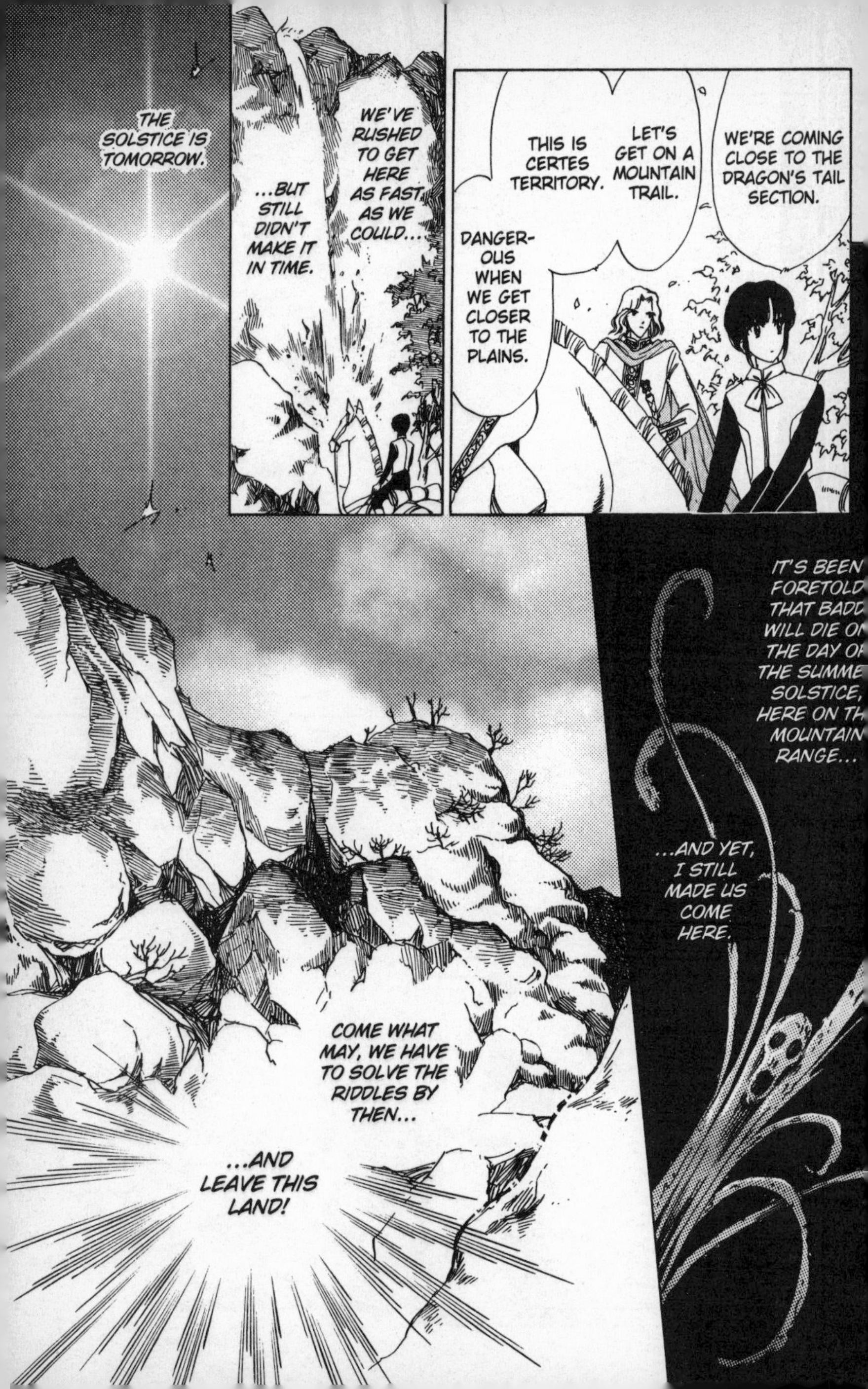
WE'RE COMING CLOSE TO THE DRAGON'S TAIL SECTION.
LET'S GET ON A MOUNTAIN TRAIL.
THIS IS CERTES TERRITORY.
DANGER-OUS WHEN WE GET CLOSER TO THE PLAINS.
WE'VE RUSHED TO GET HERE AS FAST AS WE COULD...
...BUT STILL DIDN'T MAKE IT IN TIME.
THE SOLSTICE IS TOMORROW.
IT'S BEEN FORETOLD THAT BADD WILL DIE ON THE DAY OF THE SUMME SOLSTICE, HERE ON TH MOUNTAIN RANGE...
...AND YET, I STILL MADE US COME HERE.
COME WHAT MAY, WE HAVE TO SOLVE THE RIDDLES BY THEN...
...AND LEAVE THIS LAND!

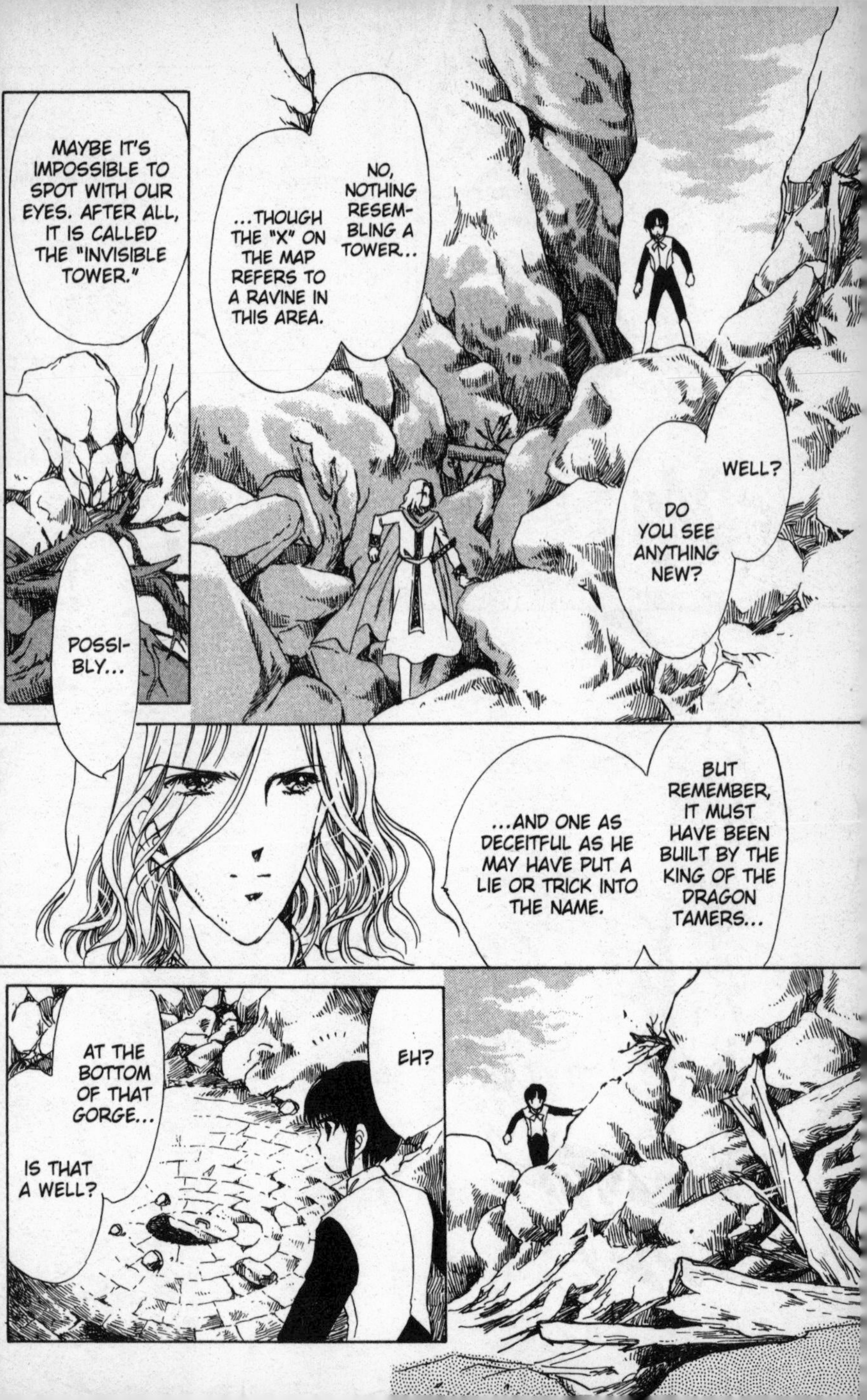
WELL?
DO YOU SEE ANYTHING NEW?
NO, NOTHING RESEMBLING A TOWER...
...THOUGH THE "X" ON THE MAP REFERS TO A RAVINE IN THIS AREA.
MAYBE IT'S IMPOSSIBLE TO SPOT WITH OUR EYES. AFTER ALL, IT IS CALLED THE "INVISIBLE TOWER."
POSSIBLY...
BUT REMEMBER, IT MUST HAVE BEEN BUILT BY THE KING OF THE DRAGON TAMERS...
...AND ONE AS DECEITFUL AS HE MAY HAVE PUT A LIE OR TRICK INTO THE NAME.
EH?
AT THE BOTTOM OF THAT GORGE...
IS THAT A WELL?

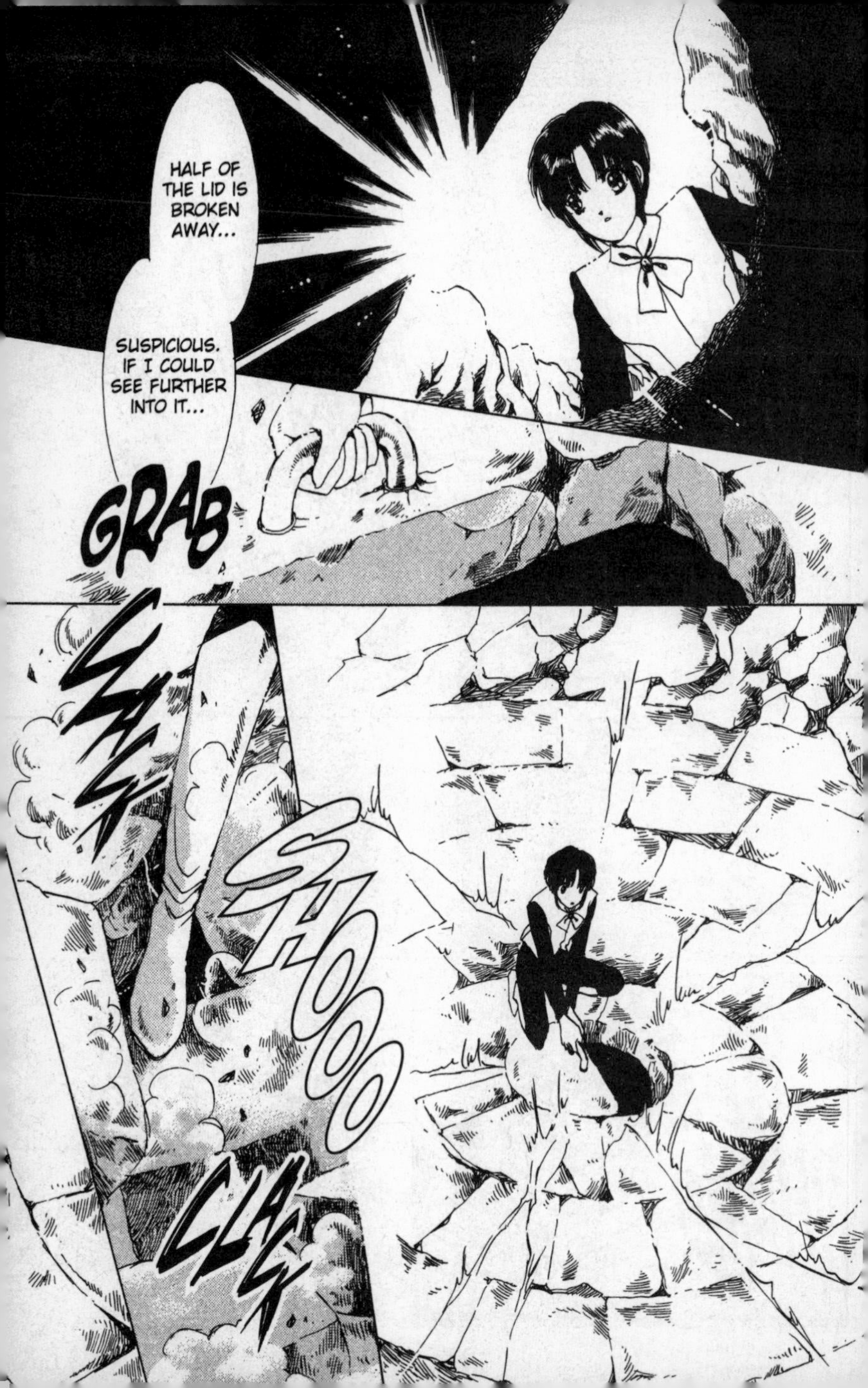
HALF OF THE LID IS BROKEN AWAY...
SUSPICIOUS. IF I COULD SEE FURTHER INTO IT...
GRAB
SHOOOO
CLACK
WHACK

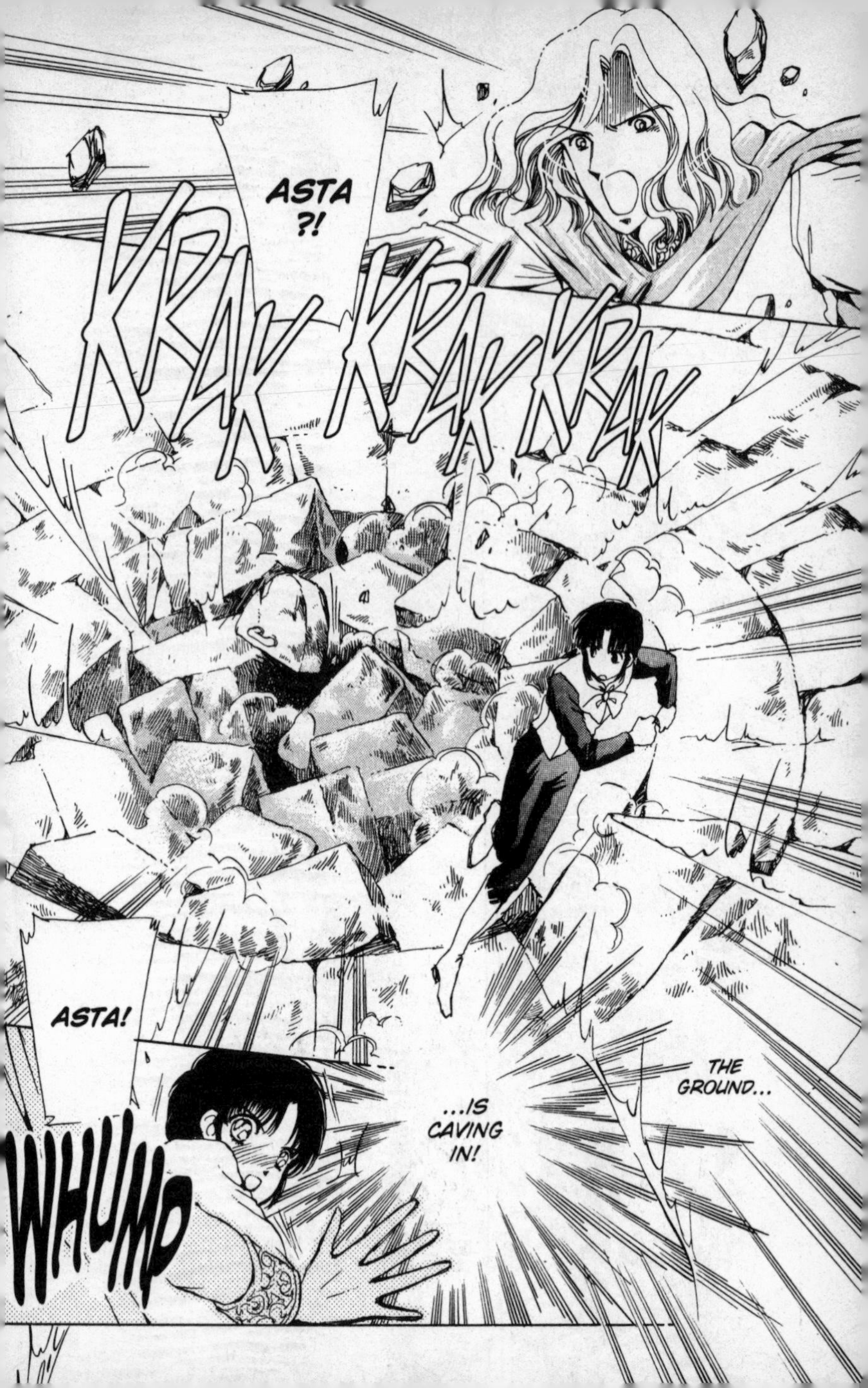
ASTA ?!
KRAK KRAK KRAK
ASTA!
THE GROUND...
...IS CAVING IN!
WHUMP

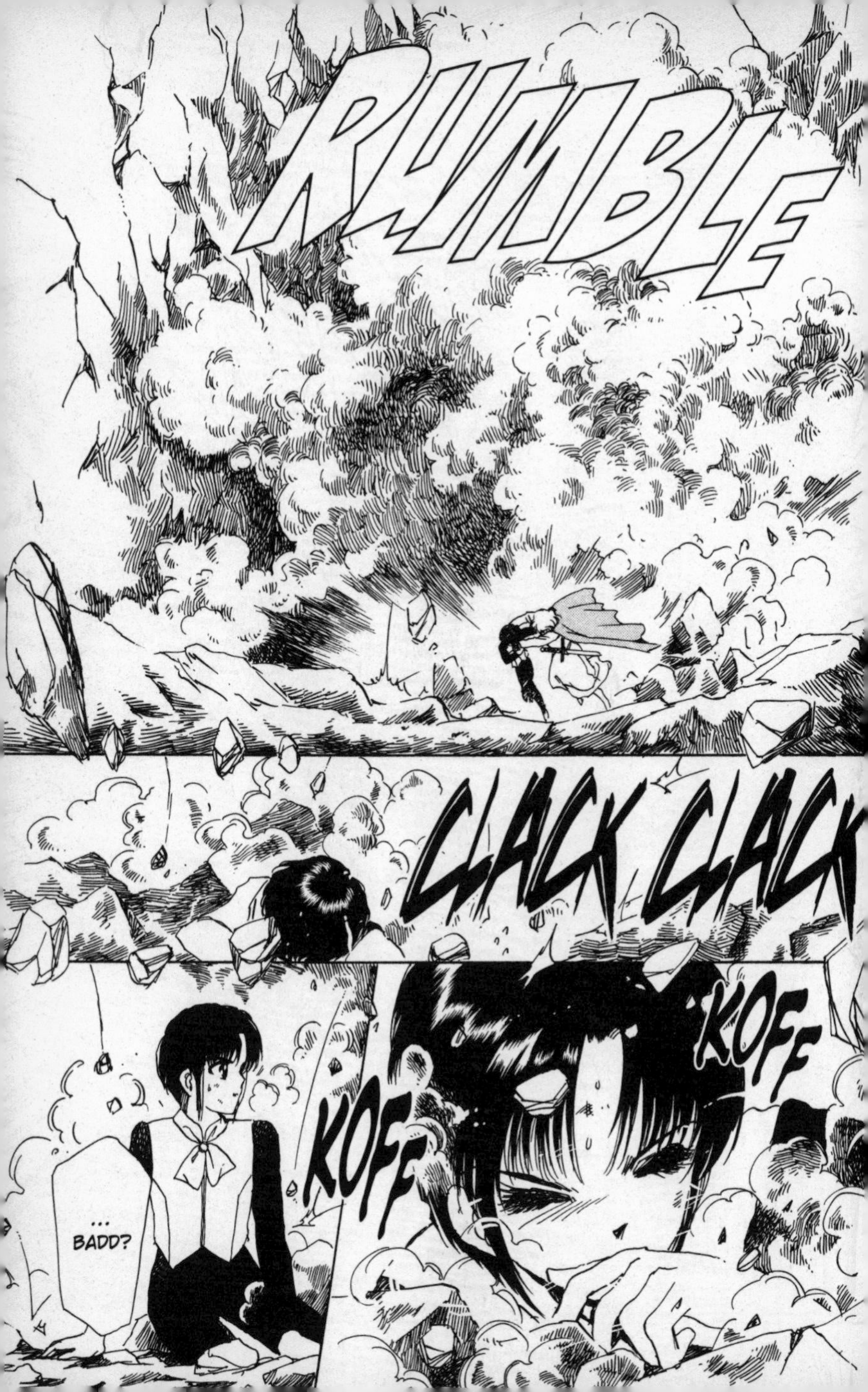
RUMBLE
CLACK CLACK
KOFF
KOFF
... BADD?

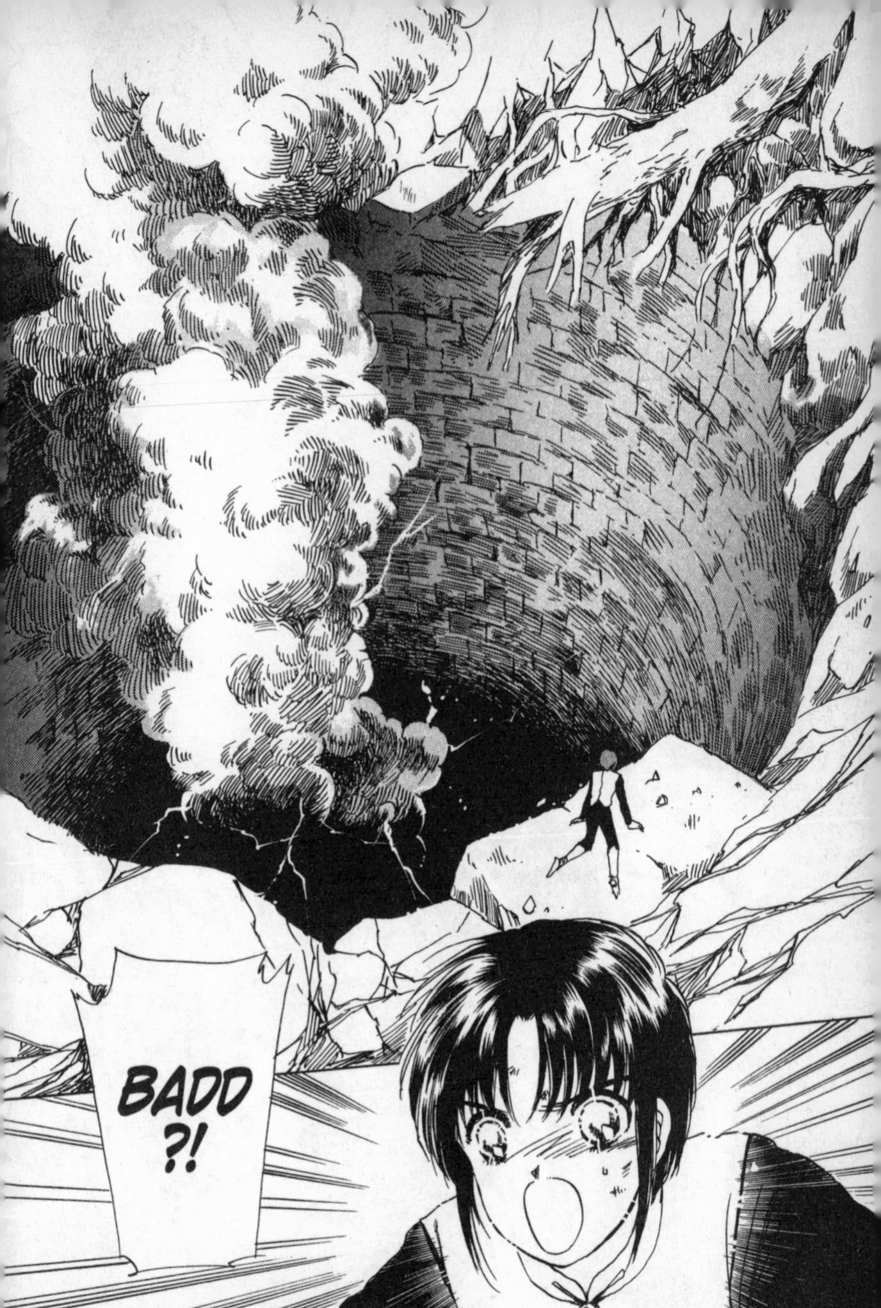
BADD ?!

Chapter Fifteen: The End

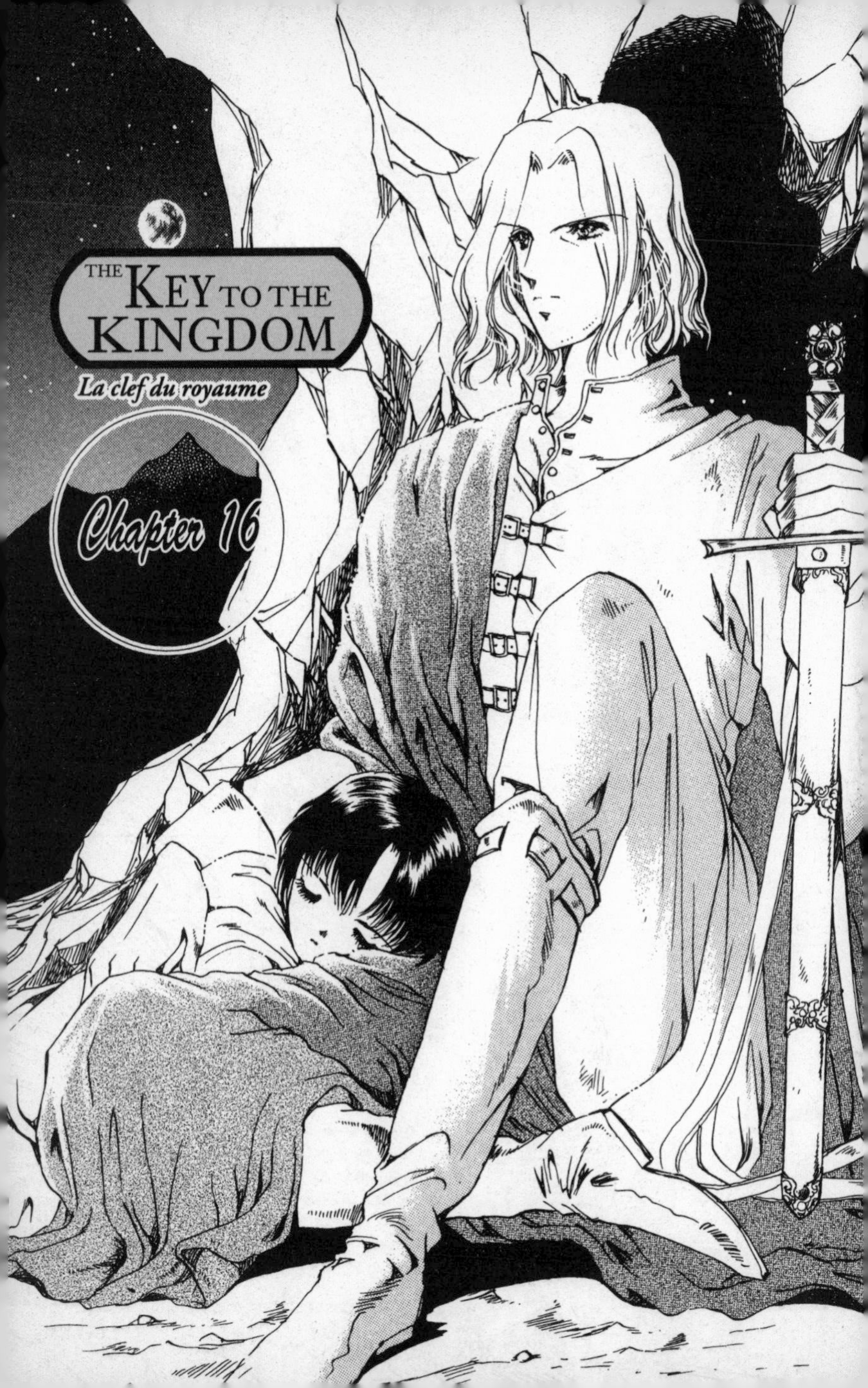
THE KEY TO THE KINGDOM
La clef du royaume
Chapter 16

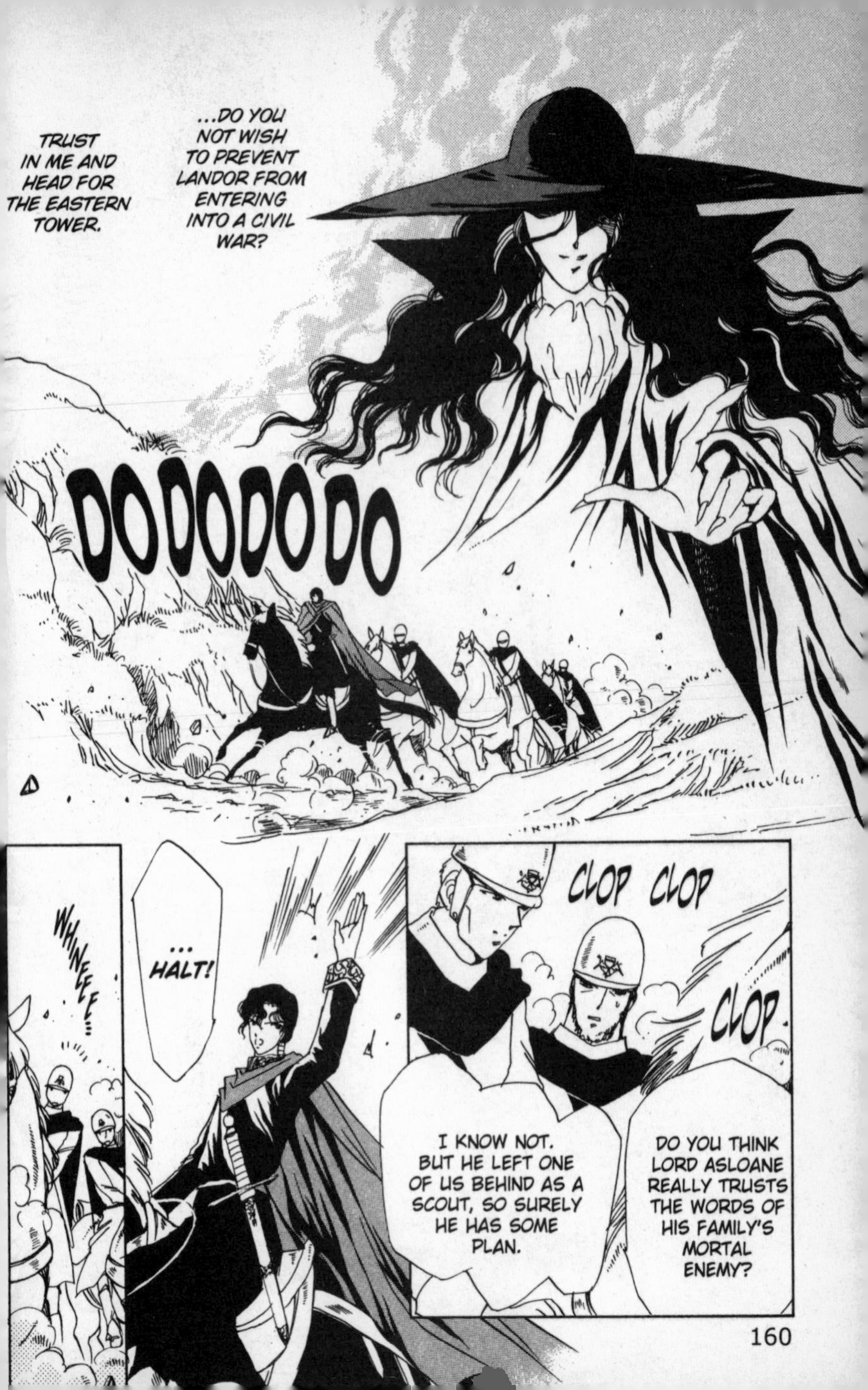
...DO YOU NOT WISH TO PREVENT LANDOR FROM ENTERING INTO A CIVIL WAR?
TRUST IN ME AND HEAD FOR THE EASTERN TOWER.
DODODODO
CLOP CLOP
CLOP
DO YOU THINK LORD ASLOANE REALLY TRUSTS THE WORDS OF HIS FAMILY'S MORTAL ENEMY?
I KNOW NOT. BUT HE LEFT ONE OF US BEHIND AS A SCOUT, SO SURELY HE HAS SOME PLAN.
... HALT!
WHINEEE...!

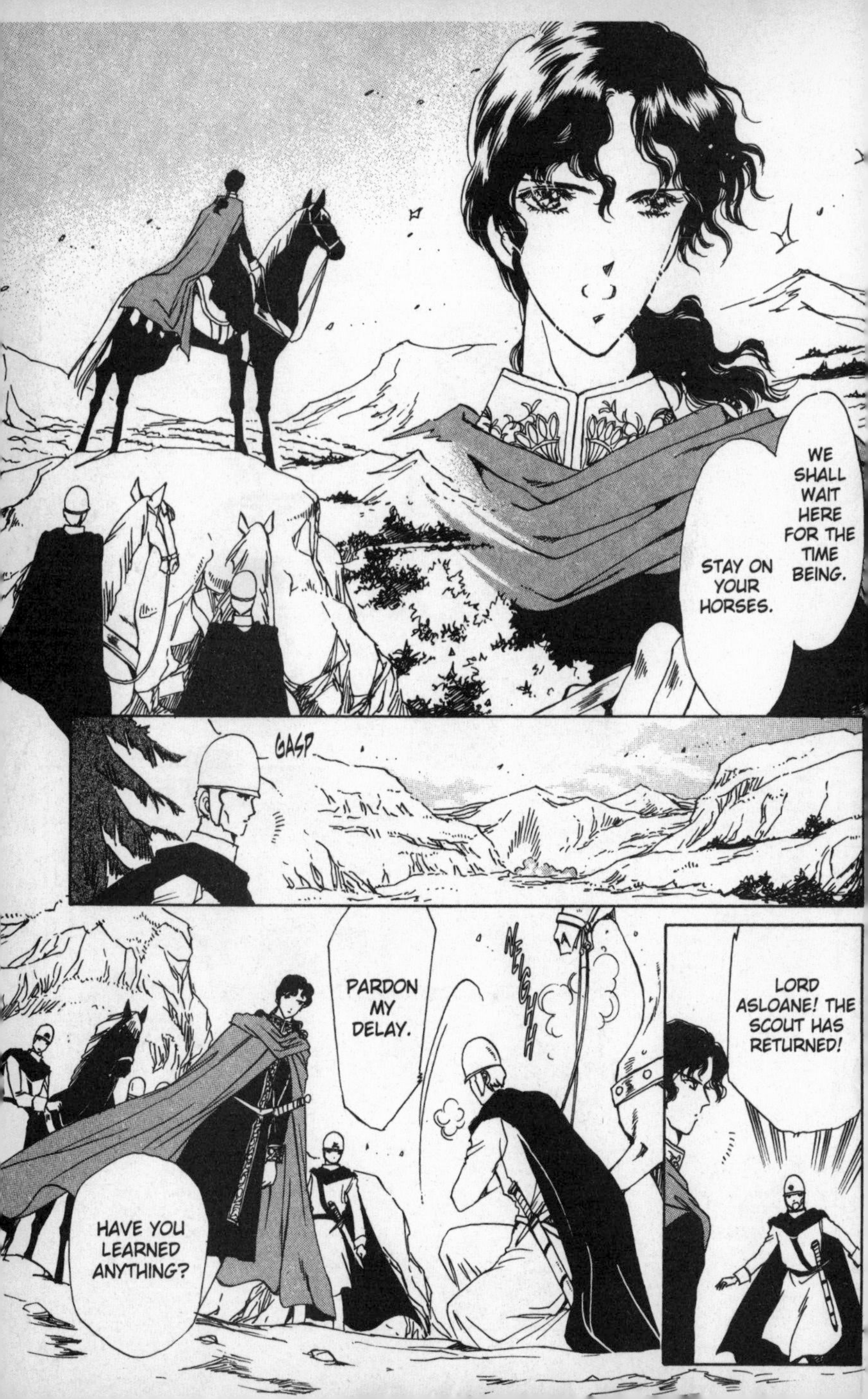
WE SHALL WAIT HERE FOR THE TIME BEING.
STAY ON YOUR HORSES.
GASP
LORD ASLOANE! THE SCOUT HAS RETURNED!
NEIGHH
PARDON MY DELAY.
HAVE YOU LEARNED ANYTHING?

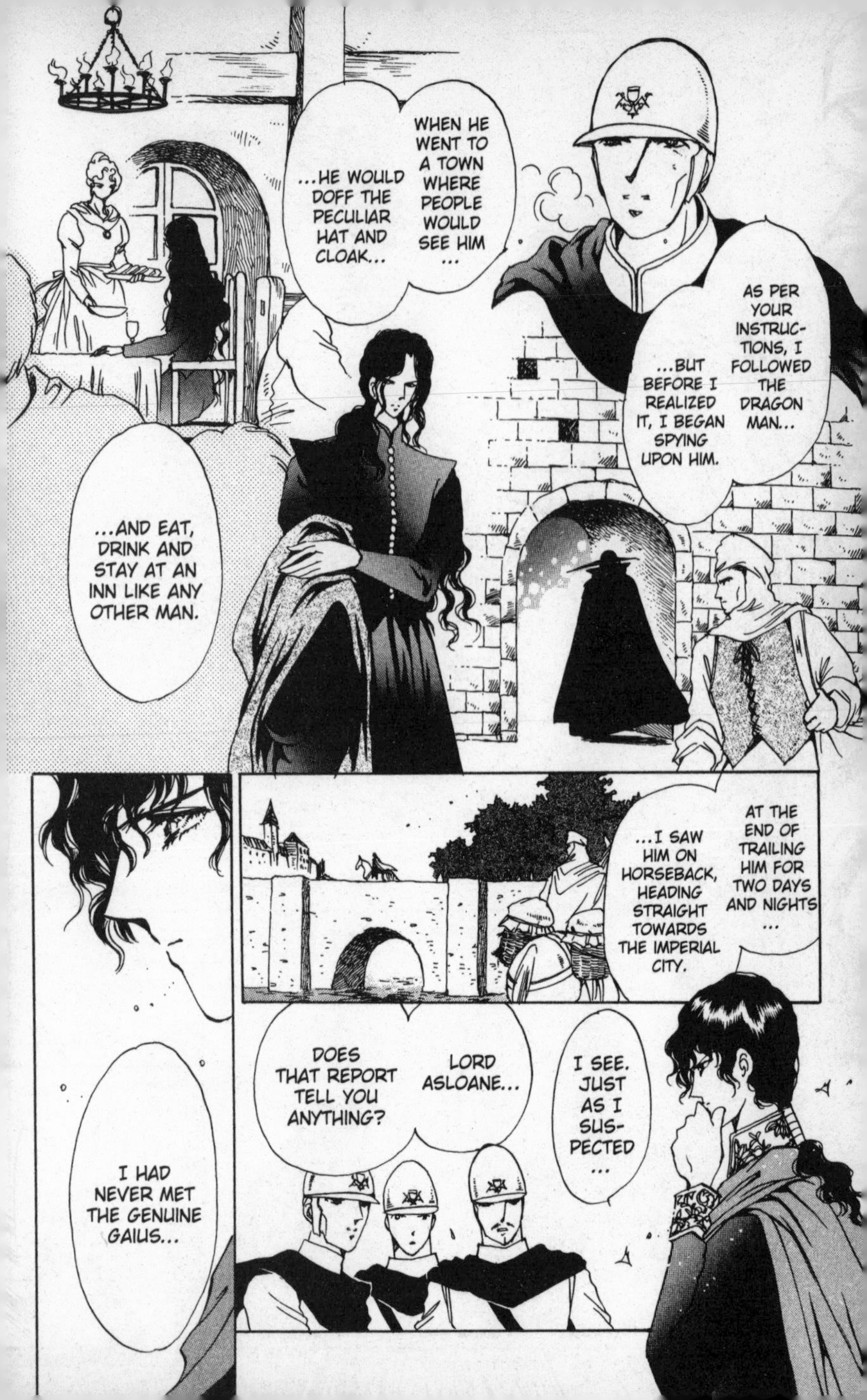
AS PER YOUR INSTRUCTIONS, I FOLLOWED THE DRAGON MAN...
...BUT BEFORE I REALIZED IT, I BEGAN SPYING UPON HIM.
WHEN HE WENT TO A TOWN WHERE PEOPLE WOULD SEE HIM...
...HE WOULD DOFF THE PECULIAR HAT AND CLOAK...
...AND EAT, DRINK AND STAY AT AN INN LIKE ANY OTHER MAN.
AT THE END OF TRAILING HIM FOR TWO DAYS AND NIGHTS...
...I SAW HIM ON HORSEBACK, HEADING STRAIGHT TOWARDS THE IMPERIAL CITY.
I SEE. JUST AS I SUSPECTED...
LORD ASLOANE...
DOES THAT REPORT TELL YOU ANYTHING?
I HAD NEVER MET THE GENUINE GAIUS...

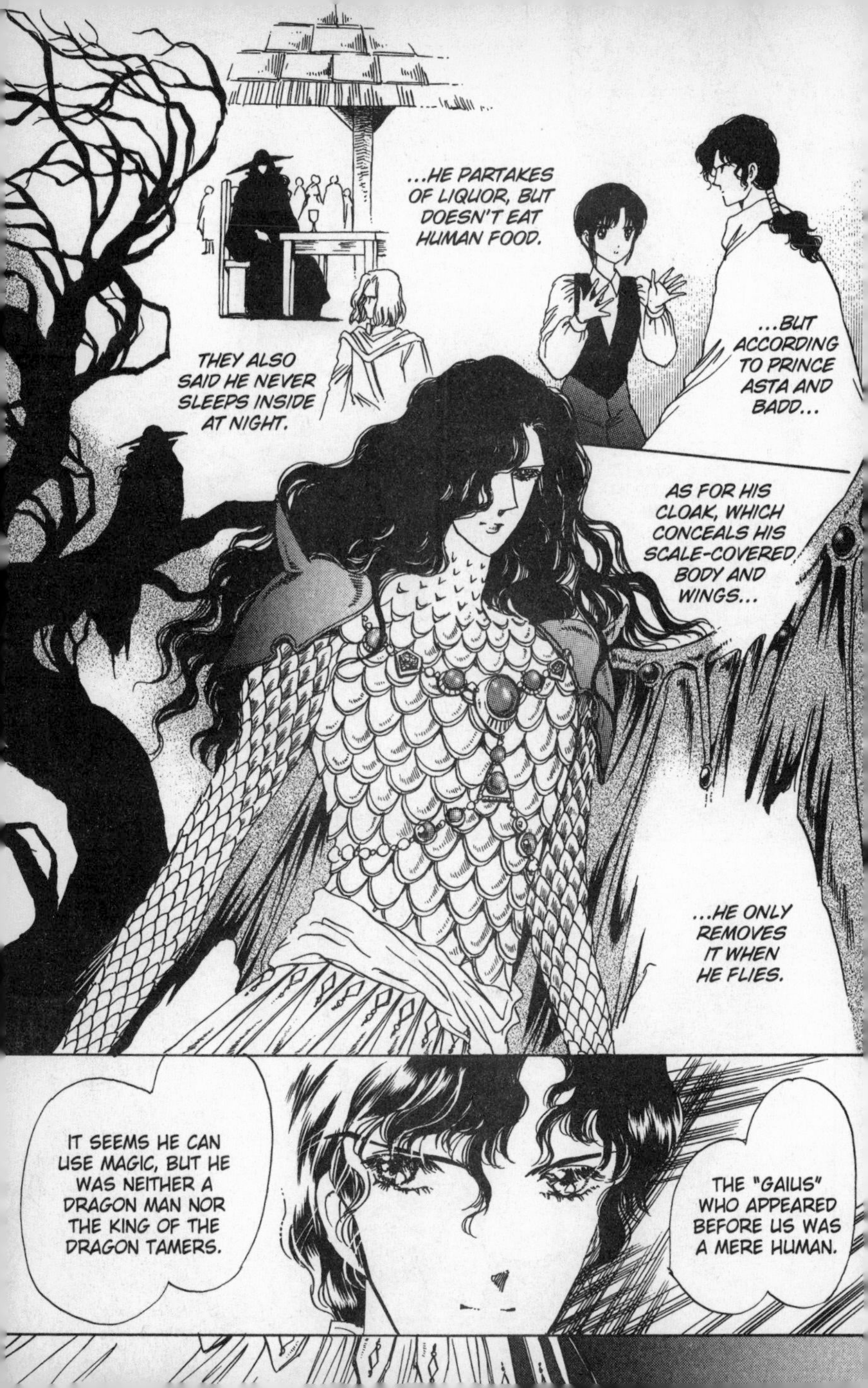
...BUT ACCORDING TO PRINCE ASTA AND BADD...
...HE PARTAKES OF LIQUOR, BUT DOESN'T EAT HUMAN FOOD.
THEY ALSO SAID HE NEVER SLEEPS INSIDE AT NIGHT.
AS FOR HIS CLOAK, WHICH CONCEALS HIS SCALE-COVERED BODY AND WINGS...
...HE ONLY REMOVES IT WHEN HE FLIES.
THE "GAIUS" WHO APPEARED BEFORE US WAS A MERE HUMAN.
IT SEEMS HE CAN USE MAGIC, BUT HE WAS NEITHER A DRAGON MAN NOR THE KING OF THE DRAGON TAMERS.

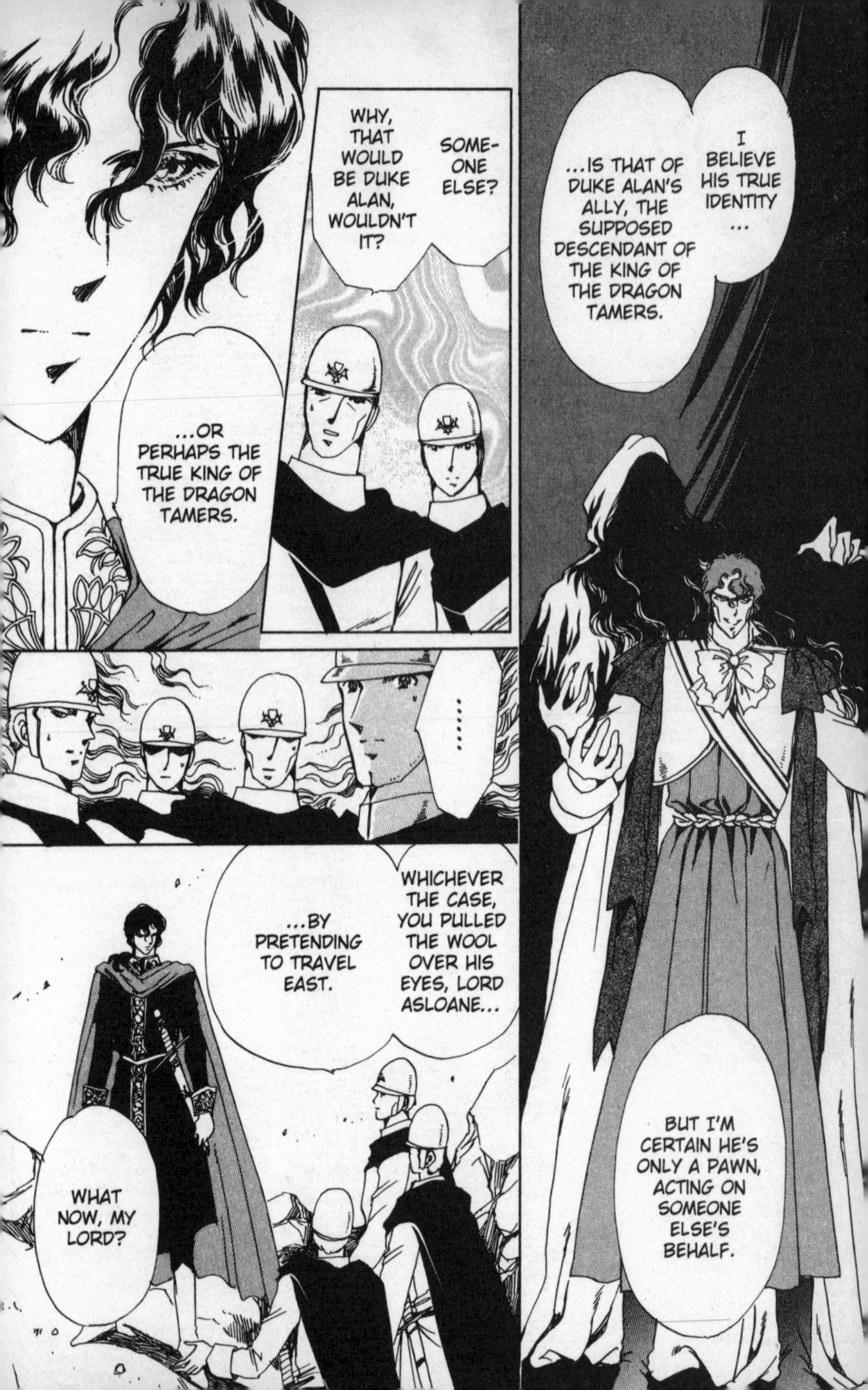
I BELIEVE HIS TRUE IDENTITY ...
...IS THAT OF DUKE ALAN'S ALLY, THE SUPPOSED DESCENDANT OF THE KING OF THE DRAGON TAMERS.
BUT I'M CERTAIN HE'S ONLY A PAWN, ACTING ON SOMEONE ELSE'S BEHALF.
SOME-ONE ELSE?
WHY, THAT WOULD BE DUKE ALAN, WOULDN'T IT?
...OR PERHAPS THE TRUE KING OF THE DRAGON TAMERS.
......
WHICHEVER THE CASE, YOU PULLED THE WOOL OVER HIS EYES, LORD ASLOANE...
...BY PRETENDING TO TRAVEL EAST.
WHAT NOW, MY LORD?

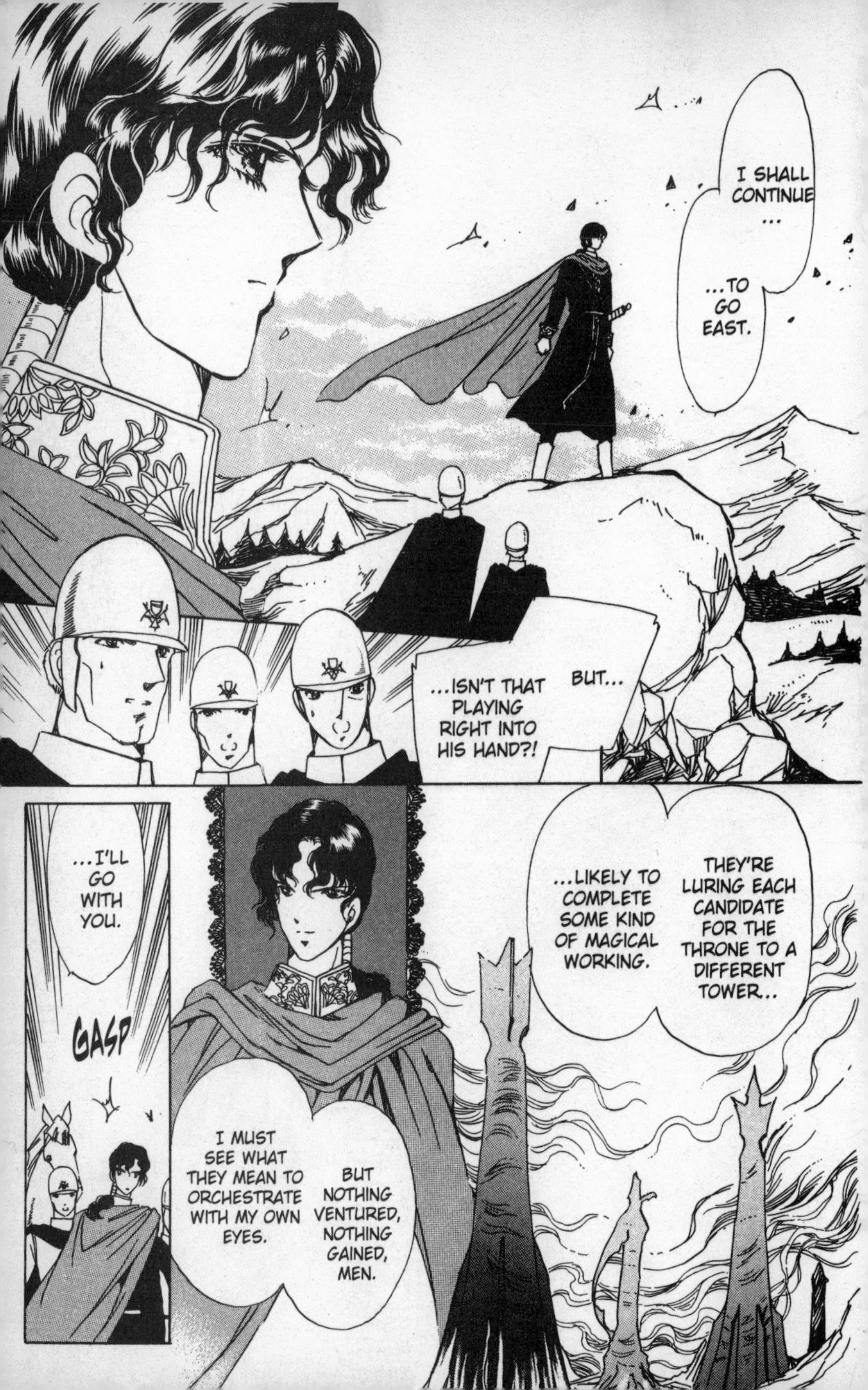
I SHALL CONTINUE ...
...TO GO EAST.
BUT...
...ISN'T THAT PLAYING RIGHT INTO HIS HAND?!
THEY'RE LURING EACH CANDIDATE FOR THE THRONE TO A DIFFERENT TOWER...
...LIKELY TO COMPLETE SOME KIND OF MAGICAL WORKING.
BUT NOTHING VENTURED, NOTHING GAINED, MEN.
I MUST SEE WHAT THEY MEAN TO ORCHESTRATE WITH MY OWN EYES.
...I'LL GO WITH YOU.
GASP

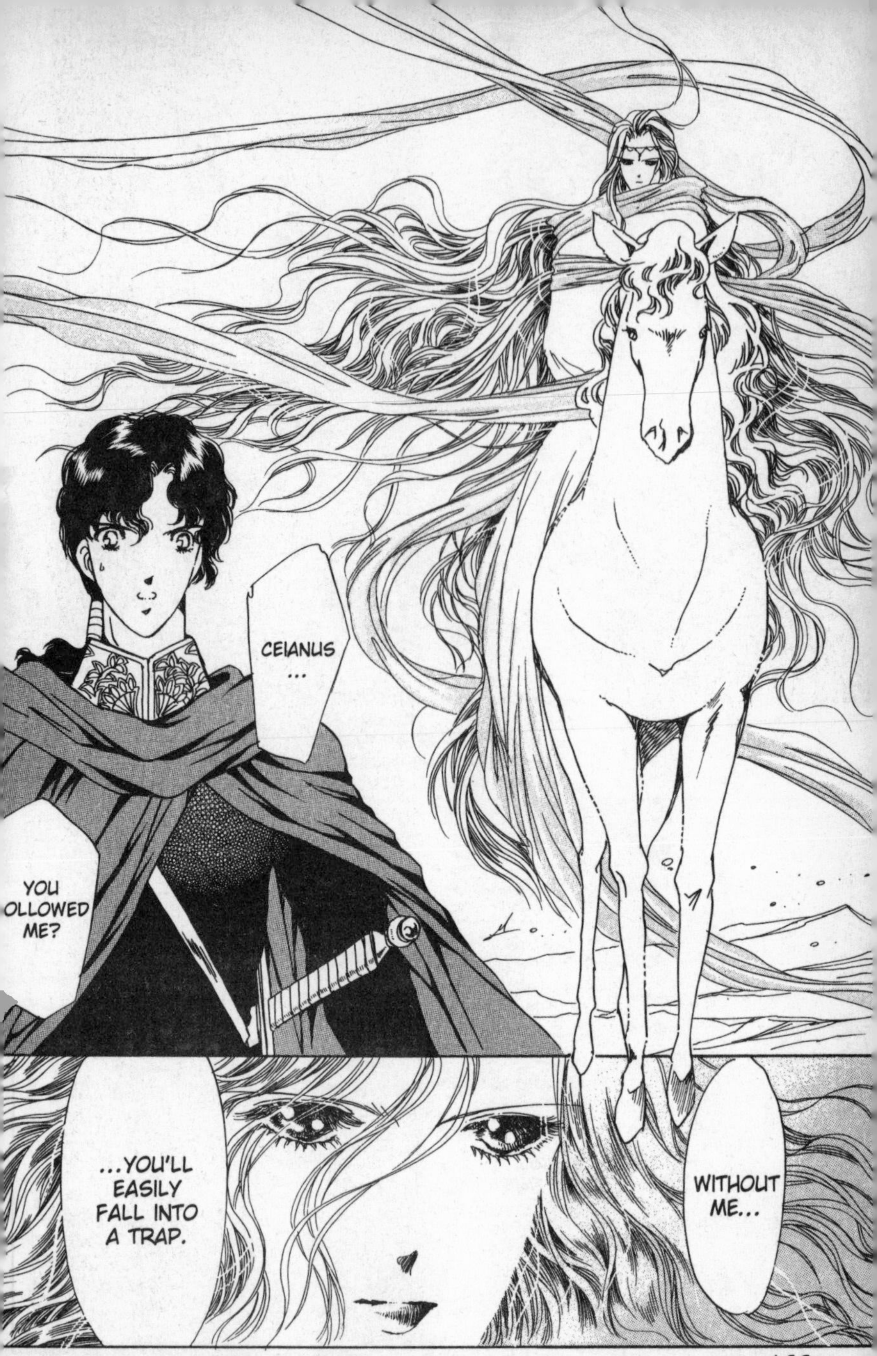
CEIANUS ...
YOU OLLOWED ME?
WITHOUT ME...
...YOU'LL EASILY FALL INTO A TRAP.

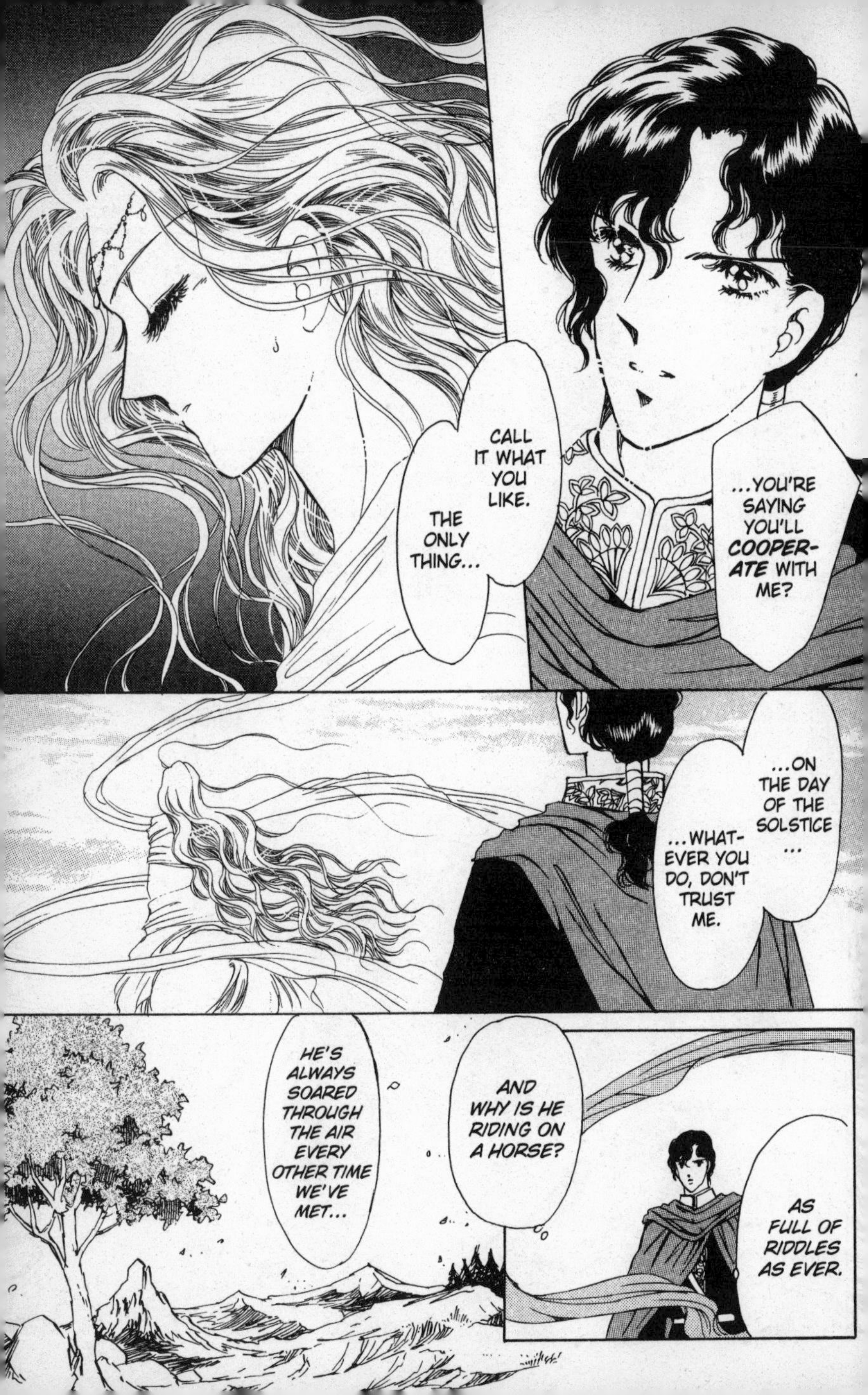
...YOU'RE SAYING YOU'LL COOPERATE WITH ME?
CALL IT WHAT YOU LIKE.
THE ONLY THING...
...ON THE DAY OF THE SOLSTICE ...
...WHATEVER YOU DO, DON'T TRUST ME.
AS FULL OF RIDDLES AS EVER.
AND WHY IS HE RIDING ON A HORSE?
HE'S ALWAYS SOARED THROUGH THE AIR EVERY OTHER TIME WE'VE MET...

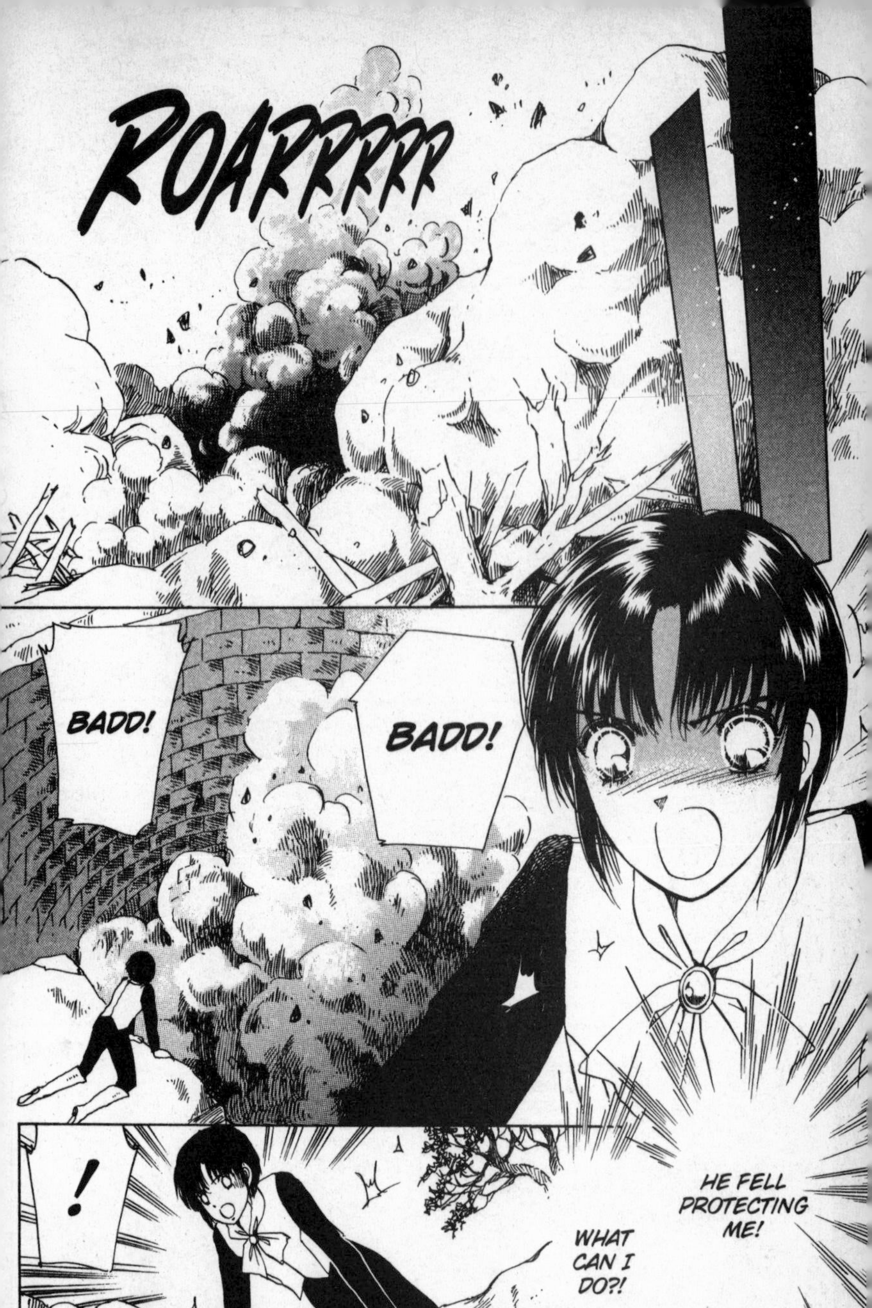
ROARRRRR
BADD!
BADD!
HE FELL PROTECTING ME!
WHAT CAN I DO?!
!

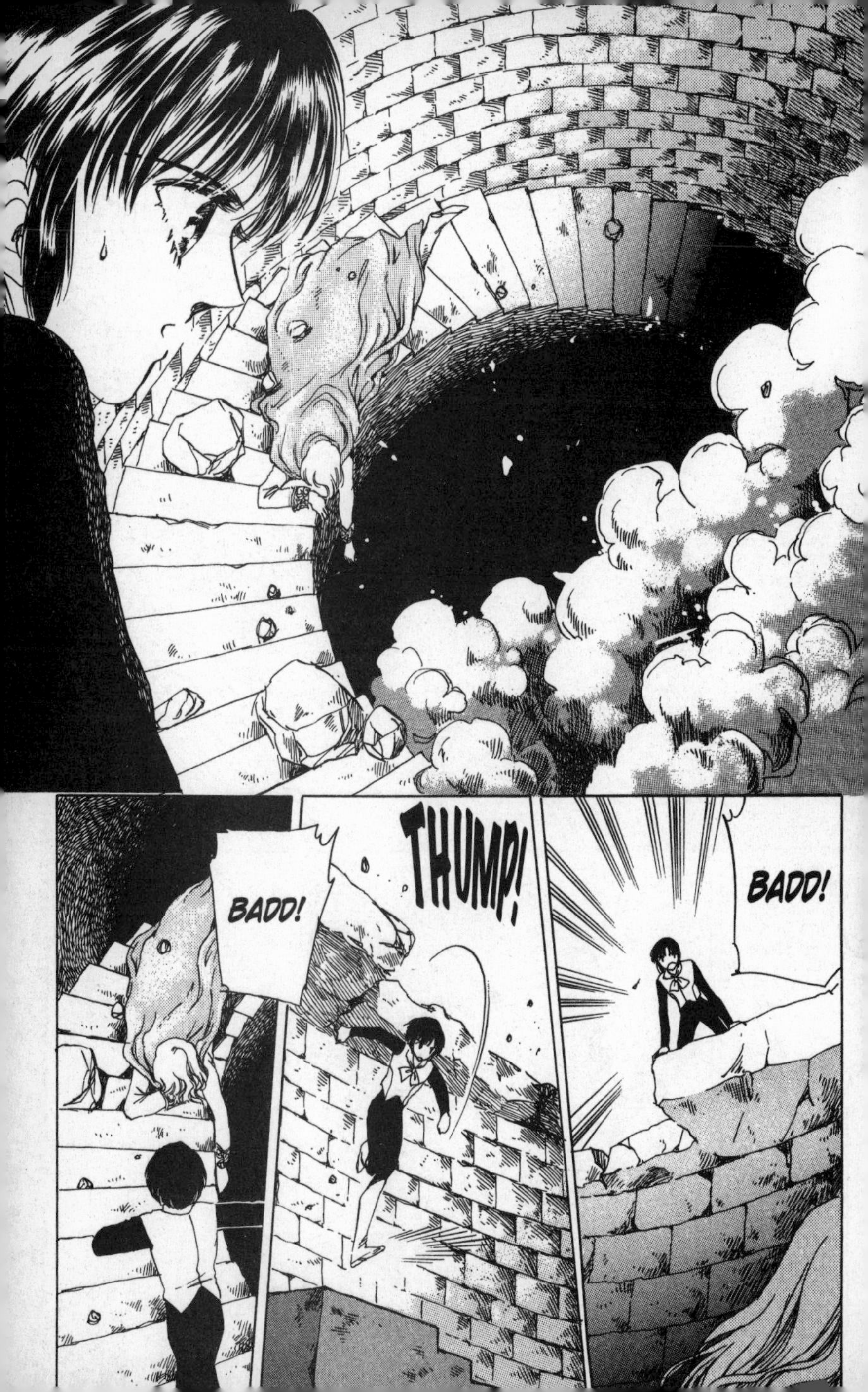
BADD!
THUMP!
BADD!

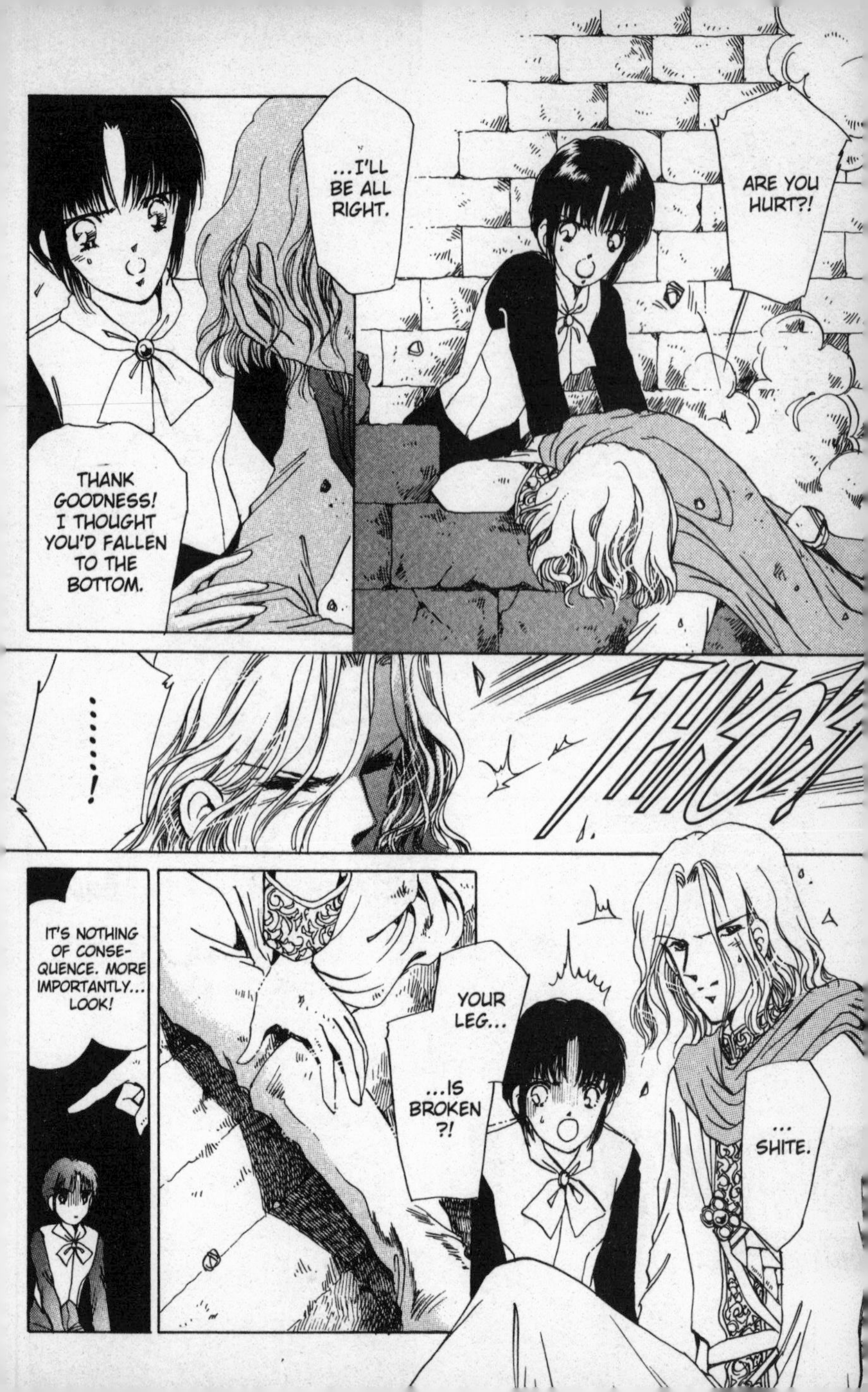
ARE YOU HURT?!
...I'LL BE ALL RIGHT.
THANK GOODNESS! I THOUGHT YOU'D FALLEN TO THE BOTTOM.
THROB!
......!
YOUR LEG...
...IS BROKEN?!
...SHITE.
IT'S NOTHING OF CONSE-QUENCE. MORE IMPORTANTLY... LOOK!

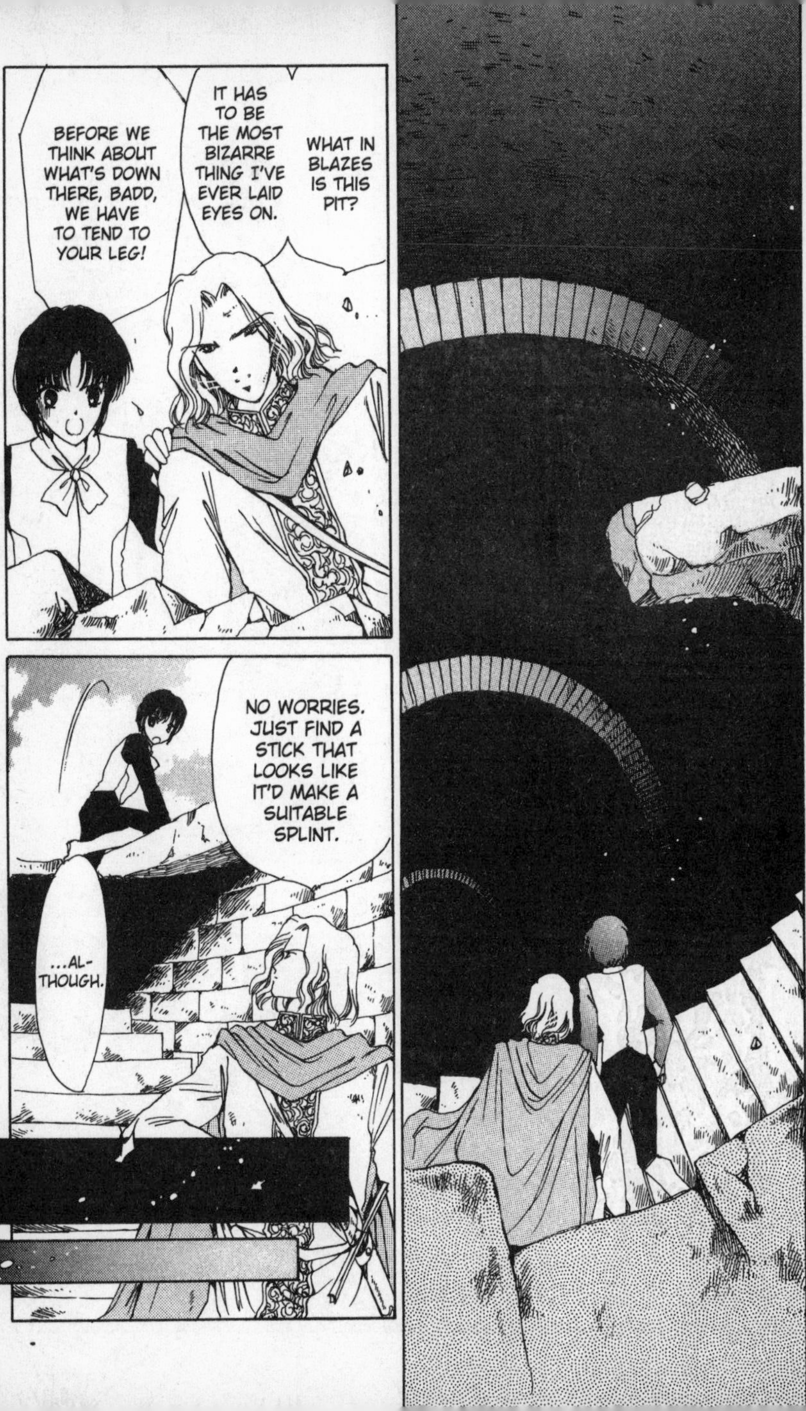
WHAT IN BLAZES IS THIS PIT?
IT HAS TO BE THE MOST BIZARRE THING I'VE EVER LAID EYES ON.
BEFORE WE THINK ABOUT WHAT'S DOWN THERE, BADD, WE HAVE TO TEND TO YOUR LEG!
NO WORRIES. JUST FIND A STICK THAT LOOKS LIKE IT'D MAKE A SUITABLE SPLINT.
...AL-THOUGH.

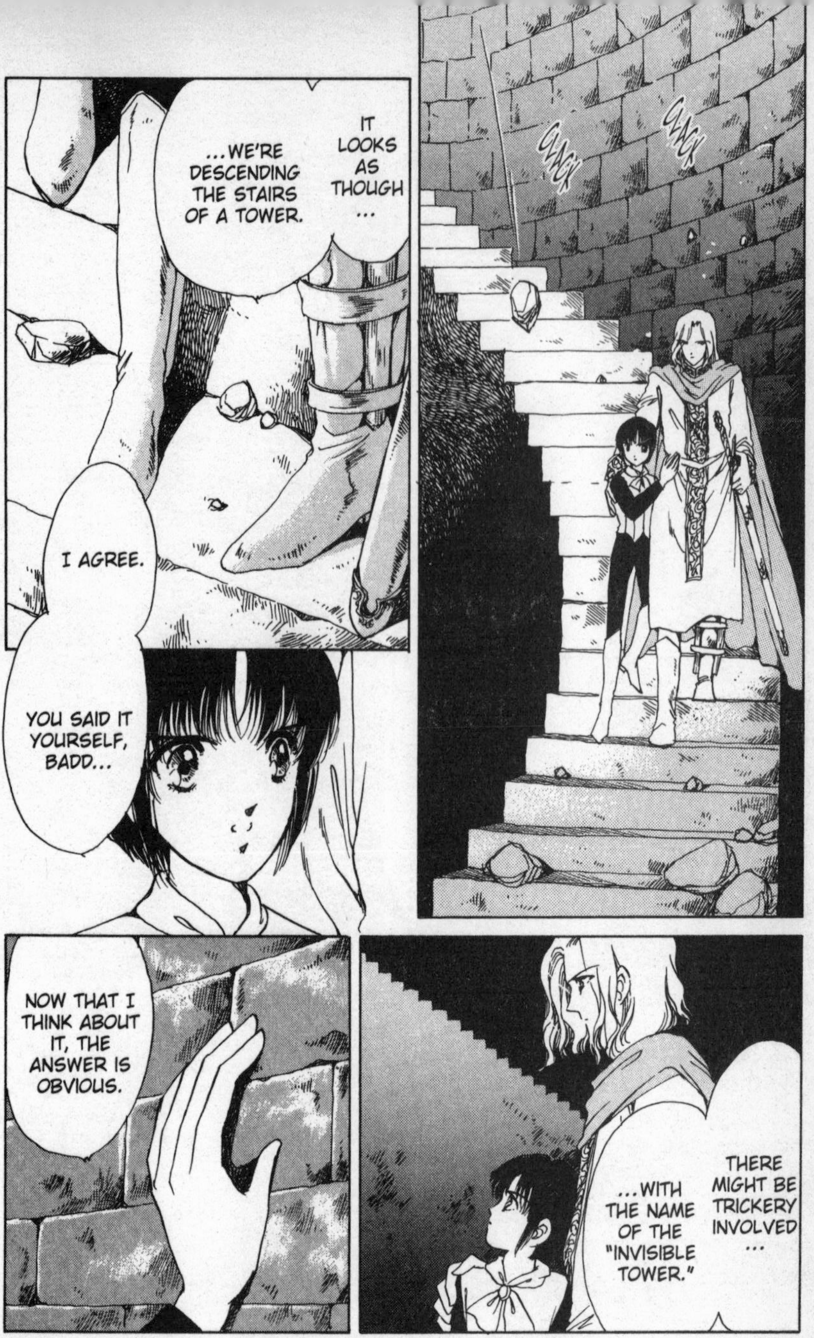
CLACK
CLACK
IT LOOKS AS THOUGH...
...WE'RE DESCENDING THE STAIRS OF A TOWER.
I AGREE.
YOU SAID IT YOURSELF, BADD...
THERE MIGHT BE TRICKERY INVOLVED...
...WITH THE NAME OF THE "INVISIBLE TOWER."
NOW THAT I THINK ABOUT IT, THE ANSWER IS OBVIOUS.

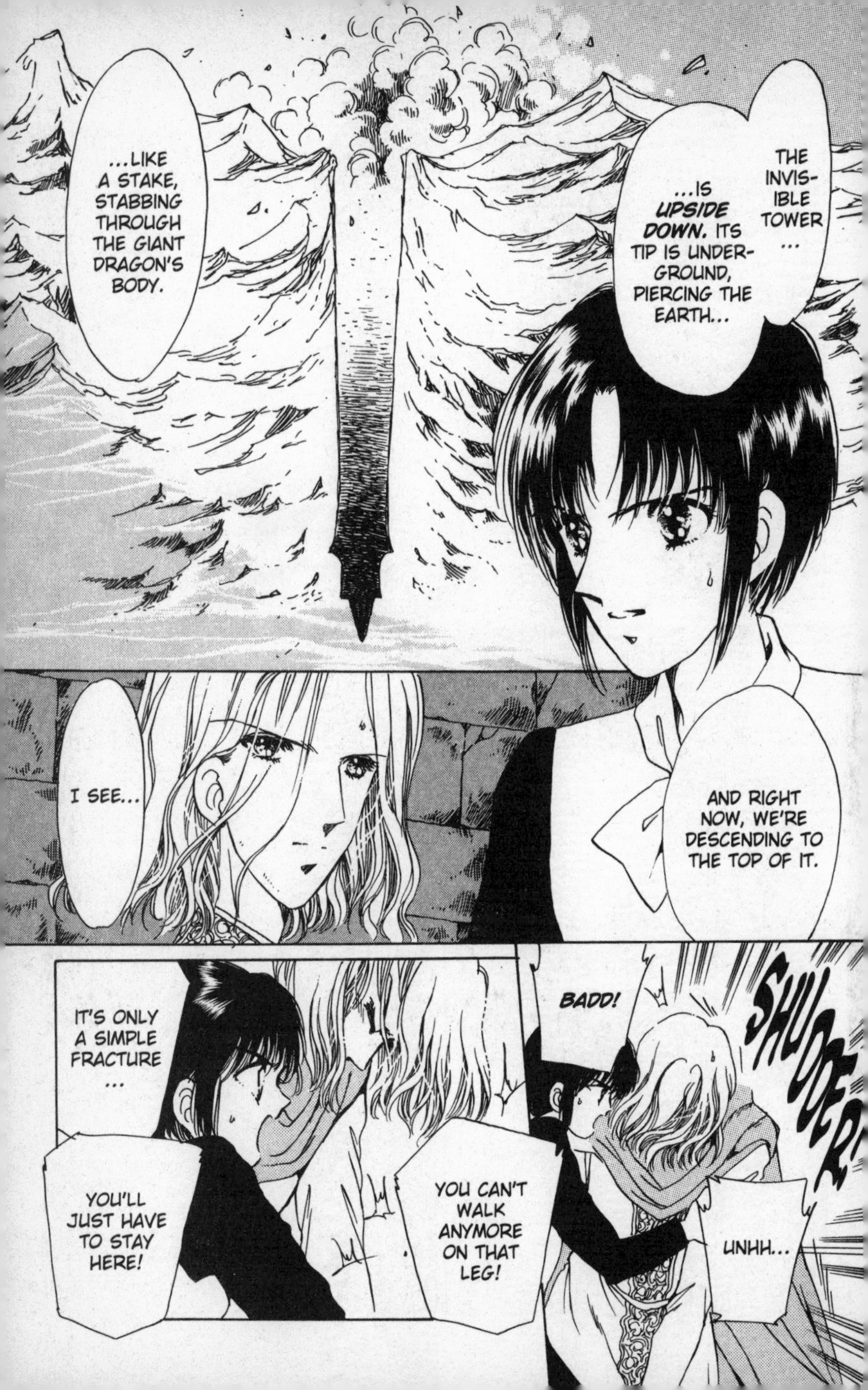
THE INVISIBLE TOWER...
...IS UPSIDE DOWN. ITS TIP IS UNDERGROUND, PIERCING THE EARTH...
...LIKE A STAKE, STABBING THROUGH THE GIANT DRAGON'S BODY.
AND RIGHT NOW, WE'RE DESCENDING TO THE TOP OF IT.
I SEE...
SHUDDER!
BADD!
UNHH...
IT'S ONLY A SIMPLE FRACTURE...
YOU CAN'T WALK ANYMORE ON THAT LEG!
YOU'LL JUST HAVE TO STAY HERE!

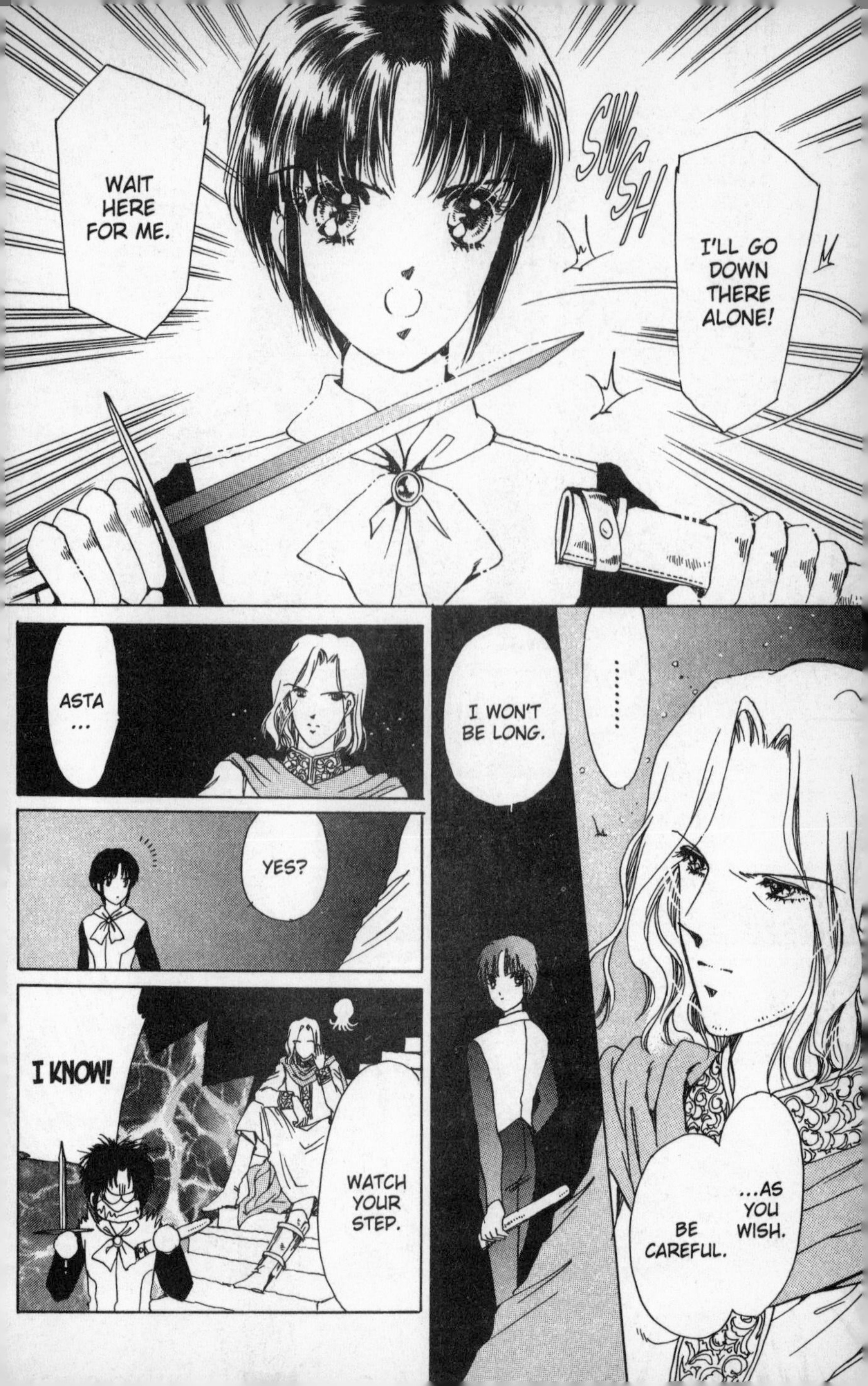
I'LL GO DOWN THERE ALONE!
SWISH
WAIT HERE FOR ME.
......
I WON'T BE LONG.
...AS YOU WISH.
BE CAREFUL.
ASTA ...
YES?
WATCH YOUR STEP.
I KNOW!

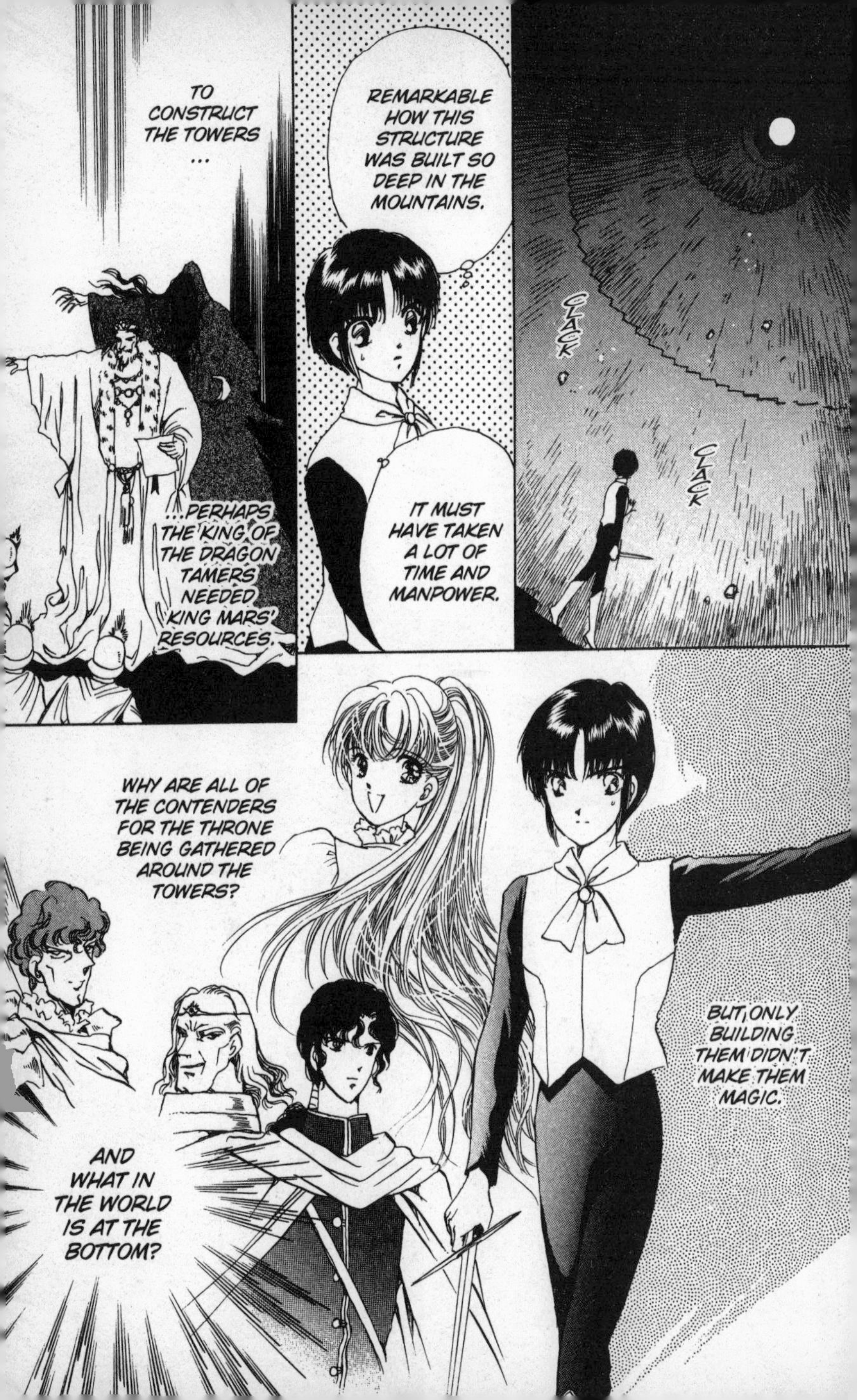
CLACK
CLACK
REMARKABLE HOW THIS STRUCTURE WAS BUILT SO DEEP IN THE MOUNTAINS.
IT MUST HAVE TAKEN A LOT OF TIME AND MANPOWER.
TO CONSTRUCT THE TOWERS ...
...PERHAPS THE KING OF THE DRAGON TAMERS NEEDED KING MARS' RESOURCES.
BUT ONLY BUILDING THEM DIDN'T MAKE THEM MAGIC.
WHY ARE ALL OF THE CONTENDERS FOR THE THRONE BEING GATHERED AROUND THE TOWERS?
AND WHAT IN THE WORLD IS AT THE BOTTOM?

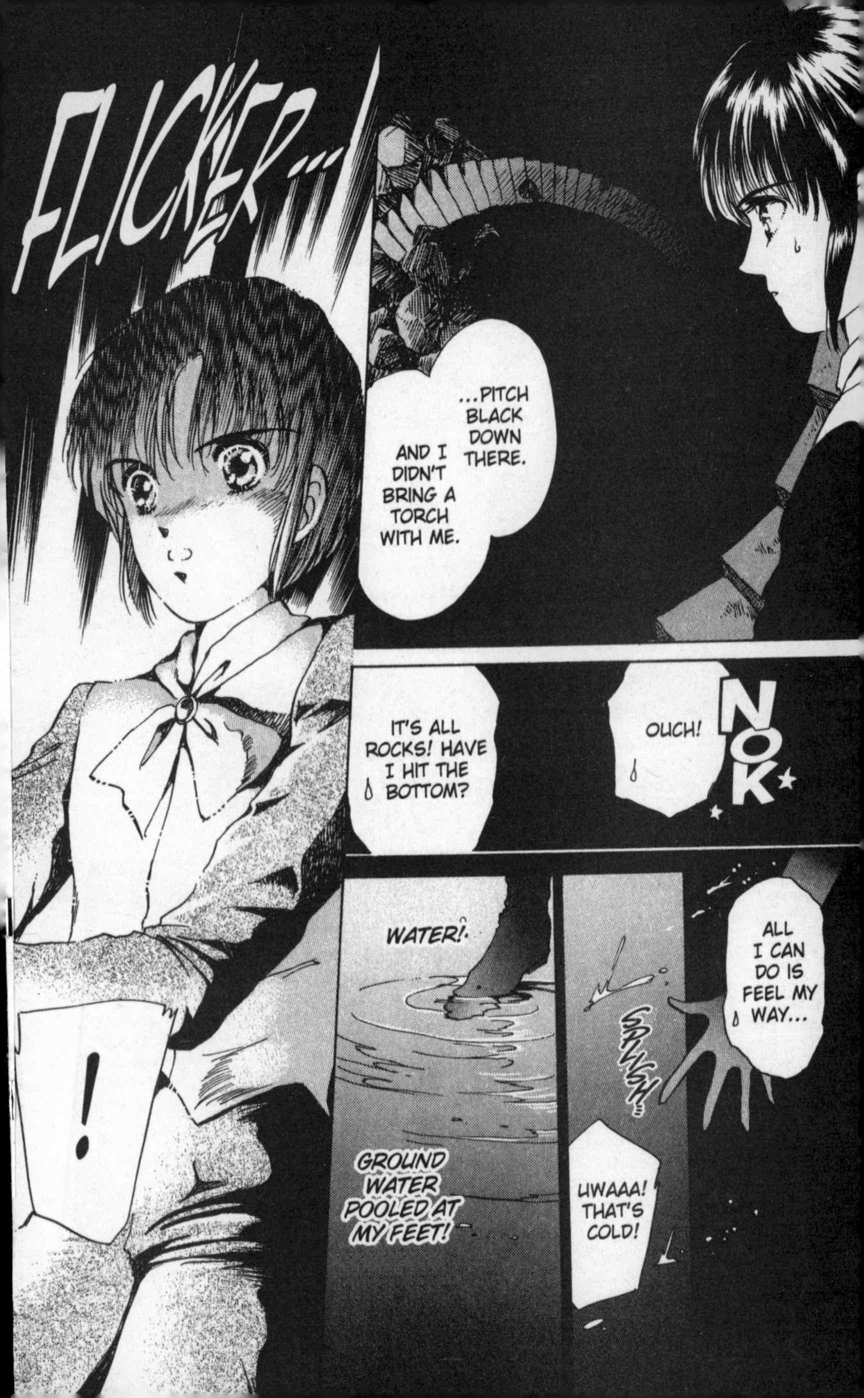
...PITCH BLACK DOWN THERE.
AND I DIDN'T BRING A TORCH WITH ME.
NOK
OUCH!
IT'S ALL ROCKS! HAVE I HIT THE BOTTOM?
ALL I CAN DO IS FEEL MY WAY...
SPLUSH...
UWAAA! THAT'S COLD!
WATER!?
GROUND WATER POOLED AT MY FEET!
FLICKER...!
!

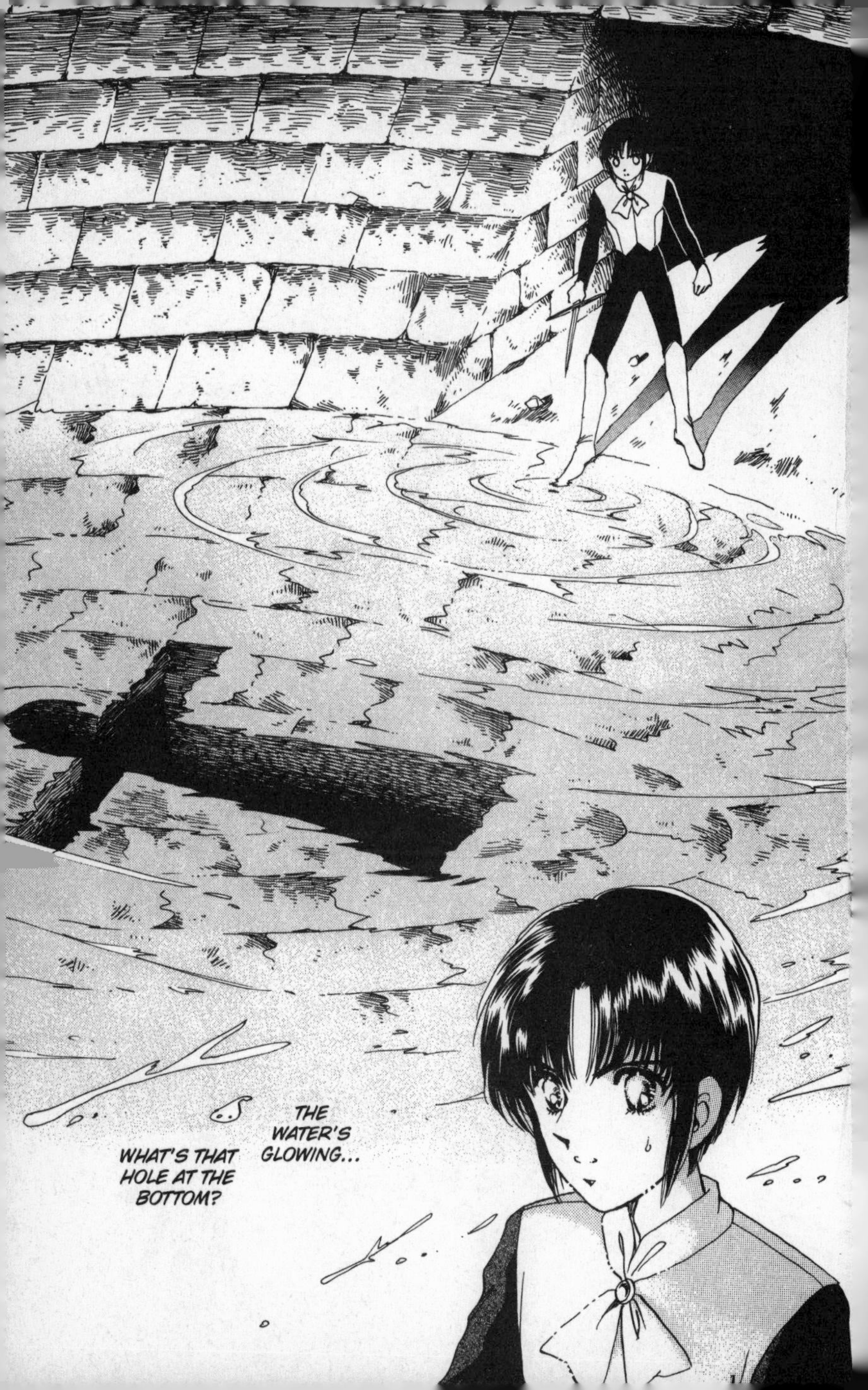
THE WATER'S GLOWING...
WHAT'S THAT HOLE AT THE BOTTOM?

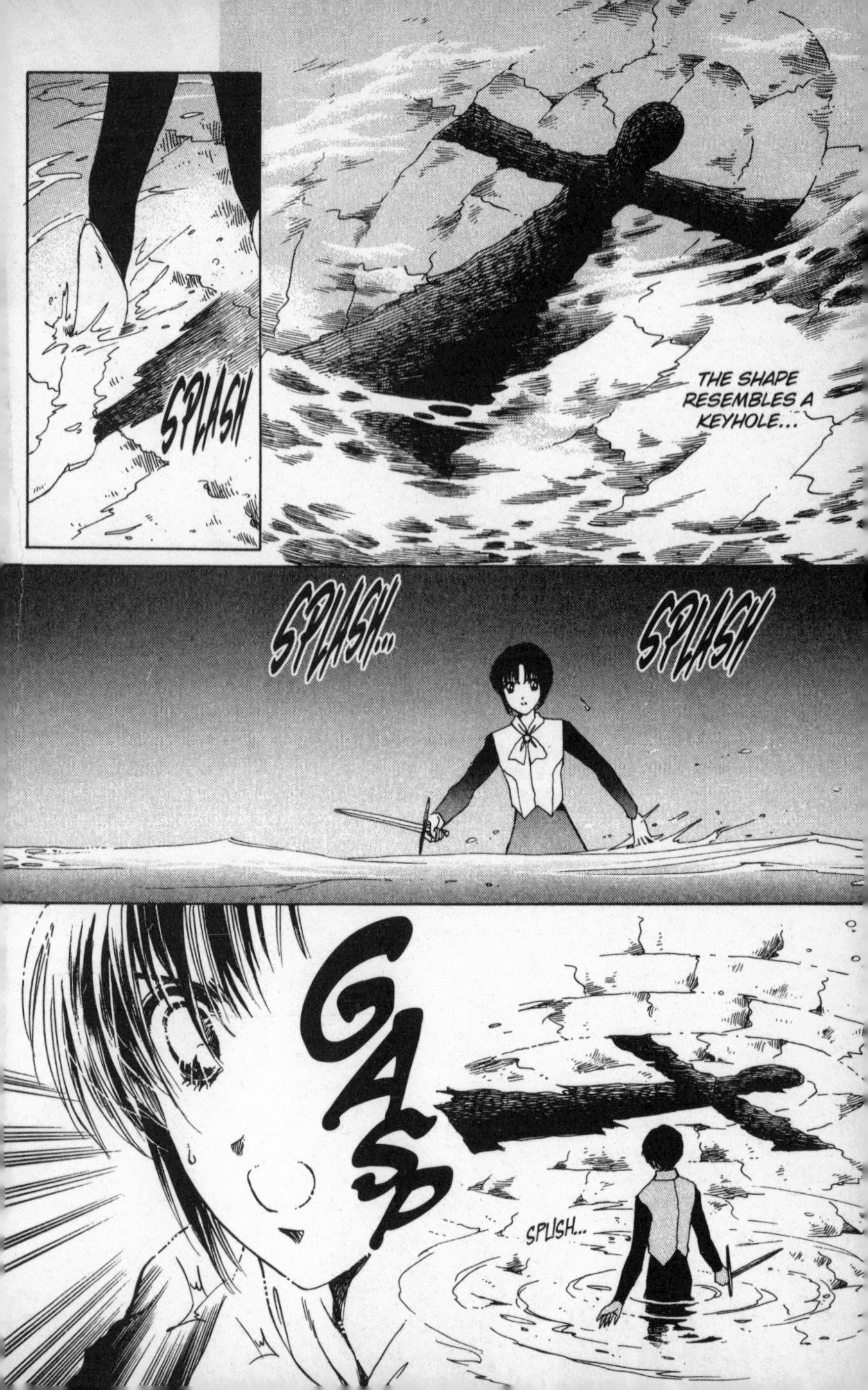
THE SHAPE RESEMBLES A KEYHOLE...
SPLASH
SPLASH
SPLASH...
SPLISH...
GASP

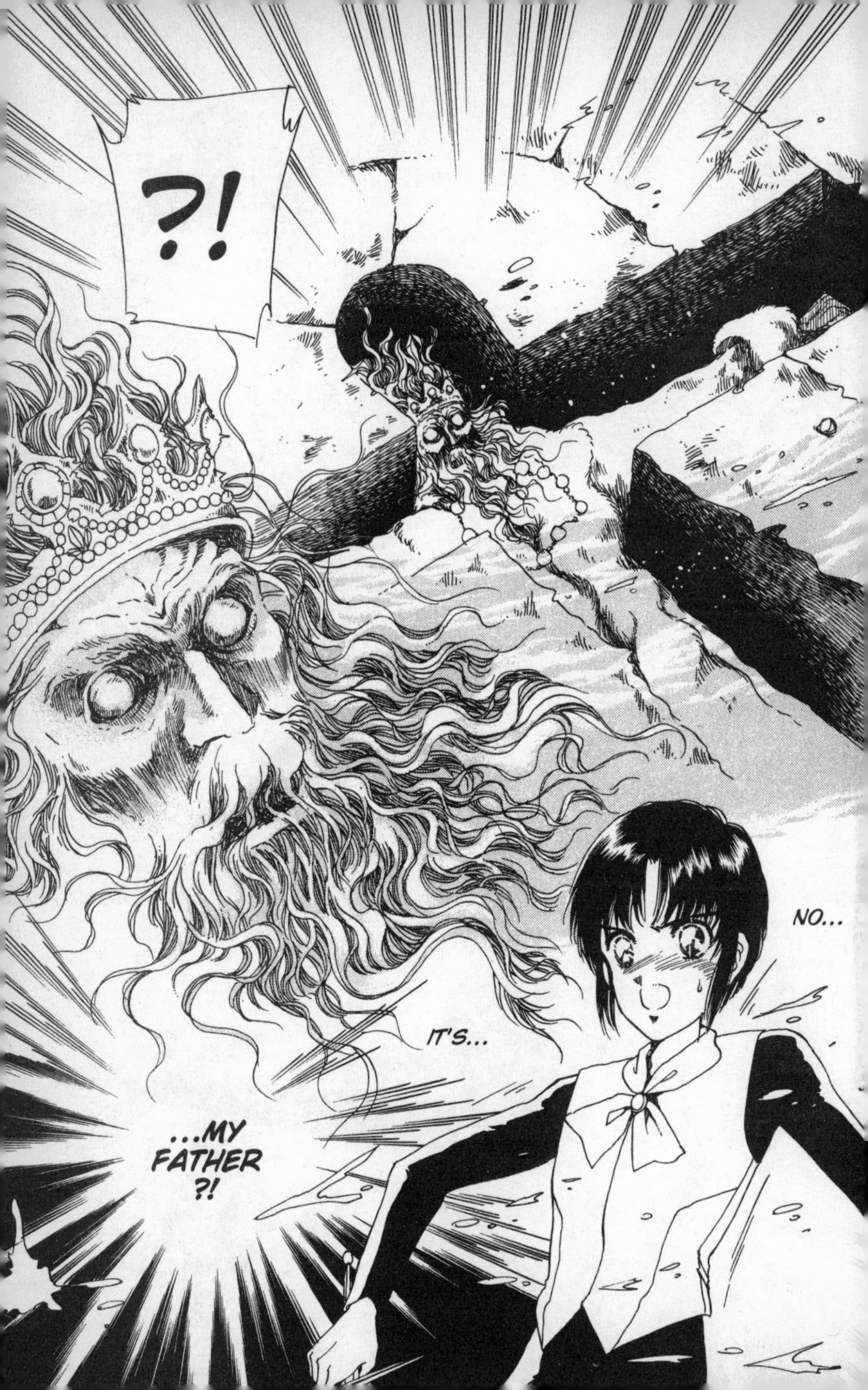
?!
NO...
IT'S...
...MY FATHER ?!

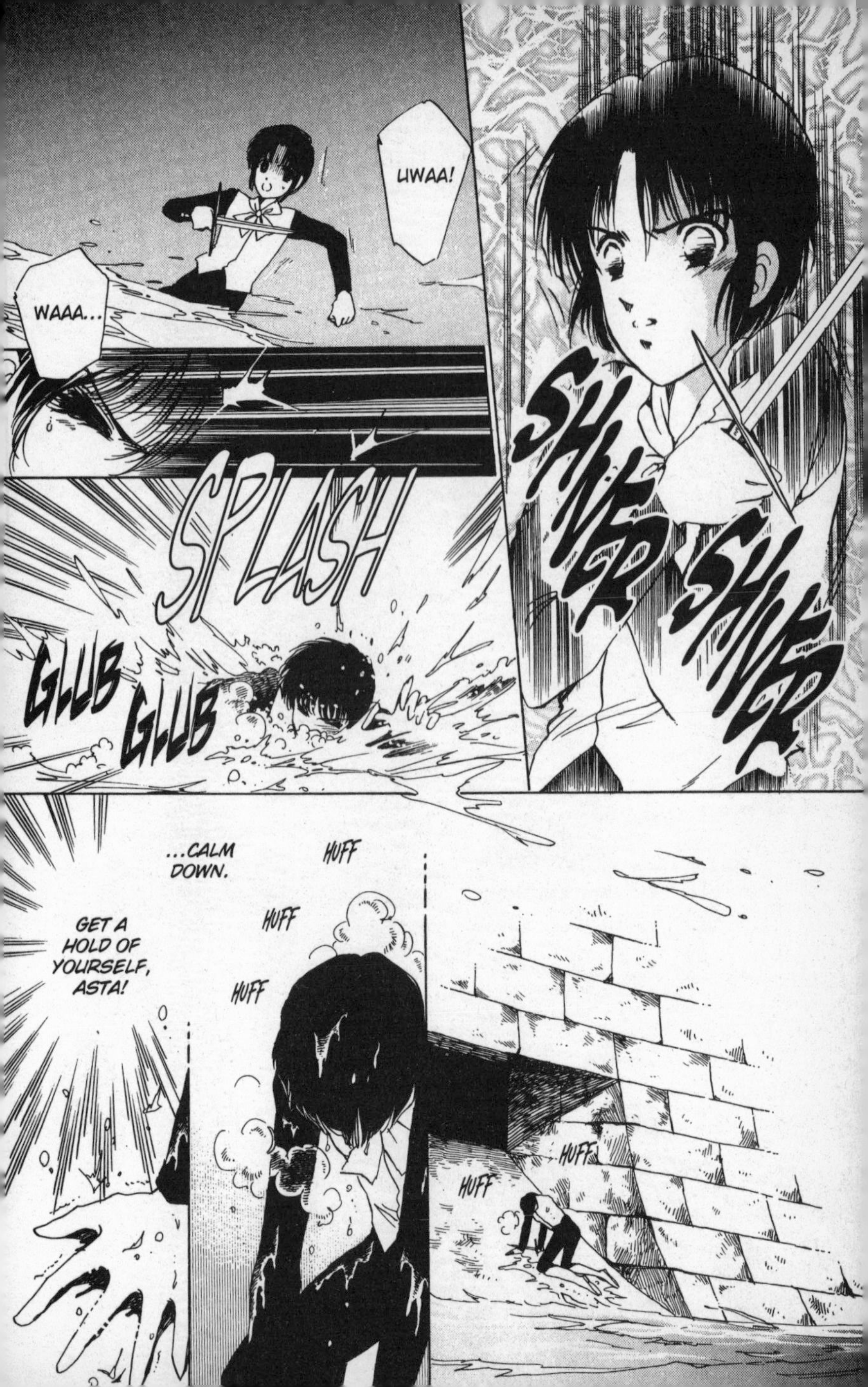
SHIVER SHIVER
UWAA!
WAAA...
SPLASH
GLUB GLUB
HUFF
HUFF
...CALM DOWN.
HUFF
HUFF
HUFF
GET A HOLD OF YOURSELF, ASTA!

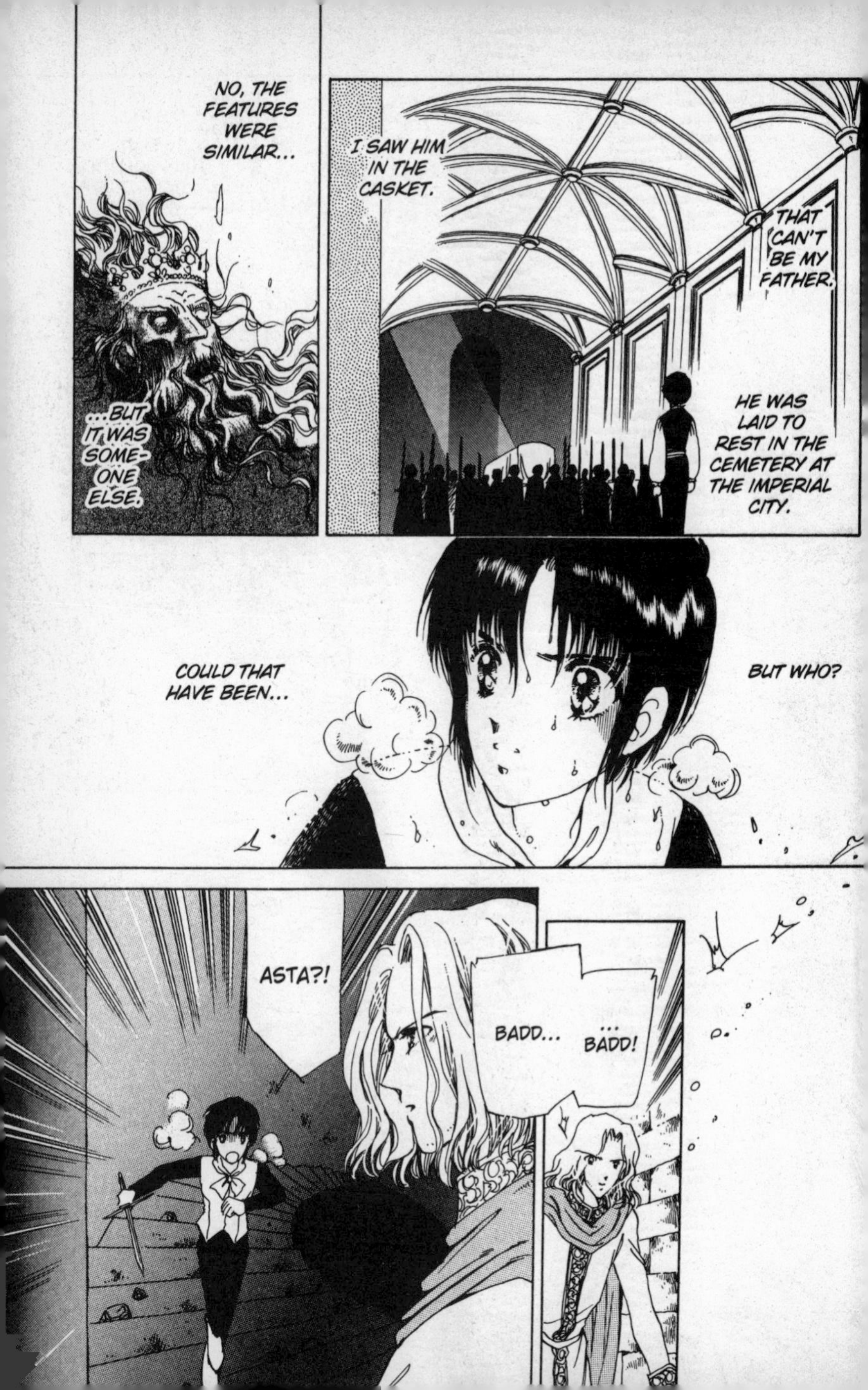

I SAW HIM IN THE CASKET.
THAT CAN'T BE MY FATHER.
HE WAS LAID TO REST IN THE CEMETERY AT THE IMPERIAL CITY.
NO, THE FEATURES WERE SIMILAR...
...BUT IT WAS SOMEONE ELSE.
BUT WHO?
COULD THAT HAVE BEEN...
BADD...
...BADD!
ASTA?!

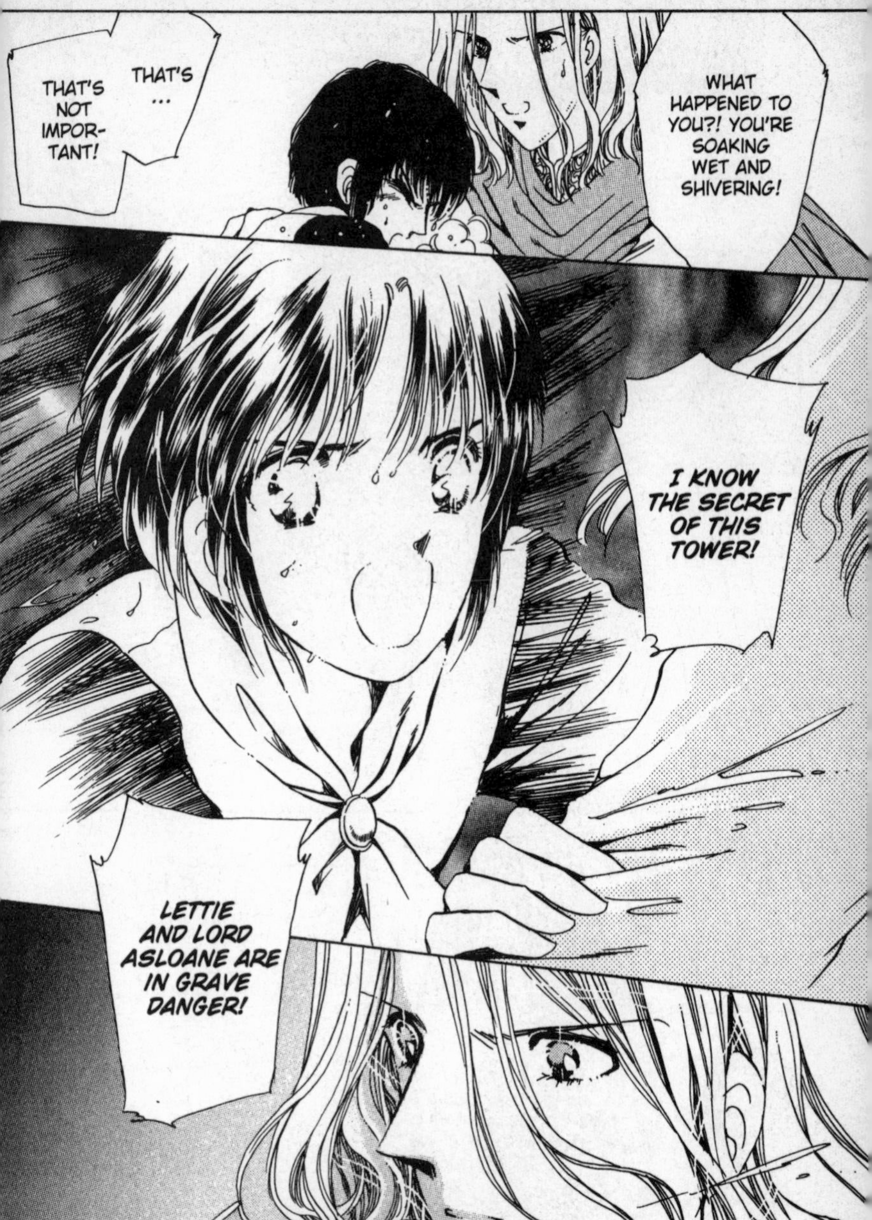
WHAT HAPPENED TO YOU?! YOU'RE SOAKING WET AND SHIVERING!
THAT'S ...
THAT'S NOT IMPORTANT!
I KNOW THE SECRET OF THIS TOWER!
LETTIE AND LORD ASLOANE ARE IN GRAVE DANGER!

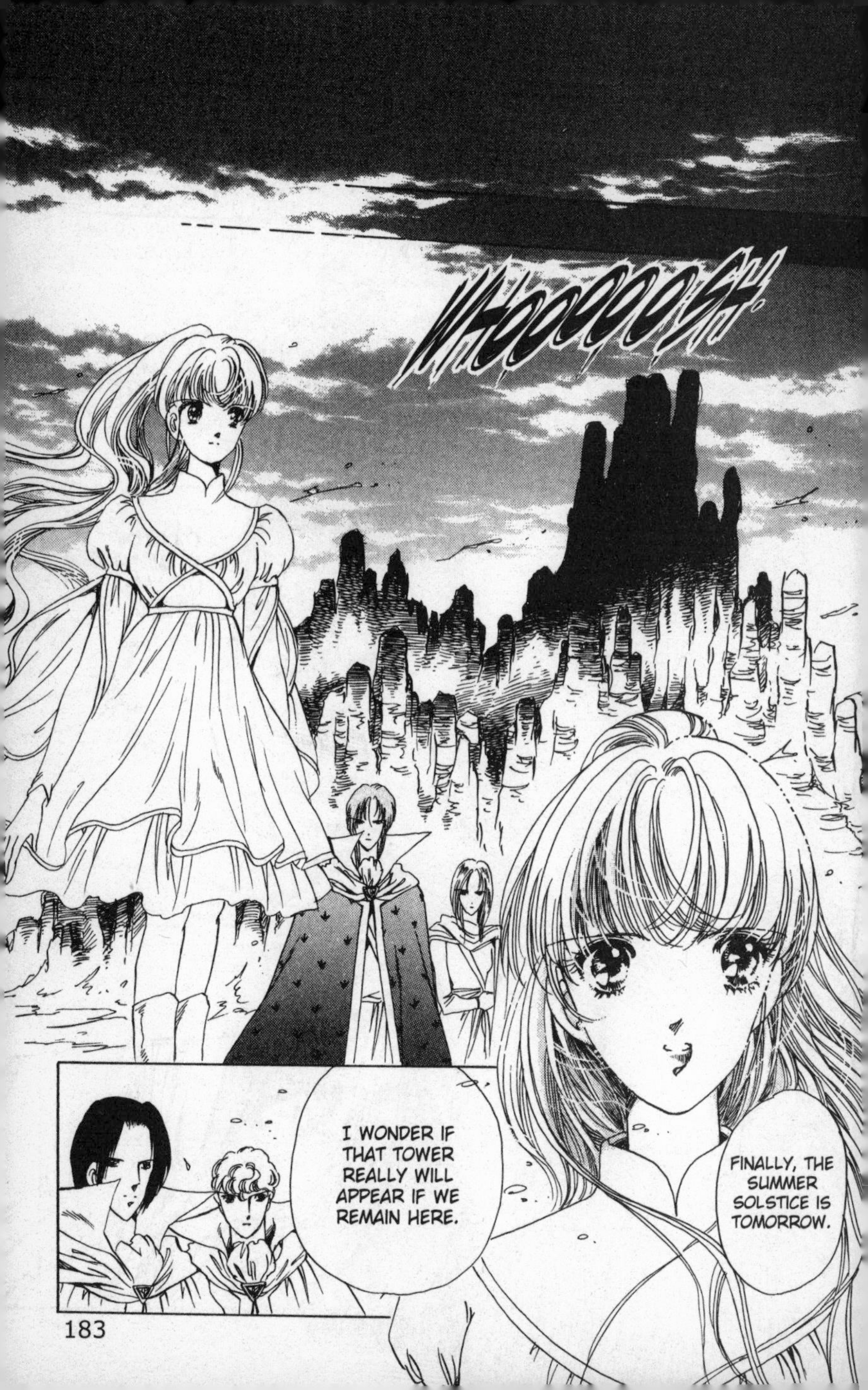
WHOOOOOSH
FINALLY, THE SUMMER SOLSTICE IS TOMORROW.
I WONDER IF THAT TOWER REALLY WILL APPEAR IF WE REMAIN HERE.

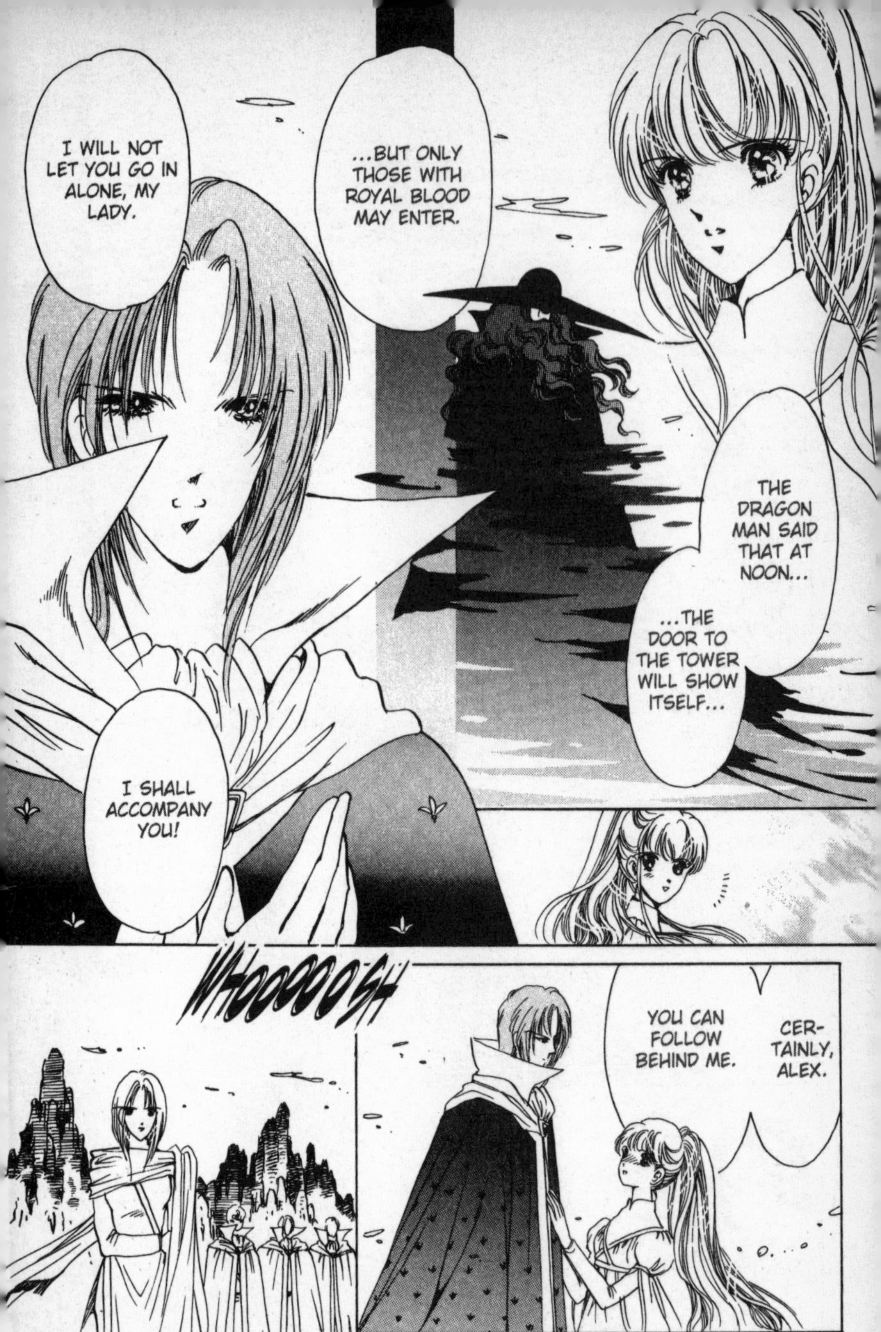
THE DRAGON MAN SAID THAT AT NOON...
...THE DOOR TO THE TOWER WILL SHOW ITSELF...
...BUT ONLY THOSE WITH ROYAL BLOOD MAY ENTER.
I WILL NOT LET YOU GO IN ALONE, MY LADY.
I SHALL ACCOMPANY YOU!
CER-TAINLY, ALEX.
YOU CAN FOLLOW BEHIND ME.
WHOOOOOSH

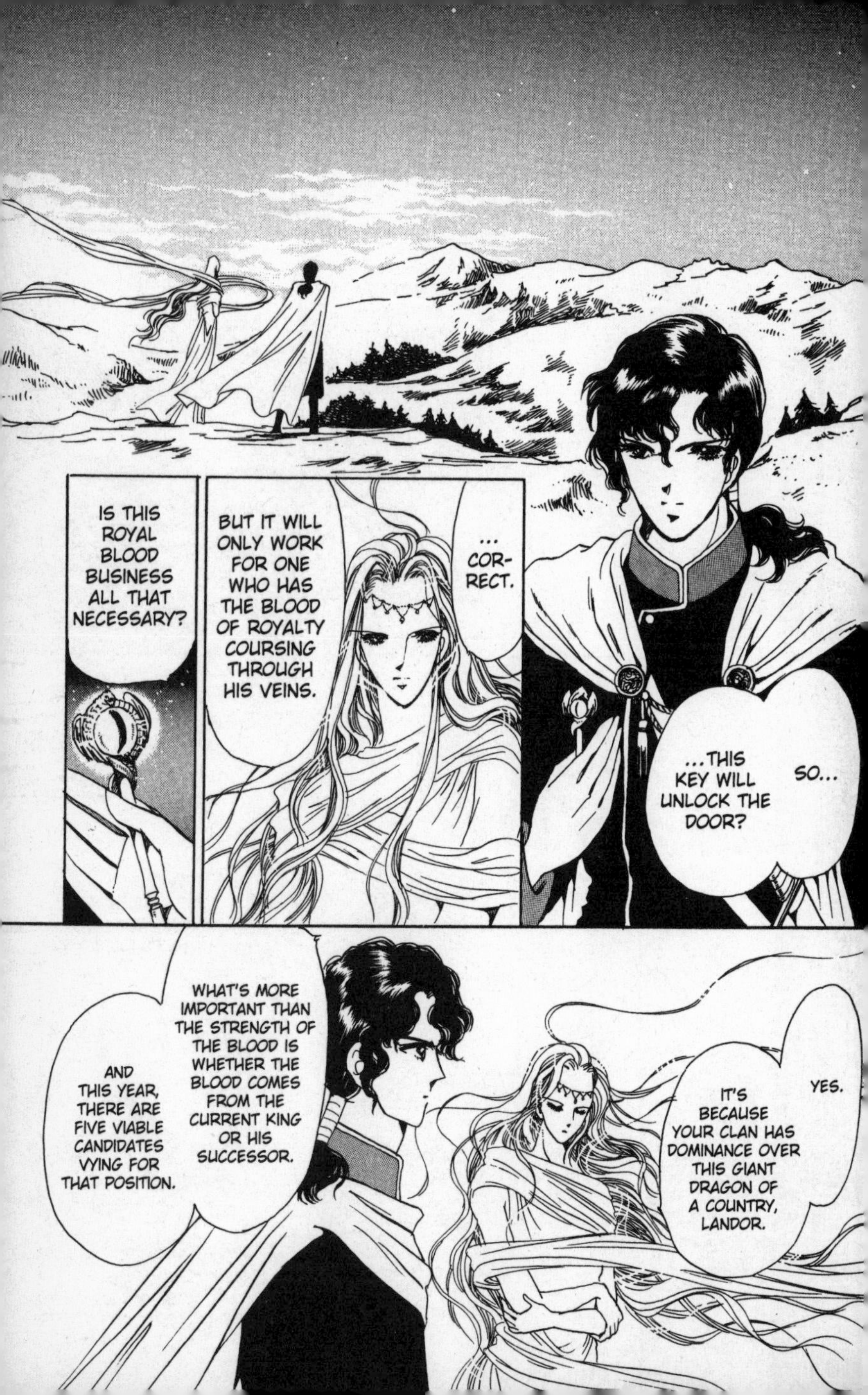
SO...
...THIS KEY WILL UNLOCK THE DOOR?
... CORRECT.
BUT IT WILL ONLY WORK FOR ONE WHO HAS THE BLOOD OF ROYALTY COURSING THROUGH HIS VEINS.
IS THIS ROYAL BLOOD BUSINESS ALL THAT NECESSARY?
YES.
IT'S BECAUSE YOUR CLAN HAS DOMINANCE OVER THIS GIANT DRAGON OF A COUNTRY, LANDOR.
WHAT'S MORE IMPORTANT THAN THE STRENGTH OF THE BLOOD IS WHETHER THE BLOOD COMES FROM THE CURRENT KING OR HIS SUCCESSOR.
AND THIS YEAR, THERE ARE FIVE VIABLE CANDIDATES VYING FOR THAT POSITION.

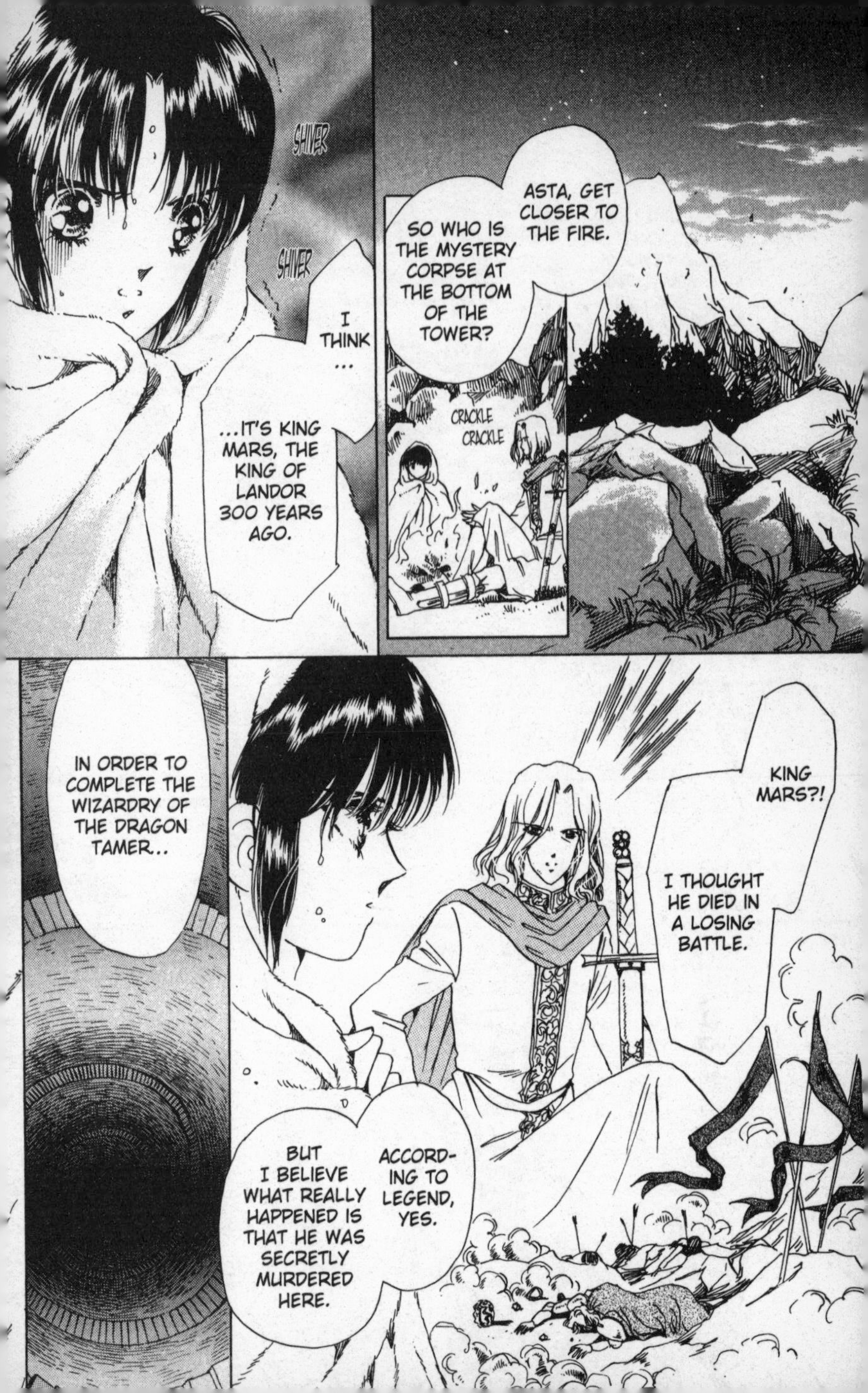
ASTA, GET CLOSER TO THE FIRE.
SO WHO IS THE MYSTERY CORPSE AT THE BOTTOM OF THE TOWER?
CRACKLE
CRACKLE
SHIVER
SHIVER
I THINK...
...IT'S KING MARS, THE KING OF LANDOR 300 YEARS AGO.
KING MARS?!
I THOUGHT HE DIED IN A LOSING BATTLE.
ACCORD-ING TO LEGEND, YES.
BUT I BELIEVE WHAT REALLY HAPPENED IS THAT HE WAS SECRETLY MURDERED HERE.
IN ORDER TO COMPLETE THE WIZARDRY OF THE DRAGON TAMER...

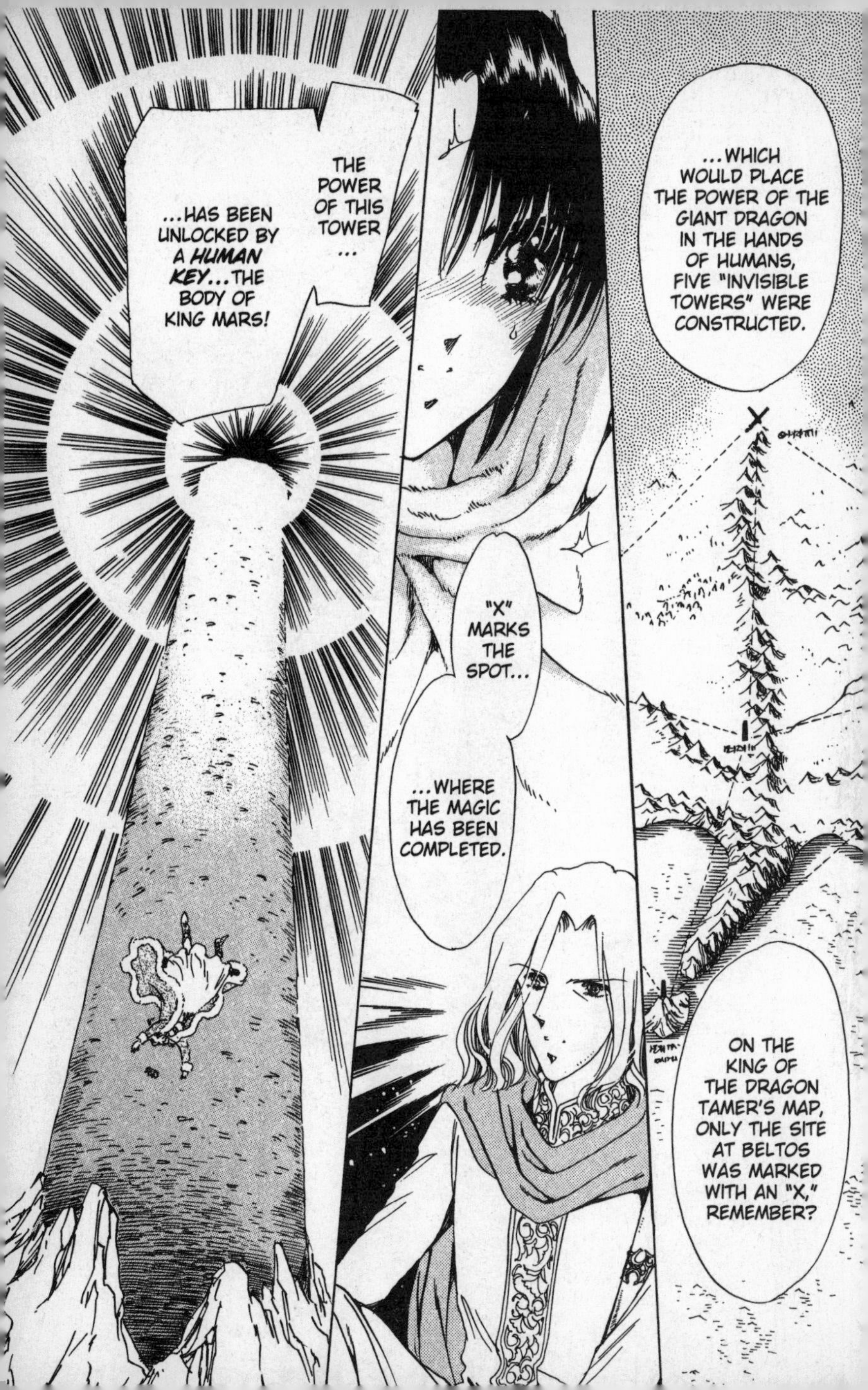
...WHICH WOULD PLACE THE POWER OF THE GIANT DRAGON IN THE HANDS OF HUMANS, FIVE "INVISIBLE TOWERS" WERE CONSTRUCTED.
ON THE KING OF THE DRAGON TAMER'S MAP, ONLY THE SITE AT BELTOS WAS MARKED WITH AN "X," REMEMBER?
"X" MARKS THE SPOT...
...WHERE THE MAGIC HAS BEEN COMPLETED.
THE POWER OF THIS TOWER ...
...HAS BEEN UNLOCKED BY A ***HUMAN KEY***... THE BODY OF KING MARS!

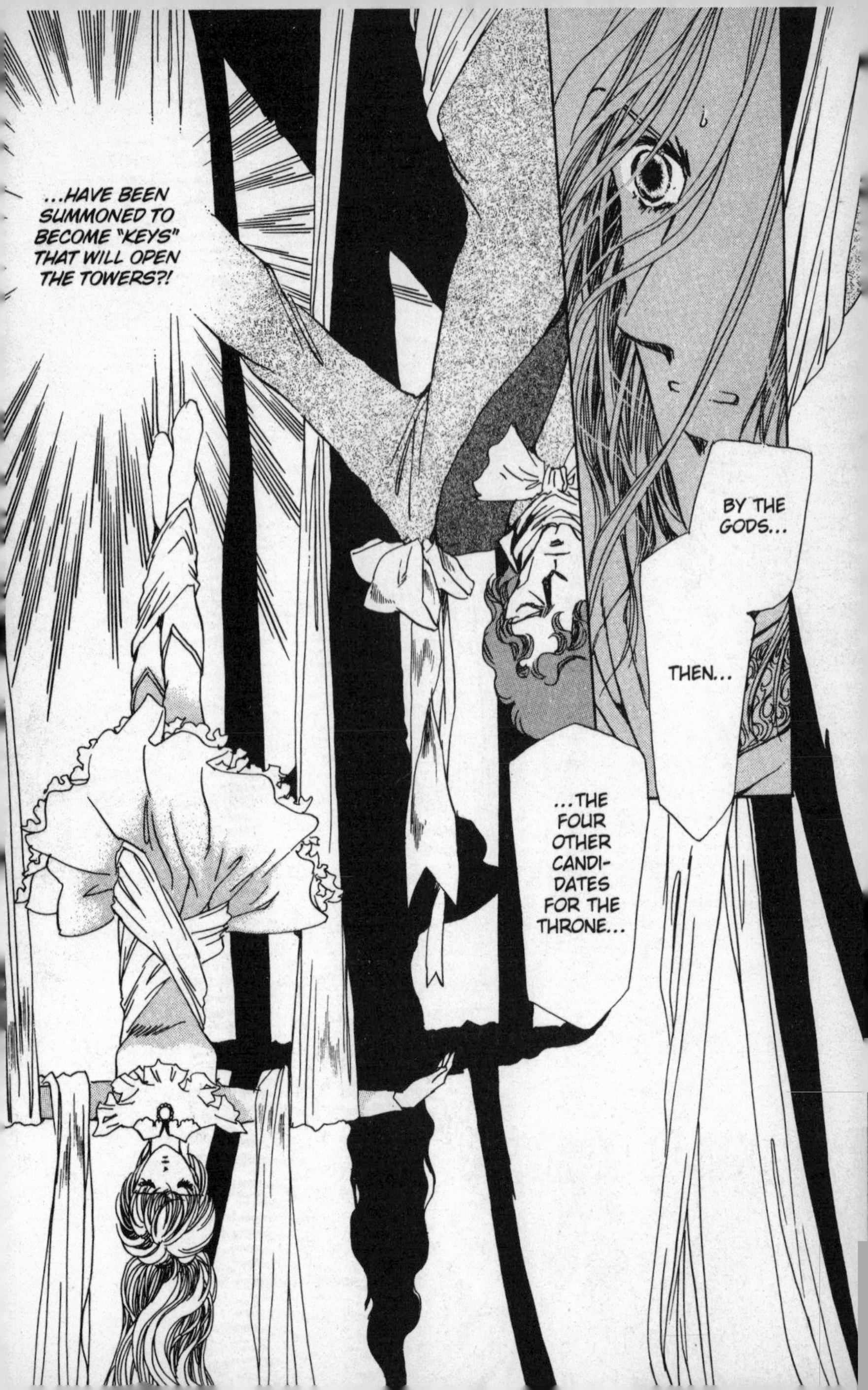
BY THE GODS...
THEN...
...THE FOUR OTHER CANDIDATES FOR THE THRONE...
...HAVE BEEN SUMMONED TO BECOME "KEYS" THAT WILL OPEN THE TOWERS?!

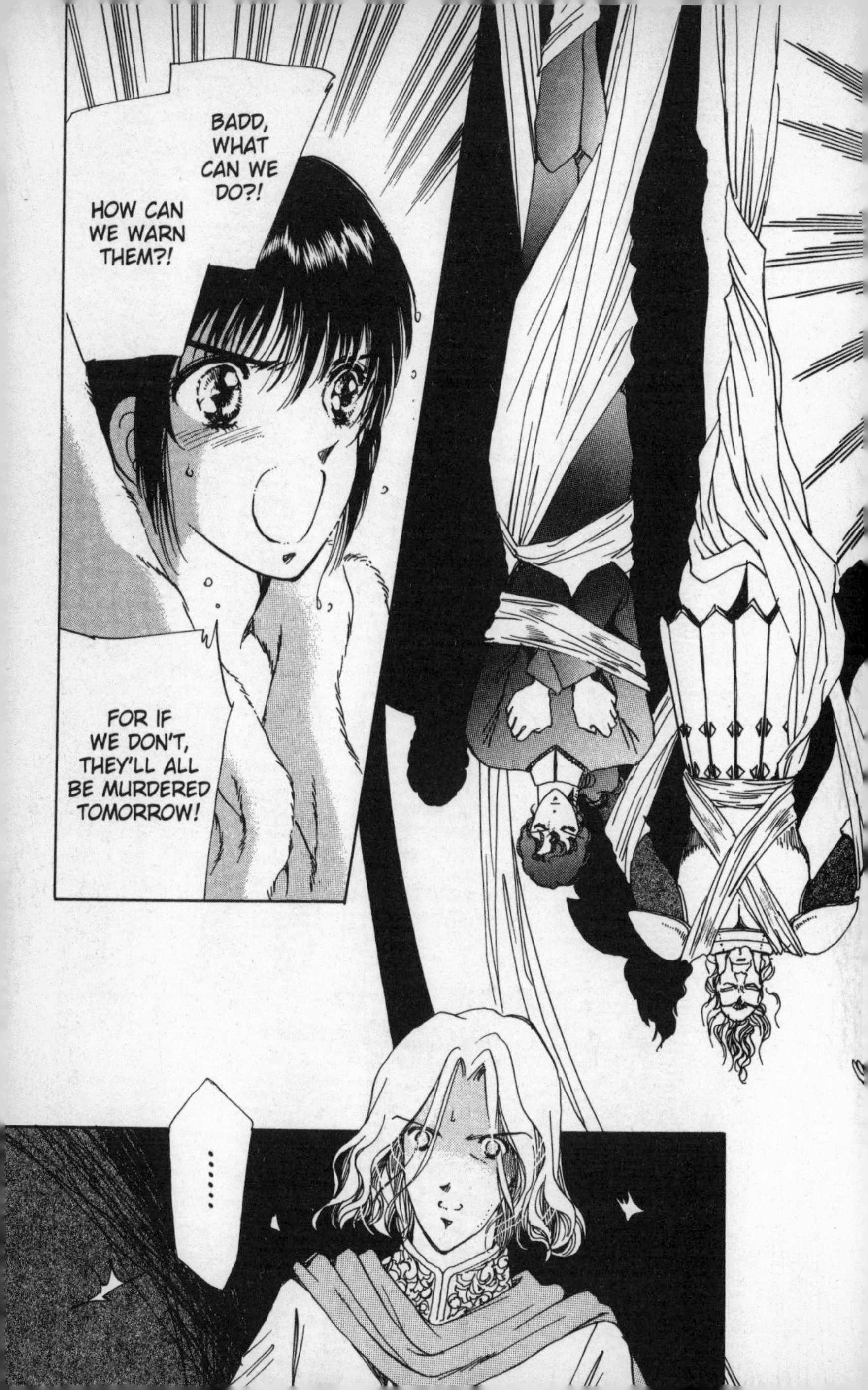
BADD, WHAT CAN WE DO?!
HOW CAN WE WARN THEM?!
FOR IF WE DON'T, THEY'LL ALL BE MURDERED TOMORROW!
......

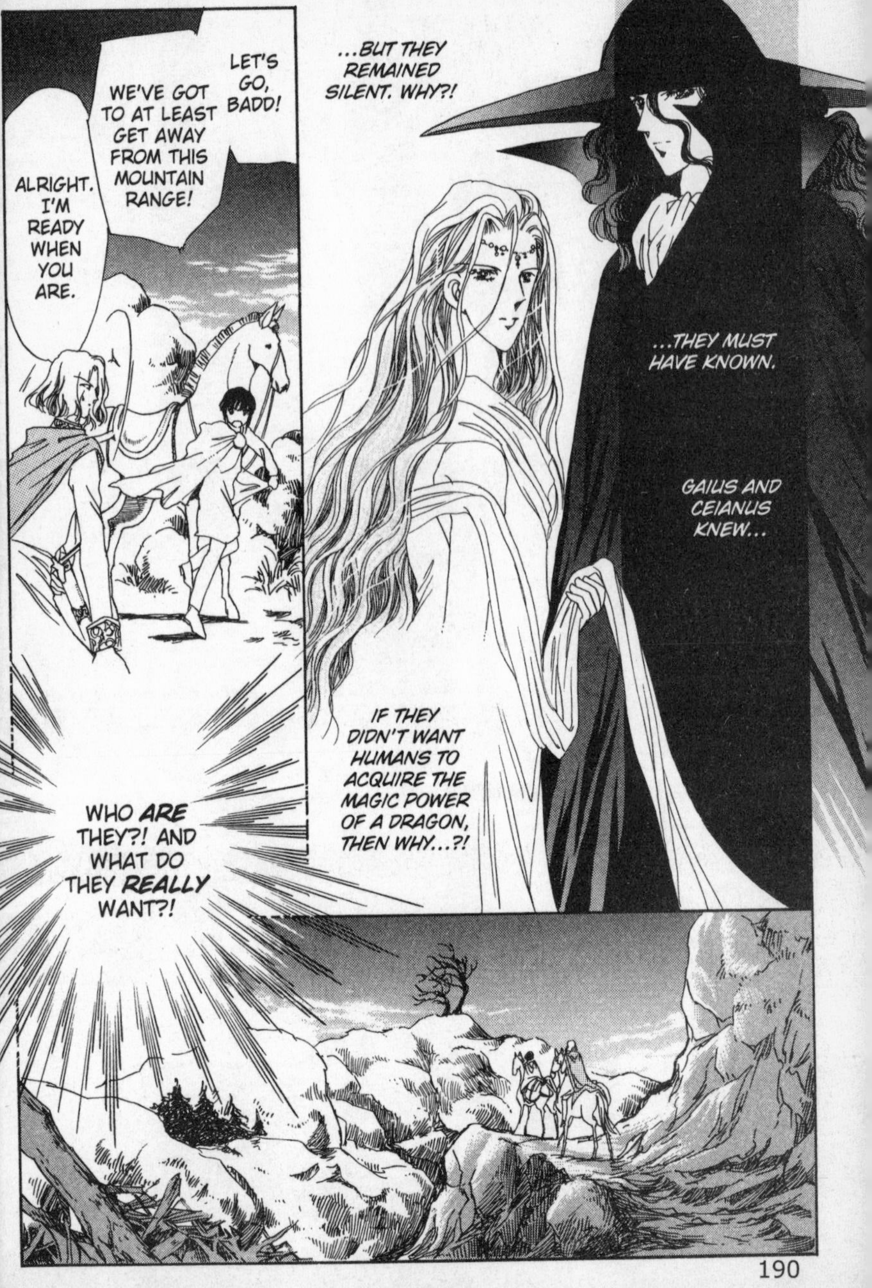
...BUT THEY REMAINED SILENT. WHY?!
...THEY MUST HAVE KNOWN.
GAIUS AND CEIANUS KNEW...
IF THEY DIDN'T WANT HUMANS TO ACQUIRE THE MAGIC POWER OF A DRAGON, THEN WHY...?!
LET'S GO, BADD!
WE'VE GOT TO AT LEAST GET AWAY FROM THIS MOUNTAIN RANGE!
ALRIGHT. I'M READY WHEN YOU ARE.
WHO *ARE* THEY?! AND WHAT DO THEY *REALLY* WANT?!

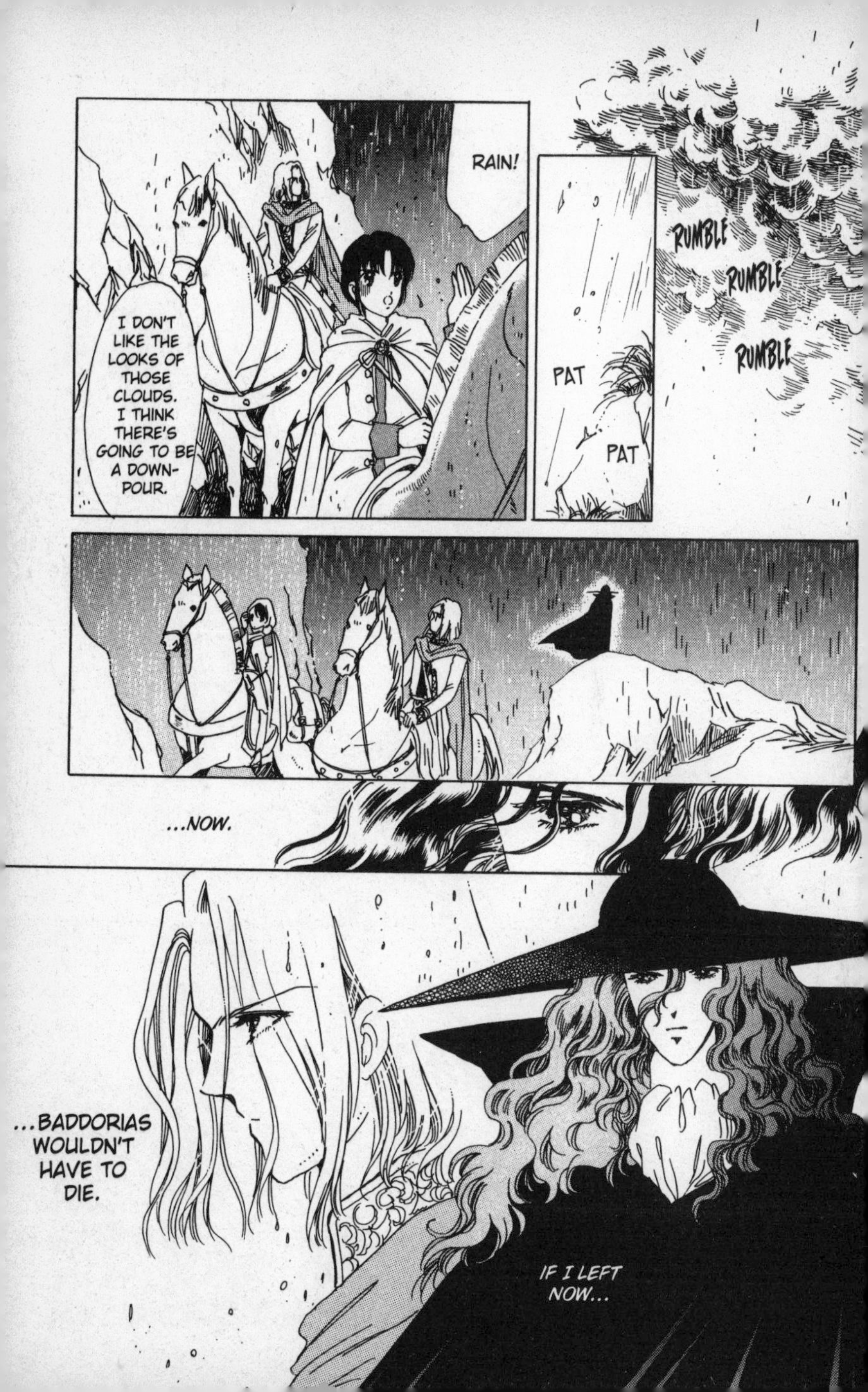

RUMBLE
RUMBLE
RUMBLE
PAT
PAT
RAIN!
I DON'T LIKE THE LOOKS OF THOSE CLOUDS. I THINK THERE'S GOING TO BE A DOWN-POUR.
...NOW.
IF I LEFT NOW...
...BADDORIAS WOULDN'T HAVE TO DIE.

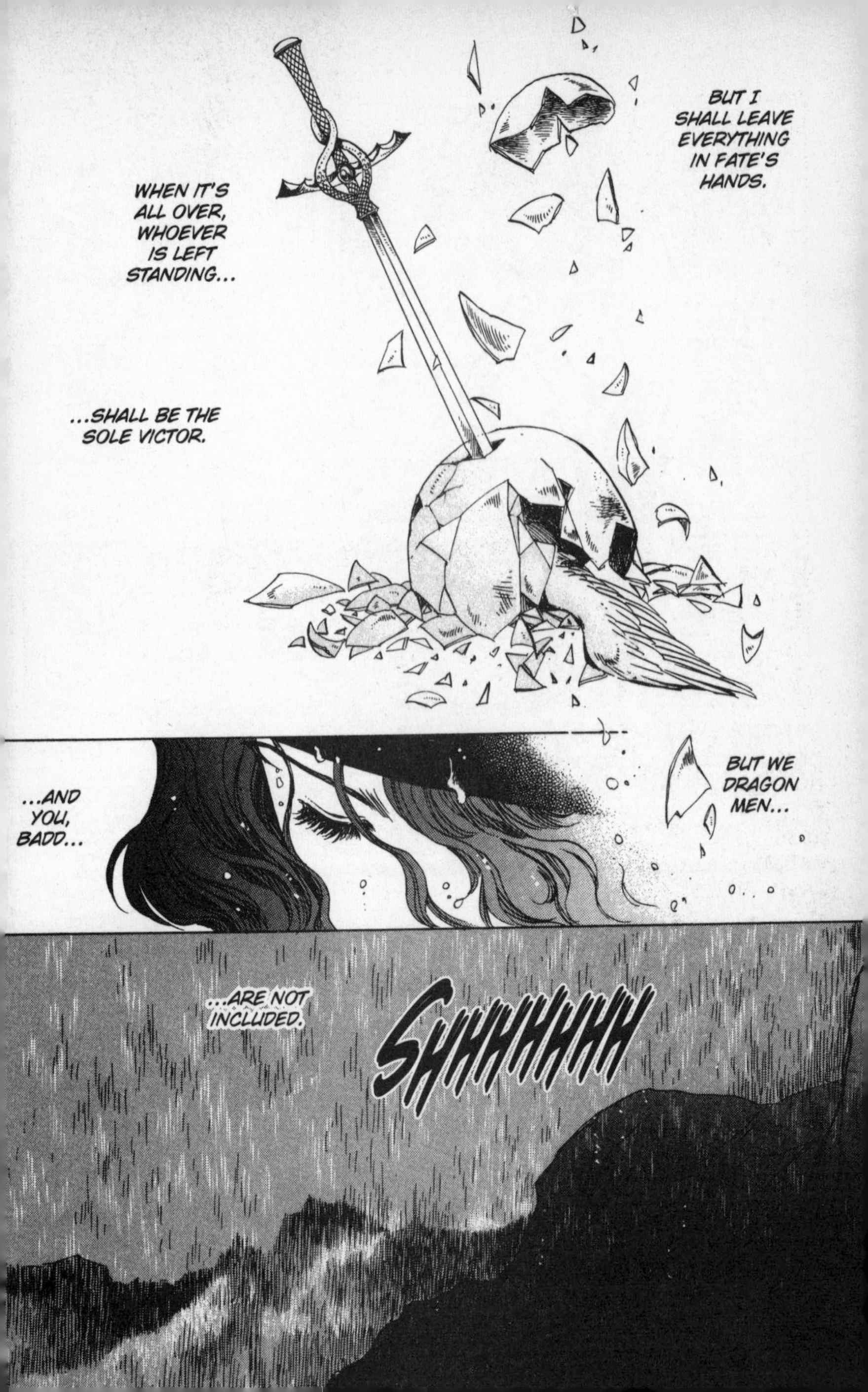
BUT I SHALL LEAVE EVERYTHING IN FATE'S HANDS.
WHEN IT'S ALL OVER, WHOEVER IS LEFT STANDING...
...SHALL BE THE SOLE VICTOR.
BUT WE DRAGON MEN...
...AND YOU, BADD...
...ARE NOT INCLUDED.
SHHHHHHH

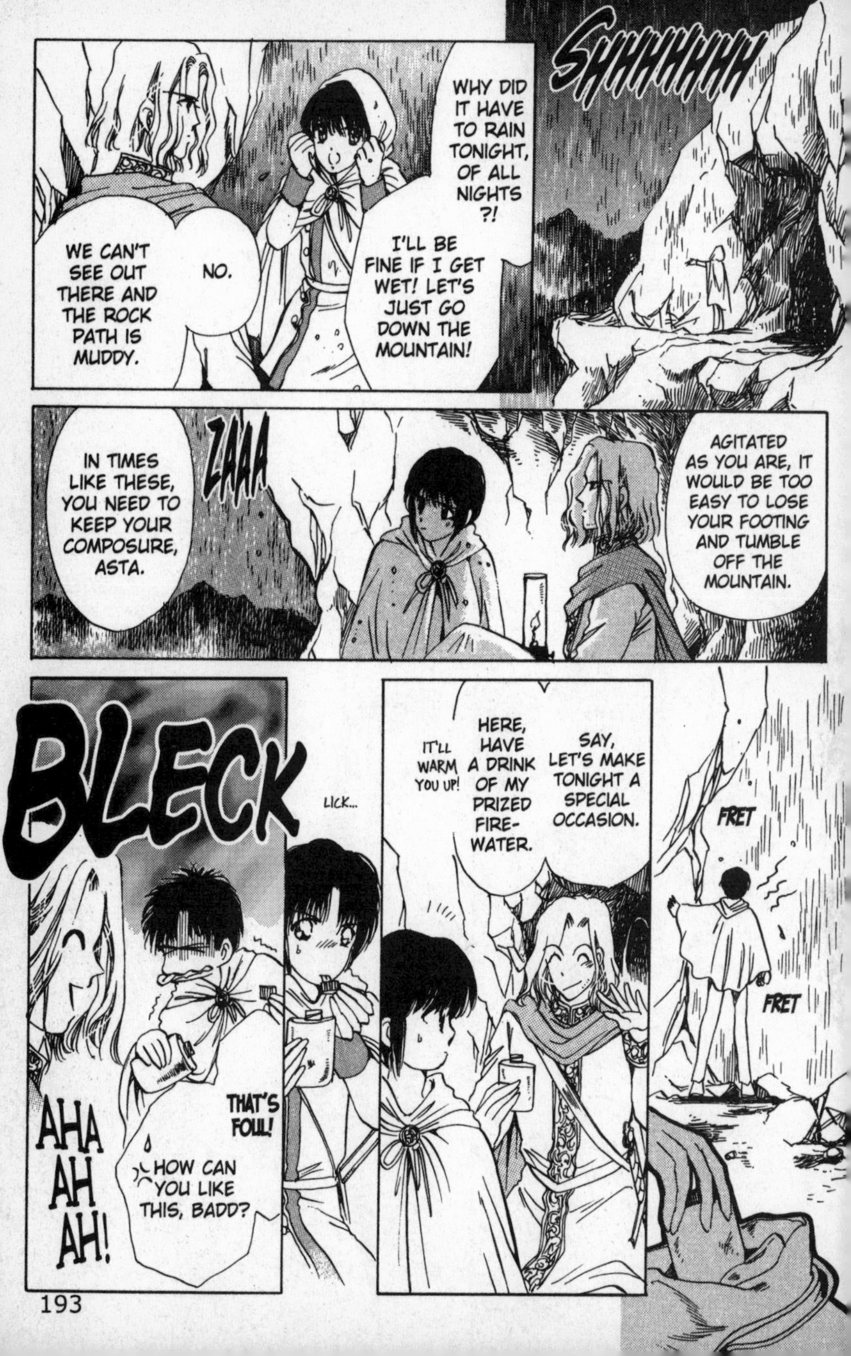
SHHHHHHH
WHY DID IT HAVE TO RAIN TONIGHT, OF ALL NIGHTS?!
I'LL BE FINE IF I GET WET! LET'S JUST GO DOWN THE MOUNTAIN!
NO.
WE CAN'T SEE OUT THERE AND THE ROCK PATH IS MUDDY.
AGITATED AS YOU ARE, IT WOULD BE TOO EASY TO LOSE YOUR FOOTING AND TUMBLE OFF THE MOUNTAIN.
ZAAA
IN TIMES LIKE THESE, YOU NEED TO KEEP YOUR COMPOSURE, ASTA.
FRET
FRET
SAY, LET'S MAKE TONIGHT A SPECIAL OCCASION.
HERE, HAVE A DRINK OF MY PRIZED FIRE-WATER.
IT'LL WARM YOU UP!
BLECK
LICK...
THAT'S FOUL!
HOW CAN YOU LIKE THIS, BADD?
AHA AH AH!

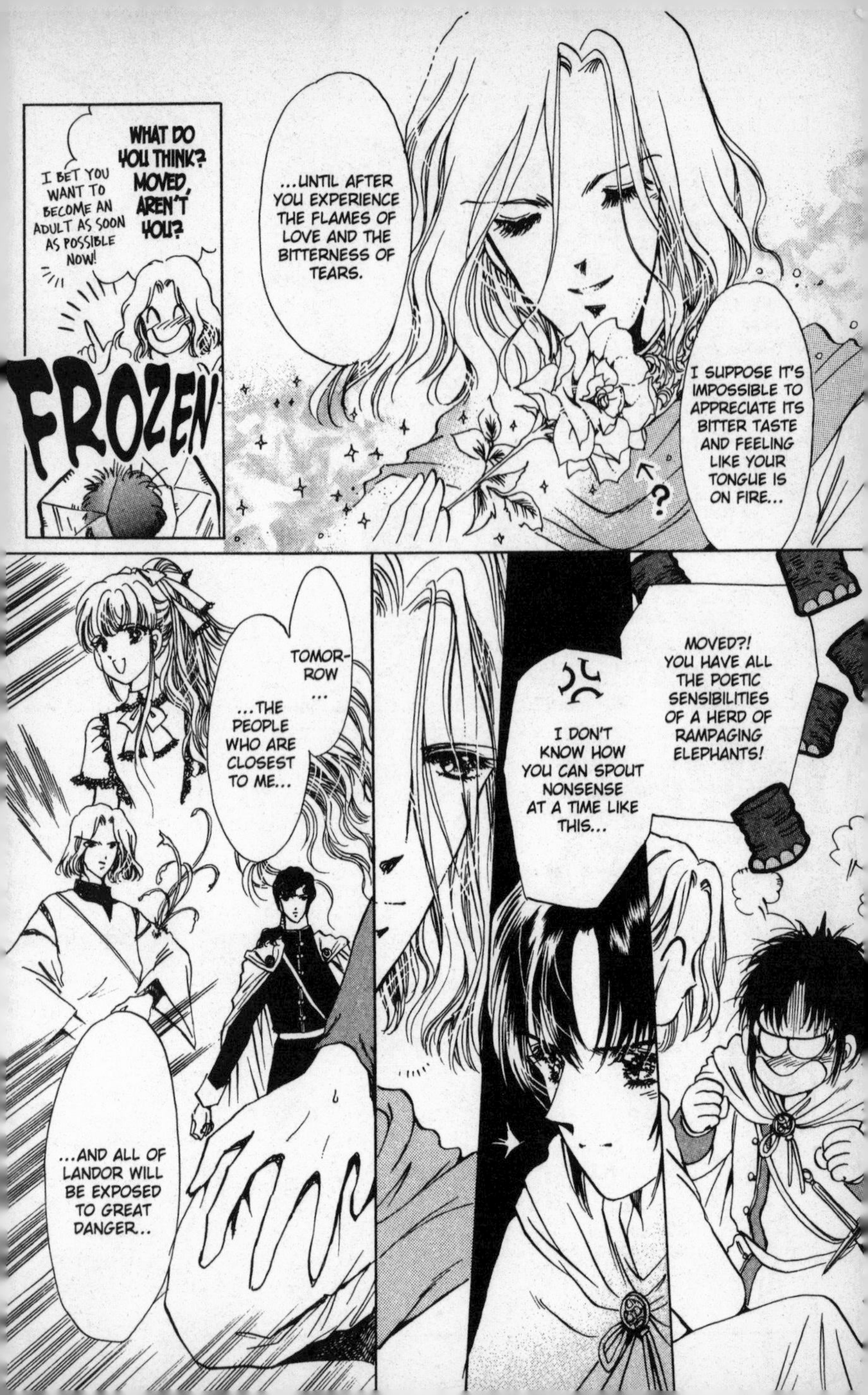
I SUPPOSE IT'S IMPOSSIBLE TO APPRECIATE ITS BITTER TASTE AND FEELING LIKE YOUR TONGUE IS ON FIRE...
...UNTIL AFTER YOU EXPERIENCE THE FLAMES OF LOVE AND THE BITTERNESS OF TEARS.
?
WHAT DO YOU THINK? MOVED, AREN'T YOU?
I BET YOU WANT TO BECOME AN ADULT AS SOON AS POSSIBLE NOW!
FROZEN
MOVED?! YOU HAVE ALL THE POETIC SENSIBILITIES OF A HERD OF RAMPAGING ELEPHANTS!
I DON'T KNOW HOW YOU CAN SPOUT NONSENSE AT A TIME LIKE THIS...
TOMORROW...
...THE PEOPLE WHO ARE CLOSEST TO ME...
...AND ALL OF LANDOR WILL BE EXPOSED TO GREAT DANGER...

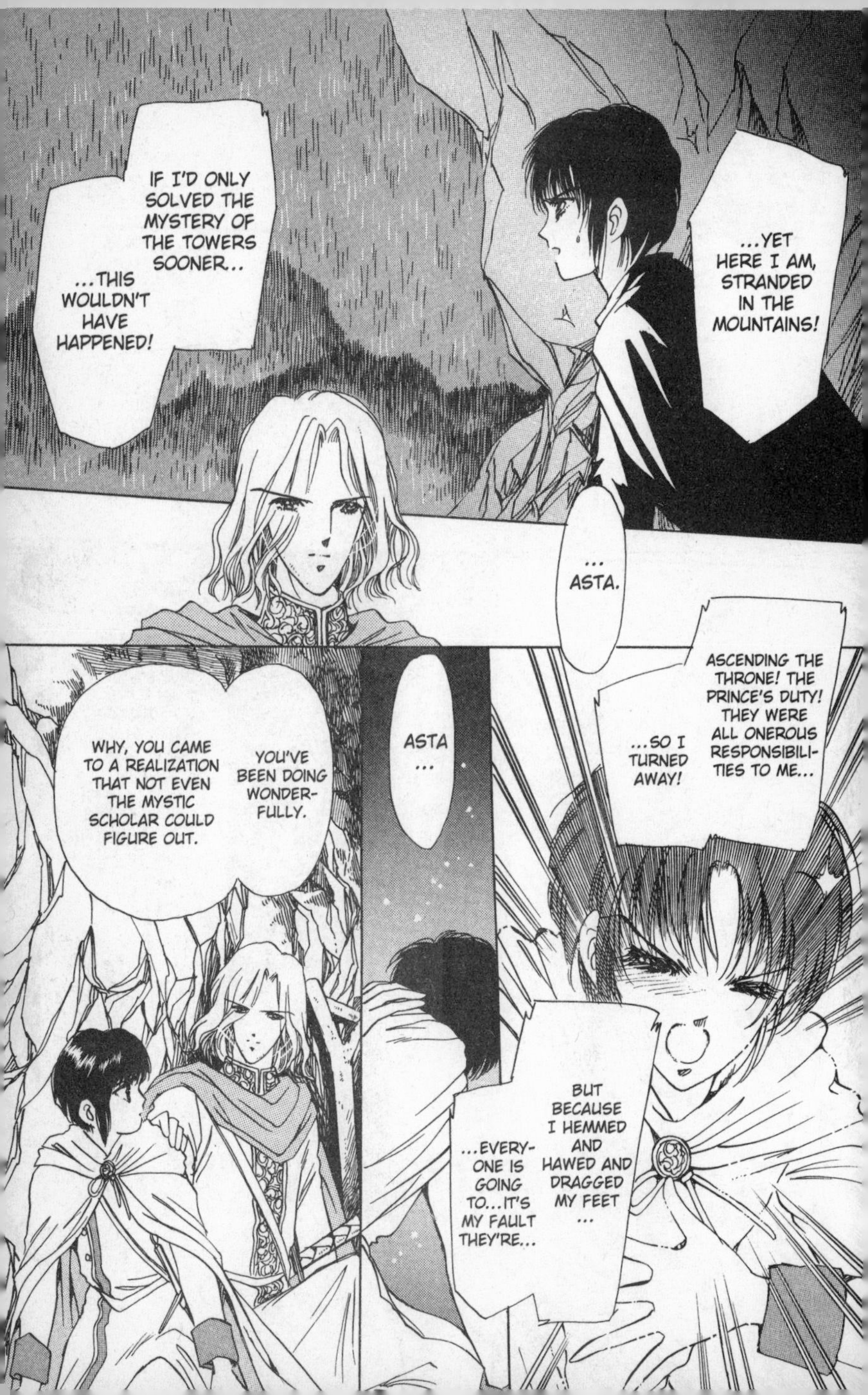
...YET HERE I AM, STRANDED IN THE MOUNTAINS!
IF I'D ONLY SOLVED THE MYSTERY OF THE TOWERS SOONER...
...THIS WOULDN'T HAVE HAPPENED!
... ASTA.
ASCENDING THE THRONE! THE PRINCE'S DUTY! THEY WERE ALL ONEROUS RESPONSIBILI-TIES TO ME...
...SO I TURNED AWAY!
BUT BECAUSE I HEMMED AND HAWED AND DRAGGED MY FEET...
...EVERY-ONE IS GOING TO...IT'S MY FAULT THEY'RE...
ASTA...
YOU'VE BEEN DOING WONDER-FULLY.
WHY, YOU CAME TO A REALIZATION THAT NOT EVEN THE MYSTIC SCHOLAR COULD FIGURE OUT.

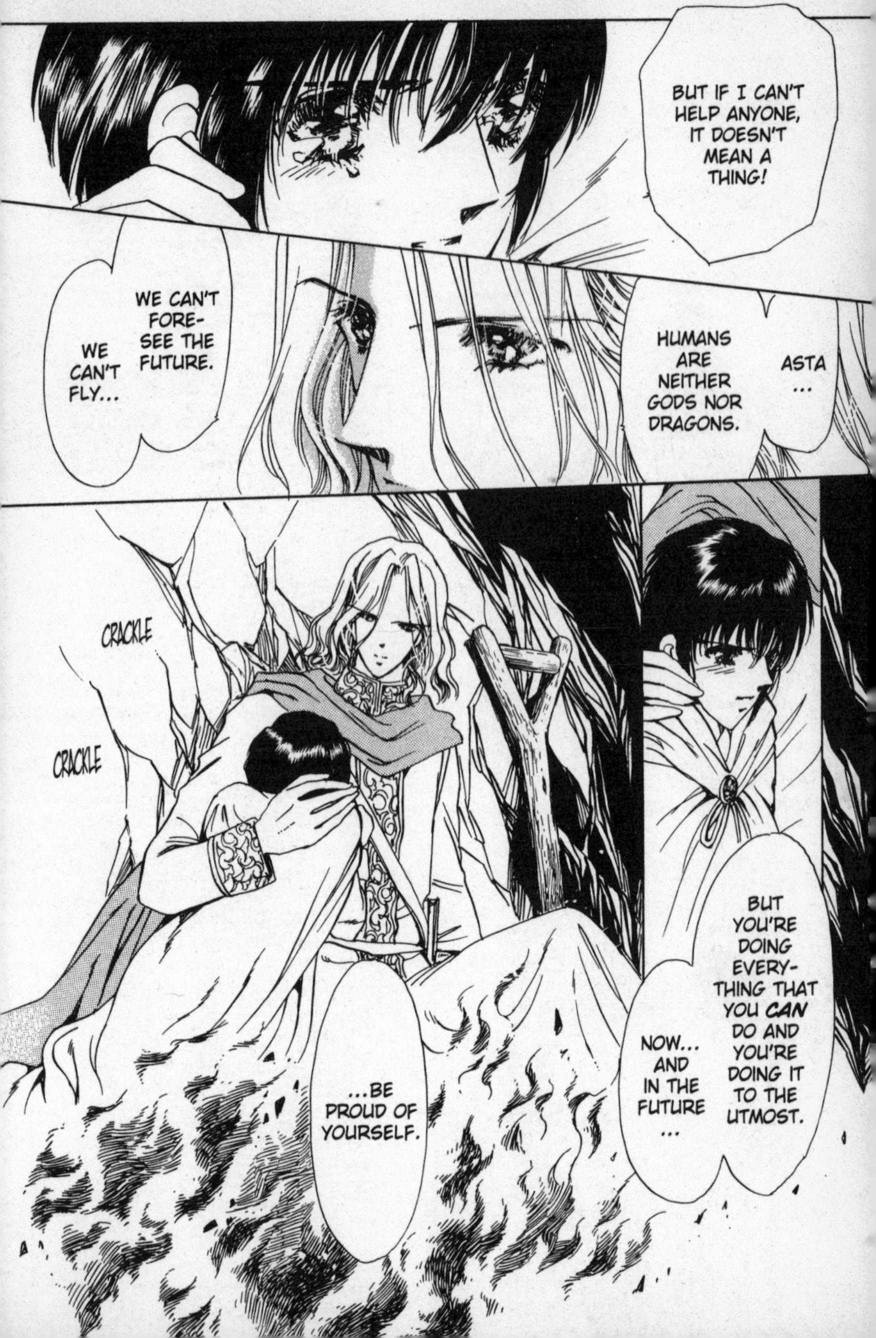
BUT IF I CAN'T HELP ANYONE, IT DOESN'T MEAN A THING!
ASTA ...
HUMANS ARE NEITHER GODS NOR DRAGONS.
WE CAN'T FORE-SEE THE FUTURE.
WE CAN'T FLY...
BUT YOU'RE DOING EVERY-THING THAT YOU *CAN* DO AND YOU'RE DOING IT TO THE UTMOST.
NOW... AND IN THE FUTURE ...
...BE PROUD OF YOURSELF.
CRACKLE
CRACKLE

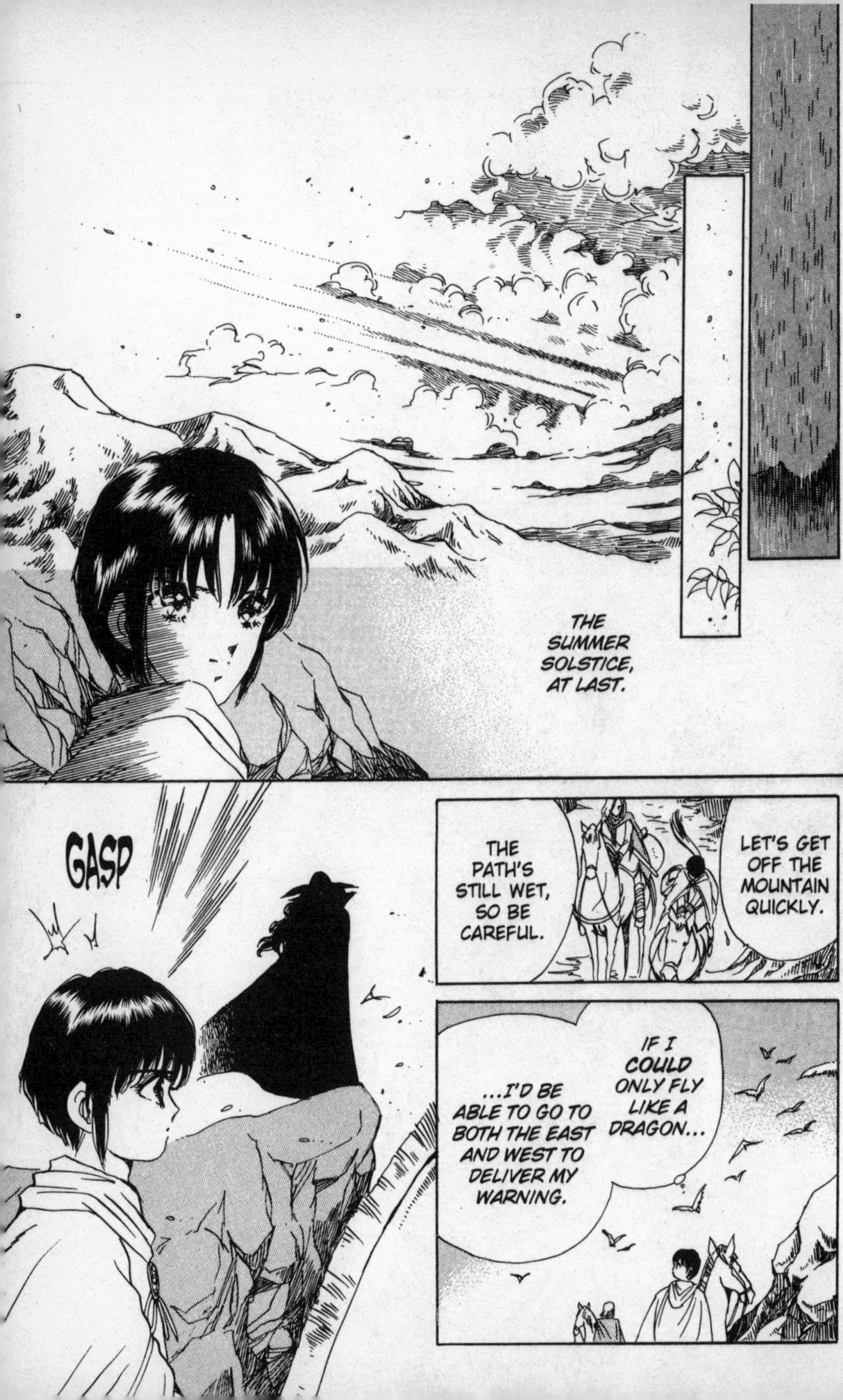
THE SUMMER SOLSTICE, AT LAST.
LET'S GET OFF THE MOUNTAIN QUICKLY.
THE PATH'S STILL WET, SO BE CAREFUL.
IF I COULD ONLY FLY LIKE A DRAGON...
...I'D BE ABLE TO GO TO BOTH THE EAST AND WEST TO DELIVER MY WARNING.
GASP

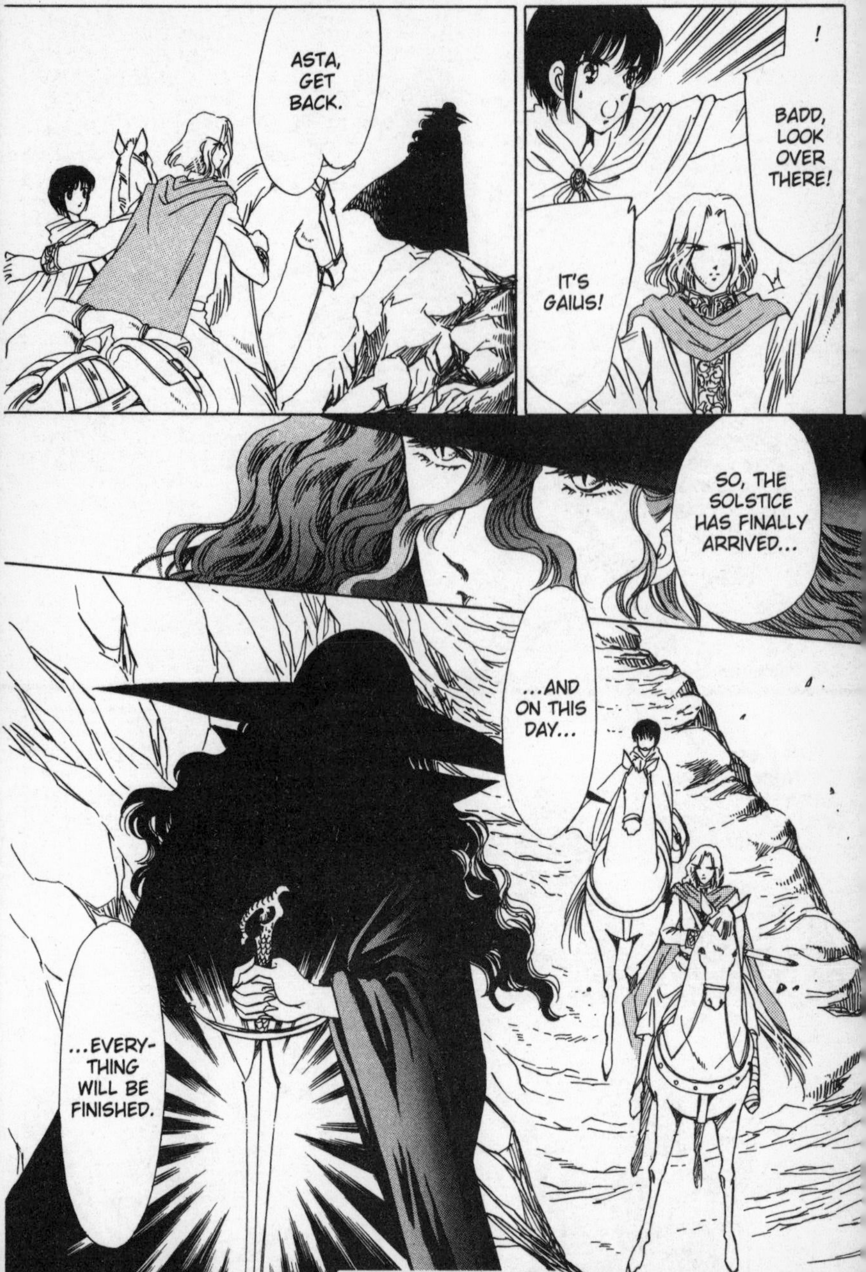
!
BADD, LOOK OVER THERE!
IT'S GAIUS!
ASTA, GET BACK.
SO, THE SOLSTICE HAS FINALLY ARRIVED...
...AND ON THIS DAY...
...EVERYTHING WILL BE FINISHED.

Chapter Sixteen: The End

Afterword

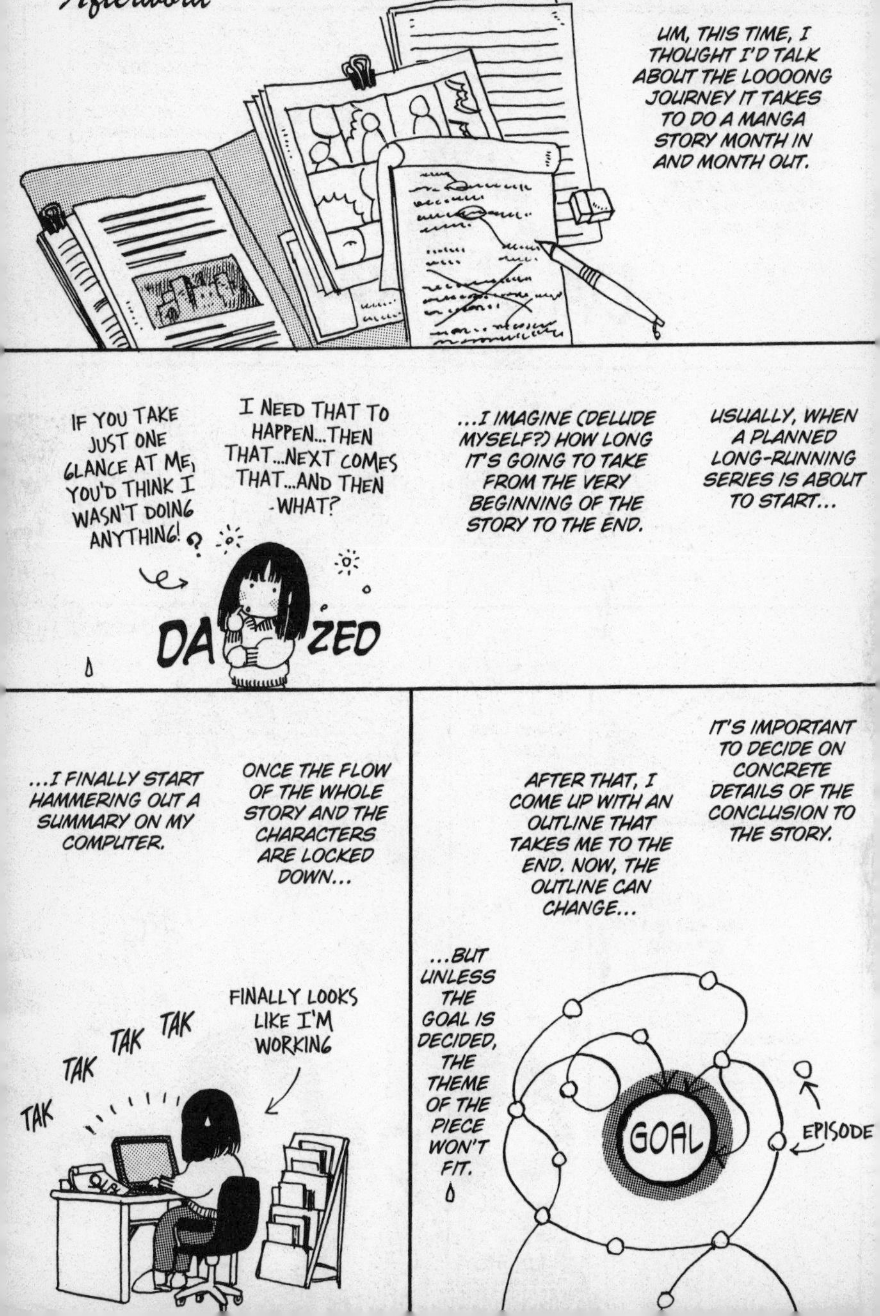

UM, THIS TIME, I THOUGHT I'D TALK ABOUT THE LOOOONG JOURNEY IT TAKES TO DO A MANGA STORY MONTH IN AND MONTH OUT.
USUALLY, WHEN A PLANNED LONG-RUNNING SERIES IS ABOUT TO START...
...I IMAGINE (DELUDE MYSELF?) HOW LONG IT'S GOING TO TAKE FROM THE VERY BEGINNING OF THE STORY TO THE END.
I NEED THAT TO HAPPEN...THEN THAT...NEXT COMES THAT...AND THEN -WHAT?
IF YOU TAKE JUST ONE GLANCE AT ME, YOU'D THINK I WASN'T DOING ANYTHING!
DA ZED
IT'S IMPORTANT TO DECIDE ON CONCRETE DETAILS OF THE CONCLUSION TO THE STORY.
AFTER THAT, I COME UP WITH AN OUTLINE THAT TAKES ME TO THE END. NOW, THE OUTLINE CAN CHANGE...
...BUT UNLESS THE GOAL IS DECIDED, THE THEME OF THE PIECE WON'T FIT.
GOAL
EPISODE
ONCE THE FLOW OF THE WHOLE STORY AND THE CHARACTERS ARE LOCKED DOWN...
...I FINALLY START HAMMERING OUT A SUMMARY ON MY COMPUTER.
FINALLY LOOKS LIKE I'M WORKING
TAK
TAK
TAK
TAK

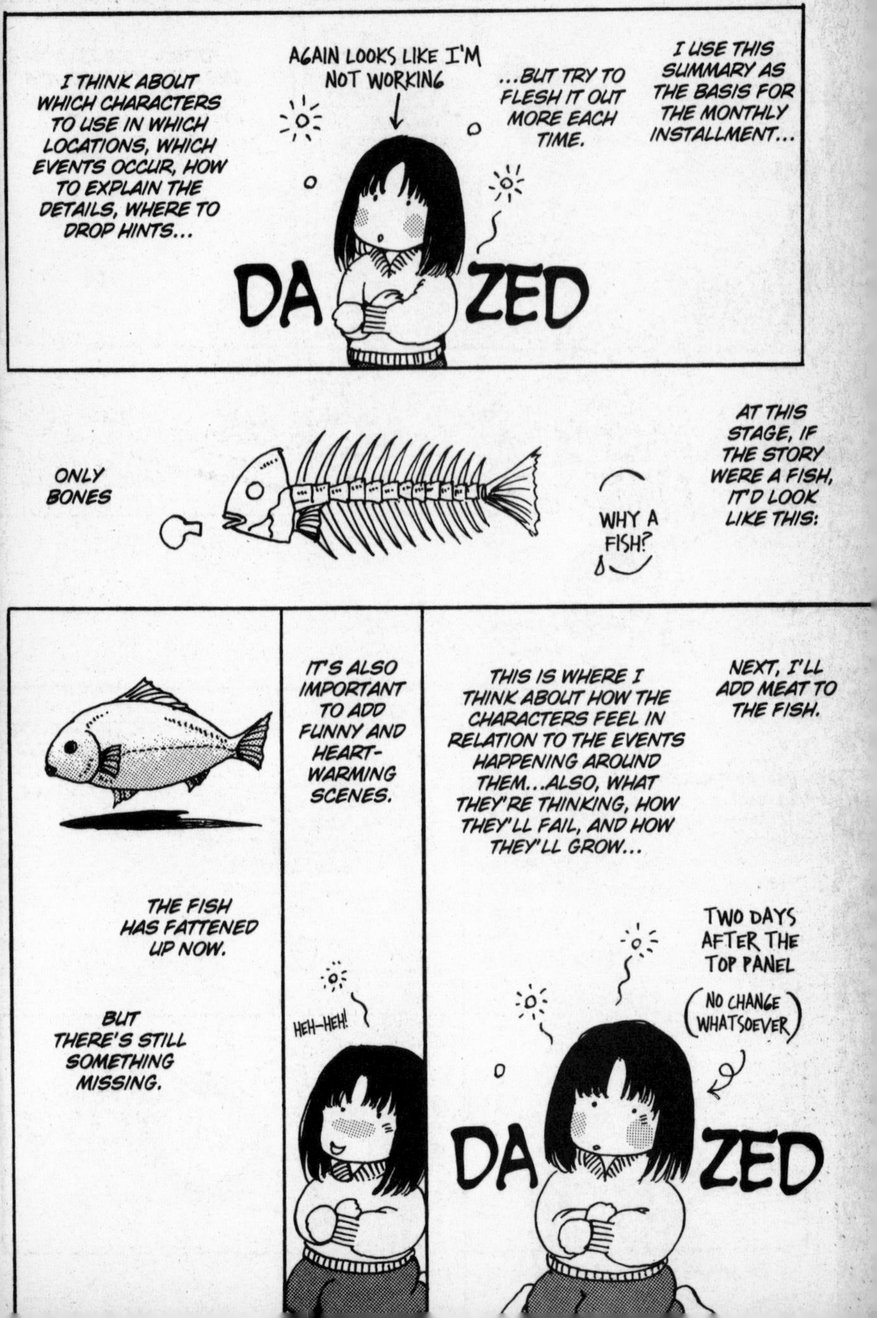
I USE THIS SUMMARY AS THE BASIS FOR THE MONTHLY INSTALLMENT...
...BUT TRY TO FLESH IT OUT MORE EACH TIME.
AGAIN LOOKS LIKE I'M NOT WORKING
I THINK ABOUT WHICH CHARACTERS TO USE IN WHICH LOCATIONS, WHICH EVENTS OCCUR, HOW TO EXPLAIN THE DETAILS, WHERE TO DROP HINTS...
DA ZED
AT THIS STAGE, IF THE STORY WERE A FISH, IT'D LOOK LIKE THIS:
WHY A FISH?
ONLY BONES
NEXT, I'LL ADD MEAT TO THE FISH.
THIS IS WHERE I THINK ABOUT HOW THE CHARACTERS FEEL IN RELATION TO THE EVENTS HAPPENING AROUND THEM...ALSO, WHAT THEY'RE THINKING, HOW THEY'LL FAIL, AND HOW THEY'LL GROW...
TWO DAYS AFTER THE TOP PANEL
(NO CHANGE WHATSOEVER)
DA ZED
IT'S ALSO IMPORTANT TO ADD FUNNY AND HEART-WARMING SCENES.
HEH-HEH!
THE FISH HAS FATTENED UP NOW.
BUT THERE'S STILL SOMETHING MISSING.

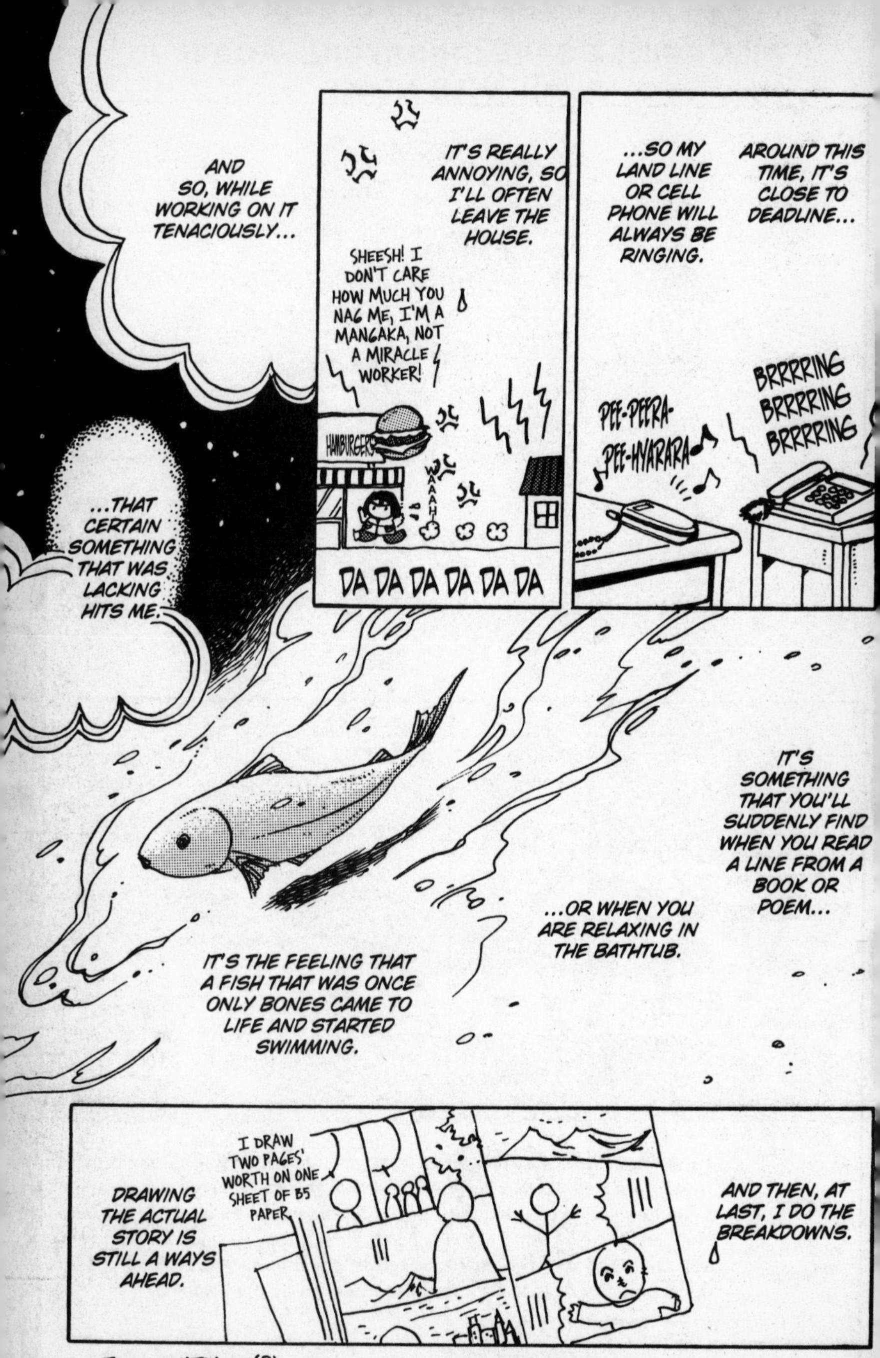
AROUND THIS TIME, IT'S CLOSE TO DEADLINE...
...SO MY LAND LINE OR CELL PHONE WILL ALWAYS BE RINGING.
BRRRRING BRRRRING BRRRRING
PEE-PEERA-PEE-HYARARA
IT'S REALLY ANNOYING, SO I'LL OFTEN LEAVE THE HOUSE.
SHEESH! I DON'T CARE HOW MUCH YOU NAG ME, I'M A MANGAKA, NOT A MIRACLE WORKER!
HAMBURGERS
WAAAH!
DA DA DA DA DA DA
AND SO, WHILE WORKING ON IT TENACIOUSLY...
...THAT CERTAIN SOMETHING THAT WAS LACKING HITS ME.
IT'S SOMETHING THAT YOU'LL SUDDENLY FIND WHEN YOU READ A LINE FROM A BOOK OR POEM...
...OR WHEN YOU ARE RELAXING IN THE BATHTUB.
IT'S THE FEELING THAT A FISH THAT WAS ONCE ONLY BONES CAME TO LIFE AND STARTED SWIMMING.
AND THEN, AT LAST, I DO THE BREAKDOWNS.
I DRAW TWO PAGES' WORTH ON ONE SHEET OF B5 PAPER.
DRAWING THE ACTUAL STORY IS STILL A WAYS AHEAD.

TO BE CONTINUED(?)

WILL ARGENT RID HIS BODY OF POISON?
FIND OUT NOW!

Apothecarius Argentum
Volume 5

By Tomomi Yamashita. Garna, the former assassin, has received a pardon from Princess Primula and is returned to his position as the royal chef. Argent feels that, as Garna's wise and resourceful ways will help protect the Princess, it is time to embark on a solo trip to cure his body of its poisonous nature. Meanwhile, there is conspiracy brewing, as a mysterious group plots the fall of all royal families, one by one.

TERU TERU x SHONEN

Volume 2

By Shigeru Takao. When Saizo was orphaned, a caring family took him in. His new brother Sasuke still sees it as his duty to protect Saizo, even as Saizo protects Shinobu. But Sasuke isn't too crazy about Shinobu, who he sees as a stuck-up, spoiled brat. Things only get worse when her mother comes for a visit. To complicate matters, there's another attempt on Shinobu's life!

DON'T MISS THESE OTHER GREAT SERIES!

MOON CHILD © 1988 Reiko Shimizu/HAKUSENSHA, INC.

By Reiko Shimizu
11 Volumes Available

CIPHER © 1984 Minako Narita/HAKUSENSHA, INC.

By Minako Narita
All 11 Volumes Available

SEKAI DE ICHIBAN DAIKIRAI © 1997 Banri Hidaka/HAKUSENSHA, INC.

By Banri Hidaka
4 Volumes Available

PENGUIN KAKUMEI © 2004 Sakura Tsukuba/HAKUSENSHA, INC.

By Sakura Tsukuba
5 Volumes Available

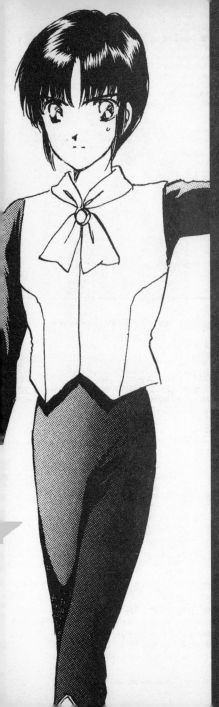

KNOW WHAT'S INSIDE

With the wide variety of manga available, CMX understands it can be confusing to determine age-appropriate material. We rate our books in four categories: EVERYONE, TEEN, TEEN + and MATURE. For the TEEN, TEEN + and MATURE categories, we include additional, specific descriptions to assist consumers in determining if the book is age appropriate. (Our MATURE books are shipped shrink-wrapped with a Parental Advisory sticker affixed to the wrapper.)

EVERYONE

Titles with this rating are appropriate for all age readers. They contain no offensive material. They may contain mild violence and/or some comic mischief.

TEEN

Titles with this rating are appropriate for a teen audience and older. They may contain some violent content, language, and/or suggestive themes.

TEEN PLUS

Titles with this rating are appropriate for an audience of 16 and older. They may contain partial nudity, mild profanity and more intense violence.

MATURE

Titles with this rating are appropriate only for mature readers. They may contain graphic violence, nudity, sex and content suitable only for older readers.

OUKOKU NO KAGI Vol. 4 © Kyoko SHITOU 2004. First Published in Japan in 2004 by KADOKAWA
SHOTEN PUBLISHING CO., LTD., Tokyo.

The Key to the Kingdom, Volume 4, published by WildStorm Productions, an imprint of DC Comics, 888
Prospect St. #240, La Jolla, CA 92037. English Translation © 2008. All Rights Reserved. English translation rights in U.S.A. arranged with KADOKAWA SHOTEN PUBLISHING CO., LTD., Tokyo, through
TUTTLE-MORI AGENCY, INC., Tokyo. CMX is a trademark of DC Comics. The stories, characters, and
incidents mentioned in this magazine are entirely fictional. Printed on recyclable paper. WildStorm does
not read or accept unsolicited submissions of ideas, stories or artwork. Printed in Canada.

DC Comics, a Warner Bros. Entertainment Company.

Sheldon Drzka – Translation and Adaptation
AndWorld Design – Lettering
Larry Berry – Design
Roland Mann & Jim Chadwick – Editors   ISBN: 978-1-4012-1396-1

IS THIS THE END OF ASTA'S MOST TRUSTED
ALLY AND PROTECTOR? FIND OUT IN AUGUST!

THE **KEY** TO THE
KINGDOM
Volume 5

By Kyoko Shitou. The day has finally arrived—the day the Dragon Man predicted that
Badd would die! A wounded Badd accompanies young Asta back from his mission, in which
the Prince learned the true meaning of the "Key"—or rather "Keys." Now that Asta knows
the identities of the sacrifices needed to unlock the Towers, he must race to save both
friends and rivals. But a Dragon Man attacks them and Badd finds himself locked in a life
and death battle.

All the pages in this book were created—and are printed here—in Japanese RIGHT-to-LEFT format. No artwork has been reversed or altered, so you can read the stories the way the creators meant for them to be read.

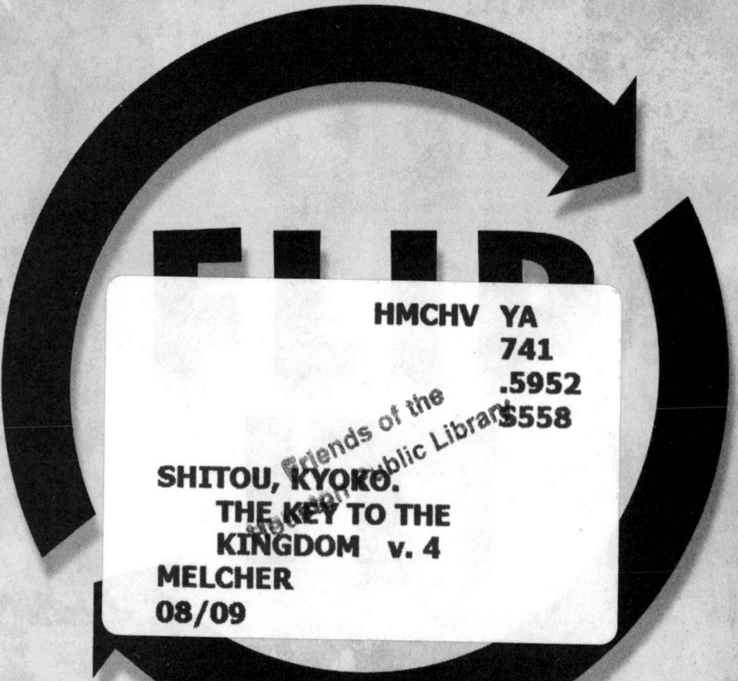

RIGHT TO LEFT?!

Traditional Japanese manga starts at the upper right-hand corner, and moves right-to-left as it goes down the page. Follow this guide for an easy understanding.

For more information and sneak previews, visit cmxmanga.com. Call 1-888-COMIC BOOK for the nearest comics shop or head to your local book store.

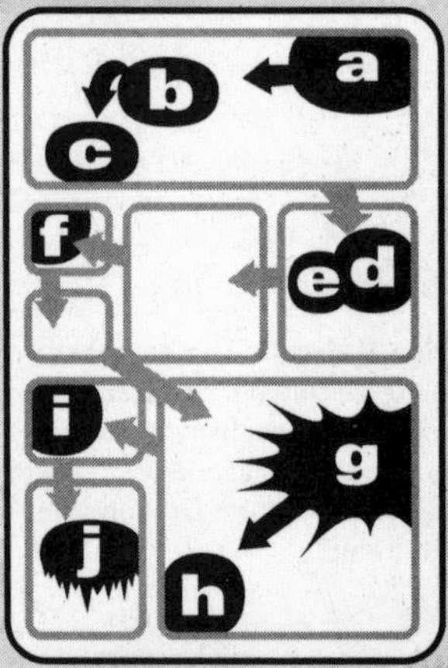
a
b
c
e
d
f
g
i
h
j